Death $\overline{\underset{A}{\text{AND}}}$ Maiden

Death $\overline{\text{AND}}$ Maiden

Infanticide and the
Tragical History
of Grethe Schmidt

William David Myers

NORTHERN ILLINOIS UNIVERSITY PRESS / DEKALB

Library of Congress Cataloging-in-Publication Data

Myers, William David.

Death and a maiden : infanticide and the tragical history of Grethe Schmidt / William David Myers.

   p.   cm.

Includes bibliographical references and index.

ISBN 978-0-87580-437-8 (clothbound : alk. paper)

1. Infanticide—Germany—Braunschweig—History—17th century. 2. Infanticide—Germany—Braunschweig—Case studies. 3. Trials (Infanticide)—Germany—Braunschweig—Case studies. 4. Schmidt, Grethe, 1646 or 7—Trials, litigation, etc. I. Title.

HV6541.G32B736 2011

364.152'3—dc22

2010041620

To my Mother, Catherine Myers

And to the Memory of Robert and Sharon Fitzpatrick

Contents

Illustrations

Acknowledgments

Acknowledgments are never easy—writing them makes it all too clear just how dependent any author is on the kindnesses of others. Fortunately, some of my debts are easy to identify. Amy Farranto and Northern Illinois University Press have been unfailingly helpful and encouraging. During hard times for university presses, Amy's enthusiasm for this project has made her a joy to work with, and I look forward to the opportunity of doing so again. Susan Bean at the press has been a strong guiding hand, and I must also thank the copyeditor, Marlyn Miller, for her amazing diligence and persistence.

A National Endowment for the Humanities Fellowship for University Teachers enabled a student of religion to learn something new and wide about the early modern world. Fordham University has been generous and patient in its support. Above all, the Herzog August Bibliothek in Wolfenbüttel and the state of Lower Saxony generously funded a year of research at the Library, which has been unfailingly supportive with its knowledgeable staff and unmatched resources. A scholar could not ask for more, but the Herzog August Bibliothek would surely find a way to provide it.

Other institutions too have played a critical role in developing this project. The City Archives in Braunschweig (Brunswick) have been consistently welcoming under two directors, and I must thank Dr. Hennig Steinführer for his help in the last year. Day in and day out, I rummaged about in their holdings, with only an occasional raised eyebrow from the staff. The same could be said on a lesser scale for the Lower Saxon Territorial Archives in Wolfenbüttel. At the Herzog August Bibliothek itself, many people deserve mention, but Jill Bepler stands out for her unflagging patience and for her meticulous scholarship and judicious advice. Christian Hogrefe guided me through the arcane riches of the library's holdings, and along with Andrea Swiderski provided valuable lessons in the culture of the Herzog August Bibliothek and of Lower Saxony. Both Ulrich Schneider and Ulrike Gleixner posed thoughtful and enriching questions about the project and early modern German history generally.

The library itself is an amazing meeting point for early modern scholars, and I was privileged to discuss this project with David Sabean, Mara Wade, Claudia Ulbrich, Otto Ulbricht, Anthony Grafton, Tom Robisheaux, and Susan Karant-Nunn, among others. All of them provided learned and shrewd advice. I am particularly indebted to Mary Lindemann for her generous help on the legal and medical culture of early modern Germany, and to Peter Albrecht for his encyclopedic knowledge of Braunschweig and the region itself—Peter saved me from numerous mistakes, though I have undoubtedly made many others. To all my colleagues among the fellows and guests of the Herzog August Bibliothek, I cannot give thanks enough, and there is not room here to name them all. Gregory Johnstone, C. Scott Dixon, and Anita Traninger were there to help frame the project at the very beginning, and it is fitting that Greg was present again at the end. Sina Rauschenbach, Isabella van Elferen, and Bethany Wiggins spent long hours discussing early modern music, history, and literature with me, and I have profited from their own work since. Jolanta Gelumbeckaite was invaluable both for her friendship and for her expertise in dealing with translation and early modern manuscripts. Leonie von Reppert-Bismarck and her husband, Thomas Rütten, helped me with my earliest attempts at translating the archival material and were consistently hospitable through-out my stay in Wolfenbüttel. I also had the good fortune of sharing the first results of my work at a Fellows' Colloquium in the Library.

Outside the environs of Lower Saxony, I remain indebted to Tom (and Kathy) Brady for their NEH seminar on German history and paleography at the Folger Library in Washington—that experience still bears fruit even two decades later. The indispensable Hubertus Jahn was instrumental in moving me to present early findings at Cambridge University, where I benefited as well from the insights of Ulinka Rublack, who was among the first to suggest that the Grethe Schmidt case could permit a look at the larger world of early modern law and politics.

Closer to home, I must also thank friends and colleagues at Mount Holyoke College, especially Joe Ellis, Chris Benfey, and Fred McGinness, for their willingness to discuss a topic far from their own specialties. Holger Teschke, Karen Remmler, John Varriano, and Kavita Khory also lent their assistance and friendship. Elsewhere, Lauren Winner, Sheryl Reiss, Susan Morrissey, and Leslie Griffin provided solid advice. Deep and special thanks are due Meredith Gill, who brought her considerable and subtle skills as a historian to bear in critiquing this project through its long history.

My colleagues past and present at Fordham continue to be a source of pride and a challenge. Maryanne Kowaleski was encouraging and help-ful on historical demography and the lives of early modern women. Dan Smail greatly enriched my knowledge of continental law, while Nancy Curtin and Tip Ragan challenged me on the subject of gender in early modern Europe. In particular, Wolfgang Mueller was generous with time and with his astonishing knowledge of medieval and early modern law, and as a native Braunschweiger he gently corrected an outsider's inevitable mistakes about his *Heimat*. I could not ask for better colleagues. Among students, Michael Conforti gave an intelligent reading of the case and encouraged me to approach a criminal case from a lawyer's standpoint. Helena Guzik was a great help in editing the illustrations. A number of sophomore classes in the Honors Program at Fordham have had to wade through the material, and the book is stronger for their assistance.

Finally, and these are my deepest thanks, from beginning to end I have benefited from the intelligence, learning, and skill of Tara Fitzpatrick. No other person did more to convince me of the value of approaching historical work in a new way, no one has suffered through the process more than she, and no one did more to see it through to completion by editing it over a long summer. Words alone cannot express my gratitude, but in a book, unlike life, words will have to do.

Death and a Maiden

Introduction

This is an account of law, justice, and power politics told through a single alleged crime in 1661. The story of Grethe Schmidt—accused, investigated, and tortured for a vicious crime—is so confounding that even one of Germany's clearest-eyed historians, Otto Ulbricht, has called it one of the "most spectacular" murder cases in northwest Germany during the seventeenth century.[1] From an apparently unremarkable arrest, the tale spiraled outward to set a defense lawyer and legal theorist against a powerful city's magistrates and then upward to a legal contest between that city—Braunschweig (English Brunswick)—and its overlord, the Duchy of Brunswick, with the city's independence and ancient liberties hanging in the balance. Lying behind the story itself were unsettled and dangerous political relations between lesser cities and the larger states seeking to engulf them. The weapons of choice were at first the criminal law of the Holy Roman Empire, fluid in practices and interpretations 130 years after its inception, and later the fragile treatises and decrees that bound the governmental entities of that empire together. The story this book tells began in the bedchamber of a house in Brunswick, but it ended at the court of Duke Augustus in the city of Wolfenbüttel. Along the way, criminal prosecution gave way to political intrigue. And yet, at the end of it all, after thousands of pages of testimony and rancorous legal exchange, it is still not clear that any murder happened.

THE STORY AND THE BOOK

In July of 1661, authorities in the city of Brunswick arrested a maidservant on suspicion of murdering her bastard child. The case at first appeared almost routine: a young unmarried woman was punished for killing in secret a child born in secret. In this instance, though, the magistrates found no material trace of a crime: no infant was ever seen, no corpse ever discovered, and no physical evidence demonstrated that Margarethe Schmidt (hereafter known as Grethe)—fourteen or fifteen at the time of her arrest—had even been pregnant. In line with the law's requirements, the testimony of witnesses justified the use of terror and torture, which resulted in a confession.

Aside from the girl's family, one person did take up her cause. Justus Oldekop, a prominent jurist and lawyer, aging and recently settled in Brunswick, became Schmidt's advocate (*Advokat*—a lawyer to represent her, roughly a precursor to the modern defense counsel). That a man of Oldekop's stature would condescend to help a poor peasant girl is itself a mystery, but help he did. Oldekop convincingly demonstrated the impossibility of Schmidt's original confession, after which the city magistrates extracted a second and entirely different confession. Oldekop so bedeviled the city's courts that, when they were done with Grethe Schmidt, the magistrates went after the lawyer himself, accusing him of sedition and libel. From the courtroom, the contest spilled into print as Oldekop publicly reviled the city's "unjust, untrue, and disgraceful" persecution of an innocent girl. The city responded in kind, vilifying the lawyer and justifying its process against an "immoral whore" who had polluted Brunswick's morals.[2] Oldekop suffered grievous wounds to his and his own family's honor. Like the impoverished family he defended, though, the lawyer remained defiant to the end.

During the 325 days Grethe Schmidt spent in jail, the prosecution labored to discover when, where, and how the girl had delivered and killed a baby. That she might in fact be innocent was a possibility that judicial officials never really considered, even though their goal theoretically was not a conviction but the truth itself. Convinced of her guilt, the magistrates interpreted the testimony of neighbors in light of the fact that Grethe fit the typical profile of an infanticide suspect as described by law and custom—a young, unmarried woman working in domestic service. Out of these basic elements the prosecution fashioned a criminal.

As intriguing as the story itself might be, the case also reveals the dynamism in the processes of early modern law and justice. The alleged murderer herself—Grethe Schmidt—was a work in progress, shaped and reshaped by the state's persistent prosecution and by her family's determination to exonerate her. The criminal processes were equally dynamic, as Schmidt's advocate sought to expand the role of the defense lawyer. The final conflict between city and duchy demonstrates the precarious, shifting balances of power in early modern Germany and the ways in which laws and courts could serve as instruments to carve out greater autonomy or to grind subjects into submission.

To unwind the complicated story of Grethe Schmidt and her ordeal, this book follows the events in chronological fashion and divides roughly into three parts, as different themes and issues come to the fore. The opening chapters concentrate on the woman and the alleged crime, while the second half of the book shifts first to the legal maneuvering over Grethe

Schmidt's fate and then to the battle of wills and words between the city of Brunswick's criminal courts and her lawyer. The book concludes with the political conflict over authority and jurisdiction between the city of Brunswick and its titular sovereign, the Duchy of Brunswick.

In looking at the materials of the Schmidt case, social historians will see much that is already familiar from the extensive studies of infanticide in German-speaking lands. Legal scholars will also recognize many of the developments traced in the book's second half. Why, then, should scholars concern themselves with this single case, no matter how gripping? Answering this question fully requires that one consider the current research on both infanticide and law in Germany. The basic argument, though, is that the deep concerns and imaginations of magistrates and rulers were at least as strong an influence in shaping infanticide prosecutions as any statistical evidence about the pervasiveness and frequency of the crime itself. The Grethe Schmidt investigation offers an intimate look at both the crime and the ways in which expectations and received wisdom combined to lay the burden of suspicion on a young woman. In short, the Schmidt case allows us to observe at close range the construction of a criminal and to ponder the significance of that fashioning for understanding the history of crime and of women. As noted below in chapter 6, the corpus delicti in this case was Grethe Schmidt herself, her appearance, and her admitted sexual activity (consensual or not). The prosecution's ability to shape the narrative without hindrance was a powerful, even decisive, tool that drove the process inexorably forward.

Another advantage to examining a single, extraordinary case is the depth of focus it permits the historian. The Schmidt process involved much more than interrogations and tortures carried out in the city dungeons. Prolonged isolation under the exclusive control of court officers was the circumstance in which Grethe Schmidt lived from the moment of her arrest. The possible cumulative effects of this experience is a factor that the historian must weigh as well. Perhaps the most intimate and crucial details afforded by the criminal record concern the process of torture and its role in shaping the identity of Grethe Schmidt as a murderer. The decision to apply torture was integral to the process of discovering the truth—physical coercion was to occur only when prosecutors had already established a high degree of probable cause.[3] Historians have also noted a substantial but uneven decline in the use of torture after 1650.[4] In this light, the routine recourse to torture in a case as problematic as the Schmidt affair seems even more remarkable. Did torture confirm almost certain conclusions resulting from testimony and other evidence? Or did the prosecutors labor to meet minimum standards permitting them to undertake terror and torture as a way of "making" a case that the evidence did not quite establish? Was the determination of probable cause left to the discretion of legal faculties who acted as judicial advisors, or to the courts themselves? One must consider that magistrates investigating serious but "mundane" crimes such as infanticide were also involved in investigating and prosecuting crimes like witchcraft. How this affected their perception of the evidence and procedures—especially in establishing a corpus delicti—is among the many difficult questions in need of an answer.

Schmidt herself was tortured twice over several months, but following the standard early modern practice this meant that she underwent a number of experiences leading up to the actual application of pain: introduction to the torturer, examination of the torture instruments, and demonstration of their use. The carefully scaled choreography of terror and actual physical pain contributed at each step to shaping the identity of Grethe Schmidt as a criminal. She went into jail a suspect, spent 325 days in the exclusive company of her jailers (save for one visit from her father), was tortured twice, and emerged a confessed murderer. While the investigation swirling outside her cell fashioned her public persona, the records also document the tremendous pressures placed upon her during the incarceration. In all of this, the question of gender—of the criminal, of the crime—played a major role.

Similarly, the extensive records covering Grethe Schmidt's defense provide an unmatched opportunity to examine the potential for a criminal defense in the hands of a skilled lawyer, as well as the ambivalent attitude toward a defense on the part of magistrates and prosecutors who saw the discovery of truth as their particular, even exclusive, domain. A close look at the work of Justus Oldekop in this case reveals an experienced advocate pushing to expand the boundaries of the process in a legal system that offered the opportunity of criminal defense only with reluctance.

Some of the issues noted above have been treated, especially for the eighteenth century. The earlier history is less well known, because although infanticide was a major crime in the minds of jurists, clergy, and rulers, its study has always been overshadowed by the attention paid to witchcraft, another crime that "flourished" in the sixteenth and seventeenth centuries and diminished in the eighteenth. Yet, save for witchcraft, more women were executed for newborn child murder than for any other crime.[5] And in contrast to witchcraft prosecutions, infanticide was much less an "exceptional crime" and more a matter of routine criminal justice. As such, an infanticide prosecution permits us to focus more on the routine workings and processes of the criminal courts. Finally, in contrast to cases of witchcraft, the very existence of which is problematic, infanticide was a deed that women may actually have committed.

To appreciate fully the significance of this singular case, then, it is necessary to place it within the context of the known world, of the generally accepted history both of infanticide and of criminal process in continental Europe. What follows is an outline of major developments, each of which will be explored more fully in the chapters to come.

INFANTICIDE

The account begins with the alleged infanticide at the beginning of 1661. In some ways, this is actually the most predictable part of the story. Over the last twenty-five years, early modern historians have delved extensively into the causes, frequency, and meaning of this particular act. What they have discovered allows us to see Grethe Schmidt both as a rule and an exception and to place the sad affair within the general context of the early modern European world. Infanticide—loosely defined as deliberately killing newborn or very young children, usually by their parents—is found throughout human history and culture.[6] In early modern Europe it was a very serious crime indeed, as indicated by the high percentage of women executed for it. This fact should not mislead us. Pervasiveness does not mean a high rate of infanticide, nor can it explain the seriousness with which authorities treated the crime. Indeed, according to one theory, frequent infanticide might suggest social acceptance, perhaps as part of a tacitly tolerated "Malthusian process" of family limitation.[7] Another theory argues that infanticide served to shape the population, with parents choosing to kill an infant based on some deformity or gender (usually female).[8]

For European history, both motives prove problematic, for a very simple reason—there was not that much infanticide overall. Keith Wrightson has concluded that the incidence of infanticide in seventeenth-century England was too low to be of use in limiting population,[9] and an important study covering England and New England from the mid-sixteenth to the nineteenth centuries has shown not only that infanticide was relatively infrequent but also that the rate actually decreased during the eighteenth century.[10] In German lands where, as we shall see, the question of infanticide was more intensely debated than elsewhere, statistics from the eighteenth century show barely one infanticide per year for every 100,000 people.[11] The second general reason   the desire to eliminate undesirables, whether because of deformity or gender—has also been hotly debated. For early modern Europe, it seems true again that no pattern can be found of *specific* infanticide of newborn girls.[12] One should note here that the question is not entirely settled, and recent evidence from Tuscan baptismal registers points to anomalies in the sex ratio of newborns brought to baptism.[13]

One might be tempted to argue that the infanticides actually prosecuted represent only the "tip of the iceberg," and that the continent of Europe is littered with the unmarked graves of victims cleverly hidden and never discovered. This gruesome vision, though, is improbable. As Otto Ulbricht compellingly argues, hiding bodies was not so easy in the early modern world, especially in the cities. Almost anywhere that a woman might stash the body, it was likely to be discovered (and from Ulbricht's evidence, usually was). Bodies buried hastily in fields had a tendency to be uncovered (and eaten) by dogs or pigs. Even if a woman could hide the body, there was the question of blood, for childbirth is and was a messy and bloody affair, hard for a woman to hide in close quarters. In contrast, the number of cases in which a body was discovered and no criminal found was relatively small. Either way, women had a hard time keeping their pregnancies hidden from the sharp eyes of watchful neighbors and employers.[14] The Grethe Schmidt case itself provides an example—unable to find an infant's corpse to pin on the girl, authorities still pursued the case, largely because of neighbors' suspicions. Yet this fact itself should also provoke caution in the opposite direction—one cannot assume that for every prosecution or conviction, an infanticide actually occurred.

Even if one were inclined to accept a mass number of undiscovered infanticides relative to the known cases, perhaps by a factor of ten, one would still be dealing with a ratio of only ten infanticides per one hundred thousand people. Of course, these statistics apply only to unmarried women carrying illegitimate children. It is impossible to know, in the end, how many *married* women or couples might have committed infanticide, since (as will be shown in chapter 2) the law was concerned only with unwed mothers. In addition, the great difficulty of determining whether an infant had been a live birth or stillborn made prosecution difficult in the absence of a clear motive. As a result, married women facing suspicion over an infant's death could claim with relative impunity that a child had been stillborn instead.

These arguments so far apply specifically to a deliberate act of infanticide. There were (and are) other, more "passive" ways to eliminate unwanted infants, possibly resulting (deliberately or not) in death. One way is through neglect of unwanted children—usually girls—with morbid results, but this practice has not been demonstrated for Europe. A more likely route to "indirect" infanticide would be through infant abandonment. Particularly during the late seventeenth and eighteenth centuries, Europe experienced a "vertiginous rise in the number of abandoned children."[15] By the end of the eighteenth century, approximately 100,000 children, "nearly all of them in early infancy," were abandoned in Europe every year.[16]

Rates of abandonment prove useful, then, in charting a rise in "unwanted" children in Europe. It is hard to argue, though, that these practices represent any Malthusian attempt to reduce the population or change its character. The fact that rising abandonment coincided with the increase in foundling homes, and in some places legal statutes requiring abandonment of illegitimate infants, suggests that "indirect infanticide" was not the goal for parents abandoning infants (though, to be sure, foundling homes had high mortality rates). As to gender selection, even the abandonment rates do not alter the fact that, during the early modern period, "up to the age of five mortality tended to be generally higher amongst boys."[17] Finally, the number of children abandoned in German lands appears to have been smaller than in France or Italy, where laws frequently required illegitimate children to be surrendered to authorities and foundling homes.[18]

Discounting the likelihood of a high rate of infanticide in early modern Europe does not diminish its significance, however. Instead, it permits us to examine the act less as a "demographic episode" than as a serious cultural and social matter. In Europe, the practice of killing or exposing newborn children had a long history tangled in the webs of religious and political strife.[19] Infanticide's true significance, though, was as a particular kind of crime that haunted the imagination and morals of Europeans from 1500 to 1800.[20] Here the loose definition of infanticide as passively or actively killing young children is too broad to be useful. Instead, Mark Jackson has used the phrase "newborn child murder" to define infanticide as a criminal act.[21] It was only after 1500 that laws and criminal courts focused on infanticide as a crime against one's own flesh and blood, thus aggravating the severity of the deed. In 1532, the new criminal law for the Holy Roman Empire (the *Constitutio Criminalis Carolina*) framed the murder of newborns in a fashion that focused on unwed mothers acting out of shame over fornication. In France, a royal edict of 1556 stated, "When they appear before our judges, women accused of this crime say they were ashamed to reveal their fault [namely, an illegitimate conception] and that their babies were stillborn." The edict then decreed:

> any woman who shall be duly convicted of having concealed both her pregnancy and her confinement, without having declared either one or the other, and without sufficient witness to one or the other, and in particular shall not be able to produce evidence of the life or death of her child as it came forth from her womb . . . such a woman shall henceforth be considered to have murdered her child and shall be put to death.[22]

A century after the *Carolina*, in 1624, the English Parliament sought to "prevent the destroying and murthering of bastard children" by "lewd" mothers seeking to escape from the shame of bearing an illegitimate child.[23]

All three legal statements refer in some way to "lewd women" committing heinous deeds against their own newborn infants out of shame over an illegitimate baby. To see how the legal theory shaped criminal practice and thinking, one need only turn again to early modern France, where fifteen hundred women and very few men were executed for infanticide between the sixteenth and eighteenth centuries. Two-thirds of all women put to death between 1565 and 1690 were executed for this one crime. Reviewing these hundreds of cases, Alfred Soman eloquently summarizes the significance of shame: "The crime designated 'infanticide' (*homicide de son enfant*) was uniformly of one type (which either excluded or absorbed all other forms of child murder): a woman conceived a child illegitimately, concealed her pregnancy, gave birth in secret, and then killed her baby or deliberately let it die in a desperate attempt to suppress the evidence of her shame and dishonor."[24]

While the murder of newborn children was a prominent crime throughout early modern Europe and the Americas as well, the issue resonates particularly strongly in Germany. One of the greatest of German legal historians referred to infanticide as the "key delict to all efforts at criminal law reform in the eighteenth century."[25] Infanticide became a capital offense there in 1532, earlier than in some other European lands. In the eighteenth century, infanticide as the focus for reforming criminal law and sexual regulations became a cause célèbre for enlightened judicial reformers such as Christian Thomasius and a literary topic for writers like Goethe, whose own close observation of a case in Frankfurt inspired the sad fate of Gretchen in *Faust*.[26] Despite the far greater attention paid to witchcraft prosecution, in many areas executions for infanticide actually outnumbered those for witchcraft. Examining the relatively large cities of Frankfurt, Augsburg, Nürnberg, and Danzig from the sixteenth to the eighteenth centuries, Richard van Dülmen reveals that infanticide accounted for 7.8 percent of all capital sentences, but 46 percent of all executed women.[28] While the second half of the seventeenth century was a time of fewer and milder punishments for men, the punishment of women in some areas was growing more severe in comparison, and executions for infanticide were increasing as a percentage of the total.[29]

One must of course recognize that these statistics reflect prosecutions rather than the number of infanticides themselves. As scholars point out, before 1500 few infanticide cases appear in the criminal courts. In German lands, as elsewhere, new laws in the early sixteenth century helped to define the crime and spur prosecutions. The promulgation of the *Carolina* in 1532 marks a watershed in the history of infanticide legislation and the beginning of a period of intensifying severity in prosecution and punishments. It was during the later seventeenth century, however, that official responses were apparently the harshest, prompting an increase in prosecutions. In Württemberg in 1658, for example, following the Thirty Years War, magistrates responded to a perceived increase in newborn child murders by promulgating an infanticide statute. The results were startling and instructive: "only fourteen infanticide cases can be traced for the whole sixteenth century, but at least fifty-five cases are known between 1600 and 1659, and a further 127 up to 1700."[30] This contrasts with other towns and cities in the region where cases of infanticide were rare throughout the seventeenth century. In Brunswick itself, for example, the Schmidt case of 1661 was followed by only two others, in 1678 (the accused was found innocent) and 1693. Despite this small number, in the 1693 case the poor culprit, Katharine Mundt, received a particularly harsh sentence for the deed—drowning.[31]

In sum, the marked concern over infanticide cannot be explained by the statistics. Infanticide accusations and prosecutions reflected less a social pathology demanding attention and more the concerns of jurists, city authorities, and even the citizens themselves. Without the involvement of a city's inhabitants—particularly women—increased prosecutions would have been very difficult. Cities and territories expected employers to be responsible for the morals and behavior of domestic servants.[32] This situation pitted an unstable, shifting population of outsiders against urban employers and citizens who could be counted on to view domestic servants without sympathy.

The Defense

The court record allows us to trace not only the ways in which the prosecution proceeded but also how the suspect responded. That even a poor family would act to protect its kin against the state is not news—the idea of an inert subject peasantry has long been refuted.[33] Women in court were also not mere passively compliant in their own doom but developed consistent sets of strategies in their own defense.[34] Just how resourceful the Schmidts proved, however, is remarkable, particularly in exploiting (with the help of their advocate) jurisdictional ambiguities to their advantage.

A close reading of the historical literature shows that after nearly 150 years of commentary and controversy, criminal procedures were neither consistent nor even smooth within, but especially between, jurisdictions.

Among the most fluid and puzzling elements of early modern continental criminal procedure involves the role of the defense. Its history is
imperfectly studied, in part because the role of the defense lawyer was
only grudgingly acknowledged by inquisitorial magistrates who trusted
themselves as the principal guardians of truth.[35] It is not that the law
excluded a defense—far from it (see chapter 10). As Alexander Ignor argues, all the elements for a defense existed in the law, which was after all
grounded upon a Roman model that included the presence of an advocate
to speak for the parties.[36] And historians have noted the relatively rare occasions in witchcraft proceedings where lawyers intervened to the benefit
of the accused. What was theoretically available in criminal procedure,
though, was not necessarily explicitly possible in practice. The nature of
the inquisitorial system itself, with the court simultaneously responsible
for prosecuting, judging, and considering a suspect's possible innocence,
could in practice lead to the defendant's complete loss of rights.[37] Lack of
clarity about the role of a criminal defense left much room for errors and
even for possible misconduct by the criminal courts to slip through, especially given the severe limitations on criminal appeals. The single-minded
emphasis on the confession in determining guilt, even under the threat or
reality of torture, could override concerns about procedural propriety and
rights. An advocate's involvement could trouble the process by challeng-
ing the trustworthiness of an investigation and its testimony.[38] It remained
for lawyers to alter the matter by either expanding or restricting the law's
reach in particular cases.

The Schmidt family's determination to protect their daughter opened
the case to wider significance, and the fortuitous choice of an advocate—
Justus Oldekop—guaranteed that Grethe's defense would test the limits of
criminal procedure. For Oldekop, then, the Schmidt affair became a test
for his own ideas about conducting a defense, limiting torture, and mounting an appeal—something generally precluded in criminal cases (see
below, chapter 3). For his efforts he ended up in exile, fleeing the city that
sought to prosecute his disobedience and curtail his insolent defiance by
maligning him in print. The city council of Brunswick denounced Oldekop
for obstructing justice and corrupting the case against Schmidt out of his
own vanity and greed. Oldekop reacted by publishing the proceedings of
the entire case while awaiting the results of his appeals to higher authority,
forcing the city to respond in kind.

Oldekop's aggressive actions and writings on the matter illuminate the
entire early modern criminal process in a remarkable way. Though Otto
Ulbricht has detailed the regular recourse to defense of some sort and has
himself brought forth a number of remarkable instances, it is unusual to

find a case in which the defense is so well detailed. This was not only due to the problematic nature of the Schmidt affair but also undoubtedly to the coincidence of such a difficult case coming into the hands of such an ambitious—and pugnacious—defender.[39] In Brunswick itself in 1663, just two years after the Schmidt case, a woman known as Tempel Anneke was accused, tried, and executed for witchcraft—at no point during the process was the question of a defense ever raised.[40]

As to the crime itself, studying infanticide rather than witchcraft shifts attention toward a crime that, even if it was not frequent, actually did occur. This opens interesting possibilities, particularly when dealing with issues of habeas corpus and, especially, torture. Confessions of witchcraft gained by torture invariably reinforce the (altogether warranted) sense of a grave injustice and provoke the question of how intelligent and educated men could become so involved in such a fantastic operation. The reality of a crime like infanticide allows us to consider the ways in which torture might actually seem a useful tool to reasonable men and women, and whether it was nevertheless still a failure. In a world that, 350 years later, is asking itself the same question about torture, the examination should prove useful.[41]

THE POLITICS OF JUSTICE

As the case of Grethe Schmidt spiraled outward, it became entangled in another dynamic element—political relations and their effect upon criminal courts and procedures. Oldekop's efforts beyond Brunswick's city walls opened a controversy over jurisdiction and standing between the city and its ambitious foe, the Duke of Brunswick-Lüneburg. Already under siege politically, with its trade routes occasionally blocked, and besieged militarily (with conquest the outcome in 1671), Brunswick and its rulers now had to confront legal challenges to the traditional autonomy of its criminal courts, supposedly guaranteed by repeated imperial decrees but potentially undermined by Oldekop's appeals.

SOURCES AND STRUCTURES

The case of Grethe Schmidt is remarkable in part for its sources—the entire criminal file is available in the city archives of Brunswick. The story might still go unremarked if it were not for the appeals that followed, the records of which are located in the Wolfenbüttel territorial archives. Oldekop's decision to challenge the city in print—and the magistrates' willingness to respond—provided yet another set of printed records, invaluable because it included the parties' extended commentary on the case. The criminal file itself is the most comprehensive, unfiltered version of the case, and it has been used as the basic source for this narrative. When the conflict moved into print, of course, Oldekop's pamphlet and the city's response became the focal point of analysis.

Because of the richness of these records and the narrative that leaps from them, the book has been structured so that (1) the sources speak for themselves, with as little interference as possible from the author; and (2) the narrative retains its original shape—whatever is gripping here comes from the story as it unfolds in the records rather than from an author's re-telling. The book is divided into narrative chapters roughly alternating with more analytical chapters geared to particular themes (e.g., law, conception, defense). The narrative chapters themselves are structured according to the particular date and place of interrogation. This too should help the reader follow a great but very confusing story with ease.

As a final note to keep in mind, whatever political and legal intrigue one might attach to the case, it is important to remember that it began with concern over a vicious and violent act involving emotions and suspicions that the historian cannot finally hope to resolve. Historical objectivity cannot obscure the fact that somewhere in this sad tale, a grave injustice occurred—an infant was or was not killed, a young woman of thirteen or fourteen was or was not guilty of the crime. In the course of the story, many characters take center stage, particularly lawyers and judges, and the law itself plays a central role. Despite all these ambitious and powerful men, however, the tale begins and ends with the girl.

Part One

Grethe

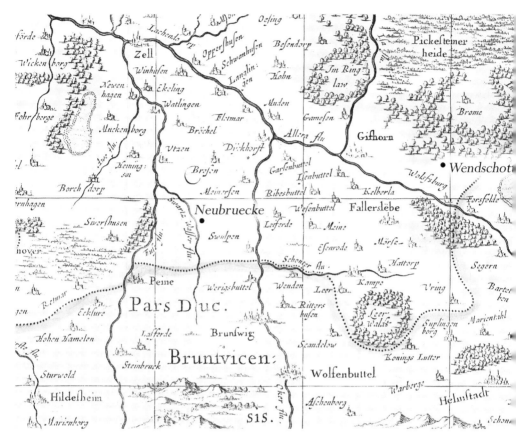

Grethe's world: Detail of the Duchy of Brunswick-Lüneburg, 1650, showing the border between the separate regions and highlighting the travels of Grethe Schmidt between 1659 and 1662. Herzog August Bibliothek Wolfenbüttel: K 7 63

1

In Brunswick, near Hannover City

The Setting

At the heart of the story stands the girl. At thirteen, Grethe Schmidt traveled from the Lower Saxon countryside to the city of Brunswick to find work. After eighteen months, though, she was forced to flee, and when she returned to the city, authorities arrested and tried her for a terrible crime—the murder of her newborn baby. Grethe migrated to Brunswick like many other women of her age and status, and she shared with them the youth and poverty that automatically drew the suspicions of authorities. Yet something singular about her behavior and character particularly provoked the magistrates. She sat in jail for five months without family or friends, indeed with no company at all except for the men who sought to condemn her and who repeatedly threatened her with physical pain. Those same men, zealously pursuing justice in the service of their city, ordered and then witnessed Grethe's torture. And still, in the sixth month of her incarceration, facing the threat of renewed torture on a cold January day, Grethe Schmidt summoned the strength to defy the magistrates of Brunswick yet again and reject the charges against her. Had Grethe been meek instead of outspoken, had she submitted easily to the prosecutors rather than defy them, had she acquiesced in interrogations rather than risk repeated torture, then her life might have turned out far differently. Grethe Schmidt's individual resolve foiled her jailers and drove the prosecution to extreme measures in order to convict her. And yet, the record of her prosecution also reveals a confused young woman whose identity and understanding of what was happening to her shifted under the burden of incarceration, isolation, and interrogation. To judge Grethe Schmidt is to judge the city prosecutors who pursued her and the ambitious old man who risked his career to defend her. Perhaps more important, judging Grethe requires assessing an entire criminal process and the practices—including torture—that supported it.

That Grethe left a historical impression at all is surprising. In a fictional New England, Hester Prynne could dominate the imaginations of the small-minded folk of a colonial town. In the real and complicated world of seventeenth-century Europe, however, the fortunes of an oxherd's daughter seldom affected the lives and reputations of respectable people. The amount of information available today about a farm girl from the distant past is unusual in itself. Ironically, the men who sought to destroy her life preserved her memory. The criminal courts of a literate and highly bureaucratic society recorded evidence of Grethe Schmidt's character, words, and reactions, in detail. Those records also make clear that, although Grethe Schmidt faced the authorities alone, behind her stood a family, in particular a resilient mother who proved endlessly resourceful, even dangerous, in defending her child.

A HARSH WORLD

The story properly begins, then, with the young woman whose sad fate allows us to know her, and the family that nurtured her. Margarethe Schmidt (referred to everywhere as "Grethe") was born in 1646 or 1647 in the small farming village of Gross Schwülper on the banks of the Oker River, ten kilometers from the city of Brunswick. Sitting on the flat plains of Lower Saxony at the foot of the Harz Mountains, Gross Schwülper barely registers with residents of the nearby city today, and even in the seventeenth century it was poor and unexceptional in every way. Brunswick, by contrast, had the power and great wealth befitting a commercial center and a member of the ancient Hanseatic League, with influence running west to London and east through the Baltic as far as present-day Estonia. Prominence and fame, though, dissipated as the Oker flowed from Brunswick through Gross Schwülper, where the village's few souls clung to a farming existence on the river's edge. The village itself belonged to the Lüneburg section of the duchy administered in the ducal chancellery at Celle.

Grethe was the second of three daughters of Andreas Schmidt and his wife, Ilse Leuthgen (married women did not yet take their husbands' names). The eldest daughter, Anna, had left home for work in Brunswick, setting a course that her sister would follow. Ilsge ("little Ilse") was the third in line and still living at home in 1661. With three children, the Schmidts were a typical household of the day, at least in number. Whatever images we may have of the sprawling and extended clans of our ancestors, the seventeenth century was not an age of large families. Scarcity forced marriage ages up and, thus, birth rates down—Andreas and Ilse themselves were probably in their late twenties when they married.

Even for the luckiest people, the world into which the three Schmidt daughters were born was a cruel one. Perhaps a third of all pregnancies ended in miscarriage or spontaneous abortions. Of infants born, a third would die in their first year. Only half would reach the age of fifteen. Even a century later, in Belm, near the Saxon city of Osnabruck, 16 percent of children died in the first year of life, nearly 10 percent died between the ages of two and five, another 10 percent between six and fifteen. The total—32 percent of the town's children dead before the age of fifteen— would fill any community in modern America or Europe with unbearable grief. Yet child mortality in Belm was comparatively low for the period.[1] Andreas Schmidt and Ilse Leuthgen had three healthy daughters, but Ilse might well have borne five or six children in all, some of whom would have died in childbirth or infancy.

Grethe was also fortunate to have been born in the countryside and not in the city, where disease and filth festered and infant mortality rates could creep up to 50 percent.[2] Poverty meant too that the girls' mother had to breastfeed her children rather than send them out to wet-nurse, and paradoxically this proved beneficial.[3] Hunger was the constant foe of growing children, and a key factor in any infant's survival was exclusive and prolonged access to its own mother's milk.[4]

Grethe, Anna, and Ilsge were lucky in another way. Both parents were still alive in 1661, defying grim odds, particularly for their mother. One out of every hundred childbirths killed the mother within 60 days, and with each new pregnancy a mother's risk increased.[5] For their time, the Schmidt family was unusually intact. By way of contrast, in the far wealthier family for which Grethe worked in Brunswick, the son Andreas had lost both father and mother and was living at home with his stepmother, Margarethe Hafferland.

This good fortune is all the more striking given the family's precarious circumstances and modest status. Andreas Schmidt worked as an oxherd. In a seventeenth-century village like Gross Schwülper, where crop yields were low, the governing commune carefully guarded access to the land and somehow cultivated every inch. Even landowning peasants had parcels too small for grazing cattle, sheep, or horses as well, so the village itself had to establish "common" pastures. This meant that someone had to tend the animals while farmers worked their fields. A communal herder for the village's common lands was a logical solution.[6] The necessity of such positions, though, did not mean they were well paid. Herders were hirelings who worked for a salary, automatically placing them below the level of landowning peasants.[7] In Gross Schwülper, the Schmidts' next-door neighbors were the local shepherd family, with a house provided by the village.

Such housing would often have to be relinquished at the end of service, so herders remained in principle homeless. As propertyless wage earners they did not qualify to become part of the village "commune."[8] Even shepherds, though, were more prosperous than oxherds. That Andreas Schmidt would later claim to have trouble paying for a legal defense came as no surprise to anyone, including his daughter's prosecutors.

Poverty and landlessness were not the only reasons for herders' low status. The work itself was dirty and difficult, involving more than lazy wandering through grassy meadows with docile herds.[9] Herders had long been marked as "dishonorable" individuals whose work rendered them distasteful in the eyes of the community, sometimes unworthy even of burial in the hallowed ground of the churchyard. Respectable people avoided them, not wanting their own "honor" besmirched by contact. This distinction had legal repercussions—dishonor disqualified individuals from membership in guilds, restricted their mobility, limited their marriage opportunities, and ostracized their children. Dishonor entailed a loss of rights that otherwise belonged to a "free" person and subject of the state.[10]

That herding folk would fall into a dishonorable category needs explaining. After all, museum walls are covered with seventeenth-century landscapes depicting herders roaming peacefully about an idyllic countryside. In fact, however, the isolation of herders' lives—lonely days and often nights spent in quiet among their animals—gave rise to suspicions about their possessing "secret" knowledge, practicing dark arts, or performing "unnatural" sexual acts.[11] Shepherds, for example, had long been suspected of theft.[12] Above all, though, herders, like executioners (another "dishonorable" profession), dealt with the grisly facts of life and death. When cattle or sheep died without having been slaughtered properly (with a knife), it was the herder's job to dispose of the body.[13]

Understanding the Schmidts means forgetting bucolic fantasies and recalling the poverty and constraints under which Andreas lived and tried to raise a family. Later, when friends and foes alike spoke of Grethe as "the oxherd's daughter," each side understood the reference. The meanings, though, could not have been more opposite. On one side stood a simple, unschooled family perennially in desperate circumstances and in need of help. On the other side, the "oxherd's daughter" automatically conjured an image not only of poverty but of distastefulness, of dishonesty, and of a natural proclivity toward criminal behavior.

Of Grethe Schmidt's mother, Ilse Leuthgen, little biographical information exists. She had worked as a servant in Brunswick before marrying Andreas, so it is probable that she too came from straitened circumstances. Despite poverty, she and her husband had raised three legitimate children in a world full of physical dangers and among the most vexing social and economic circumstances. The pastor of the parish church in Gross Schwülper testified later that, despite the family's "low and minimal status," no "bad thing had ever been heard of them."[14]

CHILDHOOD

It is impossible to know in detail what Grethe's life was like until the age of twelve. Based on her family's status, though, we can speculate about a typical girlhood of the day. Clearly, the idea of "childhood" had a more restricted meaning and a shorter duration in the seventeenth century than it does today, and the two modern activities associated with it—schooling and play—were limited. Even children as young as five would begin to help in the family's work, especially among the poor, where every hand counted and even little fingers played a role, gathering herbs, carrying water, washing clothes.[15] The idea of "child labor" as a repugnant phenomenon is a quite modern fancy; sheer necessity forced seventeenth-century children into the household economy.

As for education, it is safe to say that young Grethe Schmidt received none. Schools were available in the cities but not the country, were attended by children of higher classes but not lower, and were intended for boys but not girls. Perhaps the local Lutheran pastor Georg Weichman made some attempt at religious instruction. From Pastor Weichman Grethe would have learned that she should be an obedient child, a dutiful subject of her overlords, the Count Marenholtz and Duke Augustus the Younger of Brunswick-Lüneburg, as well as any other authorities placed over her—her parents and, later, her masters or employer. The commandment to "honor father and mother" applied to more than just the physical parents.[16] Pastor and parents alike would have drummed into her the importance of sexual purity.

Aside from these general characteristics of a seventeenth-century girlhood, court testimony provides some individual details about Grethe. Her lawyer described the young woman as "short and fat," the result of natural disposition and "liking food too much." He also repeatedly referred to her as "simple-minded" or even "stupid."[17] It is difficult to know whether he meant that she was mentally deficient in some way or merely as naïve as one would expect of a young girl from the country lacking in education or sophistication. She was, however, athletic and energetic. An employer later noted how fearlessly Grethe could mount a horse and described an episode in her garden, marveling about "how quickly she could climb a tree, and how high she could climb."[18]

Grethe Schmidt also had an independent streak that did not endear her to her "betters." The same employer who marveled at Grethe's athleticism dismissed her for being insolent. And she was undoubtedly stubborn—for nearly a year she resisted most of the physical and psychological pressures that an entire city's criminal machinery could bring to bear upon her. Strong-willed, athletic, insubordinate—from these very character traits, prosecutors would fashion a young woman criminally determined in her disobedience, intent upon her own desires. They took Grethe's disrespect for authority to be an outward sign of moral depravity lying within her. Even her robust physicality heralded a wantonness that would burst forth in lasciviousness and violence.

LURE OF THE CITY

The Schmidts' poverty and low status meant that Andreas and Ilse could not provide materially for their children's future. To have only daughters was an additional burden. Helping even one daughter find a husband and establish a household was difficult enough, but three made the task especially daunting. If the Schmidts could not marry off their daughters, then Anna, Grethe, and Ilsge might have to spend their lives working at the margins of society, perhaps as domestics.[19] Other possibilities for unmarried women were worse, prostitution among them, especially in German lands just emerging from the disaster of the Thirty Years War. Women, particularly those unattached to a family or household, were in peril of being swept along by the tides of war and the rapaciousness of soldiers.

A poor young woman like Grethe had to rely on her own efforts. Her best path to true security lay in marrying and establishing a household.[20] Marriage was crucial in the seventeenth century not only to social status, particularly for women, but also to economic well-being, even physical survival. Who but a spouse could be relied upon to tend a man or woman in case of illness and old age? Employers felt little or no responsibility to care for disabled or aged servants. Medical knowledge was primitive and medical care limited to the well-off. An ailing parent might call upon children, especially if an inheritance was in the offing, but poor sons and daughters were only able to scratch out a bare living themselves.[21] The vow "in sickness and in health" meant something quite elemental in a very harsh world.[22]

Despite the advantages of marriage, some 10 to 20 percent of women in seventeenth-century Europe would never wed, with the percentage increasing over the course of the seventeenth century, particularly in towns.[23] At any one time, more than half the women of working age were likely to be unmarried.[24] In German-speaking territories as elsewhere, the desire for marriage and children ran up against concerns over poverty, property, and illegitimacy, with discouraging results for poor women.[25] The regulatory authorities—parental or governmental—of early modern Europe did not view marriages as private affairs and might prohibit them from taking place if the couple were deemed undesirable by virtue of poverty, position—domestic servants, for example—or reputation.[26] Unmarried women might seek employment on their own, usually as urban domestic servants. Some, like Ilse Leuthgen, might work only until marriage. A woman who did not eventually marry might end up living and working on her own—a condition that today resonates with thoughts of independence, but which frequently entailed poverty and invariably brought social suspicion and often persecution.[27] For all women, a final bizarre threat loomed. Witch hunting in German lands peaked from 1590 to 1630, with minor outbreaks of persecution in the 1660s and into the eighteenth century.[28] The chief targets were older women living alone, but others, particularly single women, were potentially victims.[29] To be poor, female, and alone was an unenviable and dangerous condition.

Families like the Schmidts knew this, and so daughters would spend their teens and early twenties laboring to accumulate the resources that might make a marriage possible. Though the presence of one or two daughters at home helped lighten the labor of their parents, in order to establish a material foundation sufficient to attract marriage partners, young women had to strike out on their own, at ages that seem to modern Americans shockingly early. On average, young people—girls and boys alike—left home to live and work elsewhere at fourteen. Some poorer families could see children depart even earlier.[30] If the parents were dead or some other misfortune had befallen a family, then even younger children—between six and ten years old—might enter service. The younger the age of entering service, it seems, the more likely a child was to have experienced either tragedy or extreme poverty.[31]

For a daughter to abandon her family to enter service at such a tender age was not necessarily the cruel exploitation it seems to us. By leaving home, a girl could begin to accumulate the assets her own family could not provide in the form of a dowry. To put it more bluntly, a poor girl of fourteen could no longer afford to provide her family with "free" labor.[32] If a young woman went into service, she might be able to learn new and different skills that would be useful later, adding to her attractiveness as a prospective spouse, even though domestic service was an occupation of low prestige. The need for poor people to accumulate resources also helps explain why men and women in northern Europe tended to marry late. At the same time, during her period of servitude, a young woman might have an experience of independence for the first and perhaps only time in her life, a brief period of freedom that worried the authorities greatly.[33]

From all over Lower Saxony, indeed from all over northern Germany by the seventeenth century, country girls provided labor for growing cities. Urban households needed servants, who were frequently poor, rural women.[34] Lowly though it was, domestic service was also one of the few acceptable employments for unmarried young women seeking to move to the city, because it harnessed them to a household, hopefully one headed by a male.[35] Indeed, it was an excellent time to move to Brunswick, with the high demand for workers following an epidemic in 1657. Established labor contacts in the countryside assured employers of reliable servants, having already hired at some point a mother or a sister.[36] Rural parents like Ilse Leuthgen with a city connection hoped to ensure that their children, especially daughters, would be well treated by a known employer.[37]

Even though going to the city for work was often a rural girl's best choice, it was also risky. Leaving her home village for a distant household in a strange town, a girl could not expect to see much of her family. As she entered adolescence, a young woman had to confront not only her own feelings but also the harsh realities of male appetites. Her society placed strict restraints on all—but especially women's—sexual activity before marriage and attempted to cultivate a sense of shame in young people in order to regulate their sexual behavior. Cities expected heads of households (*Hausväter*) to protect and to police the behavior of their servants. Despite these measures, though, and without a sympathetic family there to help, a country girl needed all the courage and emotional strength she could muster just to get by.

For Grethe, the decision to leave home was inevitable and probably not hers alone. Before marrying, her mother had worked as a servant for seven years in the home of Ludolff Garsen, a citizen of Brunswick. Her experience and contacts there undoubtedly paved the way for her children. Anna, the oldest daughter, had also worked in Brunswick; next came Grethe's turn. Ludolff Garsen's widow, Margarethe Engelken, helped Ilse by finding work for her daughter. Frail and sick, Engelken already had her own servant but suggested that her niece Margarethe Hafferland, herself recently widowed, might need a new maid. Thus it was that at the end of September 1659, at the feast of St. Michael when servants were traditionally hired and their wages paid, Grethe Schmidt went to Brunswick to work for Margarethe Hafferland at her house in the Breite Strasse. She was probably thirteen years old, perhaps only twelve.

BRUNSWICK

Grethe's journey to Brunswick was only ten kilometers, but it might well have lasted a full day. Roads and paths would have been rutted and muddy from the rains that typically spread across northern Europe in autumn. The easiest path would have been to follow the Oker River, approaching the city from the flat plains of the northwest. The family would travel through fertile fields and pasture along the river's winding course—a pleasant walk, but the Schmidts were used to rural views. No doubt the sight that held them was the ever-nearer city. From this angle along the river, the looming prospect of Brunswick could fill the eye and dazzle someone accustomed to rural isolation. Great gothic churches dominated the skyline from the west, beginning with single-towered St. Andreas in the north, followed by St. Katharine's Church in the borough of Hagen, then on past the cathedral to the Altstadt and St. Martin's parish church with its distinctive double towers, and on to St. Jakob, St. Magnus, St. Michael, and finally to the hulking stone structure of St. Aegidius.

These churches dwarfed the secular symbols of power. One might glimpse the towers of the Altstadt *Rathaus* (city hall) huddled next door to St. Martin's like a smaller, humble brother. Even more imposing than the churches, though, were the walls enclosing the city, high stone fortifications covered with parapets, watchtowers, and gun turrets, notched at intervals by gates locked at nightfall and only reopened with the sun. Enclosing the entire metropolis was a moat diverting the Oker River into canals that paralleled the city walls. Cleverly engineered, the moat's water level could be raised when necessary to add an extra measure of protection. Even before reaching the moat, however, the Schmidts would pass by extra fortifications—trenches, cannon platforms, berms, and spikes.

The Schmidts would pass through one of the northern gates, and the city of Brunswick, until now partially hidden by the great surrounding wall, lay before them. It was quite a sight—a bustling metropolis of some 15,000 inhabitants, of whom 2,000 were sworn citizens of the city (burghers) and another 300 were the widows of citizens, like Margarethe Hafferland and Margarethe Engelken. These citizens gained their status through a combination of property, profession, and long residence in Brunswick. They had the right to hold office, to vote, and otherwise participate in the city's affairs. The rest of the population consisted of citizens' families—wives and children, the many people who depended upon them for work or housing, such as servants, and a very large number of workers who owned little or no property and worked for wages. Brunswick's size appears small in modern terms. Today, it is a middling city located just at

Panoramic view of the city of Brunswick, circa 1650, showing the city walls and major buildings, particularly the churches. Herzog August Bibliothek Wolfenbüttel: 6 D 6

the old frontier between West and East Germany, its glory dimmed when the Cold War shut down the highways toward the east. In the seventeenth century, however, Brunswick was a key partner in international trade with Holland and a southern member of the far-flung Hanseatic League. Its 15,000 inhabitants made it the largest city in Lower Saxony and one of the twenty largest cities in the Holy Roman Empire.[38]

For the Schmidts, whose own village was home to perhaps 100 souls, Brunswick's walls held a seething stew of humanity, bursting with new noises, sights, and smells. Long distance trade brought a bewildering array of foreign products such as English and Dutch wool, Estonian flax, spices, precious metals mined in the nearby Harz Mountains, seldom seen in the countryside. The variety of professions would fill country folk with wonder—carpenters and cobblers, coopers and wheelwrights, goldsmiths and silversmiths, bookmakers and bookbinders, millers and masons, butchers and bakers. In the textile trade alone, there were spinners of wool and flax, weavers of wool, linen, and silk, hatmakers and leatherers. And, as one would expect, Brunswickers were a thirsty lot and were not disappointed. Thirteen different burgher families brewed beer for market, to sell in taverns and to homes, and to export to northern Germany, England, and Holland, where Brunswick's red beer and "Mumme" were famous and in high demand.[39] Among the brewers was Julius von Horn, one of the city's judicial lords and later a *Bürgermeister* (mayor).[40] Also active in the brewing trade was the Möller family; an Andreas Möller would be listed as one of Brunswick's leading brewers in 1671.[41]

For a poor rural family like the Schmidts, the view of Brunswick might have produced awe and perhaps anxiety. From a different perspective, though, the city did not appear so impressive.[42] The *Bürgermeister* and *Rat* (city council) would have regarded the cityscape of 1659 with some concern. Though large for the age, Brunswick was smaller than it had been just two years earlier. A plague had swept through the city in 1657, and it had killed 5,400 inhabitants—over a quarter of the population, which was only now beginning to recover. Bitterly cold winters, the product of the century's "mini ice age," continued to afflict the city and to affect the crops. The Thirty Years War had reduced trade and hindered contact with partners and customers. The Hanseatic League was in decline, in part because rich Dutch traders, now at the height of their own Golden Age, were aggressively pushing east through the North Sea and on to the Baltic. The greatest problem, though, from the government's perspective, was reflected in the thick walls, the surrounding moat, and the variety of battlements and fortifications through which the Schmidts had passed.

All of these expensive engineering projects existed for the city's defense. For Brunswick needed defending. German cities of the seventeenth century confronted constant threats in a dangerous world. Independent though it seemed, Brunswick was technically the shared property and subject of the line of Welfen dukes who shared the Duchy of Brunswick-Lüneburg, named for the main cities in each part of the duchy. The ruler of the Brunswick part of the duchy was Augustus the Younger, who resided in the small court city of Wolfenbüttel some fourteen kilometers to the south. As much as these Welfen princes struggled for dominion and prestige among themselves, they were capable of uniting to pressure their subject cities. By a trick of history and good luck, though, the city of Brunswick's theoretical dependence had been turned into practical independence in the early centuries after its founding, when Duke Henry the Lion had granted it the rights and privileges of a "free" city while maintaining overall suzerainty.[43] Over the years, the city fathers had expanded these rights and sought from dukes and emperors the power to govern themselves and freedom from tribute or service to any overlord but the emperor. They had largely succeeded, but the accelerated decline of the Hanseatic League and the diminishing prosperity of the city lessened its ability to resist the encroachment of ambitious princes.[44] By the seventeenth century, the dukes of Brunswick-Lüneburg sought more and more to rein in the city's freedoms, tap its resources, and exploit its prosperity through taxation, customs, and tribute. And if the city would not yield legally, it could be forced to comply by threat of military attack. The duchy had already besieged Brunswick once at the beginning of the seventeenth century and would do so again.

Adding to these external troubles were divisive internal conflicts. The majority of the population were poor, propertyless laborers chafing at their political impotence. Even among the citizenry, the guildmasters and the neighborhood leaders sought stronger authority within the city council and opposed the older powers that had long dominated the government. The internal autonomy of the city's five districts meant continuous strife among them, between the powerful "old money" in the Altstadt and the more recent, less prosperous districts like Hagen, the Neustadt, and the Sack. These internal divisions had led to rebellion early in the seventeenth century, which the dukes had unsuccessfully tried to exploit.[45] From inside and out, then, Brunswick's unity and independence in 1659 lay under a great and mounting threat that would culminate in conquest just over a decade later. In 1659, for the last time in its history, the city received from the Holy Roman Emperor (Leopold I) a renewed affirmation of the many privileges and freedoms its citizens and rulers had for so long sought to maintain, and which were now increasingly besieged.

The Schmidts were likely unaware of all this. Part of the lowest level of society, their immediate concern was to establish a new life for Grethe. It was toward the Gottfried Möller household that the Schmidts headed in September 1659. After entering the city, they would wander toward the Altstadt and turn into the Breite Strasse, at the end of which stood the church of St. Martin, the Altstadt *Rathaus*, and the open grounds of the marketplace. The view was by design impressive. The Breite Strasse had been Brunswick's wealthiest and most impressive street for four centuries, concentrating in one place the oldest and best merchant houses and the most powerful of the city's leaders.[46] On the Breite Strasse, with its half-timbered houses and large, brightly colored and many-gabled buildings, stood the house where Gottfried Möller's widow, Margarethe Hafferland, awaited them with her maid and her stepson, Andreas Möller.

The New Servant

In September of 1659, Grethe began her work in the Möller household. She was not alone, joining the 13 percent of Europe's urban population that consisted of women from the countryside and the 10 percent of city dwellers, mostly women, who were in domestic service.[47] She was not alone in the Möller house, either, which had at least one other servant. Grethe had the good fortune of joining a prosperous household identified by her own mother, who had contacts with Hafferland's aunt and thus expected her daughter to be treated appropriately and to be paid her wages. If servants were notorious for theft, employers were equally reviled for their unwillingness to pay the wages due. Grethe's mother must have felt relieved that she had found her daughter a safe and relatively stable situation, something not all mothers could expect.[48]

The Möller household was a prosperous one. In a list of citizens prepared in 1671, Gottfried Möller's widow owned a large house in the Altstadt, valued at 800 thalers, as well as a smaller dwelling and three gardens to provide income through rent. Margarethe Hafferland also had 300 thalers in coins.[49] The family's history proves somewhat difficult to trace—in part because Möller was a very common name. The church registers are replete with Möller births, Möller baptisms, Möller marriages, and Möller burials. In the parish of St. Martin's in the Altstadt alone, three Andreas Möllers appear during the first half of the seventeenth century. We do know, however, that Gottfried Möller married Magdalena Passen in St. Katharine's parish in Hagen on June 12, 1620. Sixteen months later, on October 26, 1621, Andreas Möller, "Gottfried Möller's son," was baptized at home in St. Martin's parish.

Twenty years passed during which Gottfried and Magdalena had no other children, and then on June 3, 1641, Magdalena was buried "near the arsenal by the fourth linden tree." In that same year, on November 30, Gottfried Möller married Margarethe Hafferland. This second marriage was typical of an era in which the likelihood of death befalling one spouse or the other was very high. At the time of her marriage, Hafferland was forty-one years old, having been born in 1600. She may have had a daughter with Gottfried Möller; this child died in 1649 and was buried at St. Martin's. Margarethe Engelken later testified that Hafferland hired Grethe Schmidt because the widow had no more living children of her own. As for Gottfried Möller himself, he was buried on July 6, 1656, leaving behind his second wife and his son, Andreas. If Andreas was in fact the son born in 1621, he would be thirty-eight by 1659. If not, he would still be at least eighteen and probably older, since his own mother had died in 1641.[50]

As the newer maid, Grethe would perform the lowest duties on the household roster, probably those that involved hard physical labor. She would have to carry wood for fires and fetch water for cleaning and cooking.[51] A maid's job gave her ready and frequent access to the riverbank for washing laundry. Whatever the labors, all maids and other servants were expected to be obedient and humble, befitting their servile station and the scorn routinely heaped upon them. As one commentator of the eighteenth century wrote, "the most significant and most common offense of servants and apprentices is disobedience and a rebellious spirit."[52] Religious moralists attacked female domestic servants as potential whores posing a sexual danger for a household's male members, whom these unscrupulous women might seduce into promises of marriage as soon as the mistress of the house died. Should their efforts fail, then these women would fall even further into sin, leading inevitably to abortion or infanticide and final criminal judgment.[53] Other preachers referred to maids as subhuman or even bestial in nature.[54] The laws that limited the kind of clothing Grethe Schmidt could wear also were intended to govern her attitude, the demeanor expected of her in a hierarchical world that regarded her as lowly and which was determined to control her behavior.[55]

The reputation of domestics for being troublesome undoubtedly made employers all the more determined to look for servants whose families and backgrounds they knew. Young Grethe Schmidt's prospects looked good—her mother's contacts had earned her employment in a respected family living in the best part of Brunswick. Just a year after this beginning, though, Hafferland discharged her new maid, refusing to renew Schmidt's contract. The only reason Hafferland gave was that Grethe Schmidt was not the docile and obedient child that the church, society, and her employer expected her to be. Hafferland claimed Grethe was confrontational and insolent. At least Hafferland paid her year's wages. After that, though, Grethe had to find another job in Brunswick.

Once again, the family's minimal connections proved enough. Grethe's older sister, Anna, helped her sister find new employment as a servant. In October, 1660, Grethe went to work for Heinrich Lüdden and his wife, Anna Dedekind, a family who lived along the Wenden Graben (Canal) near the river in the borough of Hagen. Though not as prosperous or prestigious as the Altstadt, Hagen had a busy market and was home to many skilled craftsmen, including brewers. Grethe slept in a small alcove near the room of her employers.

Alas, things went badly here as well. According to Anna Dedekind, around Christmas, three months after Schmidt arrived, she and her husband had a stern conversation with their maid. Just a few weeks later, on the Saturday after New Year's of 1661, Anna Dedekind summoned Grethe's mother to Brunswick to retrieve her. Ilse arrived on Sunday, and after a long and difficult day, she took her daughter away. Anna Dedekind wanted nothing more to do with the Schmidt family. For the three months she worked in Dedekind's house, Grethe Schmidt received no pay. Eight months later, Grethe was in jail. All of the Schmidts' hard work to secure their daughter's future proved futile, and the sojourn begun so hopefully ended with the grim accusation of murder.

2

Anatomy of a Crime

In late July, 1661, the warden of the Altstadt jail knocked on a door in the Sack, one of Brunswick's lesser boroughs. He had come to the home of the tavern keeper Bortzfeldt in order to arrest their maid, who had been working there for some three months. The servant was Grethe Schmidt of Gross Schwülper. The warden, helped perhaps by a *Baumeister* responsible for order in the various wards (*Bauerschaften*) of the city, led Grethe to the Altstadt and its *Fronerey*, possibly a workhouse but in fact mostly a jail—one of four in the city as a whole—located near the *Rathaus*. In the *Fronerey*, Grethe was chained by the leg, and it is not clear that her cell was heated, except at the pleasure of the jailer, even as her incarceration lingered into the fall and winter. Even today, when the unconvicted are technically innocent until proved guilty, jails are not pleasant places to be. In the seventeenth century, a strong presumption of guilt attached to criminal defendants and the sordid conditions of jails were themselves a part of the process of conviction and punishment. Unlike modern lock-ups, informed by some consideration of defendants' rights, seventeenth-century jails made no provisions for exercise, fresh air, light, or even heat. Even more terrifying, the *Rathaus* dungeons had special rooms designed for carrying out a central component of early modern justice: torture chambers well stocked with implements useful in coaxing witnesses and defendants to confess. Every large city had such a chamber, manned by a professional torturer whose presence and expertise were vital if the accused or witnesses proved stubborn. The torturer, or *Scharfrichter*, took his name from the earlier practice in Saxon law (and elsewhere) of having one of the judges wield the sword of justice during executions. Now the *Scharfrichter* was often a professional responsible for what was literally "sharp" justice.[1] Normally, the *Scharfrichter* also carried out the gruesome task of executing criminals and disposing of their bodies. Lesser sentences, too, were part of the job—public whippings, perhaps, or lopping off a finger or an ear, depending on the crime.[2] By custom, torturers and executioners were held to be "dishonorable," but even so, they were integral to the criminal process, and preachers labored to include them as the honorable instruments of the divine justice mirrored in a Christian government.[3]

The criminal process launched with Grethe's arrest would last almost a full year. During those eleven months, she spent many terrifying hours in the Altstadt dungeon. Throughout her imprisonment, Grethe suffered in isolation. She had no right to visitors, nor was the city required to inform her kin that she had been arrested, although at some point, the city would contact her family to present a bill, since prisoners were expected to pay for their own food while in prison. Grethe's treatment and prison fare befitted her status as a poor individual from a low family.[4] The right to counsel existed only as a limited opportunity dependent in practice on the very judges who were prosecuting her.[5] She would face the looming ordeal alone, whatever the charge, whatever the duration. Her closest company during this time were the prosecutors themselves, who had access to her at their leisure and thus could extend their influence beyond the formal encounters transcribed by a court reporter.

The Rule of Law

The magistracy of Brunswick, exclusively male and represented by the criminal officers, had the duty of finding the truth and protecting their Christian city and its virtue from evildoers. Failure to do so would diminish the prestige of the regime in the eyes of the population and thus risk its authority, which at this point in its history Brunswick could ill afford. The magistrates also understood the task of prosecution as a Christian duty—not fulfilling it would risk the wrath of a just God. In Grethe's case, the magistrates (*Justizherren*) suspected infanticide, a specific form of murder that occurred when a mother intentionally and with malice aforethought killed a baby newly and secretly born to her out of wedlock.[6] Speaking of the mother as the culprit is no accident, for in the early modern context, discussions of infanticide concerned women almost exclusively.

This particular form of homicide held a special and heinous place in seventeenth-century criminal process. Modern criminal codes feature infanticide less prominently. When the term does appear in law or commentary, the goals are quite varied and often politically charged. The American use of "infanticide" in some partial-birth abortion statutes is an attempt to dramatize the severity of the procedure and identify it as a form of homicide.[7] In contrast, legal systems influenced by twentieth-century English jurisprudence take their cue from a statute of 1938, in which infanticide is a specific form of homicide but appears as a lesser offense occasioned by the supposedly diminished capacity of the new mother, with lighter punishment as a result.[8] This understanding of infanticide as "privileged crime" extends to Germany as well, a direct result of reform efforts undertaken in the late eighteenth century.[9]

Seventeenth-century law, though, considered infanticide an especially grievous form of murder exacerbated by the helplessness of the newborn victim. It was, in the words of the historian Otto Ulbricht, perhaps "*the cruelty par excellence*"—inhumane, unchristian, unnatural.[10] Its seriousness becomes clear in the punishment prescribed for the guilty: "she is normally to be buried alive with a stake through her. However, in order to guard the accused against despair, wherever the court has convenient access to water, the female evildoer is to be drowned instead. Wherever, in order to deter such evil women through fear, wherever such evil crime happens frequently, we decree the aforementioned live burial or, before drowning the murderess, to tear her with fiery burning pincers."[11] This horrific punishment, prescribed in 1532, was not often carried out until the latter part of the century. And, in the seventeenth century, authorities frequently substituted execution by sword. As late as 1693, though, the city of Brunswick executed a convicted newborn-child murderer by drowning her as an example for other potential killers.[12] There can be no denying the danger that confronted Grethe Schmidt in August 1661. Her life hung in the balance.[13]

The gravity of infanticide in early modern criminal law is evident in the wording of the relevant statutes themselves. The legal definition of infanticide used in the Schmidt case came from the *Constitutio Criminalis Carolina*, the basic law code promulgated for the German Empire during the reign of the Holy Roman Emperor Charles V in 1532. Known as the *Carolina*, various forms of this code remained in effect for nearly three centuries.[14]

The first relevant statute is Article 35:

> When a girl, purportedly a maiden, comes under suspicion of having secretly had and killed a child, it shall be especially *inquired* [italics mine], whether she was seen with a large and unusual body, and further, whether the body then became smaller and she was then pale and weak. When such and similar is discovered, and where this girl is a person of whom such a suspected crime could be believed, then she shall be inspected by knowledgeable women in an enclosed place, so far as that facilitates further inquiry; and if the suspicion is there confirmed, and nonetheless she will not confess the deed, she may be examined under torture.[15]

Later, Article 131 refers to "whatever woman in secret and with evil intent kills a fully formed and living child [*lebendiges Kind*]." Such a person might protest that the baby was born dead, but if that baby was born in secret, the mother would be called upon to give a plausible account of the circumstances of the birth. Should her explanation still prove unsatisfactory, she could be subject to prosecution. Furthermore, "should a woman in secret carry a living and fully formed baby, and then deliver that baby without the help of other women, its death is to be seen as suspicious. For [in such cases] nothing is more plausible than that the self-same mother, in order to hide her own criminal lasciviousness, is guilty of killing the innocent little child before, during, or after its birth."[16]

These articles specify both the victim and the necessary perpetrator of infanticide. Article 131 focuses on "whatever woman . . . kills her child . . ." and goes on to refer to a "woman who has a child . . ." and even employs the term "murderess." Infanticide, then, was by definition a woman's crime.[17] Nor did the law stop simply at murderous women in general. Article 35 describes "a girl, purportedly a maiden" (that is, a virgin), while the second paragraph of Article 131 speaks of a woman who has killed an infant deliberately delivered "in secret" and "without the help of other women," all for the purpose of hiding the "criminal lasciviousness" indicated by bearing a child out of wedlock. Prosecutors following this narrow definition would focus on women who became pregnant outside marriage and tried to avoid shame by hiding both their pregnancies and childbirths, and then, for that same reason, killing their infants.[18]

It would be entirely possible for an energetic prosecutor to focus on the first paragraph and interpret Article 131 to apply to married women who had borne legitimate children and then for some reason killed them. The reach of the infanticide law was certainly not limited to unmarried women—in theory, any woman bearing an illegitimate child was suspect, widows and wives included. Yet despite the legal possibilities, authorities mostly targeted young, unmarried women who were assumed to be trying to keep their reputations intact to preserve their chances for matrimony.[19] Why did the authorities concern themselves with these women in particular? The answer lies partly in the wording of the law, which explicitly states the motive for infanticide: "secret births," and "criminal lasciviousness." Young women were deemed especially inclined to infanticide because of the shame attached to the immoral sexual behavior that would be revealed by the birth of an illegitimate child.[20] Single young women working as domestics and fearful of condemnation might try to pass as virgins when they were not, might bear a child in secret, and might hide the knowledge of their pregnancies from other women or midwives.

Shame, then, was the source of both virtue and vice. The law enshrined the desire to avoid humiliation as the reason for infanticide and discounted other motives more familiar to modern thinking. Notably, the *Carolina* and its interpreters ignored the possibility that poor and desperate women, unable to provide for one child or perhaps one *more* child, might be tempted to kill a new infant. Such a position would have extended the law's grasp to include faithful married women and even men. It was outside the married family, however, that morals and births were scrupulously policed, and shame was the instrument of choice for enforcing moral codes.

Paradoxically, though, the shame that society employed to prevent illicit sex was also considered the motive for infanticide and only made the subsequent crime worse. What kind of person would go as far as murder just to avoid the humiliation of ill repute? Benedikt Carpzov, a towering figure in legal thinking during the seventeenth century, contrasted the motive with the crime: "what could be worse than trying to avoid the shame associated with this relatively minor crime [fornication] by committing the major crime of infanticide?"[21]

Seventeenth-century law and its interpreters presumed that women who "secretly, evilly, willingly" killed their children did so in order to maintain a false honor. In order to accomplish this, an unmarried woman seeking to pass as a virgin had to hide not only the murder itself but all signs of sexual conduct and pregnancy. Secrecy entailed premeditation from the very moment of conception. One could, of course, argue that women frightened for their reputations might seek to hide their deeds and consequences without clearly thinking ahead to the logical if gruesome conclusion. Under the guidance of the *Carolina*, however, magistrates could interpret each decision as part of something larger, more sinister. Once a woman sought to preserve her reputation through secrecy, she proved her willingness to undertake something much worse once a child was born. Premeditation began with the illicit sexual act itself and grew at each moment in a murderess's heart, just as surely as the fetus grew in her womb. Secret birth and the desire to avoid the stigma of sexual immorality pointed to newborn infants as the only plausible victims. In small villages or even in cities, women could not hide newborns for long. On the other hand, the law stipulated that the victims must have been living at birth, fully formed—that is, able to survive outside the womb. "Viability" was an issue in infanticide in the seventeenth century just as it is for abortion debates in the twenty-first, closely linked with the question of whether the infant had been born alive. These two legal conditions gave suspected women an opportunity to exculpate themselves by claiming that the baby had been born dead.[22] This could only happen, though, when the corpse was discovered and would lead inevitably back to the question of why a woman had concealed the birth in the first place. The issue of a "live" birth also gave greater latitude to prosecutors, who might afford married mothers the benefit of the doubt in cases of suspicious death while focusing even more closely on single women as suspects.

This practice of targeting only unmarried women in a statute that courts could easily extend further raises two significant issues. Undoubtedly clerics and prosecutors were at least somewhat worried about infants killed at birth. The focus on unwed mothers as the criminals to the exclusion of all other women suggests, though, that concern over infanticide was "a by-product of fornication" rather than preoccupation with the well-being of babies. The central issue may instead have been concern over a dramatic increase in illegitimate births as the possible outcome of having large numbers of ungoverned single women in early modern cities. Authorities were interested in pursuing infanticide less as a crime per se than as a tool threatening draconian measures to deter an increase in fornication and a corresponding rise in bastardy.[23] This might help explain why authorities were so concerned about discovering the fathers of living illegitimate children (to force support) but showed little interest in investigating and prosecuting the sires of dead ones.[24]

There is yet a second, and related, point to make about these paragraphs in the *Carolina*. Read as a whole, they offer not just a law but a story—a brief, self-contained morality tale that outlines characters (the wanton maid, or *Dirn*) and defines motives (shame, the desire to appear innocent) within a narrative that moves inexorably from illicit sex to corruption to murder and its penal consequences. The infanticide narrative of the *Carolina* could fire the prosecutorial imagination and then spur legal reform of sex laws in the eighteenth century. It did not, however, correspond with the social realities of the crime. The vast majority of women convicted *were* maidservants of some sort, but usually in their mid-twenties, about the same age as their partners, who usually came from the same social level, not higher. Rather than exhibit a lascivious or rebellious character, most of the women had good reputations and no prior legal trouble. Instead of pretending to virginity, most were probably expecting marriage, as a promise of which sexual relations were a very typical sign.[25] With the discovery of a pregnancy, the men fled, leaving the women to fend for themselves in dishonor. The shame that women felt and that led them to kill their newborn children was not over the loss of their virginity but, rather, over the minimal social capital they possessed and the material and economic disadvantages they would inevitably experience.[26]

For legal and religious authorities in cities and towns, though, the infanticide statutes provided a narrative that investigators and prosecutors could easily put into play, fitting the crime and the criminal tidily into the moral framework of the law. The fact that such a high percentage of convicted women displayed similar characteristics, motives, and backgrounds could mean an epidemic of sorts, or it could suggest that authorities had one story in mind as they approached the crime. If so, prosecuting infanticide did not simply mean investigation and judgment, it meant shaping the basic elements of a case into a recognizable criminal history.[27]

Bad Mothers

The law as a narrative, then, requires some explaining. In the sixteenth and seventeenth centuries, all governments, whether secular or sacred, attempted to supervise closely the sexual activity of their subjects. When the authorities arrested Grethe Schmidt, they were conforming to the prosecutorial pattern typical for the seventeenth century. They were also following a deeply ingrained logic about marriage, morality, and crime nearly five hundred years in the making. The outcome was a society in which the Christian churches exerted ever greater control over the institution of marriage, in collaboration with early modern governments that promoted family life as a way of guaranteeing order and social stability. Preachers and philosophers extolled motherhood as an exalted condition characterized by innate, natural love for children. The "good" mother played a central role in building disciplined families to produce obedient subjects of the state. "Bad" mothers could only contribute to disobedience, disrespect, and the dissolution of state and society.[28]

Ecclesiastical authorities had long attempted to bring marriage under the increasingly watchful eye of the Church. What made a medieval marriage was voluntary, mutual consent, or the promise of consent, if ratified by sexual intercourse.[29] Sexual intercourse was integral to defining the moment of marriage and consummating the contract between the couple.

Such a loose arrangement, though, made authorities uncomfortable. Marriage was too significant socially to leave simply to the capricious decisions of individuals. Towns and cities wanted to oversee the households and families within their walls. Parents wanted to influence unions that dramatically affected a family's property and economic fortunes. All patriarchal powers, in other words, had a stake in exercising control over marriage and policing the sexual behaviors that ratified it.

With the Protestant Reformation, this simmering official unease boiled over. The major reformers attacked the theory of marriage by consent alone. Protestant reformers, who regarded marriage as a public matter that must also include parental consent, condemned clandestine couplings. The new legislation and courts that emerged from Protestant success in cities such as Geneva and Zurich firmly outlawed secret marriages.[30] Without the pastor to witness it, no marriage could occur. By demanding a publicly witnessed exchange of vows, religious authorities fixed the moment of marriage and established a firmer boundary between marital and non-marital sexual activity. As noted in chapter 1, authorities in some areas of Germany could even prohibit some individuals from marrying at all.

Aided by a stricter religious definition of marriage, secular governments intensified efforts to exalt family life. Laws governing pre- and non-marital sexual activity became the central mechanisms for regulating social behavior through marriage.[31] A sharper definition of the marital state brought with it increased concern over chastity and virginity, the chief components of a woman's honor. To police the honor of women became the sacred duty of the state.[32] So it was that criminal laws from the sixteenth through the eighteenth century forbade adultery, fornication (*Unzucht*), "sleeping together too early" (*zu früher Beischlaf*), and "concubinage" (*Konkubinat*). The punishments for such crimes included imprisonment, enforced fasts of bread and water, and monetary fines. The same crimes could also be punished in another fashion, through *Schandstrafen*—shaming penalties that exposed violators (mostly women) to physical and public humiliation.[33]

To punish fornicators, of course, magistrates first had to prove that fornication had occurred. Authorities generally discovered fornication when talk of a pregnancy led them to inquire about sexual activity.[34] In most cases, such suspicions also led to questions about paternity, for magistrates in Protestant lands were concerned to find the fathers of illegitimate children. After all, the state had no desire to support these *Hurenkinder* (whores' children). For their part, mothers could sue for child support.[35] Indeed, the possibility of such support would become a factor in the Schmidt case.

Church and state officials were not concerned solely with fornication per se. They were also worried that unmarried pregnant women might seek an abortion. Abortion received harsh treatment in the Imperial Criminal Code of 1532, in a statute that condemned to death anyone who would "through force, food, or drink, abort a woman's living child, or make a man or woman unfruitful." If, however, a woman aborted a "child that was not living," then the judge should consult with other experts about the appropriate penalty.[36] This curiously worded statute, representing the midpoint of a long evolution, contains some striking elements.[37] It focuses not on the pregnant woman seeking to end her pregnancy, but on the person causing an abortion, possibly through sorcery. Startlingly, the statute distinguishes between aborting a "living child," for which the death penalty is appropriate, and one that is "not yet living." This refers to the prevailing distinction, in canon and secular law, between the "unquickened" and "quickened" fetus, depending on the implantation of the soul.

A similar division appeared later in the *Constitutions* for Electoral Saxony in 1572, prescribing death for aborting a living child and the whip for one not yet alive or for a failed abortion or "if the aborted was not a child."[38] Here the emphasis shifted to the woman herself and those who had helped her. Once again, though, the distinction appears between the "living" and "not yet living" fetus, over which jurists continued to debate. Benedikt Carpzov argued that from quickening on, the fetus should have the same status as an already-born infant. Abortion after this point became outright homicide.[39]

Despite its gradual criminalization, abortion did not inspire powerful reaction among early modern authorities. It was infanticide that provoked outrage and vigorous prosecutions. Only witchcraft, at its height in the sixteenth and seventeenth centuries, led to the execution of more women. As the witch craze subsided after 1650, infanticide became the leading capital crime of which women were accused. Indeed, the two crimes were sometimes linked: occasionally child murders were prosecuted not as infanticides but as part of a witchcraft trial.[40] But just as the larger number of women executed for witchcraft did not signify an increase in the number of witches (or the existence of *any* witches, for that matter), infanticides were perhaps not increasing nearly as rapidly as official worries about infanticide.[41]

The question remains: what made infanticide an especially vile crime— different from "mere" murder or abortion—in the centuries between 1500 and 1800? What drove authorities to seek out and prosecute with such vigor mothers who murdered their newborn children? After all, Europe in its early modern period was an exceptionally violent place by today's standards. Men of all classes routinely carried weapons, usually knives, for protection as they went about their daily lives. Everywhere, powerful men could command the allegiance of armed mobs. Even the most superficial glance at the cities of the Renaissance shows the everyday uses to which violence and murder were put—including vengeance, power, and influence. Homicide between males was a common and spontaneous occurrence. Yet the mayhem that occurred on a daily basis did not spur authorities to growing numbers of executions for murder, indeed the evidence suggests the opposite. The alleged murder of infants by their mothers, however, resulted in increasingly frequent executions and warnings, with authorities deploring the dreadful state of society.[42] What was at stake for Germany's legal and civil authorities?

In the violent culture and social tumult of the sixteenth and seventeenth centuries, infanticide became a symbol that expressed all the fears about marriage, family, and discipline that had wracked Europe since the Reformation. An unwed mother with her bastard child contradicted the sacred ideal of family, and one who went so far as to kill her offspring violated the very idea of motherhood as a woman's natural condition. The supposedly unbounded love a mother should feel for her child contrasted with a cold-blooded act performed entirely in her self-interest. Infanticide was not mere murder, but an offense against the natural order established by God.

The gravity of the crime was intensified by the fact that the victim was an innocent. While some homicides might be excused in the name of vengeance or honor, infanticide served only evil ends. Also, how could one make amends when the victim had no social status and the culprit was from the same family? Simply put, who could speak for the victim in such cases except for the state? The governing regime, along with the Christian population as a whole, was answerable to God and felt strongly the duty to avenge the blood of innocents, lest a just God should exact His own retribution, not only from the criminal but from the society that condoned her act.

This heightening anxiety over motherhood and murder coincided with increasing state power. Before 1500 infanticide was a serious offense, but cases rarely came before criminal courts, and executions for the crime were relatively rare. By the seventeenth century, however, the growth of more-efficient secular court systems in the Holy Roman Empire and the reorganization of criminal laws allowed authorities to pursue these "unnatural" women more ruthlessly.[43]

Unruly Women

The criminal law combined the general goal of promoting discipline through marriage and family life with the use of shame as a tool to keep unwanted behaviors in check. When marriage did not occur, unmarried women might end up living and laboring independently but were categorized pejoratively as women earning their own bread and were subject to deep suspicion and persecution.[44] Disapproving of this outcome and fearing the consequences of disorderly passions, authorities singled out young, unmarried women as potential infanticides. They did not have to look far. Cities and towns were swarming with single women between fourteen and thirty seeking work and eventually marriage. Grethe Schmidt was just such a young woman. The swelling numbers of single women untethered to parents and under the control of no one except their employers provided authorities with a growing population of suspects. In addition to working as domestics, most defendants came originally from the countryside and belonged much more often to the lowest rung of rural society, rarely to landholding peasants or noble families.

This was a society in which patriarchal rule over a household was the key to discipline—the hierarchical family was the model for business and for the state under the guidance of a divine father. Though young migrants provided labor, they were essentially detached from the basic institutions of control: home and parents. In their stead, the *Obrigkeit* (authorities) expected employers and heads of households to provide "parental" authority over workers and servants. Just how well could such oversight work with large numbers of unattached people moving from country to city and from job to job, or even worse, finding no job at all and falling into destitution and vice? Authorities feverishly imagined the potential for violence, rebellion, sexual misbehavior, and bastardy among the young and the restless. Magistrates anxiously pondered the potential for social and sexual mayhem unless this crowd could somehow be "mastered."[45]

In such a socially volatile age, following directly upon a massively disruptive war, the criminal law mirrored the anxieties of rulers and magistrates. As a result, women (and men) who seemed to reject the yoke of discipline and who refused to be bound by the hierarchy of the family would be made to serve as examples to others. Infanticide prosecutions were a most useful disciplinary tool—they punished women not only for murder but also for their original immorality and warned others of the consequences of rebelliousness. Infanticide trials portrayed disobedient women not only as shameful but also as unnatural. Their alleged betrayal of their own bodies and of the lives of their children were acts of defiance against the divine order. The woman who succumbed to temptation and tried to hide her sin placed all of society in jeopardy.

Following her arrest in July, then, Grethe Schmidt faced an ominous future. She was young and an outsider, just the kind of person authorities would suspect and perhaps make an example of. Who in the city of Brunswick would care about her fate? Grethe's family was in Gross Schwülper, possibly unaware of what was happening. She had been fired twice by employers. Alone now and chained in the *Fronerey*, Grethe might have remembered her first view of Brunswick—church spires piercing the heavens. How much of that inspiring vision would remain after months spent in the airless bowels of the city?

3

A Girl, purportedly a Maiden

In August 1661, the city of Brunswick opened its official proceedings against Grethe Schmidt. Despite her isolation in the city workhouse and her low status, from the very beginning the case involved people from multiple strands of urban and rural society. The prosecutors, exclusively male, ran the proceedings while the city's women provided most of the witnesses.[1] In the countryside, ducal officials, often local noblemen, questioned peasants at the city's request and mediated between the prosecutors' demands for evidence and their own duty to protect their subjects' limited rights. None of this was adversarial. Early modern magistrates undertook both investigation and judgment. The process was inquisitorial, conducted by supposedly impartial judges whose theoretical goal was to arrive at the truth, punish the guilty, and release the innocent. As inquisitorial processes initiated by the state became standard, the older custom of relying on individual accusations diminished. This protected the individual accuser but it also concentrated even more authority and responsibility in the hands of state officials. In practice, both means of criminal investigation worked similarly.[2]

For the prosecution (the *Fiskal*), the process began routinely. The matter lay chiefly in the hands of two full-time judicial officers (the *Vogten*), one for the Altstadt and one for the other boroughs (but located in Hagen). In addition, in each borough two judicial magistrates (*Justizherren*), chosen annually from a pool of citizens, sat in on the proceedings. Together, the *Vogten* and the *Justizherren* formed the *Untergericht* (the lower court), that handled most criminal matters. Once a capital case was established, in theory it would be in the hands of the city council, which formed the *Obergericht* (upper court). In the *Obergericht*, the legal expert would probably be one of the two syndics (most likely Johannes Strauch), who exercised a wide range of powers in the city and were the single best-paid governmental officials. No one in the *Untergericht* was a trained lawyer—neither the *Justizherren* nor

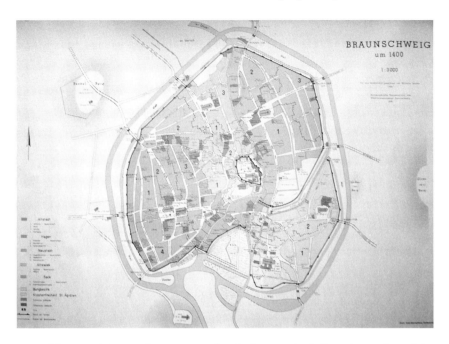

Map of the city of Brunswick circa 1400, already showing the different boroughs and the major landmarks. Courtesy of the Stadarchiv Braunschweig.

the *Vogten*, though the latter had a great deal of hands-on experience. Johannes Vellhagen had been the Altstadt *Vogt* since 1642, while Otto Theune had held the same position in Hagen since 1641. The judicial magistrates themselves also tended to be reelected repeatedly.[3] This lack of legal training was not unusual for the time, even in cities, as the number of learned jurists, especially those knowing Latin, was slow to catch up to the law's burgeoning impact. This was a cause of some concern among jurists, who pondered the potential outcome of difficult criminal cases prosecuted by men who did not fully understand the law. To compensate, learned jurists began to produce guides and treatises for judges in German and to recommend that courts seek advice from legal faculties in universities.[4] A city as large as Brunswick would have trained lawyers among the syndics in the *Obergericht*. Strauch was a doctor of laws and had been a member of the legal faculty at Jena for eight years before coming to Brunswick in 1660.[5]

Either by accusation or by official initiative—in the Schmidt case, it was never clear what had actually sparked the proceedings—officials conducted a preliminary investigation to determine whether enough suspicion existed to detain an individual and connect her to the corpus delicti. Next the suspect would be questioned, along with other witnesses. Depending on the results of that series of interviews and interrogations, a physical examination could take place (in cases of infanticide). The records would then be shipped to the legal faculty of Helmstedt University for recommendations, especially whether to undertake torture. And depending on that outcome, the suspect would be judged before the *Obergericht*. It is not clear quite when in the process the suspect and her family would have the chance to present her own case, nor the form that it might take. From the records themselves, it is also not clear that the court in this particular case ever felt the need to inform the family of what was happening, nor that the court had the responsibility to do so.[6]

In weighing criminal matters, authorities distrusted physical or circumstantial evidence and relied on witnesses' testimony. Seventeenth-century continental law had an exacting standard for conviction—certainty of the truth rather than probability "beyond a reasonable doubt." The need for certainty in practice meant that official efforts focused on a single goal: the suspect's own admission of guilt. It was the confession spoken from the mouth of the defendant that established truth beyond any doubt. Inquisitorial law involved a very sophisticated set of rules, known as *Indizienlehre*, which in theory enabled investigators to weigh the probable guilt of a suspect and allowed them to apply torture. For this reason, the pivotal moment in a serious criminal case came when officials, perhaps in consultation with higher legal authorities in a university law faculty, determined that sufficient probable cause existed to employ torture as a means to extract a confession.[7] According to the procedures established by the *Carolina*, by the time a suspect entered the torture chamber, criminal officials should be confident of his or her guilt.

Strictly speaking, the confession was not always necessary, since the *Carolina* permitted judging a suspect on the basis of two trustworthy eyewitnesses (Article 67). This was a very high threshold indeed—two individuals had to witness the deed, and hearsay was explicitly forbidden (Article 65).[8] Even then, however, the law admonished judges to seek a confession, though without inflicting torture (Article 69). In the case of a sexual delict or other "secret" crime, eyewitnesses would by definition be hard to find. For practical purposes, then, producing a confession was the central focus of the criminal process. Only in the presence of a confession did a trial take place to announce a verdict and pronounce sentence. By confessing, the defendant justified the court's involvement, released the judges from anxiety that they had convicted an innocent person, and paved the way for the condemned prisoner's reconciliation with God and society. Produced in a strongly religious society, the criminal process as spelled out in the *Carolina* required that, following judgment, the court must make time for the Church to exhort the criminal to penance. The confession, then, was critical to the process on both judicial and religious grounds, even if extracted through force.[9] Finally, the fact of a confession and the truth it expressed left little room for appeal, and except for a limited right to call upon the highest imperial court, the *Reichskammergericht*, criminal appeals from lower to higher courts were restricted in seventeenth-century German lands. The most influential jurist of the century, Benedikt Carpzov, was a notable opponent of any right to appeal.[10]

Judicial demands for a confession placed great pressures on prosecutors and suspects alike. The suspects, of course, suffered from physical torture, but the psychological stress must also have been enormous. In confessing, the suspect must accept the court's definition of her as a felon deserving punishment. Producing this acknowledgment was also an integral part of the criminal process. In the case of infanticide, though, the drive to confession merged with the story-like character of the statutes themselves, providing a ready-made narrative for prosecutors. Through the confession, the legal tale of the *Carolina* became the defendant's own story. The case constructed against Grethe Schmidt was not separable from the manner in which authorities sought to refashion her character and self-understanding in conformity with the laws of God and the city of Brunswick. To see fully how this process worked, one must review the case as it unfolded in the records.

On August seventh and eighth, 1661, the *Untergericht* interrogated three women. The first was Schmidt's second employer in the city, Anna Dedekind. Grethe herself was then called upon to explain her actions in the face of Dedekind's insinuations. Finally, Grethe's sister Anna introduced Schmidt's family into the case. These three interrogations established a narrative that would be tested again and again in the coming months as the city built a case against the girl from Gross Schwülper.

Altstadt Mint, August 7, 1661

Grethe Schmidt had worked for Anna Dedekind and her husband in the borough of Hagen from September 1660 until just after New Year's 1661. Dedekind knew much about the Schmidt family because Grethe's older sister had once been her servant. That Dedekind was the first witness is suggestive. Criminal accusations in this period could emerge either from official inquiries or from individual denunciations, which themselves were increasingly being subsumed within official investigations. It is likely that as the lead witness, Anna Dedekind was a key source for magistrates' earliest suspicions about Grethe. When the former employer appeared at the

The bridge at Hagen, 1650, showing the half-timbered building construction typical of the age. Herzog August Bibliothek Wolfenbüttel.

Altstadt Mint on August 7, 1661, however, judicial authorities confronted her with a set of twenty-seven questions drawn up on July 30. Some form of preliminary investigation had therefore already taken place.

Dedekind stated that Grethe had worked for her for just three months: from the feast of St. Michael—around September 29, when servants' contracts were traditionally made—until shortly after New Year's Day, 1661. Previously the maid had worked for a year in the house of Gottfried Möller. During the winter, Schmidt's mother had visited, presumably to check on her daughter. As far as Dedekind knew, Grethe had not set foot in the Lüdden-Dedekind house at any time since just after New Year's. Dedekind herself had last seen young Schmidt in Brunswick around Easter of 1661.[11]

Prosecutors then posed a set of apparently trivial questions about Grethe's hair. *They wanted to know whether the maid had come to the household with her hair hidden under a cap.*[12] The witness answered that in fact Schmidt had arrived with her hair cut off due to an unspecified "uncleanness." Grethe's sister Anna admitted to Dedekind that she had cut her sibling's hair for this reason, but the witness herself had not seen it happen. Nor had she given the matter much attention.[13]

Authorities then moved to the heart of the investigation. They wanted to know *whether the witness had seen or noted that the captive [Grethe Schmidt] was pregnant.* Dedekind gave a surprising answer. When Grethe first began work in October 1660, her new employer had noticed nothing and in fact believed the girl was too young to conceive. That Grethe did not appear to be menstruating was therefore no cause for her mistress's anxiety. As the fall wore on, however, unnamed neighbors started to murmur (*münckeln*), and Dedekind began to observe her servant's condition more closely. Around Christmastide she decided the rumors were true: Grethe was indeed with child.[14] Dedekind and her husband confronted the girl on the Friday after New Year's, around ten o'clock in the evening. They "spoke earnestly to her, but all the while the prisoner would neither confess nor admit anything, nor even say yes or no."[15] The couple decided to fire Grethe, and the next day summoned the girl's mother from Gross Schwülper to take her home. Ilse Leuthgen arrived in Brunswick on Sunday. When Dedekind told Ilse that she suspected Grethe was pregnant, "the mother answered that she did not know about this and wanted to question her daughter, whereupon on that very Sunday after the midday meal she went out with her daughter and did not come back to the house until evening."[16] Dedekind could not or would not say where the two women went. When the Schmidts returned, though, Grethe's mother said that things with her daughter were "different" (a widely used euphemism to describe pregnancy).[17] Disgusted, Anna Dedekind asked Leuthgen to take her daughter away. On Monday, the Schmidts left, supposedly for Gross Schwülper. The last thing Dedekind heard from Ilse was that a "rider," a cavalryman, was said to have been the father.[18]

The inquisitors pressed Dedekind to speculate about how far along Grethe's pregnancy was on New Year's 1661 and whether she was "*Grob schwanger*" (a phrase that could be translated as "great with child" and ready to give birth). Dedekind "could say nothing other than that she held Margarethe Schmidt . . . to be pregnant, and from her mother she had heard that it was a rider who had done it. But whether Grethe was close to delivery, how far along her pregnancy was, and how she returned to Gross Schwülper with her mother, these things the witness could not say."[19] It is important to keep this specific language in mind, for Dedekind would have to answer the very same question again months later. Dedekind testified further that Grethe's mother had come to gather her daughter but could not say whether Grethe had actually gone with Ilse or stayed somewhere else in the city.

The interrogation drew to a close with two final questions—*had Anna Dedekind paid Grethe her full salary for the months working in the Lüdden household? Had she noticed anything suspicious in the prisoner's eating, drinking, sleeping, or other similar activities?* No, came the firm answer, Grethe never dared return to collect her salary. Dedekind also noticed nothing at all unusual in the young woman's behavior and was even sarcastic about her appetite: "Food and drink probably tasted better to her than to anyone in the house." Whatever Schmidt's condition, it had not left her malnourished. With that last, curious question, the testimony ended.

It was a sad and typical tale that Dedekind recounted—a cavalryman seducing and then abandoning a young country girl, leaving her pregnant and unemployed. If Grethe was pregnant, it meant she had had sex sometime during 1660, and of course, non-marital sex was illegal. Fornication, though, was not the kind of offense for which a woman would likely be sought out and arrested nearly fourteen months later. In any case, Grethe had not admitted either pregnancy or sexual activity to Dedekind. So the nature of the crime, if any, was still obscure.

One should note that Dedekind also had a stake in the interview. Perhaps concerned about her own legal exposure for harboring an immoral employee and not reporting her immediately to the authorities, Dedekind fashioned a narrative to deflect criticism: she had not noticed Grethe's pregnancy. Once alerted to the fact, however, she and her husband acted immediately. And of course, they had not paid the wench any salary, which coincidentally meant the Lüdden household had received three months of free labor from Schmidt. Dedekind's testimony was itself a thin beginning for investigators, but she did point them toward suspicions about her former maid, who now had serious and specific questions to answer. The very same day, magistrates interrogated Grethe Schmidt for the first time.

ALTSTADT WORKHOUSE, AUGUST 7, 1661

All the principal actors in the Altstadt's *Untergericht* gathered in the *Fronerey* with a prepared list of forty-two questions with which to confront the girl. Both *Vogten*—Otto Theune and Johannes Vellhagen—attended. The questioning itself was conducted by the Altstadt *Gerichtsherren* (judicial lords), Julius von Horn (a future *Bürgermeister*) and Johannes Gartner. The court scribe Johannes Pilgram was there, pen in hand, ever observant. In the German fashion, Pilgram tended to paraphrase testimony and present it as indirect speech in the third person. Before these five men sat Grethe Schmidt, alone. Indeed, throughout the entire proceedings to come, Grethe Schmidt would have virtually no contact with other women, unless there was a fellow prisoner. At some point she would face an examination by midwives, but otherwise she was under the exclusive control of men. She had by now been incarcerated for two weeks.[20]

The grueling interrogation began routinely: name, family, birthplace, work experience in the city. Grethe gave her age as "seventeen or eighteen years," an incorrect response, but this was not a time of careful dating.[21] According to her pastor, she had been born either in 1646 or 1647, and so was no more than fifteen years old. The interrogation turned more serious when the judicial lords posed an impromptu question, apparently derived from Anna Dedekind's deposition: *whether Grethe had remained in Brunswick from around the Feast of Three Kings [January 6] until about 14 days before Ash Wednesday,* or February 13. Interrogators hoped to establish a timeline consistent with Dedekind's account. Schmidt testified that she had not ventured into Brunswick at all between January 1661 and the weeks after Easter in mid-April, when she began work for the Bortzfeldt family in the Sack.[22]

Prosecutors now turned to their main concern: *Whether the captive had permitted herself to sleep [i.e. have sexual relations] with someone?* "Yes," Grethe Schmidt answered simply. The interrogators continued: *where had this happened?* "In Gottfried Möller's widow's house in the Breite Strasse, indeed in Andreas Möller's chambers, near the front room, on his bed. He had laid her down there, for she needed air."[23] *By day or by night?* "In the evening around eight or nine o'clock." *And who was it who had done this to her?* "Andreas Möller, the son in the house."[24] Her candor belied the importance of the revelation. This was no roving horseman, as Anna Dedekind had testified. Andreas Möller was the son of the respected Gottfried Möller and stepson of his widow, Grethe's first employer in Brunswick, Margarethe Hafferland. The case suddenly became more complicated, for it now involved a prominent family in the Altstadt.

Prosecutors wanted more details: *Exactly when and how had the sexual encounter occurred? Had she received anything (monetarily) from Möller? Had he forbidden her to say anything afterward?* She replied that the episode took place "one or two days before Pentecost [June 10] in the previous year [1660], and it was just that single time and otherwise no more congress occurred." Even before this, though, Möller had "kissed her and grabbed her breasts, if the opportunity presented itself to him."[25] Andreas gave her no money but warned her in bed that she "should tell no one, that it would do her no harm."[26]

Grethe's responses to these difficult questions were surprisingly direct. She did not deny or hide having sex with Andreas Möller, nor did she offer any excuse. From such brief answers, it is difficult to determine whether this sexual encounter was consensual or not. Investigators, though, seemed less interested in that question than in other lines of inquiry. They turned to a matter already discussed with Anna Dedekind—Grethe's hair: *From the time of the sexual encounter, had she worn a cap? Had her sister Anna cut off Grethe's hair upstairs in Heinrich Lüdden's house?* Grethe acknowledged that she wore the cap, and Anna did cut her hair, "for she had a scab on her head."[27] The prosecutors asked whether, by cutting her hair, *she could make an excuse for [wearing a cap], saying that she had something in her hair.* Margarethe denied this: "even if it had not happened on account of the problems with her head, she would nevertheless want to [wear the cap]."[28] This exchange explains the authorities' interest in a seemingly trivial matter. Both Grethe and her interrogators understood the cap to be a sign of an altered sexual state.

The interrogators' questions so far suggest several different possibilities. Asking about money raised the issue of prostitution on Grethe's part but also implicated Andreas Möller in attempting to hide an act—fornication—that was both immoral and illegal. But the critical issue was Anna Dedekind's accusation that Grethe had been pregnant. In pursuit of this claim, prosecutors returned to the events of early 1661. *Why did Dedekind no longer want [Grethe's] services after New Year's?* Grethe replied, "because Lüdden's wife [Dedekind] believed that all was not right with her, on account of what some of her neighbors were saying."[29] The questions continued: *Had not Dedekind warned Grethe that she was held in much suspicion because she had not menstruated for a long time?* "Yes." *And because the prisoner had refused to answer either yes or no to questions about her condition, had not Lüdden's wife summoned Grethe's mother from Gross Schwülper?* "Yes." *And had not the mother on the Sunday after New Year's come to the Lüdden house and gone into the city with her daughter, returning only toward evening?* Again, "Yes."

These answers corroborated most of the previous testimony, but Dedekind did not know where the Schmidts had gone after leaving her house. Now interrogators asked Grethe, who replied, "to the old Garsen woman's house near St. Katharine's churchyard [in Hagen], and there was Gottfried Möller's widow, and she asked whether Grethe had been up to something with her stepson and whether she was soon to give birth." Grethe, though, "in the presence of her mother, told the Möller widow that she had indeed been with the stepson Andreas Möller but she knew nothing of any baby or of any childbirth."[30]

The investigators seemed a step ahead, though, and asked Grethe an unexpected question: *had her mother reserved a room somewhere, where Grethe could have her baby in secret?* Schmidt's forthright answer was equally surprising: "Not here in the city but in Neubrücke, for her mother and her mother's sister, the wife of the tavern-keeper in Schwülper, went without the prisoner's knowledge and asked the official there if they might take a room with someone."[31] Who this person was Grethe did not know. As she said, the arrangement took place without her knowledge—a critical claim, as events would later show.

The interrogators returned again to the incidents at the Lüdden-Dedekind house—*how often had Grethe returned there after the New Year? Had she not some nights later slept there in secret in the maid's bed?* Grethe answered that she had only returned in the weeks after Easter, when she came back to fetch her things before going to work for the Bortzfelts in the Sack.[32] She had absolutely not slept again in the Lüdden-Dedekind house after her dismissal.

Von Horn and Gartner's continued interest in activities at the Lüdden-Dedekind house became clear in the next questions, which finally hinted at the suspected crime: *Had Grethe brought a child into the world somewhere in the Lüdden house?* Grethe's response was careful and clear: "She has never had a child, also was never made pregnant by Andreas Möller." Her period had even resumed before leaving his household.[33] The investigators pressed her for more: *After her encounter with Andreas Möller, did she have her time [period] in the normal manner as before?* "No," came the answer. "She had previously had it every four weeks; after coitus, however, it had changed and came around the fifth or sixth week, indeed as late as the seventh."[34] Anna Dedekind, of course, had just testified that, as far as she knew, Grethe was not menstruating at all during her three months in the Lüdden house.

The officials wanted to know, then, *if she had had no baby, what did come out of her and what did it look like? What had she done with it? Had she not stashed it away secretly in her bed until the following day and then perhaps tossed it in the Oker River?* Unmistakably, prosecutors were suggesting that Grethe had borne a live baby in the Lüdden-Dedekind house and then somehow disposed of it. How would Grethe respond to such an accusation? "One day, after New Year's [presumably before her mother came to the city] in the evening in the Lüdden house as she wanted to go to bed and was already lying down, something issued from her, something very red but something not so thick and barely a finger long. . . . this mass that came out of her, she wrapped in a towel and held onto it through the night. The following day, however, at four o'clock in the afternoon, she had, in the ditch in front of the Lüdden's gate, thrown it, together with the towel, into the water [the Oker River]. Whether it floated or sank, to that she had given no attention."[35] So it was simply an unformed mass of tissue that issued from her—not a baby at all, nor something that could be mistaken for a fetus either, it would seem.

Skeptical, the prosecutors ignored the answer, persisting with questions formulated with the delivery—and death—of a live baby in mind. *What had she done with the umbilical cord? Had she cut it with a knife? With scissors? How and where had she done this?* "No response," reads the transcript. Asked who had helped in her travail, she answered, "No one." *Was it not true, though, that on the Monday after New Year's Day, 1661, she had left with her mother for Gross Schwülper or some other place? Hadn't she by then already brought the baby into the world?*

Now it was Grethe's turn to put a twist in the proceedings: her mother remained in Brunswick for a bit, she replied, but she herself went with the Garsen widow's maid, Ilse, to the home of Grethe's aunt in Mörse, about twenty-two kilometers away from Gross Schwülper. Grethe stayed there for two nights until Andreas Schmidt, her father, came to take her home. *Why did she not go directly home from Brunswick?* "Her mother said that her father would scold or grumble at her." *Well then, why did the mother stay in Brunswick and let her go on alone with Garsen's maid?* Grethe could say only that her mother left Brunswick for Gross Schwülper, but that the Garsen maid felt more comfortable going to Mörse, and Grethe deferred to her wishes. As far as Grethe knew, Ilse the maid then returned to the Garsen house in Brunswick. Asked again whether by that time a baby had already been born, Grethe refused to respond.[36]

The interrogators then changed course and showed again that they had done some prior investigating: *Why was it that on the evening she returned to Gross Schwülper, she was in such misery in her father's house that the neighbors—the cowherd and his wife—could hear them? Was it not true that her father had wandered through the house, whining and lamenting, "Oh dear God, oh dear God, what will come of it all?"* Grethe said that "she had not heard such a thing." *On the next day, though, had not the neighbor's wife come to Grethe's room and found her lying on the bed? Did the woman not warn Grethe to behave in such a way that she could answer rightly to God and to every person?* Grethe replied that yes indeed she was lying in bed sick the next day, but the cowherd's wife told her nothing, asking only whether Grethe was perhaps ill.[37]

And now the long interrogation began to wind down, with only a few questions remaining. *Was it not true that Grethe's mother and aunt went to Neubrücke to reserve a room for the lying-in? Why had Grethe stayed behind? Was it not because she had already had the baby, in Brunswick? And who had given her the idea of what to do with the child? And finally, had she again slept with another man? With whom? When?*

To these final questions Grethe replied as she had earlier. She had not known of her mother's actions until later. A room for delivering a baby was not necessary, "because she [Grethe] was not pregnant, but . . . something, as described before, came out of her."[38] Unpersuaded, the interrogators pursued the matter—*why would her mother and aunt have decided to reserve a room for childbirth if they had not learned from Grethe herself that she was pregnant?* Grethe replied that her mother perhaps heard the rumor about sex with Andreas Möller from his stepmother Hafferland and decided to take precautions. But Grethe insisted yet again that in all her life she had never had a child, much less cast one aside. She refused to say who might have helped or advised her. And to the very last question, whether she had ever had sex again with anyone else, Grethe Schmidt firmly and repeatedly answered, "No." With that, the interrogation ended.

ALTSTADT, AUGUST 8, 1661

The *Justizherren* had used Anna Dedekind's vague testimony to extract solid information from Grethe Schmidt herself. As magistrates prepared to explore Grethe's revelations about the Hafferland household, they questioned one other person whose name came up in both testimonies. Anna Schmidt, Grethe's older sister, appeared at the demand of the city on August 8. Her deposition was much less formal, it appears, and was roughly transcribed in a one-page statement. If for no other reason, though, Anna's testimony is important because she was the first member of the Schmidt family to respond to Grethe's incarceration. She would not, however, be the last.

At first, Anna claimed that she had heard nothing about a sexual act or a pregnancy. She did acknowledge cutting Grethe's hair in the Lüdden-Dedekind house, because Grethe had a "bad head." The interrogators countered that if Grethe had not slept with someone and was not pregnant, then why had her mother and her aunt reserved a room in Neubrücke? At last Anna admitted that a visiting acquaintance of hers from the village of Lastbüttel, not far from Gross Schwülper, had recounted that the previous winter, around Ash Wednesday (February 27), Grethe's mother and aunt had gone to Neubrücke to rent a lying-in room. More than that Anna Schmidt did not know, nor had Grethe revealed the name of her seducer.[39]

A reluctant witness against her sister, Anna told the investigators little that they had not already known, except that the alleged search for a birthing room occurred around Ash Wednesday. If true, this claim would disrupt the timeline established during the previous day's testimonies. Anna's seemingly desultory statement, however, itself provides clues. After all, Anna admitted to cutting Grethe's hair at a time when Grethe might have needed someone to confide in. Who could fill that role better than an older sister? Anna, though, was wary and circumspect in answering the magistrates. Was she truly uninformed? Had she really only heard about events secondhand? Or was this shepherdess in fact much cagier about fending off her interlocutors, never giving direct testimony or exposing more than absolutely necessary?

Anna was probably the first member of the family to know of Grethe's arrest, or so the sequence of events would suggest. Anna's testimony came on August 8. On August 9, a letter from Gross Schwülper appeared before the magistrates. Georg Weichman, the Lutheran pastor in the village, wrote that Grethe's father had come to him in anguish, seeking help in responding to the apparent arrest of his daughter for "unknown" reasons. Weichman reported that the Schmidt family was devout and regularly attended confession and the Lord's table. Further, Grethe was a person of whom no ill had ever been spoken.[40]

Given the timing of Weichman's letter, it seems likely that either upon being summoned or upon completing her testimony, Anna had raced back to Gross Schwülper to inform her parents of the arrest. Pastor Weichman's letter stated that the Schmidts did not know the grounds for their daughter's imprisonment. Perhaps the shame of a disgraced daughter made Andreas Schmidt reluctant to tell the pastor the whole story, or perhaps Anna had not told him everything. It is also possible that the Schmidt family had learned from their neighbors about the city's preliminary snooping and were already preparing to respond when Anna was summoned to testify. Whatever the reason, one thing is sure: by August 9, the Schmidt family were aware of events in Brunswick. But what could they do to help their daughter?

As matters turned out, the Schmidts could do plenty. On the very same day, August 9, 1661, Wilhelm Schöneberger of the village of Neubrücke sent a letter to Brunswick: "Today, the oxherd of Schwülper and his wife have petitioned that testimony be given concerning the manner in which last winter they sought permission for their daughter's lying-in in order to resolve an act of fornication. So do I testify here before every person, that the aforementioned oxherd's wife and her sister, the tavern keeper in Schwülper, came in my absence to my wife some fourteen days before Ash Wednesday last, reporting that the oxherd's daughter, a maid of fifteen years, had been made pregnant by a brewer's servant. . . . About eight days later, however, she [the girl's mother] sent someone else to explain that things were actually different with the daughter [and that the lying-in room would not be necessary after all]."[41]

Here was a surprising turn of events. The Schmidt family itself had requested the local authority of Neubrücke to confirm that Ilse had indeed attempted to find a room for her daughter but cancelled just one week later. After Anna reported Grethe's arrest to her parents, they sought help from their pastor while simultaneously soliciting exculpatory testimony on the critical matter of the lying-in room. Clearly, the questions directed at Anna Schmidt and reported back to Gross Schwülper alarmed the parents not only about the grounds for the arrest but the evidence for the alleged crime as well. Andreas and Ilse tried to head off the prosecution by clarifying the matter immediately. Though poor and unimportant, the Schmidts were going to fight for their kin.

CONNECTIONS

Though contradictory and inconclusive, these first interrogations provide a general chronology of events, a timeline to be filled in and tested during the months of proceedings to come. From October 1659 to October 1660, Grethe Schmidt worked for Margarethe Hafferland in the Altstadt. While in Hafferland's employ, Schmidt had sex with her stepson, Andreas Möller, just before Pentecost (June 10, 1660). From October 1660 to New Year's 1661, Schmidt worked for Anna Dedekind in Hagen. By Christmas 1660, a little more than seven months after Schmidt's intercourse with Möller, Dedekind became convinced that Grethe was pregnant. Just after New Year's, Grethe claimed to have had some discharge, which she hid overnight and tossed in the Oker River the next day. On Friday, January 4, 1661, Dedekind and her husband confronted and then fired the maid. Schmidt's mother arrived on Sunday, January 6, the Feast of Three Kings, and took her daughter to speak with Hafferland. On Monday, January 7, the Schmidts left town, Grethe going in the company of a servant to Mörse, where her father retrieved her. Ilse stayed briefly in Brunswick and then returned to Gross Schwülper. On or about February 13, Ilse went to Neubrücke to reserve a lying-in room, which she cancelled one week later. Grethe was not seen in Brunswick from January 7 until after Easter (April 14, 1661). At some point after that, she began to work in the Sack until her arrest around July 25, 1661. If Grethe was pregnant, she would have left Hafferland's employ in her fourth month. If Grethe had a baby, it was between January 1 and February 20, 1661, or between the seventh and the ninth month following intercourse. Grethe, though, claimed that although the timing of her period had changed, she was in fact still menstruating before leaving the Hafferland house in October.

We can also factor Grethe Schmidt's age into this timeline. Despite her own statement that she was seventeen or eighteen, the most reliable record—her pastor's reading of the baptismal register—shows that she was born either in 1646 or 1647. The earlier birth date would make her thirteen upon entering Hafferland's employ, and perhaps fourteen when she had sex with thirty-eight-year-old Andreas Möller. By January 1661, she would have been barely fifteen, at the oldest. Of course, if she were born in 1647, she would have been twelve when beginning service for Hafferland, perhaps thirteen when sex took place, and fourteen, at the oldest, in January 1661.

Aside from establishing the tangled timeline of the case, the first testimony contains surprising elements. Among the most interesting are the repeated questions about Grethe's hair to all three witnesses. Its immediate significance becomes apparent when authorities asked Grethe if she began to wear her hair under a cap after having sex with Andreas Möller. The connection was not coincidental. Women might wear a wreath or a veil at their wedding to symbolize their changed status. In seventeenth-century Germany, a woman known to have lost her virginity before marriage might be forced to wear a *Strohkranz* (a wreath of straw) as a symbol of her fallen state. Brunswick's criminal law code of 1579 stated that "where a woman allowed herself to have intercourse and become pregnant outside marriage, she should place a veil over her head."[42] According to Schmidt's lawyer, the Brunswick custom was for fallen women to come to the *Rathaus* and don a cap with a red lion (the city symbol) on it to display their guilt.[43]

Was the city trying to confirm, first from Anna Dedekind and then from the Schmidt sisters, that Grethe had taken a cap and was therefore admitting her shame but trying to hide the fact from neighbors? It would appear so. Grethe herself claimed that "her head was covered with scabs, but even if that were not the case she would have chosen to wear the cap."[44] At least one adult woman in Brunswick, though—Anna Dedekind—saw nothing suspicious in Grethe's head covering. Dedekind, of course, had every reason not to admit to authorities that she had neglected her civic duty by allowing a wanton woman to continue working in her home.

City investigators almost never pursued the issue again. Schmidt's straightforward admission of intercourse with Andreas Möller may have made it unnecessary to investigate her sexual activity. The real puzzle, though, is whether and why she was publicly announcing her fallen state. Grethe clearly began to wear it on her own, and with no outside pressure. If she was trying to hide her sexual activity, why would she have acknowledged sex with Andreas Möller in the first place? Schmidt's best course of action would have been to deny her behavior from the very beginning. The cap might perhaps indicate that Grethe was marking herself as available for prostitution.[45] This possibility, though, never came up in any subsequent discussion of the case, by authorities or witnesses.

Another possibility is that this young country girl felt both shame and remorse over intercourse with Möller—especially if she were coerced. In other words, Grethe might have taken on herself some form of public penance. Perhaps, too, Grethe was simply confused—she was only fifteen years of age, at the oldest, when all this occurred. How much did she understand of her experience before her arrest?

Another surprising twist in the early interrogations concerns the Schmidt family. The first actions by the Schmidts—Anna, Andreas, and Ilse Leuthgen—suggest a family aware not only of the way some legal processes worked but of what they should or should not say in defending Grethe. Anna framed her testimony as secondhand information. Though their father must have known the general nature of Grethe's dilemma, Andreas Schmidt refrained from explaining it to Pastor Weichman. Ilse and Andreas sent right away for testimony from the authorities at Neubrücke, confirming prosecutors' information but seeking to blunt its impact. The stage was set early on: the prosecution of Grethe Schmidt would not go uncontested by one of the lowliest of families in seventeenth-century society.

Still, the fact remains that Grethe had admitted to sex with Andreas Möller, and two weeks before Ash Wednesday, Ilse Leuthgen had tried to procure a lying-in room, then cancelled the request just a week later. Even Grethe's own mother, it seems, at some point believed that she was pregnant. Another statement in the Neubrücke letter is also enigmatic: the father of the "whore's child" (*hurenkind*) was reported to be a "brewer's servant" (*knecht*), rather than a brewer's son or a cavalry rider. Had the witnesses in Neubrücke simply misheard the facts? Had Ilse herself misunderstood who was responsible? Or had Grethe's mother for some reason misrepresented the alleged father's identity?

The gaps in the city's information, though, are notable. What was the actual evidence that Grethe had even been pregnant, much less killed her infant? Dedekind could only assert her claim that Schmidt appeared pregnant, but she knew nothing more. None of the questions from August 7 even hint at the discovery of a corpse. Where was the baby's body, live or dead? To put it bluntly, the city of Brunswick did not conclusively know whether any infraction beyond fornication had even been committed, much less what it was. Prosecutors had leads and witnesses. They had a suspected criminal. But did they have a crime?

4

Family Values

From the very first testimony, the case against Grethe Schmidt runs against conventional expectations. The time-honored conventions of detective and crime stories demand either a corpse or perhaps a single witness pointing an accusing finger at the lonely girl from Gross Schwülper. But so far the prosecutors had asked nothing about a corpse and witnesses had not mentioned one. Rather than demanding an explanation of a newborn's mangled corpse, prosecutors asked first about Grethe's hair.

A drama did emerge in the first week of testimony: the clash of two families with reputations in jeopardy and lives to protect. After Anna Schmidt's interrogation the Schmidts scrambled to explain their actions and rescue Grethe. In Brunswick itself, however, magistrates now confronted another family with its honor at stake. Grethe had named Andreas Möller as her despoiler—if she had delivered (and killed) a baby, he was presumably the father. Local officials also insinuated that Andreas and his family had paid Grethe, either for sex or for her silence about the pregnancy. These accusations seriously imperiled the Möller family's reputation. According to the criminal code of Brunswick, he could be fined and possibly banished, and he could also be made to pay restitution to Grethe's family, compensating for her lost honor and ruined marital prospects. And of course the law required him to provide for the child.[1] The fact that it was Andreas Möller who stood accused of despoiling Grethe Schmidt, though, was no favor to the young woman. As noted earlier, modern research reveals that most women prosecuted for the crime had sexual partners from their own, invariably lower, social class. The narrative that dominated the early modern German world, though, whether it came from Reformation-influenced moralists or indignant Enlightenment reformers, involved maidservants and their employers. Grethe Schmidt's tale does not fit the modern statistical profile, but it ran true to the worst expectations and fears of preachers and prosecutors alike.[2]

It was therefore in Andreas Möller's interest to exculpate himself and blame Schmidt for whatever happened in his stepmother's house in the summer of

1660. Of course, Möller himself had another option, one closed to Grethe but open to all the Andreas Möllers from the dawn of time. He could flee the city and his responsibilities until the whole affair blew over. It will come as no great surprise that in her testimony to investigators his stepmother, Margarethe Hafferland, begged the court's indulgence, explaining that her stepson Andreas "left around Pentecost and since then had not returned home."[3] Apparently he had gone on a long-planned journey to Holland. It is not clear from the record when, or even if, he ever returned.

Throughout the year-long investigation and trial, while magistrates repeatedly interrogated Grethe Schmidt, Andreas Möller never faced a single question from Brunswick's authorities. Nor did the city make any attempt to summon him back. The criminal record contains no hint that authorities even thought of looking for him. Andreas Möller was from a prosperous family, and circumstantial evidence suggests that he may have known at least of the magistrates (Julius von Horn). The investigators had reasons to protect an affluent and respected burgher, especially against an outsider of little means and less repute.[4] Whatever the cause, though, Andreas Möller was far away from Brunswick when Grethe was arrested. The burden of saving the family's good name now fell to his stepmother, Gottfried Möller's widowed second wife, Margarethe Hafferland.

Defending Andreas's and her own reputation would not be easy for Hafferland, as the authorities' next three interviews showed just how thoroughly entangled she was in the matter. Investigators first questioned Hafferland's aunt by marriage, the widow Margarethe Engelken, to whose house in Hagen the Schmidt women had gone on the Sunday after New Year to confront Hafferland. Engelken would point the magistrates to her own maid, Ilse, who had allegedly accompanied Grethe out of Brunswick the next day. Finally and most important, the magistrates confronted Hafferland herself about events that had allegedly happened under her own roof. Hafferland, it turned out, had good reason to shape the matter in a way favorable to her family's reputation.

HAGEN, AUGUST 12, 1661

Margarethe Engelken

The first woman to be interviewed on August 12 was Ludolf Garsen's widow and Hafferland's aunt-in-law, Margarethe Engelken. Engelken was seventy-four, sick, and would die the next year, but she had information critical to the case. According to Grethe Schmidt's earlier testimony, it was

in Engelken's house that Schmidt's mother confronted Margarethe Hafferland on the Feast of Three Kings, January 6. Because of Engelken's poor
health, her interview took place in her home near St. Katharine's church
and was conducted by the judicial personnel of the borough (*Weichbild*) of
Hagen. Investigators bluntly asked about the "suspicious whorish matter"
of which they suspected the accused, and Engelken made plain her moral
outrage.[5] She recounted that Grethe's mother, Ilse, had "earned her bread"
as a servant in the house for seven years while Ludolf Garsen was still
alive. Schmidt's mother had served so "truly and faithfully" that Engelken
wanted her to stay on after Ludolf Garsen's death. She therefore had good
reason to refer Ilse's daughter to Margarethe Hafferland, Engelken's niece
by marriage. Hafferland had no living children, and Engelken hoped that
she would benefit from Margarethe Schmidt's youth. On Engelken's recommendation, Hafferland hired Grethe in September 1659.[6]

Fifteen months later, around the Feast of Three Kings (1661), Hafferland and the two Schmidt women paid an unexpected visit to Engelken's
sickbed. Engelken knew immediately that "unrighteous matters" (*un-
richtige Handel*) were at hand and that "things with the girl might not be
right." Engelken told the authorities she had wanted nothing to do with
the affair. She turned her face to the wall and refused to listen, forcing the
three women to conduct their meeting in another room. Out of "hatred
for godless ways," however, Engelken was "moved to tell her old maidservant, Ilse [Schmidt's mother], that she should knock this godless female
[Grethe] to the floor."[7] Though she heard later that the young woman had
refused to admit to wrongdoing, that night was the last time Engelken had
seen Grethe Schmidt.

But Engelken did see Ilse Leuthgen again. Just three or four days after
Ilse came to Engelken's house with Grethe and Hafferland, she turned up
again on Engelken's doorstep. This time, Ilse threatened to go to the authorities (presumably to accuse Andreas Möller of fornication and immorality). Engelken was unmoved—she reported that she had told her former
servant that she could do whatever she pleased, but that she, Engelken,
"wanted nothing to do with her and her goings." Schmidt's mother had not
crossed her doorway after that.[8]

The old woman's anger at the "godless" girl was vehement. The authorities, though, coolly responded to Engelken's righteous outbursts with a
number of skeptical questions gleaned from their interrogation of Grethe
Schmidt herself. *Didn't [Egelken's] own [current] maid accompany Grethe
Schmidt from [Engelken's] house toward Mörse [in January 1661], and
before leaving the house, didn't the witness give Schmidt five gulden and*

admonish her?[9] Engelken's response seemed suddenly to turn more wary than impassioned. She could not say exactly what had happened, but the truth was that her maid, Ilse, had long sought permission to visit her own family near Wolfsburg. It was Engelken's understanding that Grethe Schmidt was to accompany the maid to Wolfsburg, where Schmidt was supposed to remain until everything had been worked out. That Schmidt and the maid had ended up in Mörse (on the way to Wolfsburg) was news to her.[10] Engelken, however, claimed that she had neither commanded nor organized this journey, so perhaps Margarethe Hafferland might be able to provide more information. Engelken must have immediately regretted reintroducing her niece into her testimony, for she hastened to add that whatever Hafferland had done sprang from a "true heart." As to money exchanging hands, Engelken personally knew nothing of it and had nothing more to report. Finally, in Margarethe Engelken's opinion, if Schmidt's condition were indeed as suspected, then the girl deserved whatever happened to her.[11]

The old woman's testimony ended, as it had begun, with anger and regret: she was now seventy-four years old and no longer troubled herself with worldly affairs. She had not wanted to be questioned about the "lascivious whore." Nonetheless, her testimony was important, because it confirmed the outline of those important days in early January. On or just before the Feast of Three Kings 1661, the Schmidt women and Hafferland had met in Hagen to observe and discuss Grethe's condition. On the following Monday, Grethe Schmidt left Brunswick with Engelken's servant and headed toward Wolfsburg. As Grethe Schmidt's testimony had recounted earlier, though, the pair got only as far as Mörse, because Schmidt's father came to fetch her home.

Margarethe Engelken might be forgiven for her confusion about the details—sick and old, she seemed profoundly distressed by contact with this tawdry affair. It is also possible, though, that her vagueness resulted from caution. Engelken admitted to knowing very little, except what she had heard from others. More important, her testimony about the maid's journey seems at best disingenuous. Her maid had long wanted to visit home—why had the widow waited until now to give her consent? Was it mere coincidence that Grethe Schmidt would go along, and is it possible that Engelken only knew of this in passing? And while explicitly absolving her own niece by referring to Hafferland's goodness of heart, Engelken placed responsibility for all arrangements squarely on the shoulders of Margarethe Hafferland. Authorities therefore left Engelken's house with many unanswered questions, but at least now they knew whom to ask next. As to the old widow, her testimony did reveal a critical fact: Grethe Schmidt had provoked deep anger among some of Brunswick's women. Whatever the girl had done, she could not rely on the kindnesses of women strangers.

Altstadt Mint, August 12, 1661

Engelken's Maid, Ilse

From St. Katharine's churchyard in Hagen, investigators returned to the Altstadt mint for the day's two other interviews. First was Engelken's maid, Ilse, who had witnessed the confrontations in Hagen and then accompanied Schmidt out of Brunswick. Ilse had worked for Engelken for three years. Like Grethe, she came from a village outside Brunswick, Wendschott, in the vicinity of Wolfsburg (forty-one kilometers northeast of Brunswick). Ilse remembered well that on New Year's Day 1661, Margarethe Hafferland visited her aunt's home and asked Ilse to fetch young Schmidt from her current employer in Hagen. Schmidt and Hafferland spoke together but Ilse had no clue about the subject or content.[12]

On the following Sunday, however, the Feast of Three Kings, Ilse the maid herself went to the Hafferland house to ask a favor. Her father in Wendschott was very ill. Ilse wanted to visit him and hoped that Hafferland could "lend a helping hand" and look after her mistress during the maid's absence.[13] At that very moment, though, Herr Möller (who was rumored to have had "fleshly relations" with Schmidt) entered the room to speak with Ilse in the presence of his stepmother. He suggested that perhaps Grethe Schmidt could accompany her to Wendschott, where she might stay for the six weeks supposedly remaining until "things were resolved."[14] According to Ilse's testimony, Andreas wanted to be available around Ash Wednesday (February 27) to see if he had some responsibility for a new child, because at Pentecost 1661, he would be leaving for Holland.[15] Hafferland listened to the proposition—she thought that getting Grethe out of town was a good idea—and gave Ilse half a thaler for expenses along the way. Andreas Möller also told Ilse that whatever happened, her father would be compensated for all expenses (e.g., for Schmidt's room and board, and whatever care the child might need).[16]

The next day, Monday, Hafferland went again to the old widow's house. This time Grethe and her mother also came. They waited as Ilse the maid got ready, and then about eleven o'clock in the morning, mother, daughter, and the maid left the house and walked the Long Canal toward the city gates. Schmidt's mother eventually turned back to the city. The two maids continued in the direction of Mörse (twenty-eight kilometers), where they stayed overnight with the tavern keeper. When they finally reached Wendschott, Ilse explained to her parents that Schmidt also once worked for the Garsen widow's niece and asked that Grethe be allowed to stay (this contradicted Grethe's claim that they had traveled together only as far as Mörse). Grethe stayed several days at the family home in Wendschott. On Friday night, though, Grethe's own father appeared at the door, saying that he would give food and shelter even to a dog and so was determined to care for his own daughter himself. Early the next morning, Andreas Schmidt took Grethe back to Gross Schwülper.[17] That day too, Ilse left with her brother Hans and went to Flechtorf (nineteen kilometers from Braunschweig) where she met some companions and returned to Brunswick.

The listening magistrates found some of these details highly coincidental: *how was it that Ilse chose just that moment—the Feast of Three Kings—to decide to visit her father?* The maid explained that her father was quite ill and had already asked Ilse to come visit or risk the chance of never seeing him again. Ilse had repeatedly asked her mistress for permission to go but had never received it. On the Sunday of Three Kings, however, Margarethe Engelken herself suggested that Ilse could visit her father if she so desired.[18]

Skeptical still, the prosecutors asked *whether Ilse went on her own initiative to the Hafferland house, since the defendant and her mother showed up unbidden on the very next day at the Garsen house?* In truth, replied Ilse, she could no longer clearly remember whether she went to Hafferland unbidden or whether someone else had suggested it.[19] She did remember that Schmidt and her mother were present in the Garsen house when Ilse received permission to go. That same day, Hafferland had also come to the house after Ilse's request for help. In fact, the witness finally recalled that it was Margarethe Engelken herself who first suggested that Ilse go to the Möllers' home.[20]

The magistrates wanted to know *whether Grethe Schmidt had received five gulden for the trip.* Ilse "could not say," other than that she herself had received an extra thaler from Hafferland for nourishment along the way. She did hear later in passing that on the Friday Schmidt's father came to Wendschott to collect his daughter, Grethe's mother and aunt were in Brunswick and received five gulden from Hafferland.[21]

Finally, *hadn't the witness spoken with the prisoner's mother in order to find out about her suspicious actions?* No, said Ilse Engelken, nor had she paid the least attention to the matter. On the way to Wendschott she always walked a little way ahead and looked back only to see if Grethe were following. Still, the magistrates wanted to know, *while under way had she not noticed that Grethe was pregnant?* No, Ilse had noticed nothing other than that Schmidt had a thick bosom. She had heard that Hafferland suspected Schmidt was pregnant and that Andreas Möller was the culprit, for Schmidt expressly stated that she had slept only with him. In sum, Grethe "was not to be thought of as a virgin, but then she had not pretended to be one either."[22]

Ilse's testimony confirmed what investigators must already have suspected from Margarethe Engelken's deposition: granting Ilse permission to travel home just when the Schmidts appeared at Engelken's door was no coincidence. Ilse's report, though, contradicted Engelken's claim to have been removed from the matter. If, after refusing permission so often, Margarethe Engelken now herself broached the trip home to Wendschott to Ilse, then it seems clear that Engelken and her niece Hafferland had agreed upon a course of action. Further, asking Ilse to seek out Hafferland for help, only to have Andreas Möller suddenly propose that Grethe Schmidt could accompany Ilse on her journey, was suspiciously convenient. Möller's claims of responsibility could have been sincere, but they also helped present him in the best possible light given the circumstances. Apparently, Hafferland and Margarethe Engelken had worked out a plan to remove the embarrassing former maidservant from their midst with the least amount of trouble. Rumors circulating about Andreas's guilt for Schmidt's pregnancy must have spurred him and his stepmother to try to limit the damage.

To untangle these very confusing accounts, the magistrates would now have to concentrate on the stepmother's tale. They called Margarethe Hafferland, Schmidt's first employer in Brunswick, to testify. The picture she painted of Grethe and the Schmidt family was a dark one indeed. In the telling of it, however, Hafferland revealed much about the tensions that existed in her own household between stepmother and stepson, and about the importance of reputation in seventeenth-century Germany.

Margarethe Hafferland

Margarethe Hafferland lived in her deceased husband's house, but unlike Margarethe Engelken, another widow, she did not live alone. Instead, the other very real presence there was Gottfried Möller's son by his first marriage. The relationship between the two, personal and financial, is difficult to sort out. If Andreas was in fact thirty-eight, then he was already in his thirties when his father died in 1656, and thus no doubt a powerful figure in the house. At the youngest, Andreas was nineteen or twenty by the end of 1660 and very likely to be asserting his rights. Hafferland therefore had to tread very carefully in dealing with her stepson, although in the census of 1671, following the conquest of Brunswick, she was listed as a property owner of some means in her own right.

Hafferland received more respectful treatment from the authorities than Grethe Schmidt or even Anna Dedekind. Hafferland gave her account with only occasional requests to clarify or expand. Grethe Schmidt had worked for her about a year, from St. Michael's Day in 1659 until the same feast day in 1660. Hafferland employed her for a whole year even though she found Grethe "quarrelsome" and "rebellious,"[23] and so did not renew her contract at the end of the year. Later, after dismissing Grethe, Hafferland heard from another former employee, Gertrude Wilmers, that local women were spreading the news that things with Schmidt were "different" (*anders*, a common euphemism for pregnancy). Upon hearing these rumors, on the Sunday before Three Kings Day (December 31, 1660), Hafferland went to the house of her aunt, Margarethe Engelken, and summoned Grethe. In a room just behind the door, Hafferland told Schmidt that everyone in town thought she was pregnant. When the girl denied it, Hafferland looked Grethe in the face and warned that if Schmidt had something else in mind, something "not good" (e.g. infanticide or abortion), she would fall under grave suspicion.[24] Instead, Hafferland testified, she urged Grethe to tell the truth—when she'd had sex, and with whom. Hafferland reported that she then asked Grethe point blank if she'd had sex with Andreas Möller. Schmidt answered that she had had nothing more to do with Andreas than "a good day, a good way"—that is, she had only spoken to him politely to wish him a good day. Hearing this, Hafferland decided she would get no more information out of her former maid and dismissed her.[25]

Any relief Hafferland might have felt about Grethe's denial that her stepson was involved was short-lived, because around the same time, Schmidt's parents in Gross Schwülper learned what was happening. Hafferland recounted that just "three or four days later," Grethe's mother came to the Engelken house, where she spoke to both Engelken and Hafferland and "behaved very badly."[26] Ilse Leuthgen claimed that her daughter had explained the whole affair and had admitted "that she [Grethe] had known no person other than the Möller widow's son [Andreas]."[27] Hearing this, Hafferland bolted from Engelken's house and raced home to the Breite Strasse to confront her stepson. Andreas denied the claim at first. Finally, though, he acknowledged that, possibly, the accusation might just be true, though he fervently hoped that Grethe was not pregnant. But even if she were, he told Hafferland, he had a plan. His stepmother should consider taking Schmidt to a place outside the city where she would be cared for. Andreas proposed that Schmidt might go to Wendschott, the hometown of Margarethe Engelken's maid, Ilse, there to await "the time" for the baby's birth.[28] Hafferland reckoned that Grethe was seven or eight months pregnant, so that same day, she summoned Schmidt's mother to the Engelken house again and presented the plan, to which both parties agreed.

Hafferland's opening statement ended here, and the magistrates began to question her. They asked first about Andreas Möller—*how had all of this happened and in what circumstances?* Hafferland said that Andreas was her stepson. As a respectable and honorable matron, she did not hesitate to speak with him about the matter. He was so insistent and forceful (*mächtig*) in his speech, however, that she could not get very far. Had Andreas been her real son, she knew right well what she would tell him, and then the outcome would have been different.[29] Implicit in this statement is Hafferland's concern about her relationship to her stepson and her position in the household.

Next, the magistrates pressed Hafferland about the proposed journey to Wendschott: *how much money was the defendant promised or given for her journey?* Hafferland admitted to providing the defendant a pair of sausages and Ilse the maid a gulden for upkeep but otherwise asserted that she gave the defendant nothing, nor any promise of more to come. Just a day after the two servant girls departed, however, Schmidt's mother and aunt appeared at Engelken's house to convey the news that Grethe's father was entirely unwilling to go along with the plan—the Schmidts and no one else would care for their daughter. According to the two women, Andreas Schmidt had already gone to retrieve Grethe from Wendschott. He wanted her to deliver the baby closer to home, and Grethe's mother and aunt had found a room for the lying-in in the nearby village of Neubrücke. The room cost only fourteen gulden, but Ilse and her sister lamented that they had no money for it. Hafferland thought this was a terrible idea but now realized she was dealing with "stupid people" (*thorick Leuthe*) who could not see the possible consequences for Grethe.[30]

Then Hafferland's tale took a darker turn. Stubbornly set in their foolish decision, Hafferland told the authorities, the Schmidt women grew greedy. They told Hafferland that if Andreas Möller would give them one hundred gulden, the Schmidts would blame someone else and promise never again to invoke Andreas Möller's name. In fact, they had already named another person as the father to the people in Neubrücke.[31] Hafferland refused.[32] At that point, Schmidt's mother and aunt threatened to go immediately toward the Hafferland home in the Breite Strasse, and "raise such a ruckus that the entire street would awaken."[33] Later, upon arriving home, Hafferland relayed the Schmidts' threat to Andreas Möller. Andreas replied that when the time came and everything worked out, the Schmidts would have their money.[34]

In her statement to the magistrates, Hafferland bitterly complained about the Schmidt women, perhaps feeling betrayed and disillusioned because the defendant's mother had worked faithfully as a servant in her aunt's household. Finally, though, Margarethe Hafferland admitted that, in an earlier meeting at the Engelken house, she had indeed given five half-gulden to Schmidt's mother in order to let the matter drop. Hafferland hoped that in doing so she had not sinned, for she had done everything in order to avoid disgrace and in memory of her stepson's honored father, who held the son in high regard and had such great hopes for him.[35]

Telling this story was no doubt hard for Hafferland. The Schmidts appalled her, but her own stepson seemed no less determined to drag the widow into unseemly, disgraceful acts. The authorities ignored her discomfort and pressed further, taking another direction. *During the time Grethe was employed, had Hafferland noticed whether her maid had her regular "time" or "work" [i.e., her period]? During the time when the defendant left service, or when next seen in the Engelken house, or when she left for Wendschott, did Hafferland think she was pregnant?*[36] Hafferland had to respond carefully for two reasons: first, the questions implied that she had been a negligent "housemother" by permitting immorality under her roof. Second, if Hafferland knew of Grethe's condition (a crime, after all), she should have reported it to authorities rather than allow Schmidt to take up new employment.

The widow replied that at the beginning of Grethe's service, the young woman seemed impertinent (*vorwitzig*), a trait Hafferland attributed to her extreme youth. One Saturday, though, as Grethe rode on a horse through the marketplace, she raised many eyebrows among the onlookers, offending Hafferland with her apparent immodesty.[37] Another time Hafferland was able to see on Grethe's shirt the signs of her "womanly time," although Hafferland could not remember whether it was before or after Pentecost 1660 (a crucial detail because Schmidt acknowledged that the sex had taken place just days before Pentecost). Hafferland once watched the girl climb a tree in the garden, "so high and with such speed," that the older woman could never have believed her to be pregnant, indeed would have argued strenuously that Grethe could not be. Of course, Hafferland told her interviewers, had she known that Schmidt was pregnant, she would have reproached her sternly and would not have permitted the maid to enter the employ of another.[38] It was only after Grethe had been gone awhile, working at the house of Heinrich Lüdden and Anna Dedekind in Hagen, that "evil talk" about her arose. Hafferland then heard from Schmidt's mother about the liaison with Andreas Möller and began to consider the possibility of pregnancy. According to Hafferland, when Grethe left Brunswick for Wendschott, she looked very "round."[39]

This explanation did not satisfy the questioners, who pointed to Hafferland's earlier answers: *had she not heard directly, from the prisoner's mother herself, that her daughter knew no one other than Andreas Möller? Had the prisoner's mother not said that her daughter was with child by the witness's stepson?* Hafferland responded that Schmidt's mother had claimed that Andreas Möller alone was responsible, and that a child was indeed at hand, expected soon. The witness also remembered seeing Grethe for the first time in several months upon summoning her to Engelken's house, at New Year's. Grethe would confess nothing, said Hafferland, and above all, "did not want to be looked at, could not stand the witness touching her, but with both hands pushed and turned the witness's hands from her."[40]

Then the interview took an unexpected turn. The magistrates asked whether, when "the child murderess was brought out in the Breite Strasse," Hafferland saw Schmidt standing near the Hafferland house, watching the accused killer and ripping her white cap away while covering her head with her apron. This is the first hint that sometime in 1661 another young woman in Brunswick had been arrested and punished for infanticide, though the city's archives today hold no record of the event. Schmidt's actions—tearing at her cap while watching another poor sinner's fate—implied anguish, shame, or perhaps guilt that she was suddenly trying to conceal. Hafferland responded that she had indeed seen her former maid that day but could not remember Schmidt's actions. Hafferland did remember quite well that, while still in her employ, Schmidt felt an "evil dampness" on her head and allowed her sister Anna to cut her hair.[41] Once again, Grethe's hair came to the fore as a possible sign of her status and shame.

The questioners, though, were for the time being concentrating on this other arrest or punishment of an infanticide in the city and wanted to know *whether, while watching in the Breite Strasse, Hafferland had said that Schmidt before long would have her own punishment or had earned the same punishment [as the arrested woman]?*[42] Hafferland explained that she was standing next to a Frau Hildebrand from the Neue Strasse, who commented, "Look, there is your old maid, Grethe." Frau Hildebrand then related that a tenant of hers had traveled to Gross Schwülper and there asked Grethe's mother how the girl was. Ilse Leuthgen said that her daughter had been terribly sick with a toothache but was now well and working again in Brunswick. Hearing this, Hafferland told Hildebrand only that Grethe and her family would have to answer if the so-called sickness and toothache turned out to be something either evil or suspicious.[43]

Finally, the city prosecutors shifted their focus back to what Ilse Leuthgen had told Hafferland directly: *while staying with Grethe in the Dedekind house, did not Schmidt's mother report . . . that the defendant was pregnant and had a living child within her?* Hafferland responded that after Ilse had spent the night with her daughter in the Lüdden-Dedekind house, Hafferland asked her whether Grethe was pregnant with a living baby. Hafferland wanted Ilse Leuthgen to place her hands on the girl's body and confirm the fact.[44] Schmidt's mother replied that it was quite certain Grethe was pregnant—"the girl's legs had swollen so thickly that she could barely take off her stockings." She had not, however, touched her daughter's stomach to feel a living baby move, for she had returned very late to the house where Grethe was sleeping.[45]

According to Hafferland's statement, that same morning—Monday, January 7—she spoke to Schmidt in Engelken's kitchen as the young woman prepared to depart for Wendschott. The older woman asked whether, things being as they were, Grethe would admit when the baby first moved within her, perhaps around the Feast of St. Michael's (September) or St. Martin's Day (November). Grethe Schmidt, though, would neither affirm nor deny but mumbled something inaudible.[46]

CONNECTIONS

With three extensive interviews of reluctant witnesses in two separate locations, the authorities were gradually adding details to the sequence of events between Christmas 1660 and the Feast of Three Kings, January 6, 1661. On the Sunday before New Year's Day, Hafferland received distressing news about Grethe Schmidt and Andreas Möller. She summoned the girl but could get no information. On the following Sunday, the Schmidts confronted Hafferland, who in turn confronted her stepson. With Margarethe Engelken's help, Hafferland and Andreas Möller hastily hatched a plan to remove Grethe from Brunswick, preserving Möller's honor while covering up his deed. That same night the Schmidts agreed to send Grethe to Wendschott and the next day left the city. Grethe went with Engelken's maid, while Schmidt's mother returned to Gross Schwülper. The plan went awry, though, as Andreas Schmidt determined to fetch his daughter home that Friday, January 11. Meanwhile Ilse Leuthgen returned to Brunswick for yet another confrontation with Margarethe Hafferland, reporting that Andreas Schmidt had brought his daughter home and demanding new payments to cover up the entire affair.

The authorities' tough day appeared well rewarded: all three witnesses provided information that added sinew to the case against Grethe Schmidt.

Now, the lurid tale spun by Engelken, her maid, and especially by Margarethe Hafferland implicated the Schmidt women in a web of extortion and
blackmail: if Hafferland's testimony was true, the Schmidts had attempted
not only to hide Grethe's pregnancy but also to exploit it for gain. They
had threatened to ruin Möller's life if he did not accede to Ilse Leuthgen's
demands for money. And the Schmidts had gone even further, offering to
place the blame on someone else, perhaps falsely subjecting an innocent
person to criminal prosecution.

It was a wretched tale indeed. The testimony about blackmail sullied the
Schmidts, but it also drew Hafferland and Engelken into the deceit. Despite
their outraged morality, however, the two old women had clearly colluded to
make Schmidt disappear quietly. And though Hafferland appeared troubled
by her stepson's behavior, she nevertheless made excuses for it and for his
continuing absence. Some of this effort undoubtedly resulted from concern
over her husband's estate—as stepmother, her control over the property was
very much tied to her stepson's fortunes and wishes.

Of greatest potential worry to Hafferland, though, were the officials'
persistent questions about money. The problem is obvious. For Andreas
and/or his stepmother to have attempted to buy the Schmidts' silence
placed them uncomfortably close to a possibly heinous crime. At the very
least, Hafferland could be seen as trying to cover for Möller's fornication.
Hafferland had the further difficulty of explaining why a young woman of
low morals, possibly pregnant, had been allowed to change jobs in the city
with impunity. In short, Hafferland could be seen as betraying another
citizen of Brunswick, Grethe's new and unwitting employer. As to Andreas,
he had clearly left the entire mess for his stepmother to clean up.

Certainly the combined testimony of August 12 made it appear as though
the Schmidt women sought to profit from Grethe's shame. If so, though,
why did the Schmidts change course? Was it the father's determination
that the family itself and no one else would care for their daughter? Did
the Schmidt women then try to make the best of the situation by renting a
lying-in room and demanding payment for their silence—a move that very
nearly worked since Andreas Möller, according to his stepmother, agreed
to the deal? And according to the letter from Neubrücke about the lying-in
room, Ilse had indeed named a brewer's servant as the culprit, potentially
corroborating Hafferland's claims of blackmail. Finally, just how much did
Grethe Schmidt herself have to do with these decisions?

A final connection from Hafferland's testimony concerns her stepson.
Andreas Möller was undoubtedly an aggressive participant in the decisions about how to handle Grethe Schmidt's situation. From Hafferland's
tale, one could easily conclude that it was Andreas himself who hatched

the elaborate plan to remove the inconvenient maidservant from Bruns-wick, leaving his stepmother and other women of the house to work out the details. No matter how disapproving, Margarethe Hafferland felt the need to comply, even to the point of acquiescing in blackmail. Andreas had obvious control over money, and he clearly was able to intimidate his sixty-year-old stepmother. One might infer from Hafferland's description not only that Andreas Möller was indeed much older than twenty but also something much more important. His forcefulness and his conniving, combined with a character that can only be described as overbearing, sug-gest that Grethe Schmidt at thirteen or fourteen may have had little choice about what happened between her and the stepson. The magistrates, though, ignored this possibility and kept their eyes squarely focused on the maidservant chained in the *Fronerey*.

Gaps and contradictions continued to exist in the sequence of events. Most crucially, it was unclear if, when, and where a baby had been born. If the childbirth took place in Anna Dedekind's house at New Year's, as authorities asked Grethe, why did her family look for a lying-in room in Neubrücke? Officials of the *Untergericht* suddenly had more, not less, work ahead of them. They had to investigate not only Grethe Schmidt but her entire family. They had to find confirmation of Hafferland's actions, perhaps from the other people Hafferland herself had named. This meant widening the arc of the investigation; now a larger circle of Brunswick's women became involved.

5

Common Repute

Women and Neighbors

Just one day after Hafferland's dramatic testimony, the search for witnesses expanded. The *Untergericht*'s opening strategy of focusing on the principal actors in the case had paid off handsomely. Each witness strengthened the wave of suspicion about the girl from Gross Schwülper that now extended to her entire family and threatened to engulf even Margarethe Hafferland's. Yet, however powerful the testimony of Anna Dedekind, Ilse Engelken, and Margarethe Hafferland, the prosecution witnesses themselves had reputations at stake and secrets to protect. Dedekind and her husband had not reported Grethe's condition to the authorities; Margarethe Hafferland had been complicit in her stepson's attempts to remove Schmidt from view and had even given the young woman money to go away. The story was in no way complete.

Even after the damaging testimony of August 12, the case against Grethe Schmidt still seemed full of holes—there was no corpus delicti and no iron-clad witness who knew with certainty that Grethe had been pregnant, let alone that she had murdered her baby. What the prosecution had, instead, was a chorus of local women from the neighborhoods of Brunswick who could testify to rumors and their own suspicions.[1] All this testimony would have to be checked for accuracy—"hearsay" was theoretically as inadmissible in the seventeenth century as it is in the twenty-first.

Anna Dedekind had testified that her original belief that Grethe was too young to menstruate dissolved as rumors about her pregnancy coursed through Hagen. During their investigation in August 1661, authorities tried to follow that train of rumors, interviewing a number of Brunswick women in a quest to fortify the case against Grethe Schmidt. The women were a motley array of Brunswickers high and low—within certain constraints, gossip was a remarkably egalitarian affair.[2] The chorus that testified about Grethe Schmidt included a soldier's spouse, a cobbler's wife, several maidservants, a collector of herbs and plants, and a mysterious old woman dispensing unofficial medicine and advice. The different social and employment situations of these women would even prove to be an advantage. An itinerant peddler living as a tenant was low in the social order, but she was able to relate and to hear information from a wide variety of sources and places then convey them throughout the city via her connection to a landlady.[3] City authorities, lacking their own police force, depended upon these women to trace Grethe Schmidt's actions. In their turn, the witnesses revealed several strata of Brunswick's life. Some were still married and living with spouses, while others were widowed and living presumably alone, and others were clearly women who fended for themselves—typically to the scorn and consternation of authorities.[4]

ALTSTADT MINT, AUGUST 13, 1661

The Cobbler's Wife

Margarethe Hafferland had already described her brief encounter with "Frau Hillebrand." Authorities wasted no time in calling this woman—Anna Sacharitz, the wife of a cobbler—to bear witness. In her rambling statement, Sacharitz stated that she had indeed gone to the Breite Strasse in order to see an accused infanticide, "in order to see whether she was familiar." While there, Margarethe Hafferland came by, and both women saw Grethe Schmidt standing in the street and watching as well. Sacharitz remarked, "See, there stands your old servant Grethe, what might she now be thinking?" Sacharitz had heard rumors that Schmidt had been at some point "womanly" (*frauenhaft*, i.e., pregnant).[5] Hafferland answered only, "Yes, what might be thought indeed." Other onlookers, though, were saying to one another "that there might be some among them, who had earned [the same fate]."[6] Sacharitz made no mention of Schmidt's own actions as she witnessed this other poor sinner.

The interviewers wanted to know *from whom the witness had heard that Grethe, now prisoner, was believed to be so womanly.* Sacharitz answered that she had a tenant—a widow named Anna Försten—who peddled "all sorts of tools, pots, and small herbs such as marjoram, thyme, and the like . . . in the villages nearby." Once, having just returned from a journey, Försten reported to Sacharitz that "a maid, namely the current prisoner, had gone into service . . . in the Sack [i.e. the Borzfeldt house] and she appeared quite womanly."[7] Försten further told Sacharitz that she had been in a village, which the witness could not name, in a house which, the witness believed, was not far away from the prisoner's father's house, to which came the prisoner's younger sister, who gave the Lohman widow [Försten], whom she perhaps knew, to believe that her sister, the current prisoner, was sick and her body ailed her. Now whether the said Lohman's widow gathered something from the general talk of the prisoner going around Neubrücke and elsewhere, and then diligently asked the little girl about Grethe, the current prisoner, this the witness could not know, for the Lohman woman had already known the captive well, when she served in Gottfried Möller's widow's house, and had brought her sometimes to the house of the witness's husband, in order to fix shoes.[8]

The upshot to this dizzying story was that when Försten returned to Brunswick, she told Sacharitz that Schmidt's sister had said Grethe was at home sick in the village—that is, in Gross Schwülper. Further, Försten said that the Schmidts were rumored to have reserved a lying-in room in Neubrücke. Sacharitz believed the rumors, and she claimed that her suspicions were confirmed when, several months later, after Schmidt had returned to Brunswick to work for the Bortzfeldts, Grethe brought Sacharitz's husband a pair of shoes to repair. At that point, Grethe had a "full bosom and seemed somewhat womanly."[9]

Anna Sacharitz's winding tale stretched from the city streets to the surrounding countryside and back to Margarethe Hafferland's house, where the two women exchanged remarks about Schmidt. What part of Sacharitz's story could the authorities consider credible? At first glance, she seemed to know a great many details about the case. Sacharitz confirmed that she had spoken with Margarethe Hafferland about Schmidt. Further, from Anna Försten she had learned that Schmidt's younger sister had said Grethe was sick, that the family had rented a room in Neubrücke, that Grethe appeared "womanly." Sacharitz also knew where Schmidt had gone to work upon returning to Brunswick.

For all this information, though, Sacharitz merely confirmed the elliptical conversation with Hafferland, a conversation the authorities already knew about. Neither woman would confirm the key dramatic detail of that episode—the moment when an apparently distraught and frightened Grethe Schmidt ripped the cap from her head and buried her face in her apron. That information must have come from another person observing the event and overhearing the two women, but it never appeared in any testimony.

Even the conversation itself proves treacherous as evidence, for what Hafferland claimed to have heard differed in crucial ways from what Sacharitz claimed to have said. Hafferland had indeed mentioned a woman living in Sacharitz's house. This woman, however, had supposedly been to Gross Schwülper and spoken directly with Grethe's mother, who acknowledged that her daughter had been sick, "with toothache." According to Sacharitz, though, Anna Försten was a widow whose itinerant life as a peddler of herbs permitted her to move back and forth from city to countryside and from village to village. She had gleaned all the details of the case from her wanderings and passed the rumors along to her landlady, Sacharitz, who was thus able to exchange knowing remarks in the Breite Strasse with Margarethe Hafferland.

In fact, Anna Sacharitz had very little firsthand evidence to give in her deposition. She had seen Schmidt three times—once while the maid worked for Hafferland, once in the Breite Strasse, and finally later when Grethe was working in Brunswick again and brought shoes to Sacharitz's husband. Sacharitz said that Grethe looked "womanly," but this conclusion had already been well prepared through secondhand sources. More significantly, by the time Grethe appeared at the cobbler's door, her alleged infant would already have been several months dead. Sacharitz's claim about Grethe seeming pregnant or "womanly" in the spring or summer of 1661 would have to be viewed with great suspicion.

The Dutiful Friend

Another woman of Brunswick proved more formidable in her testimony that same day, August 13. Gertrude Wilmers, the wife of a local soldier named Philip Becker, had already appeared briefly in Hafferland's deposition—she was the woman who informed Hafferland of the gossip about Grethe's pregnancy. Wilmers's account, though, makes plain that Hafferland was aggressive in discovering Schmidt's condition and planning to evade responsibility for its consequences. Wilmers had for years done washing and other chores in the Möller/Hafferland household and knew the couple so well that Gottfried Möller was godfather to one of her own children. The ties of long service and friendship with a patron had created a strong sense of obligation toward the Möllers. After Gottfried's death, Wilmers remained in touch with the widow.[10]

Wilmers told the authorities that at Christmastime of the previous year (1660), Hafferland asked Wilmers to perform a delicate task. Grethe Schmidt was by then gone from the Altstadt and working for Anna Dedekind. Would Gertrude ask Grethe to the Becker house and inquire "with all diligence" about what was going on? If things were as Hafferland feared, Wilmers should determine how far along Schmidt's pregnancy was. Hafferland wanted Wilmers, who lived in Hagen, not far from where Grethe was working, to keep her eye on the girl and determine if she was indeed pregnant, and "if so, make sure that she does right by it."[11] If Wilmers could get Schmidt to confide in her, she should also "strongly warn the prisoner, for it would be a baby or a human being." In other words, Wilmers should tell Schmidt not to harm the child she was carrying.

Gertrude Wilmers was reluctant to take on this task—surely things could not be so bad with Grethe! And wouldn't the girl become suspicious if Wilmers started asking her personal questions? Hafferland persisted, though, and Gertrude finally agreed to do what her former employer asked. Sometime after Christmas (she could not remember the exact date—was it New Year's Day, or perhaps the Feast of Three Kings?) Wilmers invited Schmidt to her house "to see what presents the holy Christ child had given."[12] Grethe came that very day after attending church, at about one o'clock.[13] Gertrude led her to the bedroom and earnestly inquired about her condition, for she "was pretty round and had a large bosom." Had she been up to something with Andreas Möller or perhaps with someone else? Grethe confessed that yes, "once he laid her on the bed, to have his way with her." She insisted that it was with "no one other than Herr Möller."[14] Gertrude Wilmers grew alarmed. Though acting at Hafferland's request, she seemed truly concerned about Grethe. Wilmers sternly warned the girl that "this was no mere snowball [*schnee Klumpen*] and would not just melt away," that Grethe would be held in suspicion and must do the right thing.[15] Schmidt stood stock still and uttered not a single word in response. Wilmers tried to get Grethe to look her straight in the eye, but the girl refused to meet her gaze and "bowed her face and eyes again and again."[16]

Gertrude then asked when Grethe had last had her period, but the girl said only that she did not know. Wilmers exclaimed, "See, you don't know, therefore tell me if Herr Möller has been with you, you should be well helped, you have a rich father [for the baby], who must provide for you what you want. Just tell me where you were with him, there are so many places, if your current work is so unpleasant, where someone can accommodate you [for the witness did not know that the girl still had (living) parents]." These exhortations, though, fell on deaf ears, for Grethe would admit nothing. Gertrude Wilmers finally gave her two or three apples, warned her again "to do the right thing," and let her go. Describing the encounter to Hafferland afterward, Wilmers stated that she could learn nothing from Grethe Schmidt and wanted nothing more to do with the matter. Indeed, in later callback testimony, Wilmers swore that she had not seen the accused again but had only heard from other women some weeks later that Grethe had left Anna Dedekind's employ.[17]

Gertrude Wilmers's testimony reveals the anxiety Margarethe Hafferland felt in the weeks before Christmas. She had heard the rumors about Schmidt, and she wanted to know for sure if the girl was pregnant and if her stepson was the father. Rather than confront Grethe directly, she called upon bonds of loyalty forged through service. Wilmers's Christmas ploy certainly worked to lure Schmidt to her home. What the older woman saw and heard, though, surprised and saddened her. Wilmers's sense of duty conflicted with alarm and even compassion as she saw the pitiable girl bow her head in shame. Despite growing misgivings, Wilmers persisted in trying to elicit information, trying to comfort Grethe with the idea that, if only the girl would tell Wilmers the truth, Andreas Möller would have to care for her and had the resources to do so. Was Wilmers sincere here, perhaps trying to convince Grethe not to abort the infant or murder it? Or was she simply trying to gain information for Hafferland's benefit? Apparent in the last sentences of her statement is growing concern but deepening resignation about what Schmidt might do.

Wilmers's testimony gave authorities the most persuasive and reliable evidence to date. Unlike Sacharitz, Wilmers relied neither on gossip nor on secondhand information but testified only to what she herself had observed. She precisely described the physical changes in the maid and astutely assessed her psychological state of shame and uncertainty. Unlike Hafferland, Wilmers had no obvious stake in the matter aside from obligation to a patron and pity for a young woman's plight. Yet for all Wilmers's apparent sympathy, sharp questions, and clever ruses, she got no farther with Grethe Schmidt than a ready admission of (apparently forced) sex with Andreas Möller. Schmidt refused to confess anything more. Was it shame or stubbornness that kept her silent? Or was she perhaps guilty of fornication, as she consistently admitted, but innocent of anything more, as she continually claimed? Like so many other episodes in the case, the meaning of this moment is unclear, yet it holds a key to Grethe Schmidt's state of mind and conscience.

Gertrude Wilmers was not the final witness against Schmidt that week. One by one, the main witnesses came back to correct or expand their statements and, more important, to swear to them under oath. Anna Sacharitz, as noted above, excused herself from the oath on grounds that she might have misunderstood Anna Försten's words. Yet recalling these witnesses was not at all pro forma. Despite lengthy statements made earlier, both the maid Ilse Engelken and Margarethe Hafferland had plenty to say when they sat again before the judicial lords.

Hagen Rathaus, August 14, 1661

Ilse the maid stuck to the basic story she had told on August 12, but her corrections strengthen the sense of anxiety and despair that increasingly marked events for both Hafferland and the Schmidt family. According to her second deposition, Ilse's supposedly chance encounter with Andreas Möller—during which he suggested that she accompany Grethe to Wendschott—took place not in the front room of his stepmother's house but in a chamber opposite, in order that other servants would not overhear.[18] This small change in testimony makes it even more clear that Ilse's sudden permission to visit Wendschott was not spontaneous but part of a plan perhaps conceived when Hafferland asked Gertrude Wilmers to observe Schmidt's condition.

Most of Ilse Engelken's new testimony, though, concerned the trip to Wendschott with Grethe. According to Engelken, the day was cold and the going difficult because of ice. Schmidt, whom Ilse did in fact believe to be pregnant (*welche Zeugin bey sich für schwanger gehalten*), had a hard time of it and grew sour, especially after she twisted an ankle upon leaving. Ilse tried to chat during the long journey. She asked Grethe how she had been able to "get together" with Herr Möller, who was after all a distinguished fellow.[19] Schmidt replied that, if he wanted to be alone with her, then he most likely could do so (the implication being that his prominence and position in the house allowed him to do whatever he wanted). Then Schmidt exclaimed, "Pfui!" That "fat guy" now sat warm behind the tiled stove (*Kacheloffen*) in his own home, while *she* had to leave and wander away through ice and cold.[20]

During their journey, Grethe recounted to Ilse a curious incident. Sometime after her encounter with Möller, Grethe and another maid in the household fashioned a straw doll in the form of an infant and hid it in Andreas's bed. The next morning, though, Andreas came and tore the doll limb from limb in front of her, and as Grethe turned red warned her not to try to frighten him.[21] To the truth of these events and to her entire testimony, Ilse Engelken swore an oath.

In Ilse's testimony the prosecution would see much to confirm their suspicions. On the way to Wendschott, Schmidt had given details about her relations with Möller, and her little game with a straw baby doll suggested that, even while still in the Hafferland home, the possibility of pregnancy had been on her mind. Furthermore, Engelken stated for the first time that, from the beginning of the journey, she believed Schmidt was pregnant. This was a considerable change from her earlier refusal to speculate, when she would say only that she knew Grethe was no virgin.

Having heard more incriminating evidence in this testimony, the magistrates seemed uninterested in its other implications. Ilse's new deposition suggests yet again that Grethe's sexual liaison with Möller was not just youthful high spirits, perhaps not even a consensual encounter. In the Engelken maid's retelling, Grethe appears as a young woman trapped by her position and resigned to the attentions of her mistress's stepson. If so, the final months of Schmidt's time in Gottfried Möller's house must have produced in her a difficult mixture of fear, anger, and defiance, which might well have contributed to the behavior that made Hafferland fire her. Was Hafferland herself, despite protestations to the contrary, aware that something was awry? After all, another maid had helped Schmidt fashion the straw doll—Hafferland seems to have been the only person in her own household who did not know what was going on.[22] Is it possible that this woman could be so naïve about what was happening right under her own roof?

ALTSTADT MINT, AUGUST 14, 1661

The magistrates certainly wanted to hear more from Margarethe Hafferland, who testified right after Gertrude Wilmers's callback on August 14. Although Hafferland did not change any of her previous testimony, she felt compelled—"before taking the oath with her hand upon her chest"—to add one more very surprising and confusing event. Some eight days after Schmidt's departure for Wendschott and eventual return to Gross Schwülper with her father (approximately January 15), Schmidt's mother, Ilse Leuthgen, came to Hafferland's house on the Breite Strasse with a startling revelation. She and her daughter had visited a woman in Brunswick to have Grethe's "water" (i.e., her urine) inspected. This woman, to whom Hafferland referred simply as the "Frankish woman in Hagen" (*Fränkische in Hagen*), reported that in fact Grethe was not pregnant, because her "water" was cloudy (*auffgeschlagen*).[23] As a result, Schmidt's mother regretted reserving a room for her daughter in Neubrücke. Hafferland doubted these claims, telling Leuthgen that women like the *Fränkische* who claimed to inspect other people's "water" were often deceived, if not outright deceiving, and usually did not know what they were talking about. Hafferland offered to inspect the urine herself in order to determine Schmidt's condition.[24]

But Hafferland only saw Grethe Schmidt's mother one more time. Around Easter 1661, her aunt Margarethe Engelken summoned Hafferland to Hagen and told her that Schmidt's mother and aunt had to come to Brunswick with a request. Would Hafferland write a letter stipulating that Grethe Schmidt had never had a child in the city? They wanted to send the letter to an official in Neubrücke, where the Schmidts had earlier reserved a room for the lying-in. Hafferland waited in Hagen for the pair, but they never came back. Hafferland herself returned to the Altstadt after telling her aunt that the "women would wait a long time before they receive[d] any such letter from her."[25] With those defiant words, Hafferland finally took the oath and swore to all her depositions.

These two striking episodes had a direct bearing on events, and it is odd that Hafferland had not offered this information in her first deposition. Each event could be taken either as exculpatory or incriminating: were the Schmidts trying to explain their behavior or disguise it? Had the whole matter been a tragic mistake, or was Ilse Leuthgen marking a trail of tests and testimonials that would point falsely to Grethe's innocence? If the latter were true, then one must believe that from the very first weeks of January 1661, the Schmidt women, perhaps including Grethe herself, had plotted a dark course of deception and premeditated murder. Yet this conclusion still remained elusive for the magistrates. For now they had to ponder the testimony of yet another witness, known to them only as "the *Fränkische* in Hagen."

HAGEN, AUGUST 15, 1661

Margarethe Hafferland had given the authorities no other clue about the woman's identity or whereabouts, but apparently they had no trouble finding her, for on August 15 the bailiff Otto Theune appeared at her home. Strangely enough, even in the deposition the woman went entirely unnamed—she was for all intents and purposes simply *die Fränkische*. She appears to have been yet another woman working for her own living on the margins—this time barely—and most probably alone. The record makes no mention of a husband, or of her being a widow. She was interviewed at home, because she was sickly and had "not left the house for some years." Otto Theune posed the following questions: *Whether around New Year or the Feast of Three Kings of this year (1661), a woman from Schwülper brought "water" for her to inspect? What was her name? Whose water was it? What advice was the woman seeking? What advice was given?*[26] These were predictable questions, trying to pin down the Schmidt family's actions, based on Hafferland's statement.

The next question, however, went in an interesting and very different direction: *Was she [the Fränkische] asked perhaps to make something, perhaps a drink of some sort? What kinds of herbs and other ingredients were necessary to make such a drink good, or useful? And how much money did she receive for it?*[27] Perhaps Grethe Schmidt's mother had sought something more than mere advice, or so the authorities suspected. Was it possible that the Schmidts had come to the *Fränkische* to buy a purgative that would induce abortion? Suddenly, this marginal and anonymous old woman held a vital clue to the case.

Yet if the magistrates hoped to extract detailed information, they were disappointed. Warned to speak the truth, the *Fränkische Frau* responded: "Indeed people do come for her to inspect their water but she could not remember or recall at that time any woman from Gross Schwülper bringing water. Further she paid no attention whence or whither the people came or where they belonged, sometimes they were entirely unknown to her and she seldom asked the reasons."[28] To the other questions, one after another, she answered, "No," she had nothing to report.

This response could be understood as the addled ramblings of an aged and sick woman, but of course another possibility seems more likely. The *Fränkische* was a woman trading in unofficial medical advice and prescriptions and possibly sold purgatives (used as abortifacients) to women hoping to terminate their pregnancies. She therefore would not want to know too much about her clientele. To such a woman, visits from the *Vogt* or from suspicious lovers or parents might have been common, and the consequences possibly unpleasant. Confusion and apparent ignorance were excellent safeguards against this occupational hazard.

The magistrate persisted, though, and asked again *whether around the New Year or Three Kings a woman from Schwülper brought urine to inspect explaining that it was her daughter's, with whom things were "different," and asking her to make a "drink"?* The *Fränkische* was equally adamant: "No, that did not happen. She did make a drink for people who had some damage in the liver or lungs or some other malady in their bodies, and for that she needed a few means from people whom she, through God's grace, had helped. That she had made someone a drink for such a purpose as they [the magistrates] suggested, no one could in truth say such a thing. She was just a wretched, broken-down old woman who knew nothing of such things, had little to do with such matters. This she would swear to God in highest heaven, she most emphatically knew nothing to report."[29]

As in her first answer, the old woman gave some vague information while indignantly rejecting the main thrust of the question. For the magistrates, though, yet another possibility in the case had opened up. Grethe Schmidt denied having killed a living baby, and there was still no evidence of a child, where it had been born, or how or where it had died. Was it possible that she was telling the truth in some way, that rather than murder Schmidt's crime was abortion? One must also keep in mind that the *Fränkische Frau* seemed to fit the profile of a woman who could be suspected of witchcraft—this may explain her defensive protestation that any success she had in helping people was entirely through God's will. Among the crimes attributed to witches were abortion and infanticide. Both the *Fränkische Frau* and the Schmidts could run afoul of dark suspicions that continued to place women in peril. Indeed, it was only in December 1663 that Brunswick's magistrates executed their final witch.[30]

CONNECTIONS

With her final protestation of ignorance, the curious tale of the *Fränkische Frau* ended. And with her interview, the magistrates came to the end of one phase of their investigation. They had sought information from the women of Brunswick, who in their various ways—some reluctantly, some a bit too enthusiastically—had let the authorities into the circle of rumor and intrigue that eventually became "knowledge." Anna Försten's itinerant life visiting village after village allowed her to collect more than herbs as she gathered tidbits of gossip in one place and then deposited them, in somewhat different form, elsewhere. Out of this hodgepodge of half-truths, Anna Sacharitz had forged definite opinions, culminating in the conversation with Hafferland as the pair watched Grethe Schmidt's anxious behavior in the Breite Strasse. Yet the impression one gains from this testimony is that the women of Brunswick had their eyes on Grethe Schmidt but seemed disinclined at first to act. Sacharitz purposely went to the Hafferland house in order to test Margarethe's reaction but did nothing more than confirm her own suspicions.

Margarethe Hafferland demonstrated her own influence in several ways. She had one servant, Ilse Engelken, act as companion for the defendant while the family sought to conceal Andreas Möller's dishonorable behavior. Hafferland exploited the influence and reputation of her late husband to persuade Gertrude Wilmers to act the detective on her behalf. Wilmers reluctantly coaxed Schmidt into confiding in her, eliciting information to return to her patroness. Despite the subterfuge, Wilmers also provided the only tangible sympathy Grethe Schmidt ever received from this circle of women.

Finally, there was the *Fränkische Frau*, to whom the Schmidt family may have turned for a way out of their daughter's predicament. Despite her self-serving self-deprecation, the *Fränkische Frau* was also a mediator in her own way, providing knowledge, medicine, and perhaps abortifacients to the residents of Hagen. Ilse Leuthgen allegedly had visited her, Hafferland knew of her, and the authorities knew where to find her.

Yet despite all the testimony of these varied women, what could the authorities now claim to know? Only Wilmers and Ilse the maid had given solid testimony, and each of them could only report that yes, indeed, Schmidt admitted that she had lain with Andreas Möller, and yes, both women thought her pregnant. And yet, in her very first interrogation, Grethe Schmidt had acknowledged the sex and denied the pregnancy. How far then had the authorities really gotten in the case? The prosecution's next move depended on the stipulations of the law itself, which pointed the prosecution toward considering seventeenth-century medical science.

6

Corpus Delicti

I will greatly multiply your pain in childbearing; in pain you shall
bring forth children, yet your desire shall be for your husband, and
he shall rule over you.

Genesis 3:16

With each testimony, the authorities of Brunswick found some detail to
add to their case against Grethe Schmidt. Yet each new witness seemed
further removed from the central action and participants, and for all their
suspicions, investigators lacked the most crucial evidence—the corpse of
an infant. That did not deter these authorities from zealously prosecuting
Schmidt. After all, a body was already at hand in the form of the young
woman herself. The living Grethe and not her allegedly murdered offspring
was the true corpus delicti, in fact if not in law, and pregnancy was the central issue under investigation. Grethe had admitted to having sex but denied
having ever been pregnant. Her neighbors, however, whispered about her
body: her breasts had grown full, and the girl looked pregnant. Without a
scientific test to establish her condition, Schmidt's allegedly pregnant body
was built out of the memories, expectations, and imaginations of others.

To seventeenth-century eyes, the signs and meanings of conception
and pregnancy were difficult to apprehend, even under the most favorable
circumstances.[1] For a single woman of poor means, the signs of her pregnancy announced the social and legal troubles she would face as a sinner
and an outcast. A pregnant single woman would have every reason to hide
her condition from employers and family members.[2] She might even try
to deceive herself, a fact that helps explain why so many single women
described their babies as suddenly shooting out from them unexpectedly
and in the most unlikely places, such as fields and streams.[3] These women
might also hope that some "accident" would rescue them before the truth

would become known or they were forced to make awful decisions. The magistrates of Brunswick, in contrast, understood it as their duty to discover and punish such poor, sinning folk. Each side in this case relied on a common stock of "facts" and a manner of thinking that conditioned their approach to Grethe.

CONCEPTION

It may be true, as the modern joke goes, that a woman cannot be "a little pregnant." Seventeenth-century women would not have laughed, for both their understanding of conception and the medical science that interpreted pregnancy were very different from what we believe today. Two momentous shifts have fundamentally conditioned the modern view of pregnancy. The first is "the Nilsson effect," as the historian Barbara Duden terms it, referring to Lennart Nilsson's color photographs of a developing fetus that appeared on the cover of *Life* magazine on April 30, 1965.[4] The unprecedented images of "the drama of life before birth" signaled a change in the way people viewed the process of pregnancy and the nature of the "life" residing in the womb. Duden notes that such photography helped reorient (indeed, created) the identity of the fetus, making it seem to have a life of its own, separate from the mother. That image continues to resonate powerfully in today's debates about abortion, birth control, and stem-cell research. To historians, though, "the Nilsson effect" also signals the modern capacity to examine in detail what occurs in the uterus. A pregnant woman today can directly witness the process through sonograms, for example.

Accompanying the newfound subjectivity of the fetus is the growth over two centuries of a highly developed clinical system that places most pregnant women, at least in developed countries, in the hands of medical professionals and interprets their experiences accordingly. Scientific testing determines whether a woman is pregnant, and doctors focus equally on the health of the mother and the baby. A test establishes pregnancy, and a woman begins an established routine determined by modern medical "facts."[5] Motherhood "becomes the carrying out of a learned process of reproduction, baby care, and education."[6] This does not mean that women have in some way become alienated from their bodies, or that a modern American or European woman has less control over her pregnancy than her ancestors could ever imagine—far from it. But her perception of the process has changed. Now she must incorporate the demands of a battery of tests and advice devised by experts for her and her fetus's benefit; she ignores these at her peril.

The transparency of modern pregnancy contrasts with its obscurity in the past. Whether we consider the definition of stages of gestation, the means of diagnosis, or the way a woman understood her experience, pregnancy was an event shrouded by the flesh that separated the womb from the world without. Given the opacity of a woman's body, how did early modern science understand pregnancy? How was it detected and diagnosed? And above all, how did women define and then experience their condition?

Science and medicine in the seventeenth century presented previously un-imagined wonders. Just as the era's physicists and astronomers were summarizing in elegant mathematics the uniformity and precision of the universe, early modern biologists and chemists were describing the human circulatory system and the nature of oxygen. At the beginning of the century, Galileo Galilei had pierced the heavens with his pioneering telescope and viewed the rings of Saturn. In 1676, Antony van Leeuwenhoek peered through his newly invented microscope and detected the presence of "little seed animals"—sperm—in his own semen.[7] New observations brought the life sciences to the brink of a great transformation that was only fully realized in the nineteenth century. Despite these promising novelties, though, seventeenth-century embryology and anatomy remained firmly within the framework established more than a millennium earlier by Aristotle and Galen.

It was Aristotle, so fundamental to Western science and philosophy, who laid down the terms under which fetal development, for two thousand years, would be interpreted. Aristotle contrasted two possibilities for conception. In preformation, a miniature of the individual already preexists entirely in either the male or the female seed and then slowly grows to full size. This formula implies that only one true parent exists, the other providing either a stimulus to growth (e.g. the male semen) or an environment in which to develop (e.g. the female womb). Aristotle favored instead an *epigenesist* model, in which "each organism is gradually produced from some initial undifferentiated mass by means of a series of steps and stages during which new parts are added."[8] Galen followed Aristotle in this regard, but over the centuries both theories gained adherents and alternated as the favored paradigm for scientists.

Aristotle deprecated the mother's contribution to conception. Though the woman, like the man, produced "sperma," her seed was "cold" and inferior (even barren), while male seed was "warm" and dominant. A woman provided only unformed matter to which male semen gave definitive form.[9] Her menstrual fluid provided first matter and later sustenance for the embryonic life shaping within her. Lest one think that the ancients, physically blind to events in the womb, nevertheless pictured the gestation process as resembling Nilsson's luminous photography, one should consider that Aristotle likened it to churning milk into cheese.[10] According to the Greek philosopher, "The action of the semen of the male in 'setting' the female's secretion in the uterus is similar to that of rennet upon milk. Rennet is milk which contains vital heat, as semen does."[11] This image is not limited to Aristotle but appears in Scripture, in the Koran, and in the visions of Hildegard of Bingen.[12]

Galen, the other giant of ancient medicine, followed Aristotle in many ways but differed in a crucial respect: he argued that the female contributed more than unformed matter. Women's semen, injected into the womb during intercourse, mixed equally with the male to form the fetus, which menstrual fluids would then nourish. It was this view, more sexually "egalitarian" than Aristotle's, that held sway until the end of the seventeenth century. Galen based his theory in part on the idea that female genitalia were in fact defective and inverted versions of the male organs—that is, the uterus is a scrotum turned inside out for lack of the heat necessary to make it perfect and therefore male. Curiously enough, this meant that to inject semen into the womb, a woman must also achieve orgasm, and so medical manuals concentrated rather unexpectedly on female sexual pleasure, or as the seventeenth-century embryologist William Harvey wrote, "the male and the female dissolve in one voluptuous sensation, and inject their seminal fluids into the cavity of the uterus."[13]

The traditional understanding of conception underwent profound transformation in the late seventeenth century, as Harvey and others focused attention on conception as the fertilization of eggs. The mechanism remained unclear: did the semen contribute some substance to the egg or merely "infect" it as a "contagion," rendering the entire female body fertile? The egg fertilization theory also gave new predominance to the idea of preformation throughout the eighteenth century. Scientists and philosophers even argued that all the human beings that ever were "preexisted" in the seed of the earliest humans, a notion congenial to Christian theories of predestination prevalent in Protestant countries at the time.[14] Even with the revolution in the science of generation, Europeans remained light-years away from the modern image of conception. The "mammalian ovum" itself was discovered only in 1827. Only at the end of the nineteenth century did researchers first observe the union of sperm and egg.[15] These changes happened decades or centuries after the arrest of Grethe Schmidt and lay bare the intellectual chasm between her world and our own.

Conception and gestation were not the only elements of pregnancy debated in the learned world. From the beginnings of Western science until today, scientists and philosophers have differed on the exact moment of animation or "ensoulment." From Greek tradition, three possible moments of animation existed. Some ancients placed animation at the moment of conception, an idea favored among Christians. Because the conceived seed contained all the elements necessary to human life, it *was* human life, some even arguing that the seed contained the soul like a kind of "condensed steam," which was then released at conception.[16] At the other extreme were those who held that the soul was breathed into an infant at birth, literally appearing with a child's first gulp of air. It was Aristotle's middle position that fixed the debate until the eighteenth century and even beyond. At some point, the fetus—that coagulating female matter given "form" by the male seed—became animated, that is, it received a human or rational soul. The embryo metamorphosed from a basically vegetative state to a more perfect form as a human fetus. This was the position that held sway, even among Christian theologians, through the eighteenth century, though it gradually gave ground to the idea of immediate animation at conception. Aristotle believed that the moment of animation differed by gender, the male at forty-five days and the female at fifty.[17] This thinking is reflected in laws and customs that condoned attempts to purge or induce miscarriages until the fortieth day. Of course, because the moment of conception itself was not fixed before the seventeenth century, the moment of animation fluctuated accordingly.

Less learned than philosophers, ordinary people in the seventeenth century also pondered the nature of conception. Relative lack of learning did not necessarily put the average person at a disadvantage, for neither the scientist, the midwife, nor the prospective mother could look inside the living womb. Homespun traditions and sophisticated speculation suffered from the same blindness. Ordinary folk were not as prolix in their analyses as the philosophers, and their words are not so well preserved. Still, a wealth of images remains from the early modern period, often in court records or doctors' reports. Obvious references to the unborn as "fruit" ripening were pervasive.[18] Yet there is little available discussion of the ways this metaphor might have worked, and some historians have argued that it did not become a common image for German women until the eighteenth century, perhaps under the influence of learned doctors. Until that time, women might simply refer to the "child" that grew inside.[19]

Other associations also crowded the imagination and may have been more decisive for ordinary people's understanding. Strikingly, Aristotle's ancient description of conception as "cheese-making" appeared in the Middle Ages among European peasants in the Basque region and among the Cathars who peopled the village of Montaillou.[20] Among the Basques, it was understood that the "white blood" (semen) of the male curdles the red blood of the woman, which then "sets." A similar image from the same region compared conception and the gradual swelling of a woman's pregnant body to the fermentation of yeast in bread: "Sainte-Engrâce women are 'curdled like milk' at conception and 'rise like bread' during pregnancy."[21] In contrast, the obsession with purging impurities and expelling "growths" indicated a continuing association of pregnancy with filth.[22] Human beings were begotten in the womb: "Between the regions occupied by the most filthy and vile excrements which exist in the body . . . between the lower intestine or entrails near the rectum and the bladder used for urine."[23]

SIGNS

The many conflicting beliefs about conception at both the scientific and the popular level show just how puzzling the generation of a human being was before the age of precise anatomy and observation. Of course, everyone knew that sexual intercourse produced babies in a span of approximately forty weeks, but the exact process remained enigmatic. Not all intercourse resulted in pregnancy—why in some cases and not others? And when did pregnancy itself begin? Modern medicine has precisely located the moment of insemination, but seventeenth-century medicine had not yet described the process or even accepted the fertilization of egg by sperm. If male semen acted as "rennet," just when did curdled female semen begin to ferment? If the male seed "infected" the woman's entire body like a virus, then when did this contagious fertility produce an embryo?

Blind to the womb's inner workings, doctors and women alike waited for visible signs of the invisible developments below the skin. One might imagine that detecting pregnancy would be a relatively straightforward reading of commonplace symptoms—sensations of nausea, cessations of menstruation, changes in physique. But in the tangle of daily life, illness, and seventeenth-century assumptions about the body's workings, these seemingly clear events could signal many different conditions. Doctors and midwives agreed that pregnancy was hard to certify, and false diagnoses were quite common.[24] Conversely, some pregnant women were reported to show no signs at all.[25] Only over a period of weeks and months would a woman's true state reveal itself, both to her and to her neighbors.[26] Changes in menstruation and body shape were among the chief clues then, as they remain today.

Given the role of blood in theories of conception, it should be no surprise that the sudden absence of menstruation was the first sign of pregnancy, for learned doctors and women alike.[27] The fact that, for the most part, pregnant women did not menstruate confirmed for many the idea that blood, particularly the mother's, provided the substance of the fetus and was diverted after conception to provide sustenance. Preoccupation with the quality of blood and commonly expressed fears over the effects of "stagnation" indicate just how great a role blood played at every moment, from conception to birth. Women knew that when the flow of blood ceased, a child might be at hand. Less fortunate women forced to confess their crimes of fornication, abortion, or infanticide also spoke of the sudden end of menstruation as the first indication of trouble.[28]

One might imagine that the "monthly purgation" was a private sign, but the closeness of everyday life in the seventeenth century could render all secret things public, and for a woman hoping to avoid criminal charges a bloody sheet, gown, or dress could be exculpatory evidence. Certainly, because so many of those accused of fornication were maidservants living in close quarters with their mistresses, the sudden absence of bloody sheets or clothing could prove suspicious and had to be explained.[29]

Blood, though, could lie. Some medical experts held that bleeding could continue during pregnancy. In fact, some argued that continued bleeding might indicate that a pregnancy was progressing nicely, with the woman's blood moving well and not stagnating.[30] Johann Georg Sommer's *Nothwendiger Hebammen-unterricht* of 1676 cautioned that the absence of menstruation was no sure signal that a woman was pregnant, nor did a continuing period exclude the possibility that she was indeed with child:

> It is an entirely deceptive and ungrounded opinion to conclude that if menstruation should continue in the first months, that a woman is not pregnant, or if in these months the expected purification ceases the women is pregnant, particularly since these two opposites contradict themselves in fact, because with certain pregnant women this purification in the first and second month not only does not stop, but continues in its accustomed order through the first half of the pregnancy, and it is not unheard of for such women to produce healthy children, most of them males. The opposite is also well known.[31]

Sommer's beliefs echoed those of Paolo Zacchias, the papal physician who compiled and edited one of the first great compendiums of cases in forensic medicine, the *Quaestiones medico-legales* (1630).[32]

Women themselves did not consider the absence of menses a definitive sign of pregnancy, for they thought any number of circumstances could result in a missed period. Menstruation might be a seasonal event—halting in winter and returning in summer—or result from drinking cider or eating soup, or even "wild dancing."[33] Absence of menstruation could also indicate other conditions besides pregnancy.[34] In a world that viewed blood flow as a sign of health, a missed period could mean that a woman suffered from dropsy.[35] Or it might indicate "stagnant blood" that made the womb unclean and threw the balance of bodily humors out of kilter, requiring a purge to restore equilibrium.[36] Or, as modern medical practitioners would note, it might be the result of malnutrition and famine.[37]

If missing menstruation was only an uncertain hint of pregnancy, then what other signs proved more decisive? Eventually, a pregnant woman's body would thicken and her breasts swell and harden, telling signs for neighbors and other observers. The *Carolina* itself described one grounds for suspicion—a woman would grow heavier and swollen and then suddenly return to normal or seem weak. Even the body's visible signs, though, remained uncertain. Some women claimed that their bodies were swelling because of impurity and stagnation in the womb, once again requiring a purgative. More ominously, doctors suggested the possibility of a tumor of some sort as the reason for a woman growing heavier. In the case of an adolescent woman such as Grethe Schmidt, dramatic physical changes might accompany the onset of puberty—a heavier body, fuller breasts. Of course, some women just grew heavier, as Ulinka Rublack notes in describing midwives' inability to diagnosis a pregnancy in Stuttgart.[38] This was a claim Schmidt's lawyer would later make in Grethe's defense—not only that she naturally tended to become heavier but remained so after her alleged pregnancy was supposedly over.

The difficulty of detecting a pregnancy through external clues was particularly acute in the early months. Eventually, though, the developing fetus made its presence known, at least to the mother—it began to move. The moment of quickening had far-reaching consequences in every area of life. It was described differently in learned traditions and popular understandings. Christian theologians, for their part, understood this perfecting as the moment at which God infused new creation with a soul, making it a human being. From that point, whatever affected the fetus would affect its soul as well. Jurists considered it the moment at which criminal penalties would apply to the embryo's destruction. In everyday life, feeling the fetus kick was the most certain indication a woman experienced that she was indeed pregnant, carrying from this point on a "living child."

Unlike the "objective" animation of the embryo described in learned medicine and philosophy, physical quickening depended on a woman's "subjective" experience of the baby moving within her, occasionally as early as the fourth month but more often in the fifth.[39] The mother herself would sense movement much earlier than examining midwives and doctors could detect it.[40] Quickening was the event that confirmed what all the other symptoms could only suggest.[41] By the time a woman feels the fetus move today, she has usually already been medically diagnosed as pregnant. Well into the nineteenth century, though, the fetus's movement and its implications could come as quite a shock. The moment abounded with psychological, social, and legal meaning. Until a woman felt her child move within her, the fact of pregnancy was in doubt, as the symptoms could point to a variety of conditions for which she might require a purgative or some other medicine to induce menstruation. Even women who suspected a pregnancy did not necessarily believe the embryo to have life yet and so might try to induce a miscarriage. Once a woman felt the fetus stirring within her, though, the consequences of her actions changed—abortion after quickening became a sin and a crime. Now a woman was compelled to adjust to the demands and social expectations of pregnancy. Even so, fetal movement remained outside the sphere of legal and forensic testing.[42]

Quickening was interpreted by different women in distinct ways. Whether they responded joyfully or with resignation, married women could expect special treatment once their pregnancy was proved. Unmarried women, however, would dread the first kickings and experience this definitive sign with great anxiety. Quickening could convince a single woman that she was now an outlaw, facing criminal charges once her condition was discovered. Even worse, once her pregnancy became known to others, an unmarried woman would face the suspicion of her neighbors as they wondered whether she would be tempted have an abortion or commit infanticide. In Grethe's case, suspicious neighbors admonished her over and over to "do the right thing"—presumably to deliver a living child rather than seek to terminate the pregnancy. What the neighbors meant, though, may well have changed with each successive stage of the alleged pregnancy.

Although expectant mothers tried to record the auspicious moment of fetal movement exactly, quickening too proved uncertain in the face of numerous anomalous conditions that could be mistaken for a true pregnancy.[43] The greatest German midwife of the seventeenth century, Justina Siegemundin, took up her career precisely because she had been falsely diagnosed as pregnant until the very moment of delivery. Her story makes for harrowing but instructive reading. Considered pregnant "by all of the midwives," Siegemundin prepared for labor at the appropriate time, but after three days, no child appeared. As many as four midwives conferred and agreed that Justine would have to continue in the exertions of labor, with the probable end result that "I would have to die along with the child." Finally, a soldier's wife who was also a midwife came to examine Siegemundin and concluded, "there was no child but a clogging of the blood, and, moreover, a serious disease of the womb and a fallen womb." In fact, she was suffering from a prolapsed uterus, and a doctor's "medicament" finally provided relief.[44] More famously, a century earlier in 1554–1555, Mary Tudor, the queen of England, experienced a "false pregnancy" shortly after her dynastic marriage to Philip II of Spain. She underwent a "confinement" of two months, only to emerge from the ordeal with both her spirit and her health broken, and no heir to show for it.[45]

As the Siegemundin example shows, it was not simply the lack of expertise of so-called experts that caused diagnostic problems. Tumors and false conceptions were also thought to cause movement.[46] Throughout the early modern period, women and doctors were fascinated and puzzled by the existence of molar pregnancies. If nature were somehow to be "confused" during conception, then a false growth or "mole" might occur (*mola* or *Mondkalb*, perhaps a hydatidiform mole, as similar growths are known today). Both popular and learned literature testify that molar pregnancies were a frequent occurrence in the early modern world.[47] Today, they occur at a rate of approximately one per thousand pregnancies in Europe and America, are frequently associated with dietary deficiencies, and often appear in women under twenty years of age.[48] In early modern thinking, even virgins could suffer from moles, since according to scientists they did not require intercourse to form.[49] Justina Siegemundin described in detail her discovery and removal of such a "moon calf" from a "highborn" woman.[50] "Moles" deceived women and doctors, who sought to distinguish the specific kind of movement typical to them. The renowned French midwife Louise Bourgeois compared the movement of a true child to "the beating of wings of a small bird." In contrast, a mole was like "a cat stretching out in front of a fire."[51] The midwife, in such cases, must resort to her experienced and expert sense of touch.[52]

CRIMINAL CONSEQUENCES

The main signs of pregnancy, then, proved hard to read with accuracy. The uncertainties were especially significant for single women, who had reason to dread pregnancy in a world that legally proscribed non-marital intercourse and took punitive actions against illegitimate pregnancies. The *Carolina* stated explicitly that young women who suddenly grew heavy and then just as suddenly became thin again could be suspected of infanticide. At earlier stages, an enlarged belly or breasts could invite criminal investigation for fornication, even before the question of abortion or infanticide arose. Parents and authorities would launch the search for the father as accomplice in the crime.

Ambiguous in themselves, the visible signs of pregnancy depended on the viewer—just how much physical change was enough to arouse curiosity or suspicion? Frequently the other members of a household, whether family, servants, or employers, were surprised by an illicit pregnancy among them.[53] Familiarity may have caused the household to overlook what was apparent to outsiders. On the other hand, neighbors were likely to be more critical of domestics who were newcomers to the city and whose general reputation was suspect. The historical evidence available from infanticide cases speaks mostly of instances in which witnesses' suspicions were borne out by finding a corpse. The records are generally silent on the question of how often women suspected of being pregnant turned out to be innocent.

The early modern understanding of pregnancy and its signs played a crucial role in the case of Grethe Schmidt. It also illuminates some of the witnesses' seemingly perplexing claims and actions. One of the continuing controversies during the case was whether Grethe menstruated during the months she served as a servant in two different households. Anna Dedekind saw no evidence of this and so assumed that Schmidt was too young to conceive. Later, Schmidt's mother and aunt would claim that the resumption of menstruation demonstrated that Grethe had never been pregnant in the first place. Schmidt did not fall under suspicion until November or December 1660, at least six and perhaps seven months after her one admitted encounter with Andreas Möller. Schmidt's neighbors were clearly concerned about more than just her growing "fat"—they described Grethe as increasingly "womanly" (*frauenhaft*), which could indicate a number of changes most commonly associated with pregnancy. At what point did her body begin to seem "womanly"? Grethe's own employer, the person most likely to have seen her up close, was among the last to suspect her. Schmidt's changing body seemed normal enough to Anna Dedekind until neighbors convinced her to look again. Finally, some of the changes potentially indicating pregnancy—in Grethe's weight, or in the shape and heaviness of her breasts—might also suggest the physical transformation resulting from puberty. After all, Grethe Schmidt was no older than fourteen at the time of her alleged pregnancy.

In her New Year's confrontation with Grethe in Engelken's house, Hafferland noted Schmidt's refusal to be touched. Later, Hafferland asked Schmidt's mother directly about whether a "living child" was present. She wanted to feel the girl's body and find out for herself. The elder Schmidt allegedly answered that Grethe had indeed been pregnant—she had grown so fat that she could barely remove her stockings—but whether there was a "living child" at hand was a different matter, because she had never felt her daughter's belly. Grethe herself refused to answer when or whether she had felt any movement.

This tug-of-war between Hafferland and the Schmidts shows that both knew what was at stake in allowing the girl to be touched. Hafferland wanted to certify with her hands the evidence that seemed so clear to her eyes, while the Schmidts desperately sought to avoid that telling moment and were perhaps already establishing lines of defense. Yet even more was going on, and all the women knew it. The issue was not just Grethe's pregnancy, a fact that her mother allegedly had already admitted. The more serious question was whether the child had already quickened and was therefore "alive" in the eyes of the women and of the law.

Hafferland had another reason to try to establish the date of conception. It might show whether Grethe had indeed had sex under her roof with her stepson, Andreas. A later conception date might eliminate his guilt for the pregnancy and could reveal Schmidt to be promiscuous or even a prostitute. Hafferland, by probing to determine the status of the pregnancy, might herself be sifting through the acceptable options for saving her family's reputation, though she would of course never admit favoring an abortion. The Schmidts, refusing to acknowledge a quickening, were perhaps preserving some freedom of action—perhaps a purgative was in order to restore the blood flow and expel some false growth. But if they admitted that the fetus had moved, such recourse would be a capital crime.

In the absence of firm evidence that Grethe, if pregnant, had experienced quickening, the prosecutors were left with a high degree of uncertainty about the case. In her own testimony Grethe mentioned a red mass that issued from her at some point. Was she saying that she had miscarried or that some form of "false conception" or mole had grown inside her, merely appearing to be a pregnancy? If so, could this also account for the fact that there was no baby, no corpse to be found? Here was another potential line of defense.

Possibly Grethe Schmidt herself wanted to believe that she had never been pregnant. If she were innocent, then her refusal to be touched could be accounted for by modesty, shyness, or offense. If she were indeed carrying a living child, however, her behavior indicated that she was determined to conceal the fact and deny her accusers the most definitive proof available. Missing menstruation was only suggestive, the thickening body could prove only so much. Whatever Schmidt's motives, the truth is that no accuser ever touched her to feel whether a baby moved inside. Whether by accident or design, the single best proof of a pregnancy remained unconfirmed. For all the testimony produced against Margarethe, the authorities still could not prove that she had killed her baby, or even that she had ever been pregnant. The flawed testimony of witnesses now gave way to the professional judgment of trained medical professionals. Prosecutors would now call on another group of women—the official midwives of Brunswick.

7

Knowledgeable Women

The Midwives' Tale

After two weeks of intense testimony, Brunswick's authorities had a crucial decision to make. Between August 1 and August 14, prosecutors interrogated Grethe Schmidt and her sister Anna, the two employers Anna Dedekind and Margarethe Hafferland, Hafferland's dying "aunt" Margarethe Engelken, and her maid, Ilse. Authorities followed their leads to solicit testimony from Philip Becker's wife, Anna Sacharitz, the Lohman woman, and the enigmatic *Fränkische Frau* in Hagen. Unsolicited material flowed to the judicial lords from Neubrücke and the Schmidts' pastor in Gross Schwülper. No body had turned up to prove the magistrates' darkest fears, but they were confident that the maid Schmidt, an unmarried female servant, had had illegal sexual contact resulting in a pregnancy she sought to hide from friends and denied to employers and authorities. The time for a baby's appearance was long past, yet Schmidt had produced neither an infant nor an explanation. Did this not suggest some criminal act?

For their next move, the magistrates turned back to the law. Certainly in their eyes, Grethe Schmidt was, as the *Carolina* stated, a "person of whom such a suspected crime [infanticide] could be believed."[1] She had confessed her sexual transgression with Andreas Möller, acknowledged that others believed her to be pregnant, admitted that her mother had reserved a lying-in room in Neubrücke. What more was necessary?

Her obstinacy to date convinced the judicial lords that it would take more than mere verbal pressure to get Grethe to admit the truth; it would take at least the threat of torture. In order to take this step, though, prosecutors had first to measure their evidence against the law's demands. So far the evidence, compelling as it seemed, did not quite add up: they had no body, nor any eyewitnesses to the suspected crime of infanticide itself, though the law made allowance for an act that by its nature went unseen by others.

Accordingly, the prosecution decided to subject Grethe to a physical examination to see if they could find in her body the clues to an infant's death: "she shall be inspected by knowledgeable women in an enclosed place, so far as that facilitates further inquiry: and if the suspicion is there confirmed, and nonetheless she will not confess the deed, she may be examined under torture."[2] The "knowledgeable women" were two professional midwives from the Neustadt, Grete Voges and Jillian Wilckens. Sworn to serve the city in cases of illicit pregnancies and suspicious births, they conducted their exam and made their report on August 20, before Julius Von Horn, the *Gerichtsvogt* (court administrator) Johannes Vellhagen, and the ever-attendant judicial scribe Johannes Pilgram.

Standing alongside the judicial personnel was Laurence Gieseler, the official city physician and medical examiner. Gieseler had not himself inspected Grethe and in all likelihood did not attend the examination, a fact that requires explanation. The easy response, of course, is that the law specifies "knowledgeable women." In fact, pregnancy and childbirth were among the few areas in which the judgments of women—so often casually dismissed, especially in court—carried some authority. The grounds for these women's participation lay deep within European history and life. And yet, even as Voges and Wilckens were testifying, their roles and practices were being challenged across the continent.

EXPERT WITNESSES

Using midwives in court was nothing new in 1661. In fact, midwives were the first medical personnel certified as "expert witnesses" in the European legal tradition, occupying an entire chapter of the sixth-century *Corpus Juris Iustiniani*. Their duties were many. Midwives examined condemned women to determine if they were pregnant (and therefore not to be executed until after the birth) and tried to establish virginity, pregnancy, or female impotency. Famously, midwives determined the virginity of Joan of Arc during her trial in 1431.[3] In medieval Europe, male impotency was one of the few grounds for divorce, and clerical judges sought out midwives for help. To determine male impotence, midwives even participated in the traditional *congressus*, in which they alone or perhaps with a group of physicians would observe a married couple attempt copulation. *Congressus* was only abolished in France in 1677, under intense pressure from physicians and jurists who argued, reasonably, that the presence of witnesses was not conducive to male sexual performance. Midwives also conducted physical examinations of women who claimed to have been raped. Here the midwives would seek not only traces of lost virginity but of violence.[4]

Of midwives in the Middle Ages, particularly in Germany, relatively little is known, though medieval legends about antiquity suggest their duties.[5] At Jesus' birth, for example, Joseph supposedly found two midwives—Zelemi and Salome—to assist and care for the newborn Christ. Incredulous at Joseph's claims of Mary's virginity, the two women inspected her physically and discovered that it was indeed true.[6]

Whatever their social status, midwives were thought to be necessary, which by the seventeenth century improved their lot considerably. As Mary Lindemann has written of the period, "More Europeans came in contact with midwives than with any other medical practitioner."[7] Even if most births were uneventful (and up to 90 percent were, no matter who attended), the knowledge and skills a midwife brought to the birthing chair could still prove crucial. The ability to turn the fetus in the uterus could mean the infant's survival, while delivering the afterbirth and tying off the umbilical cord could prevent fatal hemorrhaging of the mother. A successful birth meant that the midwife had the honor of carrying the infant to the church for christening and received a gratuity.[8] If everything failed, the midwife could at least baptize the unfortunate baby, a function that provides the first evidence of the Church's attempt to regulate midwifery in the later Middle Ages. Synods ordered that midwives be instructed in the correct procedures of emergency baptism.[9]

In rural areas of France and Germany, women who had distinguished themselves by their skill in attending their neighbors, who had successfully (and in wedlock) borne their own children but were perhaps no longer encumbered by caring for them, and whose moral reputations were good might be selected by their peers as official midwives for a village or region.[10] These "wise women" (*sage-femmes* in France) might also have prepared for the job by working with a more experienced midwife or a family member.[11] On many occasions this was the only training available.[12] Once appointed, a midwife could expect a fee for her services, though in general she could not support herself solely through these earnings. Of great significance were the various gifts a "birth-helper" might expect from the family for her attentiveness after the delivery, during the baptism and subsequent "purification" of the new mother, all events that the rural midwife expected to attend as testimony of her success.[13] To many village authorities, though, participation in all these social events kept skilled midwives from being available for other births and had therefore to be limited in the name of productivity.[14]

Urban midwives had a different experience. From the mid-fifteenth century, city officials tried to oversee practitioners, who might spend a year or more in apprenticeship, take an examination, and then swear an oath to follow the city's rules and procedures. At first these examinations took place before the city council, but gradually city authorities ceded the responsibility for oversight to "honorable women" of the upper class. Was this because close involvement with women of the lower orders was distasteful to patrician males?[15] Or was it because these same men acknowledged (no doubt with great relief) that childbirth belonged to women, who were likely to know more about it? At some point university-trained physicians entered the process and began to exert authority over midwife examinations. These male doctors, though, were trained through reading classical texts going back to Galen and may never have witnessed a single live birth or even examined a woman physically, in contrast to midwives whose experience was exclusively empirical and might extend to dozens of live births. City officials seemed to recognize the importance of experience—only in the late seventeenth century did statutes recommend that midwives seek out physicians for advice on delivering babies.[16]

In fact, experience and tradition counted greatly before the eighteenth century. Practices prescribed in midwifery statutes remained largely the same between 1450 and 1750.[17] This is not surprising, since most births took place without serious incident for mother or child, so authorities had no reason to change. Perhaps more important, though, tradition and modesty meant that male physicians could not touch female patients nor even inspect their intimate parts without permission. Women touched women, and men touched men. The catastrophe of a fetus's death allowed male surgeons to enter, cut up the fetus, and remove it from the mother's womb.[18] Toward the end of the seventeenth century, as medicine became more "professionally" organized, university-trained males began to monopolize medicine and oversee its diverse practitioners. Until then, firm boundaries defined the separate spheres, and this worked both ways, for the midwife's role was clearly circumscribed. She could not prescribe medicines, a prerogative of apothecaries and doctors, and once surgery began, her authority ended.[19]

The image of "wise women" ruling over the sphere of birth and new life in sympathetic communion with their sisters and without the presence of men might seem pleasing. The true picture is much different, though, for the work of midwives, particularly in cities, was always regarded with some distaste. It belonged mostly to women of the lower classes, to artisans' wives or widows, and fees were low, depending always on the charity of clients. Patrician city councils avoided contact with midwives as much as possible. Physicians considered the work beneath them, "the most filthy and lowly part of surgery," as one eighteenth-century doctor described it.[20] And it involved physical contact with blood in great quantities. Like menstrual fluids, the effluvia of birth caused alarm, so much so that the Christian churches required "purification" rituals into the nineteenth century.[21] In the early modern world, wherever blood was spilled, the potential for dishonor followed.

In the ancient world, the midwife also worked to secure supernatural intercession for successful childbirth.[22] Pregnancy and childbirth, especially up to the point of baptism, were times of great uncertainty, for which women and families sought all the help they could get. City ordinances regulating midwifery always warned practitioners against using "superstitious" methods to protect mothers and infants. Midwives' instructions drawn up for the Duchy of Gotha in 1658 demanded that they

> hear God's word diligently, receive the blessed Lord's Supper at the appropriate time, diligently visit the hour of catechism, and apply what they have learned to faith and Christian life. In contrast, all superstition and misuse of God's name and words . . . , blessings, characters or letters, especially the making of gestures and crosses, detaching the umbilical cord with certain questions and answers, . . . and the like, are not only entirely forbidden to them, but also, should they note such unchristian and blameworthy beginning in others, [the midwives] should admonish them, and also in any case point these out to the pastor or to the government.[23]

On occasion, the language of such regulations suggests a contest between the false powers of idols and reliance on the true Christian God. The Brunswick instructions of 1685 admonished: "The midwife should under no circumstances use superstitious words, gestures, or blessings, but the work of God, and she should in the beginning, the middle, and the end use devout prayers."[24]

If superstitious practices were noted and forbidden, even when their intent was to protect mother and child, the possibility of midwives using magic for harm alarmed the authorities.[25] Especially in the sixteenth and seventeenth centuries, official suspicion hung heavily over all midwives. After all, they had access to blood and to other matter that was useful to witches—the placenta and the umbilical cord.[26] The *Malleus maleficarum*, the fearsome *Hammer of the Witches*, published in 1486, claimed that midwives were especially susceptible to Satanic seduction. They might brand newborns with the sign of Satan, make brews out of the bodies of infants they had either disinterred or murdered, and cause women to be infertile or to miscarry.[27] Numerous trials charged midwives with harming mother or child, and as late as 1687 a midwife was executed for witchcraft in Tübingen.[28]

One other element about midwifery concerned magistrates. The fact that midwives were experts in delivery and alleviating the pain of childbirth suggested that they would be capable abortionists. The ancient Babylonians threatened death for midwives who helped women to abort their children.[29] This was true as well for medieval Europe and was implicit in the *Carolina*'s anti-abortion strictures. Purgatives were an integral tool for midwives during and after childbirth. As labor began, a midwife might use some concoction to help it move along, since difficult and long labors were not only painful but thought to be very bad for mother and child alike. Once the baby was born, expelling remnants of the afterbirth and quickly restoring the mother's menstrual flow were thought to help bring her fluids and humors back into balance, so that her milk would be pure and not tainted by retained blood.[30] The fact that midwives were skilled in concocting purgatives as well as potions for restoring the flow of menses raised alarms among physicians, officials, and the "wise women" themselves.

Midwives, then, met with very mixed responses and frequent official suspicion. Midwives' participation at an event so critical and fraught with physical and social dangers could, however, serve the purposes of discipline so dear to magistrates and pastors. First, the issue of emergency baptisms prompted ecclesiastical attempts to train midwives in the procedure and appropriate circumstances of its use. Infant baptism remained important to the main Protestant churches,[31] and Protestant magistrates even expected midwives to serve as preachers during labor and childbirth. In difficult moments, the midwives of Brunswick were to pray devoutly and exhort the other women present "through prayer to offer the little child up to the love of God."[32] This was in fact more important than immediately performing a baptism, which would only cause distress to the family. In case of misfortune and stillbirth, the midwives upon removing the fetus "should nevertheless thank God the Lord, and also as best as possible console the woman in her childbed that they have diligently commended the little child to God in prayer, and therefore her [the mother's] labor has not been in vain."[33] Finally, midwives were to remind women in the midst of their labor pangs that this was God's will, His merciful punishment, which women must bear:

> they should know, when they come into anguish and need, that God has laid such [sufferings] upon them graciously, that He spoke to Eve (Genesis 3): "I will create pain for you when you are pregnant. In pain will you bring your children into the world." Is that not a gracious punishment? I hear well that He says much about pain, but along with that He says that He wants you to be pregnant and to give you children.[34]

The seventeenth-century woman who in the throes of labor was tempted to question God's wisdom and actions would receive a stern warning from the devout midwife.

MIDWIVES AND CRIMINAL INVESTIGATIONS

The midwife's function as Christian counsel was less important to government officials than her other potential role—policing a suspected crime scene. Ceaselessly wary of the disorder posed by single women, authorities in cities and villages alike worried about the harmful consequences of fornication—unwanted pregnancies, followed by abortions, and above all infanticides. Magistrates could direct a local *Hebbame* (midwife) to inspect suspicious women for signs of illicit sex and especially of pregnancy, despite the dubious accuracy of such indicators. A negative diagnosis could potentially exculpate women who had been denounced or accused, while a positive certification from the midwife would bring greater scrutiny and intense pressure to reveal the name of the father, both to exact punishment and to guarantee that an infant would receive paternal care rather than become a burden to town or village charities. Where one midwife could not decide, others would be called in, and it seems clear that authorities needed only one affirmative diagnosis to prove their case.[35]

From the sixteenth century, officials required midwives to report the details of illegitimate births. Statute after statute demanded that, when called to an unknown or unmarried woman's bedside, midwives must energetically inquire after the father. Midwives in cities like Strasbourg were also to judge whether any birth occurring less than nine months after a marriage was full term—if so, the father could face expulsion from his guild.[36] More ominously, governments noted that unmarried mothers might resort to abortion through potions or medicines. For this reason, midwives in the city of Nürnberg were warned not to assist in illegitimate births nor to bury any dead child without informing the officials.[37]

In Brunswick, the *Bademütter* (midwives) summoned to help "unchaste" women were enjoined to ask first about the father of the baby and even withhold assistance until he was named, a practice seen also in the Brandenburg countryside.[38] The most painful moments of labor seemed an opportune time to ask for the father's name.[39] The midwife should not help such a woman "hush up" the birth and must admonish her to care for the infant. To this end, the midwife was to return frequently to make sure the "whore" was not neglecting her offspring. In her oath, the midwife swore to inform the authorities and the local pastor in any case of illegitimate birth.[40] The varied tasks assigned to midwives—aiding mothers or assisting prosecutors—demonstrate that their role in early modern life depended on the status of the pregnant women they attended. For the married woman hoping for an heir, the midwife was critical not only to a successful childbirth but also to the comfort and even spiritual health of mother and baby alike. For single women carrying illegitimate children, the midwife represented the intrusion of the state and the end of any hopes for keeping a birth secret, terminating the pregnancy, or otherwise avoiding the wrath of the law or the enmity of neighbors.[41]

Whether in the everyday practice of their profession or in the area of forensic medicine, though, midwives faced increasing challenges, particularly from male doctors. Using midwives to conduct examinations had long offended some physicians who sought greater control over the medical "profession." Doctors' objections were both social and technical. Learned physicians ridiculed the origins of most midwives. In words dripping with scorn, Johannes Bohn noted in the eighteenth century that the average midwife sprang from the lowest castes, from the cattle stall and the ranks of swineherds and ox-tenders,[42] the very orders from which Grethe Schmidt herself emerged. As far as their competence to investigate infanticide cases, midwives' own suspected involvement in the deaths of infants disqualified them in the eyes of some doctors and jurists. They were far more likely to join in plotting with murderous mothers, to turn newborns over to the devil, or to sell infants' joints and fat as medicines or potions. Some authors excoriated midwives specifically on grounds of gender, arguing that women's vanity, curiosity, and inclination to evil made them untrustworthy witnesses.[43]

Doctors' objections focused mainly on the use of midwives in court proceedings to establish virginity and sexual impotence. Some early modern "forensic medicine" treatises ridiculed the idea that a woman's virginity could be tested either by the presence of the hymen or the narrowness of the genital passage. Many anatomists frankly doubted the very existence of the hymen but argued that, in any case, it was easily disrupted and of little use as proof.

Despite mounting criticism in learned circles, though, one should be wary of placing midwives and doctors in automatic opposition. Both were responsible for serving the judicial courts, and midwives had as great a stake in preventing evil and punishing crime as did the other honorable women of Brunswick. Indeed, suspected as they often were, midwives perhaps had extra incentives to display their own competence and sense of duty. While it is true that many traditional legal duties of midwives had been curtailed by the late seventeenth century, local criminal courts across Germany still relied on midwives not only to examine infanticide suspects for traces of birth or motherhood but to certify illicit pregnancies as well. It also seems clear that authorities accepted their testimony, especially when more than one midwife was involved and both came to the same conclusions.[44] Conversely, in criminal matters, a split opinion would lead prosecutors to pursue a matter further.

It also seems clear that by 1660, the actual examinations conducted by midwives went beyond the basic stipulations of the *Carolina* itself. Article 35 provides for the examination of unmarried women suspected of fornication, suggesting strongly that the law's intent was quite traditional—to look for signs of virginity or its violation. Article 36 specifies a breast examination—looking for lactation—as the way to detect birth. Because some commentators cast doubt on the presence of milk as a sure indicator on its own, the *Carolina* recommended a wider inspection by midwives. Women of sixty or seventy years who were no longer menstruating and even men and newborn children had been seen to have milk in their breasts. If, however, someone was the kind of woman who could be suspected of harming a newborn, then not only could her breasts be "visited," but her stomach could be felt in order to see whether it was "creased."[45]

Touching a woman rather than simply looking at her was therefore a very important part of the examination, another reason for excluding males, even physicians. Thus, a woman would be taken to a "secret place," a room where she would be alone with the midwives, asked to strip, and then her breasts, stomach, and pelvis would be inspected.[46] From the manuals for childbirth, one thing is clear—midwives were not squeamish about touch. The hands of midwives were well accustomed to feeling and manipulating women's bodies—they would not shirk from the task of examining Grethe Schmidt.

With Grethe, the midwives faced a peculiar task. The *Carolina*'s Article 35 concerns women pretending to maidenhood. The midwife's examination, then, seemed intended primarily to establish or dispute virginity. In the Schmidt case, magistrates and defendant had already agreed that Grethe was no virgin. On the other hand, Article 36 appears to have been irrelevant because at least seven months had passed since the alleged birth—whatever happened, Schmidt was not lactating. The examination, then, had to seek evidence that she had actually borne a baby, whether alive or dead. Out of all the cases of childbirth and infanticide included in the new compendiums of forensic medicine, not a single example involved a prosecution and examination so long after the alleged birth. The Grethe Schmidt episode violated many common expectations of criminal prosecutions, and this was one more.

What then was the point of the examination? Was it simply a formality, following the law to the letter? This possibility must be considered, but the prosecution clearly expected to have their suspicions confirmed after so much suggestive and incriminating testimony. Still, the prosecution was aware that a prima facie case did not yet exist. One must remember that the decisive proof in early modern continental law was the defendant's confession of wrongdoing, a fairly high threshold of proof that might require torture to achieve. In practice, investigations established "sufficient indications" of guilt (or in modern American jurisprudence, "probable cause"), permitting recourse to torture. In the case of infanticide, rumors were not enough, there had to be some greater evidence to justify so significant a step. Grethe had admitted a sexual liaison, which intensified the authorities' suspicion. Now the prosecution hoped to clinch its case.

ALTSTADT, AUGUST 20, 1661

> *Present: Julius von Horn (Judicial Lord), Johannes Vellhagen (Vogt), Johannes Pilgram (Court Scribe)*
> Witnesses: Grete Voges & Jillian Wilckens, midwives

Grete Voges, Frantz Racken's widow, official midwife in the Neustadt, having been reminded of her midwife's oath and other matters in the presence of Dr. Laurence Gieseler, the physician, reports that, following instructions, she visually inspected the captive [Grethe Schmidt], and using her hands as the case required, as much as possible explored the neck and entrance of the womb ["collum et ostium Matricis"], that she then concluded that the sexual organs of the captive were narrow and closed, that the same [captive], in the midwife's opinion, never had a child, much less that a child has ever passed through that place.

Asked, whence she comes by such knowledge? She [the midwife] says, when she comes to a person who has already brought one or more children into the world, then it is much different, than with this prisoner who in that place was entirely and completely closed.

Jillian Wilckens, Hennig Cordes's wife and sworn midwife in the Neustadt, having been admonished, reports that, following her instructions, she inspected the prisoner Margarethe Schmidt in her legs [where women after the birth normally have blue veins], and her breasts and her navel, but found nothing, especially however in the birth regions, at the joints and the pubic bone, she found the captive to be entirely uninjured, and everything therefore narrowed, so that the midwife for her person could not say, that from the captive a child ever came to the world or was born, and that the captive's womb until now was still very closed.[47]

This startling affidavit presented the authorities with the first indication that Grethe Schmidt might have been telling the truth. Importantly, the testimony came from witnesses required by the *Carolina* itself and chosen by the prosecution. The older midwife, Grete Voges, appeared to have no doubts about the matter—"no child ever passed through the [womb]." The city, no doubt stunned by her testimony, followed up to ask how she could be sure. Voges was firm, basing her conclusions on direct experience with other cases.

The midwife from the Neustadt, Jillian Wilckens, pointed to other specific evidence from her visual inspection. Her conclusion, though more qualified than Voges's, seemed equally certain: "the midwife for her person could not say, that from the captive a child ever came to the world or was born, and that the captive's womb until now was still very closed."

These women's natural sympathies probably rested with the magistrates of Brunswick and the local women who had testified against Schmidt, rather than with the poor outsider accused of a particularly heinous act. Yet Wilckens's and Voges's reports are striking for the firmness and consistency of their findings. It would be one thing to profess uncertainty and say they did not or could not know. Ambivalence from the midwives about Schmidt's condition, combined with her own admissions of sexual activity and the observations of her employers and other Brunswick women, would probably have sufficed to make torture necessary, especially in the absence of any exculpatory evidence. Now, however, the city's painstakingly laid-out trail of rumor and suggestion ran up against the confident and unambiguous conclusions of experienced professional witnesses. Rather than indicate probable cause, sufficient to threaten Grethe Schmidt with torture, the midwives had undermined the entire case. All the while, Laurence Gieseler remained silent; there is no indication that he disputed the midwives' accounts in any way.

ALTSTADT, AUGUST 28 AND SEPTEMBER 2, 1661

For three weeks, the city's case had proceeded without a hitch. Suddenly the midwives' testimony upset its inexorable progress toward the *Rathaus* dungeon's torture chamber. This may be one reason why on August 28 the judicial lords looked at earlier testimony and called Anna Försten to confirm Anna Sacharitz's August 13 account of the itinerant peddler's journey to the villages around Gross Schwülper and what Försten had heard there. Confronted perhaps with the implications of taking an oath, Försten was much less forthcoming than she had supposedly been with Sacharitz. She claimed that yes, indeed, she had considered Grethe Schmidt to be "womanly" because the girl had a "full bosom."[48] But Försten insisted that Sacharitz had misunderstood and misrepresented the alleged encounter between Försten and Schmidt's little sister in Gross Schwülper, which Försten said had never taken place. Rather, in Neubrücke, Försten had merely heard it rumored that the younger sister had been talking of Grethe's condition. Further, the idea that Schmidt's mother had rented a room in Neubrücke "was making the rounds back and forth" (*weren hin und wieder in schwange gangen*).[49] In other words it was simply gossip. So Försten had not heard of Grethe's supposed "sickness" from a family member in Gross Schwülper but, instead, from an unidentified person in Neubrücke. Anna Försten was willing to swear (*mit Cörperlichen Eide bestercken*) only to this more limited testimony.

Hoping to clear up the discrepancy between Försten's testimony and Sacharitz's deposition, the authorities called back Anna Sacharitz, who admitted she might have misunderstood Försten's words, and so begged to be spared an oath—which, if her testimony later proved false, could result in torture. Whatever role Anna Sacharitz played in bringing Grethe Schmidt to the attention of authorities, her own statement in the case was legally next to worthless, and the magistrates knew it. Summoned again days later (September 2), Sacharitz too affirmed her testimony with an oath. It would seem the authorities were determined on the matter.

They might have had good reason to apply pressure to Sacharitz. On August 30, a petition appeared, pleading for Grethe's release and entreating the magistrates not to listen to wild tales and rumors spread without a shred of evidence. Signed by her parents and close relatives, this document is the first recorded evidence that the Schmidt family would not meekly accept the magistracy's judgments in the case but was prepared to fight in court. The peculiar case—unique in so many particulars—now became even more complex as other actors emerged to give old evidence a new look. The only constant was the young woman awaiting judgment.

8

Legal Maneuvering
and the Question of Torture

The petition presented to the city's investigators on August 30 moved the investigation of Grethe Schmidt's deeds into a new phase. For the first time in the case, the prosecutors—who so far had complete control of the witnesses and the story—came under scrutiny. The petition, "signed" by Andreas Schmidt and numerous relatives (all of them male and all in the same hand), raises the issue of a criminal defense, not just for Grethe Schmidt but in early modern courts generally. The law did guarantee some right to be heard before torture could be applied. How far that right extended and in what way will be addressed in chapter 10. For now, though, it is enough to note that, in exercising this basic and minimal privilege to be heard, the Schmidts looked to professional counsel to protect Grethe.

The petition itself is worth examining. At first glance, the Schmidt family's entreaty seems hesitant and modest—they were dismayed by Grethe's incarceration, sure of her innocence, and confident of the authorities' Christian charity. A closer look, though, shows that the Schmidts were not naïve about the case, nor should the obsequious language of dutiful subjects obscure their dissatisfaction. Noting that Grethe had languished in prison for close to a month with no resolution in sight, her blood relatives could not stand by passively. The petition quickly sets out a defiant line of defense. Her relatives reject as "sheer madness" any accusation that Grethe went about with a "heavy body" (i.e. that she had been pregnant) or that she somehow murdered its "fruit." Because Grethe's youth and inexperience prevent her from demonstrating her innocence, "we her closest relatives are bound and responsible, out of natural love and Christian justice, to give her our help." Therefore, the family requests that copies of all acts (documents) produced in the case be sent to them and that the magistrates hear their response.[1]

So the Schmidts would seek to exonerate Grethe; it is quite clear that she had no hand in organizing her defense. There is no evidence of contact between her and her parents during August 1661. Nor had the authorities communicated with the family—the Schmidts must have remained unaware of the midwives' examination, for example, or this petition would certainly have mentioned it. To gain access to the investigation, the Schmidts would have to force their way in. Whether the city was negligent in this regard is a question that took on great significance later.

As so often in this case, though, the Schmidt family's actions suggest a canny approach to the criminal process, surprising for a barely literate family in a world in which the law was still written and expounded upon in Latin. Even judicial personnel were frequently flummoxed by the arcane details that were the glory of lawyers and professors. During the seventeenth century, legal scholars translated important commentaries specifically for untutored judges, whose ignorance of law and procedure impeded the full implementation of the *Carolina*. That the Schmidts challenged the procedures intended to incriminate their daughter suggests great determination and a practical familiarity at odds with their education and social status.

One should consider, for example, the family's dismissive rejection of the charges as baseless, mere gossip "floating" about. By referring to the "madness" from which the accusations emerged, they were trying to undermine the case as built on rumors—from the very outset impeaching testimony the content of which they did not yet know. They appeared to know that no body had been found, for the petition neither mentions a corpse nor tries to explain it away. It is also interesting that the petition emphasizes Grethe's youth, innocence, and ignorance, thus permitting the family to intervene on her behalf.

Couched in this line of defense, though, is another argument. The Schmidts were shrewdly suggesting that they only learned the charges in the swirl of rumor after Grethe's incarceration. It was all news to them! Were they trying to inoculate themselves against suspicion while defending her? Her family did have reason for concern—though without access to the court records they might not have known it. The magistrates had now heard from reputable women about the unsavory, even criminal behavior of the Schmidt family. Grethe's aunt had allegedly returned with her mother to Brunswick to blackmail Hafferland. Shortly after questioning Grethe's sister Anna, the authorities received a letter from Neubrücke solicited by the Schmidt family. Andreas Schmidt allegedly traveled to Wendschott to fetch his daughter, for reasons only poorly explained. In the magistrates' eyes, every member of the family was potentially involved.

These suspicions might even explain why no one seemed to have visited Grethe since her arrest. The city was under no compulsion to permit visitors, thereby increasing pressure on the defendant. On the other hand, they would have had good reason to seize Grethe's mother or aunt should either have appeared on the *Rathaus* steps or at the *Fronerey*.

The Schmidts' caginess and determination to defend Grethe do not entirely explain the petition, though, which is written in a learned hand and flowery language. They clearly had some help. Given the kind of nuanced arguments adduced even in this early petition, assistance came from a higher legal source, perhaps an advocate—a learned lawyer skilled in the written arts of law. An important city like Brunswick would house numerous advocates. It just so happened, that in 1661 Brunswick could boast of a particular man uniquely suited to addressing the legal troubles that had brought Grethe to grief—Justus Oldekop. He later described his first contacts with the family: "When her relatives and closest friends heard nothing about her release [after months] they finally with tears sought out an advocate for counsel." He told them, "if [the family] knew that the prisoner was guilty, they should not waste any money on her or her case. If not, however, they might undertake to procure copies of the records from city hall and the judicial office, and bring them to the advocate for inspection and an answer."[2]

Whoever wrote this first brief (possibly Oldekop himself in fact, despite his demurral), the petition came at a difficult time and may have provoked investigators in ways the Schmidts did not foresee. It is quite possible that Johannes Vellhagen and his colleagues saw this appeal as an affront, a defiant and unscrupulous attempt by wily lowlifes to bluff the *Justizherren* out of pursuing the truth. Whatever the final merits of Margarethe Hafferland's story, it gave the *Untergericht* compelling grounds to see Grethe's mother herself in the worst possible light, as a liar, a procuress of abortions, even a blackmailer. Now the prosecutors could imagine the entire Schmidt family as involved in greedy and unseemly scheming. Worse still, the Schmidts had a lawyer to help them.

Maneuvers

On September 13, the prosecution complied with the Schmidt request to see copies of the first interrogations.[3] One week later, on September 20, the defense responded to the evidence for the first time. The Schmidts had intervened just in time, for in theory a suspect had the right to be heard prior to being tortured, after which formal charges could be filed. As events would turn out, this was an important letter, for it constituted the single opportunity the Schmidts would have to forestall the prosecution's inclination to employ torture against Grethe.

To the City Council and *Bürgermeister* of Brunswick:

That your princely, high, and gracious majesty have so graciously permitted the defense of my arrested and still-incarcerated daughter Margreta Schmiedes, for this do I give my obedient thanks. As to me and to her mother, the admitted excess with Gottfried Müller (who, however, as a man in the fullness of his own years ought not to lead on and seduce a young woman of sixteen or seventeen) has brought heartsickness and dismay. Despite such heartfelt suffering, we are nevertheless herewith lifted up and consoled, in that the evil, for which our daughter has fallen under suspicion through women's gossip, and finally [led] to this long-lasting incarceration, can not in the smallest way be laid to her, nor attributed to her, but much more the contrary, is demonstrated through the unanimous testimony of the sworn midwives as found in the testimony according to act #14. From here we proceed to other conjectures, especially because the menstruation of my daughter according to the report in act #4, happened variously around the correct time, and stopped for some weeks. It could happen very easily that from this [stoppage] something, barely a finger long and no thicker, might have gone out from her, about which not only many knowledgeable and experienced women but undoubtedly also many learned doctors are informed. Therefore as a result not the smallest indication of a misdeed emerges. To your princely high true Graciousness therefore is my humbly pleading request presented, that you will release my daughter now, place her freely on her way, and without fee, since this matter has already proved costly for me, a poor oxherd, and let this protracted imprisonment caused through Godtfried Müller's [sic] committed excess, serve as punishment for the same: Through your high discretion, you yourselves will rationally determine, that she and her parents, through the already completed imprisonment have already been very harshly punished through the imprisonment completed thus far. . . .

Your obedient subject,
Andreas Schmidt[4]

Here in the space of two folio sheets are claims designed to halt the steady march to the torture chamber. Notably, it is addressed to the *Bürgermeister* and city council, who composed the upper court, or *Obergericht*, which could take over responsibility for more serious crimes but also dealt with the external and more learned affairs of the criminal court. The rebuttal goes far beyond the outline of late August. The petition also betrays some haste. It repeatedly uses the name of the dead Gottfried Möller when meaning to place blame on his all too lively son, Andreas. Perhaps its most telling feature, though, is the heat of the argument coursing beneath the deferential language. For the first time, with the entire prosecution evidence spread before him, Oldekop the advocate was able to test the case and found it wanting.

The new petition moves beyond the "mad rumors" mentioned in the August petition and now flatly dismissed the testimony of accusing witnesses as "women's gossip" (*weibliche plauderey*). The author turns quickly to focus instead on the reports of the sworn midwives. From their unanimous testimony that Grethe had never borne a child, it is clear that no suspicion of evildoing should fall on her. The advocate finds corroborating testimony in inquisitional act number four, which detailed the stopping and starting of Grethe's menstrual cycle. Furthermore, the petition argues, the connection between a temporary menstrual stoppage and the clotted blood that she apparently expelled is a phenomenon known not only to knowledgeable women but to doctors as well (the advocate here does not note that this particular document is the defendant's own testimony).[5] His point is that Grethe offered a plausible account of her missing periods, their resumption, and the results. Combined with the authoritative report of the midwives, the record should dispel any suspicion of evil deeds.

Within the petition the quick emergence of a strategy is evident. The defense concentrated on the forensic evidence that was the strongest exculpatory material produced so far, but the brief also hints at problems in the other testimony—not only was it based on mere rumor but worse, "*women's* gossip." This was, of course, different from the "official" testimony of the "sworn" midwives or the general medical understanding of "knowledgeable" women. The tension over women's testimony was unavoidable—so far all the relevant witnesses in the case had been women, so the advocate had to establish levels of credibility for some while impeaching others. "*Weibliche plauderey*" was a dismissive term designed with the all-male judges in mind.

The defense also sought to resolve another serious problem—Grethe had admitted to the sexual act, a criminal offense in its own right that automatically awakened more serious suspicions. The Schmidt family tried to minimize the damage here by humbly acknowledging the sexual misconduct that had, they assured the judges, brought them heartache and grief. Grethe's month-long incarceration was punishment aplenty for her "admitted excess," especially given the family's poverty, a condition that could only be worsened by having to pay a fine or court costs. The Schmidts' humility and openness stood in implicit contrast with the behavior of Andreas Möller, who had not come forward and had suffered nothing. Indeed, his culpability may have been worse—a grown man in the fullness of his years and experience ought not to be "seducing" and "leading astray" a young woman of sixteen.[6] The defense wanted to place the burden of responsibility, and therefore the merited punishment, on the adult male, not the young woman.

Admitting the lesser crime of fornication (perhaps mitigated because of seduction by an older man) in order to establish the family's obedience was a resourceful move. The defense would eventually go even further and turn Grethe's acknowledgment of vice into a virtue. Oldekop later described the petition as something that seemed simple, almost perfunctory: he "diligently read through them [the records] and realized quickly, indeed he saw clearly, not only that no evidence of the alleged infanticide was at hand but, on the contrary, that different parts of the city's own evidence worked in favor of her innocence."[7]

Because of this apparently exculpatory evidence—especially from the midwives—Oldekop saw no need for a lengthy argument and had written a "simple and humble supplication" to free the innocent captive. He expected an uncomplicated hearing and a quick release. Events would prove him quite wrong. For the time being, though, the family through its advocate had made the first informed plea for dismissing the charges. The question is whether it was compelling enough to forestall the inquisitors' determination to move forward, all the way, to torture.

The Prosecution's Response, Altstadt

The magistrates responded within a week to refute Oldekop's main contentions that the medical evidence decisively favored Grethe Schmidt's account and that malicious gossip, rather than murder, was at the heart of the matter. On September 27, the city physician, Laurence Gieseler, commented officially on the midwives' report:

> Concerning the statement submitted by the midwives in the case of the imprisoned woman, I give to my Lords and Superiors the following to consider, that their witness and testimony is not to be accorded full belief, indeed where it is not impossible then entirely doubtful, that someone, who has been corrupted by a male, also from whom an abortion or perhaps other unformed mass of flesh has issued, is actually to be distinguished from someone, who has brought a fully formed child to the world, for the female

womb is just as much changed in an abortion (miscarriage) as in true birth, and although in legitimate and perfect parturition the same parts are more open and widely separated from each other than otherwise, so do they come together again just as exactly and as hard as before the time. Therefore the midwives, in my opinion, can say with just as little certainty that no child was at hand, as that they can say that a living full fruit was there.[8]

Gieseler's testimony dismisses the midwives' report, arguing that it proves nothing, indeed in principle can prove nothing.

One must note how, from the very beginning, the contending sides perceived the midwives' testimony. To the defense, the *Hebammen* report conclusively demonstrated that no case existed against Grethe ("not in the least"). Their certainty clinched Grethe's innocence. For the prosecution, though, the uncertainty of the results, given the city physician's skepticism about bodily evidence of pregnancy and childbirth, instead justified further the drive to torture Grethe. "Painful questions" were more necessary than ever for the truth to emerge. Because of the narrative already fixed in the officials' minds after more than a month of interrogations, the burden of proof now lay on Grethe's shoulders. Given the contradictory testimony, the possibility of a confession held out to the prosecution the promise of certainty wrought in the suspect's own words. A confession, even under torture, would cut through the dubious examinations and the lies and obfuscations and, so, prove a compelling tool. The Grethe Schmidt investigation reveals an interesting paradox in the criminal process: a strong case led inexorably to the torture chamber but a weak case demanded the certain answers that only "painful questions" could extract. Either way, the prosecution would justify its determination to torture Grethe.

Gieseler's testimony raises questions of its own. In the first place, what was his own authority over the forensic examination? The *Carolina* is quite specific about "knowledgeable women" but makes no mention of male physicians. While it may seem predictable that male learning and authority would trump female wisdom and experience, the word of midwives remained compelling, a reality borne out by the writings of early forensic medical experts such as Paolo Zacchius and Paul Amann. Compounding the confusion is that Gieseler probably never physically examined Grethe, nor any other woman, during pregnancy or after birth. Male hands did not probe women's reproductive organs, especially in the intimate way that was a routine part of the midwife's trade. In other words, whatever the midwives might or might not have deduced, Gieseler could not judge their conclusions from his own experience. It is also true that early modern treatises, especially in forensic medicine, spent virtually no time on this particular issue, and no case appears in the seventeenth-century literature concerning a suspected pregnancy so many months before the woman's forensic examination.

Another question arises—why was Gieseler's opinion only offered now? He was present to hear the midwives' original report in August and did not dispute their findings. At the time, he made no comment of any sort, nor did the city solicit his judgment. Of course Gieseler was now supporting his "lords and superiors" in the face of the defense claims, and his statement would certainly help when the records were sent to Helmstedt University for the legal faculty's comment. The timing, though, makes it seem that the medical facts were less important than shoring up the prosecution's case.

GROSS SCHWÜLPER, OCTOBER 17–19, 1661

In addition to offering Gieseler's rebuttal, the magistrates moved to strengthen other testimony against Schmidt by returning to the opening days of their investigation. Grethe's first interrogation included questions about her family's behavior in Gross Schwülper, especially her father's distress. Now the city contacted the ducal official in the village to ask that he question the Schmidts' next-door neighbors, Andreas Hageman and his wife, Ilse Thiess. They were the village cowherds, and their house was separated from the Schmidts' only by a "partition." If chaos reigned in the oxherd's house, if Grethe's father wandered about crying "woe," if Grethe herself was either about to give birth or was recovering after, then the Hagemans were in the best position to have witnessed it.[9]

The thirteen questions posed to the Hagemans rely on their proximity to the Schmidt clan and perhaps hint at the earliest sources of the city's information against Grethe. The first three questions locate Grethe Schmidt in Gross Schwülper around the Feast of Three Kings and particularly at Candlemas. From there, however, the prosecutors' interest becomes more specific—*wasn't Grethe in the throes of childbirth and didn't her mother attend her need?* And then—*didn't Grethe's aunt come to the house, saying, "O God, how will this turn out?" And did not the girl's mother call to her, "Shh, Shh" meaning that she should be quiet? And wasn't the now jailed woman nursing a living, full-term child? And did she [Grethe] not ask for her child and wish to nurse it?* At this point the questions shifted to darker possibilities, involving Grethe's mother: *Did the mother not say to her daughter, "Do you want to be a whore your entire life?" What did she mean by such words? Did the mother not mean by this that the child should be killed?*

These questions suggest another possible line of attack, focusing on Grethe's mother as the true agent of death, perhaps even the actual murderer. Grethe in contrast appears almost the hapless, unwilling victim of Ilse's cold-blooded calculations. If so, the magistrates were perhaps hoping for two criminal prosecutions rather than one. They were clearly working out the implications of their earlier interviews in Brunswick, which placed the elder Schmidt in a sinister light. Now they had good grounds at least to question Ilse Leuthgen.

The appearance of this new line of argument at the very moment the Schmidt family emerged publicly to defend Grethe raises two other possibilities. First, prosecutors were perhaps hoping to intimidate the family's representative by showing that the evidence was stronger than he knew and indicted the very family he represented. A second possibility is even more devious: the magistrates may have been trying to divide the Schmidts, hinting that defending Grethe would bring unwanted attention to other family members, specifically her mother. Throughout the early records, Ilse Leuthgen appeared far more active in organizing affairs than her daughter.

The magistrates were now marshalling all the evidence in order to demonstrate both the seriousness of the matter and the strength of their case—no "women's gossip" here but complete and plausible accounts in two separate places. If the prosecution's original information came from the cowherd and his wife, people living just a wall away from the oxherd's own family and therefore in a position to see and hear much, this was an excellent moment at which to produce them. The Hagemans, landless workers dependent upon the authorities for work and housing (like the Schmidts), would presumably be compliant.

Reaching the Hagemans, though, required time and negotiation. Brunswick had no jurisdiction over Schwülper, which lay in the Lüneburg part of the duchy and was administered by Claus von Marenholz, a vassal of the dukes. Permission, then, was required to interrogate them, and the Count von Marenholz was protective, not so much of his subjects' rights as of his own prerogatives. Furthermore, the interview would have to wait until Marenholz himself was available in Schwülper to conduct it. The Brunswick *Justizherren* sent their request to Marenholz on September 27, but Claus von Marenholz did not summon the Hagemans until October 17. According to Marenholz, the couple were anxious: "Now the two persons did appear . . . however[,] as the customary admonitions and witness's oath was laid before them, they strongly rejected it, and sought to excuse themselves with their lack of knowledge, that they were plain, simple herding folk, who had never performed such an oath nor could understand it, because they passed their days with cattle in woods and field."[10] Even though Marenholz cajoled them, saying that no trouble would come of their testimony, that no one would know what was said, and that this was in any case a duty they could not escape, the Hagemans initially refused. They asked for two days to think things over and reluctantly agreed on October 19.[11]

Andreas Hageman testified first. If the magistrates in Brunswick were expecting conclusive evidence from him, they would be sorely disappointed. To one inquiry after another, about the Schmidt family's and Grethe's whereabouts or actions in January 1661, Andreas stated, "He does not know." "He has seen nothing." "He has heard nothing, says one should ask Grethe's parents." To the critical question of whether Grethe was in Gross Schwülper at the end of January, he pleaded that "he has no time to attend to such things, for he, all day long with the cattle in woods and fields, grows weary, wanting only when he would come home at night, that he lay down to rest, the parents of the prisoner in the house where she lived must also have been home, and they should be asked."[12] To one question only did he provide a simple answer. Asked about Ilse Leuthgen's alleged intention to kill the baby, "he heard nothing from the parents, but from the people there was in general talk, that the aforementioned person M. S. [Grethe] wanted to reserve a lying-in bed in Neubrücke, and that she was depending on her parents."[13] Asked whether he had anything to add, the simple man who wearied himself in the fields by day and rested by night would tell the authorities nothing more.

The cowherd's reluctance was not unique—frequently in this case, the men had nothing to say, absolving themselves by referring to their hard work and resulting absences. It was the women who provided useful information—it was in many respects entirely the women's case. The authorities thus expected more of Ilse Thiess, Hageman's wife. Asked to state her age, she answered that she actually did not know—according to her own mother, she was born sometime during the last "Brunswick war," another example of the era's casual attention to birth dates. Thiess was more careful in replying to the magistrates' inquiry. It was indeed true that around Three Kings Grethe Schmidt returned to Gross Schwülper from Brunswick, where she had been a servant. Rumor had it that she was in need of a lying-in bed, and for this reason she had come home. For the most part, Grethe stayed with her parents, except for a few days when she had visited her aunt, the tavern keeper's wife. To the third question—*whether during the night of Candlemas the prisoner was sick in the oxherd's house and what was afflicting her?*—Thiess replied that it was around that time that Grethe's mother came to her house and said, "Our Grethe is indeed grown sick." The next day Thiess asked Grethe's ten- or eleven-year-old sister, who said that Grethe's "heart is so painful" that the mother gave her *Kalmus* (*Acorus Calamus,* a plant used even today for medicinal purposes). Some three days later, in the morning, the witness was leaving her house when she saw Anna (Grethe's aunt). The following Sunday, she went into the oxherd's house to borrow a pair of onions to cook. There she saw Grethe lying on the bed and asked her mother whether the girl was still sick. The oxherd's wife answered that yes, it was nothing other than what she had in the city and was "causing great pain to her heart." Hearing this, the witness turned to Grethe and said, "Grethe, if things are as people say, you have earned great punishment from your parents," to which Grethe "answered nothing, neither yes nor no, but kept quite still." Thiess then turned to the young woman's mother and asked whether she had been to Neubrücke to reserve a lying-in bed. The mother said that she had but was sorry to discover that another pregnant woman had gone to the place first, so the family knew of no other place to take their daughter.[14]

Here was important information: Grethe was sick, and more important, her mother affirmed to Ilse Thiess that she had indeed sought a room for the girl but was too late. Thiess's testimony changed markedly, though, when the questions sought specific facts or conclusions. Whether Grethe was in childbirth, whether her mother attended to her, whether she had brought a living child into the world and wanted to nurse it—to these questions Ilse Thiess replied that she did not know, that Grethe's parents should be asked. Of Grethe's mother's intentions and motives, Thiess was ignorant. She could only say that talk went round that Grethe was pregnant and that her parents had sought a lying-in room in Neubrücke. Finally, fourteen days before Easter, she heard a bit of gossip and went into the oxherd's house and spoke to Grethe's mother, saying, "Ilse, the people cannot leave aside the suspicion, that your daughter, although you were in Neubrücke, yet had no child, to which the oxherd's wife answered 'yes, one or two people have said that to me.'"[15]

With this, Ilse Thiess's testimony came to an end. Thiess was willing to talk of the gossip going around and of Grethe's "sickness." When asked directly about an infant, though, or about any of the events that might have occurred around Candlemas, the cowherd's wife appeared as ignorant as her husband. As the next-door neighbor, Ilse Thiess had every opportunity to observe Grethe closely herself but said nothing of what she concluded. On the question of whether Grethe had been or still was pregnant, Thiess was silent. Again the reader is left to wonder just how cagey these supposedly simple folk really were. The couple—in particular Ilse—made no direct statements and were determined to testify, if at all, from a distance and without exposing themselves in any way.

The city officials of Brunswick, upon reading this interrogation, had more information than before, but even these close witnesses could not provide them with the certainty they needed. The question now was whether there was enough material to warrant torture. The city was convinced of at least one person's guilt, and the contradictory and incomplete testimony, rather than the high probability of guilt, made torture all the more attractive in order to extract the whole truth. At the same time, the law's requirements governing the use of torture demanded a higher standard of proof than the city could claim on its own. To solve this tricky legal puzzle, the city turned to the legal faculty of the University of Helmstedt for help. By now, Grethe had been in jail for nearly three months, with no end in sight.

9

Terror, Torture, and Grethe Schmidt

"So, what do you think, Meister Hans?"
"I don't know—she's pretty fat. I will do with her what I can do."
Turning to the young woman, [he said] "If you come into my hands and still
will not confess, then I will stretch you out on the rack so thin that we'll be
able to shine a light through you."[1]

This lurid account seems to modern eyes the stuff of pulp fiction or far-off
wars. In fact, though, it is Justus Oldekop's description of a conversation
that took place in the dungeons of Brunswick in early November 1661.
Can it possibly be true? And how did the next phase of the Schmidt investigation proceed?

HELMSTEDT, OCTOBER 29, 1661

To determine its next step, the Brunswick *Obergericht* gathered all the
files from the case and shipped them to the legal faculty of the University
of Helmstedt. The university's review would give no comfort to the incarcerated Grethe Schmidt. The faculty proposed nine questions for the
authorities to put to the prisoner. All nine assumed that she had steadily
and stubbornly lied: (1) Did she know she was pregnant? (2) If so, why
did she hide the fact? (3) Wasn't she *planning* to kill the baby upon its
birth? These are the questions specific to the Schmidt case. The other six
are more generic to any infanticide investigation. The faculty urged the
magistrates to ask, for example, whether the infant cried out before it was
killed. This had nothing to do with the collected testimony in the Schmidt
case but was a standard query to establish whether a baby was indeed
born alive. The goal of these questions was to fit Grethe's confession into
the recognizable pattern of secrecy and premeditation demanded by the
law governing infanticide.[2]

The response from the legal faculty carried grave implications for Grethe. It also revealed the methodical workings of the imperial criminal justice system when torture was being considered. Since the sixteenth century, the *Carolina* had recommended possible consultation with legal experts, in part due to concerns about the inexperience and ignorance of judicial personnel throughout the empire. As criminal procedure in practice struggled to keep pace with the ever-greater complexity of law and theoretical learning, this worry among learned jurists intensified and the *Aktenversand* ("sending of acts") became more common by the mid-seventeenth century. It was not universally required, though, and in some places—Rostock, for example— courts had wide latitude.[3] Even though the government of Brunswick had competent legal scholars in the form of the syndics, consultation with the legal faculty of Helmstedt was the safer route.

Asking the legal faculty for help was important to the court in another way. By design, the *Aktenversand* served to protect the suspect from judicial misconduct resulting from the judges' ignorance or malice. The reverse was also true, though, as a faculty's affirmation protected the court by providing authoritative legal justification for its decisions, especially in difficult cases. The Schmidt case certainly qualified as this, especially on the question of whether torture was justified. Carpzov and other legal authorities agreed that torture should only occur when the case was almost completely proved and the only missing element was the confession.[4] This would assume that the corpus delicti was in evidence. In the Schmidt case the midwives had been uncertain, the corpus delicti was still nowhere to be found, and so the grounds for torture seemed quite tenuous. The legal faculty's judgment thus seems somewhat surprising, even contradictory to the established customs in infanticide cases, but its authority allowed the court to proceed in confidence.

The Helmstedt recommendations retraced the rigorous choreography for the use of torture established by the *Carolina* and amplified by Benedikt Carpzov, who despite his harsh reputation for severity during witch trials was in fact concerned about the consequences of torture and fashioned a set of compromises to rationalize its use beyond the reforms of the *Carolina*.[5] The city would interrogate Grethe as before, this time using the university's questions. If she then refused to confess, she would first be "introduced" to the torturer (*Scharfrichter*), who would display the tools of his trade to "terrorize" her. If fear of physical suffering was insufficient to "draw the truth out of her," then the "painful sharp questioning" would occur, which means she would be tortured, but in a "humane fashion." This was a "first" torture, which, if it did not succeed, could be followed by a much more severe "full" torture. The truth, when it came, was to be recorded, and three days later, she would be required to repeat the confession in the absence of the torturer and his instruments. Her final statement, the *Uhrgicht*, was also to be transcribed. Potentially, then, Schmidt would face three separate but increasingly intense interrogations on the same questions over a matter of days. It is important to remember, though, that no matter how careful the choreography and how objective the language, torture was centrally about terror, fear, and pain. Carpzov recommended that it not take place just after the suspect had eaten, to avoid causing even greater physical distress. Despite the determination of legal faculties to orchestrate the events precisely, torturers and investigators had a great deal of latitude in deciding upon the degree of pain that might be acceptable or tolerable. Experience with other cases, such as witchcraft, might make magistrates and torturers more aware of the body's limits, but the experience of inflicting serious torture might just as easily harden them to the cries of pain from less resistant individuals. The effects of torture were hard to measure "objectively."

The city magistrates quickly moved to implement the decision, publishing, on November 1, a decree repeating almost verbatim the counsel given from Helmstedt, except that instead of "humane" (*menschlich*), the torture was to be "bearable" (*erträglich*).[6] It is possible that the decision to begin with a lighter torture reflects some success for the initial defense in raising doubts about the case among the Helmstedt legal faculty.[7] Grethe might have been somewhat lucky, since much greater, almost limitless torture was in fact possible, though not perhaps at this particular stage.[8] Here, then, was the critical moment when the full weight of seventeenth-century law and practice would fall on the obstinate shoulders of an adolescent woman, in an effort to crush the truth and any lingering stubbornness out of her. The testimonies, the rumors, the leads and clues of the last three months would culminate now.

At what point did the Schmidt family and Justus Oldekop learn that torture was imminent? Brunswick's decree is dated November 1. On the same day, but posted earlier in the file, "Andreas Schmidt" pleaded again with the magistrates: "It has come to my attention that our governor in Gross Schwülper, that of von Marenholz, is said to have heard some witnesses, of which we require copies for the assistance of my still guiltlessly incarcerated daughter, and I ask that these be sent to me without a fee, because I have not the means to pay for the further and detailed defense."[9] The request to waive defense fees comes as no surprise, given Andreas Schmidt's impoverished status. More interesting is the fact that the Schmidts had received no communication from prosecutors about recent events. Instead, the family apparently learned of the Hagemans' questioning from Gross

Schwülper, probably from the Hagemans themselves, though the next-door neighbors had sworn not to reveal the contents of their testimony.

This sequence may explain a curious fact in the case—one that the prosecution would later try to use against Justus Oldekop. Why had there been no contact between the Schmidts and the prosecutors in the time following the defense's first serious petition? After all, six weeks had elapsed with no record of further attempts by the family to prevent torture. The city would later accuse the advocate of negligence here. Oldekop would respond, though, that the case seemed so flimsy, so easy to resolve, that he could not imagine the magistrates would go further, until he learned otherwise.

Once again, then, the new defense had to play catch up, and in a great hurry. Certainly the city felt no need to reveal the Helmstedt decision—once a legal faculty made its recommendations, prosecutors avoided sharing any potential questions with suspects or their lawyers, in order to prevent a calculated response.[10] On the other hand, even following Oldekop's September letter, investigators had solicited two more pieces of evidence—from Gieseler and the Hagemans—about which the defense knew nothing and yet which were included in the documents sent to Helmstedt. For the Schmidts, the timing was very difficult indeed. Even if the prosecutors agreed to provide the Hageman testimony, they were already setting in motion a series of potentially decisive interviews, if necessary, using torture. In fact, this stage of the interrogation process began the day following the city's notification of its intentions, November 2.

ALTSTADT FRONEREY

The interrogations that began before noon on November 2 and continued in various forms until November 8 covered the same questions from Helmstedt over and over again. This stage of the interrogation as recorded in the records may seem repetitive, but this was part of the point. Prosecutors wanted to confront Grethe with a consistent, plausible narrative in order to wear down her resistance to the "truth." The constant repetition also schooled Schmidt in the truth as the prosecution understood it.

The progressive intensification of Grethe's questioning is evident from the venues where it occurred over the next few days. The judicial personnel (Vellhagen, Theune, Von Horn, Gärtner, and Pilgram) gathered first at the *Fronerey* where Grethe was held. Neither her defenders nor anyone close to her would be admitted to any interrogation, even during torture—perhaps especially during torture. Alone again, Grethe responded. Asked *whether she had not known she was pregnant by Andreas Möller*, Grethe answered no, only that, as she had admitted earlier, after having sex with Möller the one time she did not have her period as often as before. Frau Möller [Margarethe Hafferland] spoke to her around the New Year, saying she knew that she [Grethe] was pregnant. Still, *did she [Grethe] not intend to kill the child when it came into the world?* No, Grethe insisted that she knew nothing of any child. All she knew was that Hafferland had accused her of being pregnant because she was not having her period. To each of the next questions, Schmidt consistently denied having borne a baby. Question eight prompted her longest response: *where,* the magistrates asked, *had she buried and left the child after the killing, whether in or out of the womb* (i.e., whether she aborted it or murdered it afterwards)? Grethe responded that "she has had no child, therefore she also has killed no child, what she has already admitted, that [what] issued from her in Heinrich Lüdden's house on the Wenden Graben, was, looking at it, no child, but to tell in all honesty, a reddish filthy object, like a toe, about two fingers long, which she washed out with her shirt in the puddle in the ditch in front of Lüdden's door, at about four o'clock in the afternoon."[11]

Grethe's denials were no more persuasive to the authorities in November than they had been in August. Dissatisfied, the interrogators confronted her again on the afternoon of November 2, still at the *Fronerey.* In addition to the judicial officers another person now appeared: Claus Frölich, Brunswick's official executioner and torturer. Frölich was an old hand at torture—he had been on the job since 1645. His presence signaled a new, more ominous turn in the interrogation. Despite repeated warnings and opportunities, the authorities stated, Grethe had refused to confess the truth, and so, wrote the scribe, "in order to terrify [her] they introduced her to the torturer and his tools of pain, and assured her [the prosecutors] truly intended to use them on her, they made earnest threats and preparations, and under these [threats] they once again questioned her diligently and thoroughly."[12] As they proceeded, the interrogators had in their hands her answers from the morning session.

So the questioning began again, and again Grethe disavowed any knowledge of a pregnancy and denied as well that she had hidden her relations with Andreas Möller from his stepmother. She acknowledged that the Möller widow believed her to be pregnant but only because Grethe's period did not come as normal. Here the questioners paused and placed in front of her the bindings and thumbscrews to be used for torture, confronting her with her own testimony, her denial that what issued from her (in the Lüdden house) was "in the form of a child." Still she persisted in her denials, and the interrogators assured her that they were not satisfied and urged her on to the truth. And it was here in the *Fronerey,* facing the implacable *Justizherren* and the looming figure of the torturer, that Grethe "finally admitted that the [material] that came out of her in bed at the Lüdden house . . . two or three days after the New Year in 1661 after ten in the evening, which she had already felt happening at six o'clock, was not a "piece of filth as she recounted earlier." Instead, it was "a little piece of flesh and bone, with little hands and feet as well as a little head, though she could not tell if it was male or female, without life, as soon as it came from her, because there was no trace of life to be found in it, she left it lying in her shirt in bed until the next afternoon." Then, at four o'clock, she gathered the shirt up with some clothes she wanted to wash, took it to the ditch near the Lüdden-Dedekind house, and shook out her bundle. The little mass of flesh sank straight off, and, as the water grew higher, drifted away.[13]

The interrogators were determined to be precise, asking *whether this stuff that came from her was in the form of a child and had previously moved inside her.* Grethe answered that "some eight days prior, before it came out of her, something moved in her body a little . . . what it was and whether it was the stuff that came out of her later, she did not know." Asked further, *whether she did not consider the stuff that came out of her to be a child, and how it came to its death,* she replied, "Yes, she considered it to be a child, how it came die, though, of that she knew no reason, except that right after it moved, she had to carry two—more like three—large measures (*Himten*—a total, it seems, of about 40 kilograms) of flour from the granary mill to the Lüdden house." The implication here was that a particularly hard physical task had induced a miscarriage. Still, Grethe denied that she ever intended to kill a child or had in fact done it any harm.[14]

Shifting again from the scripted questions, the prosecutors asked, *if she laid no hand on the child and killed it, perhaps she earlier took some kind of drink* (i.e., an abortifacient)? Interrogators clearly remained curious about the purpose of Grethe's mother's alleged visit to the *Fränkische Frau*. Grethe, though, testified that she had "laid no hand on the child, except that as it came to the world, she cut the umbilical cord with a pair of scissors lying on a chest near her bed, and wrapped it with a towel so the bed would not be soiled, and tossed it in the water." As to the drink, "she took no drink, but otherwise she knew well, that the old Garsen woman [Margarethe Engelken] had advised her mother (as she later heard from her mother) that she should take a drink, to what end Grethe had no idea, but that it had not happened."[15] This was an interesting revelation—the suggestion that the Schmidts look for a purgative came from the sick old woman who so hated "godless ways." Grethe repeated that she had killed no child and referred only to what she had testified earlier. No one gave her any help, but, as she was carrying grain from the mill, she learned from another servant out of Gross Schwülper how to remove the umbilical cord.[16]

Still unconvinced, the interrogators were aware that they had somehow broken through. Now was the time to increase the pressure, as Grethe had "earnestly set herself to talk." As if on cue, the torturer closed in on her "as though he really wanted to seize her."[17] Still she refused to confess anything more, pleading instead, "even if she must die for it, the infant came out already dead into the world."[18] She acknowledged she "should have reported this to the government, as she understands now, she would certainly have summoned Lüdden's wife. God knows the truth, she has no guilt in this."[19]

In this interrogation, the power of deliberate terror becomes clear. Despite her last denial, Grethe's defiance wilted under the heat of intimidation and threat of bodily harm. Fear of pain, it seems, worked wonders, and the young woman had now acknowledged her pregnancy, the birth (or miscarriage), a place, and a time. She continued to deny a live birth and any responsibility for killing the child, but that was all.[20] Just a little more pressure might have brought forth the needed confession, but the city pressed her no further and ended the session. Unfortunately for Grethe Schmidt, the *Justizherren*, dissatisfied with the results so far, had run out of patience and decided to take the next step.

Before turning to that event, though, it is well to consider not just Grethe's answers but the actions that prompted her response. As noted, the imperial law provided grounds for using terror as a tool to induce confessions. Historians have noted the strict controls that the *Carolina* placed on the use of torture—it was no arbitrary affair carried out by bloodthirsty brutes. It is also true that the use of torture was declining in some places by the last half of the seventeenth century, and that numerous categories of individuals were exempt from it anyway.[21] The Schmidt case, though, dramatically shows what "visual and verbal terror" could entail. Here at least it was not merely a display of instruments, the uses of which were left to the suspect's imagination. The torturer Frölich did not stand stolidly by but showed the prisoner what would happen should she not answer "truthfully." And later in the interrogation, he made his presence known, menacing Grethe and even acting as though he was determined to seize her right then. No doubt this pantomime conveyed the impression that he relished the chance to wring the truth out of her.

It is not difficult to imagine, therefore, that Oldekop's melodramatic description of this session, clearly embellished for shock value, may indeed have some truth to it, despite serious inaccuracies, including his use of a stock name for the torture, "Meister Hans." The torturer's determination to make a convincing display of his talents and zeal for the job was all too real. It is interesting to note that the city's own later account of the case leaves out this interrogation entirely, mentioning only that Grethe had

been "presented with the torturer and his painful instruments" and yet refused to confess that she had borne a living child. After that, "she was given
over to the torturer."[22] Another possibility must be considered as well. By
emphasizing the threat to come, the court officers were seriously hoping to
induce a confession without going to full torture. The more frightening the
terror, the less likely it would be to have to carry it out. The interposition
of various grades of threat short of torture itself gave the suspect multiple
opportunities to tell the truth before the thumbscrews were applied, and
then later the rack or strappado.

DUNGEON OF THE ALTSTADT RATHAUS, NOVEMBER 5, 1661

The choreography of terror and torture led Schmidt and the court officers
from the *Fronerey* around the corner to Frölich's workshop with its dedicated
devices, and she was "given over to his hands."[23] The same questions were
presented, and Grethe at first responded as she had at the end of the previous
session that she did indeed know she was pregnant, even before Gottfried
Möller's wife spoke to her: "her clothes became too small and she no longer
was having her period as before." She hid this fact because she was "ashamed
. . . and did not dare say how things were with her." To question three, though,
*whether she did not have the intention to kill the infant when it came into
the world*, "No, firmly," was her persistent answer. At this point, the torturer
took the bindings and "bound her hands together in front of her. Even after
repeated questions, however, she stood by her denial of this article."[24] It is
not clear from this account whether Schmidt was stripped before the torture,
which was known to happen as standard practice elsewhere.[25] No mention of
it appears in the Schmidt case.

The interrogators then moved on to question four, *whether or not she
had brought a living child into the world*. She repeated that the child did not
come into the world alive:

> it was already dead when it came from her into the world, although it had
> moved in her eight days and then one day before it came to the world, and
> indeed on the right side of her body at eleven o'clock of the very night, about
> three quarters of an hour before it came to the world, and she had already
> begun to have pains, it moved a little in the midst of her body, and even as
> it was being born into the world it moved a little bit, and then it had for a
> quarter hour resisted before it came out of the womb and into the world, and
> then *she took the child with both hands first by its legs and then by its body and
> pulled it out of her* [italics mine]. She took it to the window and looked at it
> in the moonlight but found that it was not alive—how it came to its death

she did not know. Then, as she felt that that the child was now out of her and there was no life in it, she laid it down for a while with her in the bed, on her right side. Soon she got up and inspected it in the moonlight through a hole in the wall, but there was no life to be found in it.[26]

Unpersuaded even by this detailed account, the interrogators now began to "speak earnestly" to the bound woman. The torturer prepared to apply the thumbscrews (the "humane" torture recommended by the faculty of Helmstedt). At this dangerous point, Grethe's words flowed more freely:

the child, as it had come into the world, still moved a little and (lying between her legs) whined a little, two or three times, but she was so thoroughly exhausted that she could not move any more. A little bit later she turned over and wanted to see the child, she realized that her right leg was lying over the child's face and immediately pulled her leg back, but she realized that the child was dead. It had lived for a quarter hour, and she did not know that her leg was lying over the child's face.[27]

The magistrates admonished her again and again. It was the looming torturer, though, who tipped the scales. Just as the thumbscrews were about to be applied, Grethe confessed:

that she killed the child with her leg in the manner reported. And then the thoughts came to her, how the child had been born living into the world. She brought it around to the moonlight in the opening as she wanted to see if it was living still. If it was still living, she would not have wanted to kill it, and it had been a boy, which the next morning, in front of Heinrich Lüdden's door in the Wenden Canal, she tossed into the water, so that it would float away, as the water had gotten high.[28]

After these moments of pain, dread, and revelation, the interrogation proceeded smoothly to its end. *Where did this happen?* "In Heinrich Lüdden's house, in her bed in front of her bread-giver's [employer's] bedroom, at night around eleven o'clock." *Hadn't the child cried or made some sound?* "It whined, or meowed, like a kitten." *Hadn't she killed the child or otherwise harmed it so that it could not live, and how had she done so?* "She had, out of premeditation [*aus Vorsatz*], intentionally laid her right leg on its mouth, so that it would die and perish." *And where had she left and buried it after the killing?* "She left the dead child lying in bed until the following day, then toward evening around four o'clock, she took it and threw it in the canal in front of her master's door. All the while her mistress sat in the room and sewed." *Who had helped her?* "No one helped her, she did all this on her own." And the interrogation concluded with a final, unscripted question: *Was she not sorry that she had, with premeditation, killed her own child?*

"Yes, she is sorry."[29]

Altstadt Fronerey, November 8, 1661

Following the excruciating events in the Brunswick dungeon, the court gathered yet again, this time removed from the torture chamber. As required by law, three days elapsed so that Grethe Schmidt's final statement would be "free-willed and uncoerced." The statement itself, though, shows either that she had had some "help" shaping her story in the intervening days or, possibly, that the scribe was filling in details as he went along. The confession that emerged fit neatly, not only into the prosecution narrative but into the interpretive framework of the *Carolina*. There is no evidence to indicate that her family had been in contact with her, nor is it clear that they were aware of her ordeal.

This session ran smoothly, and the investigators scrupulously noted that her confession emerged "through torture that was initiated but not carried out, except for the bindings with which she was at first—though mildly—seized, but which were soon again released."[30] By the city's lights, it had acted in an appropriately "humane" fashion, as prescribed by law and by the faculty at Helmstedt. Precision about such details mattered in considering just how sincere the confession was, establishing a ratio between dread and pain on the one hand and truth on the other.[31] Grethe's good fortune in being sentenced to a "humane" torture now might have worked against her interests, since it had taken relatively little in the way of pain to squeeze the truth out of her.

Accordingly, Grethe now again confessed:

> three days after the New Year of 1661, in Heinrich Lüdden's house, on the Wenden Graben, at night around eleven o'clock, [she] bore in her bed in front of her housemasters' bedroom a living child which, when it was already brought in to the world, yet a few times whined, or meowed like a kitten, and then to the same [she] laid her right leg over its face on its mouth in order to smother it.[32]

This is the confession she reaffirmed on November 8, when she reiterated that "she, with premeditation, pressed the child with her right leg and killed it."[33]

Grethe once again had to answer the nine Helmstedt University questions, which now could provide the substance of a formal confession. She affirmed that she knew she was pregnant but had not wanted to admit it out of shame, and that at first she had no intention of killing the child, "but then a half hour before the child came into the world, it came into her mind to kill the child."[34] The child, she acknowledged, had lived after its birth. All of this happened three days before New Year's ("and not three days after, she now correctly remembered")[35] in Heinrich Lüdden's house before midnight, and "although the moon was not so bright, it shone enough so that she could see the child in the opening and realize that it was a boy."[36] And yes, it had grunted a little and meowed like a cat, and then she took her right leg, "indeed the upper part [thigh] at the thicker flesh," laid it over the child's mouth, "and pressed on it so that it should die and did die."[37] To be exactly sure, interrogators asked whether she placed her right leg over the baby's face *intentionally, so that it would die*. Yes, she answered, "because she very much wanted to remain a maiden, and it [the truth] would not come out."[38] Afterward, she let the body lie on her bed until the next day around four in the afternoon, when she bundled it in a clean towel, about half a table in size, and fastened it with a linen ribbon. Then she threw it into the water, on the left side of the pool so that it would sink and float away with the current of the water. As to whether someone had helped or advised her in the matter, she stated that she "had done all of this alone."[39]

The magistrates still had other questions to resolve some puzzles and fill out the picture. *Why had Frau Lüdden not noticed some trace of blood fallen to the floor?* "She took a towel and wrapped it around her body, and the following day, just as she had thrown the child into the canal the day before, she now also threw the towel in the canal so that it would float away."[40] *Had she not soiled the bed where the child was born?* Grethe replied that she had laid the towel on the bed beneath her, but nevertheless it did get a little soiled, "so she washed and cleaned it again and placed the sheet on the floor so that it would dry, but on the third day she placed it back on the bed."

These questions about material details, though, were not all the investigators had on their minds. Perhaps out of personal puzzlement, but more likely because they now had to figure out what to do with this confessed murderess, the interrogators asked two more questions: *on the night after the birth, had she slept in the same bed again, and did she feel no sense of dread because she had killed the child?* "It did not bring her dread, but instead she lay on the bed and cried, for she was very sorry that she had killed her child."[41]

With these words, the confession came to an end. Painful and remorseful though it appears, Grethe Schmidt's statement also fit the narrative which the law, the prosecution, and the university all shaped. Schmidt, for example, now offered as motive the desire to be considered a virgin (*Jungfer*)—just as the *Carolina* expected of such women. Even the language of her confession follows the presumed model of an infanticide. And now, she had confessed that she intended beforehand to kill the child, that it was no spontaneous action. This also conformed to the stipulation of the law, which assumed not just intention but premeditation. There was no temporary insanity, no spur of the moment reaction, only cold-blooded planning. And, of course, guilt in a Christian land required not only a confession but regret. The end of the criminal process was not simply punishment but the miscreant's recognition of guilt and sorrow for it.

Grethe's responses were clearly not solely of her own devising. Her confession was a formal matter, and it is likely that, after her ordeal, the prosecutors gave her a sense of what they now expected. In the days following her breakdown in the dungeon, Grethe was alone and entirely at the mercy of the jailer and the *Justizherren*. As Christian men they may also have hoped that Grethe's compliance and repentance would save her soul, if not her body. Once again, there is no trace in this evidence of any attempted contact—from either side—with her family or lawyer.

As to the rest of the confession, Schmidt filled out the details of the account, telling how she carried out the deed, how she inspected the child in the moonlight, where she tossed the baby, even how she hid the whole episode from her employers. The confessed method of murder was in line with what many women convicted of the crime admitted—smothering (or perhaps drowning) the infant rather than beating it (as was the case a century later with Susanna Margarethe Brandt in Frankfurt). According to Otto Ulbricht, psychologically women might have used this means of murder as a way of denying to themselves that they had done violence to their offspring.[42] Grethe told a sad and macabre tale to the prosecutors, and they now had a murderess and a full admission of guilt. At this point, the story should have ended, with Schmidt left to her punishment. There were, however, some problems. Schmidt's confession of concealment driven by her desire to be considered a maiden, for example, perfectly fit with Article 35 of the *Carolina*, but it flatly contradicted her previous statements as well as her earlier behavior in the city. Even her accusers acknowledged that she had neither hidden nor denied her sexual misconduct. And there was the puzzling and consistent use in the transcription of the phrase *mit Vorsatz* or *aus Vorsatz*, meaning "with intention" or "out of premeditation," terms familiar to a scribe and a prosecutor but undoubtedly less expected from an illiterate farm girl. Had she actually used the phrases or was she simply affirming the prosecutors' questions, which the scribe then summarized?

Finally, and most important, there were the dramatic details about the birth, death, and disposal of the infant's body. The story posed a dilemma: if Schmidt's confession was true, then all the testimony given by neighbors, by fellow servants, by employers, and by expert midwives, was false. If the earlier evidence was correct, then Grethe Schmidt could not have killed a newborn in Anna Dedekind's house in Brunswick three days after New Year 1661. The prosecutors may have been pleased with the success of their efforts, but they were dead wrong.

Part Two

Justus

Frontispiece for Justus Oldekop's *Contra Carpzov*. Herzog August Bibliothek Wolfenbüttel: M: Rm 121

10

Case for a Defense

On November 8, Grethe Schmidt repeated her confession in the Altstadt *Fronerey*. The court officers might have thought their work was nearly done. So the letter that arrived four days later on November 12 may have seemed mostly a formality. Signed by Andreas Schmidt, the letter pleaded, "According to God's word and all spiritual and worldly laws" that before someone was "damned," Grethe's defense must be heard and she must have access to an advocate with whom she could confer alone. Further, the judge or the government had the duty to pay all the expenses relevant to a defense. Because of Grethe's "notorious" poverty, her parents unable even "to buy a pair of shoes," and her wider family burdened with children, the city of Brunswick should appoint, at its own expense, a learned advocate to represent her. Finally, the city should provide copies of all materials gathered in the case until now, again without requiring any fee.[1]

The Right to a Defense

Once again, the Schmidts asserted a legal right to defend Grethe, this time more aggressively in the aftermath of her interrogation under threat of torture. Because of their dire poverty, the family petitioned for a learned advocate to be paid for out of the city's treasury. The advocate needed access to Grethe and the opportunity to speak with her alone and in private. And the advocate needed all records through the torture and final confession. The Schmidts' claim not only to a defense but to the particulars—the right to confer in private and to view all evidence, at the public expense if necessary—should not be taken for granted in the seventeenth-century context and requires some explanation. For Grethe, her defender, and the prosecution, the nature and extent of that right would eventually come to dominate the proceedings.

The criminal system was in flux during the sixteenth and seventeenth centuries, especially in German-speaking lands, where the Holy Roman

Empire's introduction of Roman law on top of more customary Teutonic codes and practices produced great friction. At the same time, German courts were in transition from "accusatory" to "inquisitorial" practice—that is, from a system that began criminal proceedings on the basis of one individual's accusation against another (as in civil practice) to one in which courts undertook investigations and prosecutions on their own initiative. This compounded the confusion over how the criminal process ought to run.

Nowhere was this uncertainty more evident than in the discussion over criminal defense, its conduct, and the personnel who could be involved.[2] With the advent of inquisitorial process, the state's judges theoretically were themselves responsible for investigating and discovering the truth.[3] The suspect now became an object of the state's attention rather than an agent in the proceedings, as had been the case in the accusatorial process. The scope and operations of any defense pursued by the suspect herself shrank accordingly, in theory to be compensated by the active work of the court itself on her behalf. Even granting the possibility of a defendant's representative, though, what was he to do?

Generally speaking, representation came through two kinds of legal experts. In court itself, a procurator handled the vocal arguments and proceedings for the defense, for which his training was largely practical in nature. Written legal arguments, which were considered far more important and decisive, were the responsibility of an advocate, though, a learned lawyer with an extensive university education. Given their higher educational demands and wider learning, advocates were generally of a higher social class than procurators. Indeed, during the seventeenth century, it appears, advocates increasingly usurped the lesser duties of the procurator and assumed a combined role, for practical and economic reasons.[4]

Even so, judges did not automatically or universally recognize the role of the advocate—or of the defense itself, for that matter. Once again, the promulgation of the *Carolina* in 1532 proved to be a landmark moment. For all the attention to torture and executions recommended in the *Carolina*, the law code in fact contained a number of quite modern features. Two separate statutes asserted a basic right to criminal defense. According to Article 47, if a suspect should claim innocence, then "the judge should, at the expense of the accused or his family, diligently investigate, or if, at the discretion of the judge, the accused or his friends want to call witnesses . . . such a request should not be rejected without good grounds."[5] Article 73 referred to situations in which both accused and accuser assembled and reviewed evidence and witnesses. Perhaps the most revolutionary feature of the *Carolina* stipulated that all parties to a criminal accusation had the right to inspect and question the prosecution's evidence.[6]

The extension and interpretation of that right might vary, though, depending on how the case was introduced. In the case of a private accusation, commentators gave wider latitude to constructing a defense, including the choice of a defense lawyer or advocate and greater access to the records of testimony.[7] Because such a process appeared more a private matter between individual parties than an official investigation under the power of the state, the court did not necessarily view its own prestige and authority at stake. Inquisitorial process, though, was a different matter.

Given the central role of the judge in inquisitorial process, initiating a defense lay more in his hands than in the defendant's. In theory, the defendant had only to deny her guilt, at which point the judge was required to investigate her claims.[8] This could cut both ways in practice: if the defendant (or others on her behalf) did not plead her innocence, a literal-minded judge might overlook the possibility of a defense entirely.[9] Increasingly, though, commentators on the *Carolina* sought to establish the right of a defense and the court's responsibility for ensuring that one was provided. The eminent Saxon jurist Benedikt Carpzov grounded the natural right to a defense in the Bible, noting that before God expelled Adam and Eve from paradise, Adam was given the chance to explain himself. The Schmidt petition began with just such a claim to divine sanction. Both the *Carolina* and commentators permitted "parents and closely related friends" to act on the accused's behalf, language echoed in the Schmidts' reference to Grethe's "closest relatives and blood friends."[10] To Carpzov this was especially necessary when the defendant was an "innocent, simple, and incompetent person,"[11] language the Schmidts employed in justifying their intervention for Grethe. Indeed, depending on circumstances, Carpzov argued, the judges themselves were obliged to work on behalf of a defendant who protested her innocence.[12] Most commentators agreed that poverty should not hinder a defense—if necessary, the state must bear the cost.[13]

According to early modern commentators, no defense procurator or advocate could attend the initial interrogations of the suspect.[14] But from the moment charges were formulated until the final confession was certified in court, the accused could conduct a defense, at any point and no matter how great the alleged crime. Even if a first attempt at exculpation failed, new evidence and new witnesses might still be heard a second or a third time.[15]

The claims made by Carpzov in favor of the defense belie his reputation as a ruthless hunter of witches. In fact, Carpzov was a champion of clarifying and streamlining legal process. His discussion of torture, along with his insistence on sending the materials out to a faculty for review, suggest concerns over the justice of the system and the possibility for abuse.[16] In practice, of course, these lofty notions worked out imperfectly.[17] In prosecuting witches, for example, judges frequently overlooked or refused recourse to any kind of defense.[18] Carpzov's ringing endorsement of a natural right to a defense, based ultimately in the Bible, wrestled with the everyday facts of criminal law and the conviction, deeply grounded in Lutheran belief, that God had ordained the magistrate to uncover and punish evildoers. Practical matters affected criminal investigations at every turn. Inquisitions happened in the pressured aftermath of serious misdeeds. By the time the inquisitors arrested a suspect, they were confident of the "truth" and practically concerned, like prosecutors everywhere and always, with getting a conviction, which in the seventeenth century required a confession.[19] It is not clear that prosecutors viewed exculpatory information as anything more than an obstacle. In the absence of any capacity on the part of the accused to insist on the kinds of legal rights Carpzov had begun to adumbrate, a true defense was likely to be minimal or non-existent.

Seventeenth-century jurists also shackled the defense at every turn. The tendency of inquisitorial process to concentrate all the power in the hands of the judges ought to have impressed upon them the responsibility of attending to the suspect's possible innocence. Instead, it could lead in practice to the defendant's complete loss of rights.[20] A presiding judge was allowed to undertake the defense duties himself, thereby excluding all outside counsel. Carpzov's treatise on Saxon law suggests that, in particularly atrocious and notorious crimes, the judge should limit the suspect's access to a lawyer. What would be the point other than to impede justice? In modern Anglo-American jurisprudence, the claim is astonishing, but much less so when one remembers that early modern law was about the truth rather than balancing claims—to Carpzov a defense was less a fundamental right than a means to uncover the truth.[21] Procedural restraints abounded in the legal commentary. The defense had to wait until after the suspect had been interrogated and formally charged in order to prevent her from knowing in advance what questions would be asked and how to answer them.[22] It also raised questions about precisely when charges had to be formulated and what kind of latitude the prosecution had beforehand. These prosecutorial options cut back severely on the time available for gathering exculpatory evidence, even though a successful defense demanded that the advocate have access to the records as early in the process as possible.[23] As the first month of the Schmidt investigation demonstrates, exclusive control over the evidence allowed prosecutors to shape the contours of a case entirely on their own terms. By the time Grethe's family formally entered the process, the magistrates had already interviewed Anna Dedekind, Grethe herself, Margarethe Hafferland, Margarethe Engelken, and others twice, conducted the midwives' examination, and digested its results. The result was a formidable narrative tailored by and for the prosecution.

As finders of fact, responsible for discovering—and defending—the truth, the inquisitorial courts of the Holy Roman Empire carried a different goal and burden than "adversarial" systems developing in England or even the accusatorial process that was in the process of being superseded. One of the issues that becomes clear in the Schmidt case is the conflict between a world in which judgment resided securely in a single institution, the authority of which depended on its ability to see the truth correctly, and the real world in which truth was hard to know with any certainty and yet vehemently contested by opposing parties fierce in their convictions. The institutions of justice resisted a full defense in part because to welcome conflict from the outside meant accepting knowledge as fragmented and partial. The *Carolina* and its commentators—who had sure ideas on how inquisitions were to begin, interrogations were to be made, and tortures were to be conducted—were much more muddled, and divided, when thinking of how, when, and even whether an accused person should establish his or her innocence, and who should be in charge.

As the *Carolina* decreed, the defendant and her advocate were permitted to know the names of witnesses testifying against them and to inspect and respond to the evidence assembled.[24] Some historians see this possibility of peeking behind the curtain and viewing the evidence as the fundamental component of the right to a defense.[25] The substance of this right, though, remained controversial in the seventeenth century. Was the defense at every turn to be given copies of all the evidence and testimony compiled by the prosecution, as assumed under Roman law? Or should that access be more restricted?[26] Once again, in the accusatorial process the rights of the defendant to access evidence and testimony were wider than in inquisitorial procedure.[27] Carpzov relied on the *Police Code of Electoral Saxony* (*Churfürstliche Sächsische Policeyordnung*) of 1612, which referred to "the suspect and his advocate . . . examining the inquisitorial acts and testimony of witnesses set before them in the presence of the judicial personnel."[28] This Saxon custom was preferable, Carpzov explained, because copying the acts "takes up time, needlessly drawing out and scattering the inquisition process, which should be fast and expeditious."[29] Carpzov's advice to move with "all deliberate speed" would force an advocate to review materials quite hastily, relying in the end only on notes and memory.

Carpzov's opinion that evidence only be viewed in the presence of court personnel potentially allowed prosecutors to try to influence or hamper the defense's review. They would also be privy to conversations between advocate and client while examining the records, effectively crippling any "defense strategy." Others extended the requirement to all meetings between suspect and lawyer.[30] Restrictions concerning the *Akteneinsicht* (inspection of the records) display all the tensions between the theoretical right to a defense and its actual practice. What seems obvious today may only have been implicit in the seventeenth century, turned into a reality by ambitious lawyers seeking to extend the domain of their craft. The *Carolina* did not become a "modern" law code on its own.

What emerges from influential legal commentaries and statutes is a deep-seated suspicion concerning defense lawyers and their motives.[31] The magistrates conducting a special inquisition might consider the defense a nuisance or a hindrance, even if they grudgingly permitted one. Even worse, according to contemporary critics, the advocate fed upon his ability to manipulate and stall proceedings. Advocates of the seventeenth century (lawyers, after all) were renowned for obfuscating the truth and confounding the plain sense of the law. They filed frivolous briefs that served no purpose other than to fill up more paper (and therefore create more expense for any court that agreed to provide copies), extend the process indefinitely, and line their pockets at the expense of defendants and prosecutors alike. This was even more infuriating in the case of a poor defendant whose court costs must be borne by the government. Commentators sought to curb these frivolous antics. Brunnemann's *Guide to Criminal Practice* firmly states that the judge was not required to go along with the defendant's choice of defender: it was within the judge's discretion to appoint an advocate.[32] As noted above, Carpzov gave the judge the option to exclude an advocate entirely in especially serious cases. In fact, the legal treatises of the age are replete with exasperated complaints about grasping lawyers and proposals to forestall their greedy ways.[33]

The subject of the defense, its possibilities and limitations, raises another significant question in early modern criminal courts—at the end of the process, with the confession recorded and the defendant sentenced, was there any recourse left for the accused? Was it possible to appeal a criminal verdict? Like the right to a defense itself, the right to appeal was drastically limited. Carpzov conceded the right of an appeal in Roman law but argued that it was not applicable to German practice.[34] The fact that the *Carolina* and the courts relied so heavily on the suspect's own confession meant that, whatever problems arose during the process, the defendant herself had acknowledged the deed, lending an air of certainty to cases.[35] Even in civil cases, many cities and territories had wrested from the Holy Roman Empire the privilege of not allowing an appeal beyond the city's or territories' jurisdiction. The city of Brunswick, for example, had long cherished its "right of no appeal," meaning that only in very limited situations—civil rather than criminal—could a plaintiff appeal beyond the magistracy to the *Hofgericht* (the central ducal court) in Wolfenbüttel. The city's right to administer its own courts and justice was a fundamental element in the edifice of autonomy that the city fathers had labored so long to build and maintain.

There was, however, one particular avenue for a convicted defendant to pursue beyond the local criminal court. The Imperial Chamber Court (*Reichskammergericht*), roughly a kind of empire-wide supreme court, permitted in its constitution of 1555 an appeal in particular situations that offended "natural reason and equity." Chief among these offenses was the complete absence of a defense of any sort on the part of the court.[36] Should this occur, then even a court's "privilege" not to permit an appeal beyond its jurisdiction would not stand. Such cases were rare, in part because to mount an appeal an individual would need financial resources unavailable to most poor criminals.[37]

ADVOCATES FOR THE DEFENSE

Numerous voices in the mid-seventeenth century objected on both practical and legal grounds to the constraints that jurists placed on advocates. The cries grew especially insistent in the wake of witchcraft trials, the methods of which caused great unease. These voices hoped to legitimize the defense's role in a system that tilted heavily toward the prosecution, held defense lawyers in low regard, and did not always equate the protection of the innocent with the need for outside representation.[38]

In 1659, the Hildesheim lawyer and legal scholar Justus Oldekop produced two treatises arguing against the positions of Benedikt Carpzov The first, *De Appellatione in Causis Criminalibus*, rejected Carpzov's position on criminal appeals. Oldekop had long argued for the possibility of appeal, particularly in cases of witchcraft, but he applied the same principle to all serious criminal matters.[39] The second treatise, *Decades tres Quaestionum ad processum Criminalem necessarium*, struck at the heart of Carpzov's interpretation of procedure right from the beginning—the opening question asked whether the defense in a criminal case must be given copies of the evidence against the suspect. Carpzov, as noted above, saw no such obligation, basing his conclusions on "Saxon custom." For Oldekop, though, the suspect's and his defender's access to the records was a matter of right based not only on Saxon custom (specifically rejecting Carpzov's contention) but also on Roman law generally, which Oldekop's treatise cited at length.[40] It was also a practical necessity born of common sense—how could the suspect establish her innocence without recourse to the evidence being used against her?

Even where a flagrant crime seemed to leave no doubt about the suspect's guilt, Oldekop upheld the right to a full and unfettered defense—for the hidden or special circumstances of a seemingly obvious crime might alter an individual's guilt or mitigate the kind of punishment meted out. To Oldekop, Carpzov's idea of denying a full defense in serious crimes was not only unjust but simply illogical—it was precisely in prosecuting the most heinous offenses that a defendant was most exposed, and in which the consequences would be the most grave. To employ a medical metaphor, it was the sickest patients who stood most in need of a doctor.

Justus Oldekop's work reflects an understanding of criminal defense that was strikingly expansive in the German juristic world of the mid-seventeenth century. Above all else, Oldekop aggressively championed the role of the advocate as integral to the criminal process rather than as a necessary evil to be watched over at every turn. His support may have derived, of course, from the fact that he was himself a professional lawyer making a living from just those practices that so exasperated judges and jurists like Carpzov. Yet his own life suggests that long-standing principle played a great role in his thinking.[41] As early as 1633, Oldekop disputed the methods employed in witchcraft prosecutions and other criminal matters in his *Cautelarum criminalium*, published only two years after Friedrich Spee's *Cautio Criminalis*—the most famous attack on the witch prosecutions of the sixteenth and seventeenth centuries. For Oldekop, the inquisitorial practices that corrupted the courts during witch hunts had the potential to affect the conduct of other kinds of criminal cases as well: prosecutions in the absence of a corpus delicti might lead to torture without specific grounds and indiscriminate incarceration and might limit the suspect's defense to the advice of the ruling judges rather than an independent advocate. Throughout his professional life, Oldekop demanded that the criminal process be "transparent" (using modern language) to the suspect; the defendant should have full knowledge of the evidence, the witnesses, and the charges against him or her as well as the right to respond. Even more, Justus Oldekop consistently opposed the easy use of torture and of physical punishment generally—he was well aware that "painful questions" could extract confessions even from the innocent. Torture was too hard for suspects to endure, but too tempting for inquisitors to resist.

Oldekop's first book, the *Cautelarum criminalium*, was printed in Brunswick, and the city is, in fact, not far from the places where Oldekop spent much of his life. A doctor of laws by training, Oldekop had been a diplomat and counselor, first in Hildesheim, where he was born in 1597;

then in Hannover, at that time still a modest city in the Lüneburg section of the Duchy of Brunswick-Lüneburg; and finally in Halberstadt, east
of Brunswick. During the Thirty Years War, the conquest of Hildesheim
by imperial troops had brought Oldekop into contact with powerful
men such as the famous general Tilly and had forced Oldekop, a devout
Protestant, to flee the wrath of Catholic conquerors in 1635. He therefore
knew war and exile well. Controversy too was a familiar theme in his life.
From 1650 to 1659, he was himself a syndic in the city of Halberstadt. In
1660, at the age of sixty-three, he moved with his family from Halberstadt
to Brunswick. Like Grethe Schmidt, he was an outsider in Brunswick, an
alien. Unlike Grethe Schmidt, whose great hope at the beginning of her life
was to eke out a living and establish a basis for a relatively secure existence,
Oldekop's goal near the end of his life was to capitalize on the possibilities
for a learned man in a vibrant city and to leave an indelible mark on the
public and intellectual life of his age.

It is, however, striking that in the very year Oldekop's two treatises appeared (under the title *Contra Carpzovium* in 1659, in Bremen), Grethe
Schmidt went to work for Margarethe Hafferland, and that in 1660,
Oldekop himself was living in Brunswick. All of this was coincidence, as
was the fact that, in 1661, Grethe Schmidt would need a lawyer. That her
advocate would be Justus Oldekop, though, seems more like destiny. Her
case involved all the problems and procedures over which Oldekop had
struggled passionately throughout his life. The Schmidt case would allow
Oldekop not only to test his own theories but also to push the limits of
what a defense lawyer could do. Oldekop's offhand remarks about how he
came to be involved in the case—an impoverished family in tears seeking
assistance for their daughter—should be taken with a grain of salt. For
Grethe Schmidt, the issue was her very life. For Justus Oldekop, it was the
chance of a lifetime.

Setting the Stage

The *Obergericht* answered the Schmidts' request on November 13. The
magistrates responded carefully: "because of the prisoner's alleged poverty,
a regular advocate from the *Fiskal* will be appointed for her defense, according to proper procedure, with a hearing to be scheduled after a term
of fourteen days." To this end the advocate was to "inspect the acts." The
Council also directed the *Justizherren* to visit Anna Dedekind as soon as
possible in order to determine whether she had really not noticed any sign
of childbirth in the captive or the home. Dedekind's affirmative testimony
could powerfully corroborate Schmidt's confession and diminish any pro-

spective defense. It is possible, though, that the prosecution had already become uncertain about the validity of Grethe's admission.[42]

In the prisoner's plea and the council's response, the tensions over the meaning and extent of the right to a defense are plain to see. The city agreed to pick up the cost for defending the impoverished girl from Gross Schwülper. Compared to the family's request, however, the council's offer fell short—no copies of the records were to be provided, but the court's representative would inspect them on Grethe's behalf. A strict time limit would be placed on the defense, and the response ignores the request for a chance to confer in private. Most important, though, the city council had decided to conduct Grethe Schmidt's "defense" from within the prosecutor's office itself. If Oldekop had expected to be named Grethe's advocate, he would be sorely disappointed. The city had opted for limited representation, rejecting the arguments of one of the seventeenth century's most aggressive champions of an expansive right to a defense.

Exactly one month later, on December 13, the city received a one-hundred-page response with the title, "Deductions of innocence and the nullifications of indications [of guilt] in the case of the *unjustly incarcerated* and *illegally tortured* [italics mine] Margarethe Schmidt." The brief raised the stakes dramatically, not only outlining Schmidt's innocence in the starkest of terms but also impugning the legality, propriety, and even the motives of the proceedings. Suddenly the case against a poor, foreign maidservant became a test of the competence and motives of the city's judicial personnel. The brief also did not come from a city-appointed counsel, whom the Schmidts apparently rejected. Instead, it was Justus Oldekop writing on behalf of the oxherd's daughter.[43]

Not even a Sow

The Case for Grethe

"I wouldn't even convict a sow with this evidence."

—Justus Oldekop, *Wahrhafte Beschreibung*

On December 13, Justus Oldekop responded to the entire process with outrage and scorn, very different from his milder pleas in September. His anger was no doubt exacerbated by the *Fiskal's* decision to pass him over and appoint an "in-house" representative to defend Grethe, but this was only part of the problem. According to Oldekop himself, even though Grethe's "father and relatives" had pleaded and asked for assistance, the city did not appoint an official advocate until after the girl—incarcerated for eighteen weeks—was terrorized and then tortured. Appointing an advocate out of the *Fiskal* itself and then limiting his work could not provide real justice: even with the best of intentions and the most Christian character, the appointee would, because of his office, be more inclined toward the prosecution than the accused.[1] The same office that had produced an illegitimate inquisition was now appointing itself to defend the victim of that process. The family would not accept this offer—what was required was a non-partisan advocate who would be reimbursed or paid directly by the city itself and who would be free to conduct an appropriate and full defense. Indeed, as Oldekop would later describe the moment when the prosecutor first offered the Schmidts a defender, Andreas Schmidt initially replied that the family would have to discuss the matter with their own advocate, Dr. Oldekop. At this, the prosecutor "bared his wolf's teeth" and told them that Oldekop would cost them a lot and they were but poor people who "did not have the best." The prosecutor, in contrast, would "graciously" help them at the expense of his masters in the city.[2] The Schmidts, though, could see that this would be of no use to them—

in fact it would only make matters worse. Of course, Oldekop was and had been acting unofficially as the family's advocate since the beginning of September, a fact the city would focus on later. The question now was what kind of advocacy the city would permit—and who would pay for it. The entire process, though, confirmed for Oldekop the suspicion that the investigation was not only flawed but also corrupt—the prosecution was determined to condemn Grethe and cover its tracks by preventing any outside intervention. He concluded that to seek truth from lies was like distilling cabbage and expecting gold to result.[3]

Yet another element was central to Oldekop's change in tone. As noted earlier, Oldekop seemed at first to think the case was routine—there was no corpus delicti, no physical evidence against Grethe, and the midwives' official testimony appeared decisive. He had written a "simple and humble supplication" to free the innocent captive and expected an uncomplicated hearing. Instead, he believed, the *Fiskal* arbitrarily, without consultation or notification, "against all indications of innocence and without the knowledge of her parents or her advocate . . . first terrorized and then tortured the poor prisoner, left unheard and undefended."[4] It was this "unheard of, entirely irresponsible terrorizing and torture" that spurred the advocate to present his case to the city. His anger was intensified by the constant delays and the *Fiskal*'s unwillingness to provide copies of the files. Given the seriousness of the situation, Oldekop did not ponder the consequences of his accusation. "The truth," he noted, "is bitter."[5]

THE DEFENSE BRIEF

Oldekop's long, sometimes rambling, but always vehement argument in Grethe's defense can be divided into three parts. First, he attacked the prosecution's procedure in opening the investigation in the first place; second, he sought to undermine the central interrogations under torture in order to invalidate the final confession; finally, he presented a full set of arguments in favor of Grethe's innocence and explicitly accused the prosecution of neglecting its duty to explore them. The result was a powerful—and often personal—indictment of the Brunswick *Untergericht* that raised the hackles of the city council and lifted the case to a new and more dangerous level.[6]

The Fatal Procedural Flaw

The foundation of Oldekop's defense was the absence of the corpus delicti itself. Not only was a corpse missing—the city literally had no carcass—but there was still no evidence that any crime had been committed in the first place. Worse yet, the files did not even contain a detailed description of what the crime itself might have been. Oldekop noted that there was not the "smallest mention" of an accuser or a crime in any of the records, even though all judicial theory clearly demanded that before launching "a criminal inquisitional or accusatory process," authorities must have the body of the crime.[7]

According to Oldekop, the files were even silent about how the judges became aware of a potential crime, whatever its nature. Oldekop here referred specifically to Article 188 of the *Carolina*, which states, "Where, however, the complaint issues ex officio and not from particular complainants, then there shall be transcribed how the complaint came to the judge, also what the accused responded to it, and what thereafter occurred in all stages of the proceedings in accord with this our ordinance."[8] To this point, though, the prosecution had done nothing to describe how the complaint came to them, which made it unclear whether the magistrates were responding to a specific event or to individual denunciations with unspecified, possibly personal, motives against Grethe and the Schmidts, as Oldekop himself believed.[9] The prosecution had thus violated the provisions of the law itself, which required magistrates to consider the possible grounds for enmity in a criminal accusation.

The sheer number of mistakes suggested to Oldekop that malice was the real motive for the prosecution. Either the city shared with Dedekind and Hafferland some unspecified hatred of the Schmidts, or the prosecutor was from the beginning simply prejudiced against a poor, simple woman from the hinterlands. The prosecution's subsequent decisions, Oldekop argued, were an attempt to cover up that fact, all the while collecting new evidence (presumably from the Hagemans) behind the Schmidts' backs and hiding it from them and their defense.

No body, no charge, no grounds—in sum, no corpus delicti: in Oldekop's view, from these failures at the very beginning of the case all the other difficulties followed inexorably. Though Grethe Schmidt should never have been incarcerated, this young person "of fifteen or sixteen years" had now languished in jail for eighteen weeks. During this lamentable and lonely time, Grethe's family and friends were not permitted a visit—excessive punishment for a crime that might not even have occurred.

Having undertaken this malicious investigation with no corpus delicti, Oldekop claimed, the court then set about creating one through maladroit interrogations. From the outset, investigators bungled the questioning of witnesses, beginning with Anna Dedekind, who was asked "whether [she] did not notice" that Schmidt was pregnant. To Oldekop this kind of "leading" question alerted the witness to the prosecution's goal, and in turn allowed the prosecution to seed the testimony with hints of the supposed crime.[10]

Tortured Logic

The sham attempt to manufacture a corpus delicti culminated in the interrogation—and especially the torture—of Grethe herself. Whatever their evidence, Oldekop argued, the magistrates wrecked their case beyond repair by repeatedly folding suggestions about the circumstances of the crime into their interrogations of the suspect. This directly contradicted Article 6 of the *Carolina*, which stipulated that a person suspected of a crime through rumor or general reputation could not be tortured until authorities had established that a crime actually had been committed. Oldekop pointed to the first interrogation of Grethe, when the city asked, "whether she had not had the baby in the Lüdden house and in what room"; "whether she had not secretly hidden the child in her bed until the next day"; "whether she had not then thrown the baby in the Oker."[11] In Oldekop's view, the city did not know what, if anything, had happened but was from the opening of the proceedings in August planting the answers Grethe would give in November. This tactic was even more evident in the torture sessions. The prosecutors asked about the "material" that came out of her, "and when the examiners gradually received the answer that they wanted to receive, they asked her further, 'didn't she consider that mass that came out of her to be a child, and how it came to its death through her.' Or 'whether she hadn't laid a hand on the child and killed it. Whether she perhaps took some drink beforehand.'"[12] Or, at the final session following torture, when examiners asked the suspect, "whether she was not sorry that she, with prior intent, killed her child?" Oldekop notes that including the term "prior intent" (*Vorsatz*) required that Grethe acknowledge both murder and premeditation at once. Through this question the examiners transformed the captive into someone who had committed child murder with malice aforethought, according to the language of the *Carolina*.[13] Tired and in pain, the young woman might not have been aware that she was betraying herself through an untruth and thereby deepening her mortal peril.

Oldekop saved his strongest language, though, for the "wretched, illegal" torture sessions themselves, in which "not even a cold bean of worth is to be found."[14] Oldekop was a long-standing foe of torture, so his brief brought a lifetime of opposition to bear on this single case. His fierce rhetoric here reflects his claim that the prosecution was willing to go to any length to undo Grethe Schmidt. As he contrasted the city's vicious terrorizing process to the victim's youth and simple-mindedness, it seemed inescapable to Oldekop "that the *Fiskal* begrudged the prisoner her established innocence, was quite anxious for her death and undertook every word and effort that the prisoner should never enjoy her innocence but one way or another would not get free of the hangman's hand."[15] Because the matter was so unclear and false, however, the prosecution turned to another way, the "unheard of, worthless, and illegal terror and torture."[16]

Oldekop dismissed the prosecution's claim that the torture really was not so harsh, or that in fact it was through the prior "terrorizing" that the prisoner validly or spontaneously confessed. Such reasoning only "prostitutes [the court] further."[17] Oldekop focused on the prosecution's use of the terms "valid" (*gütlich*) and "spontaneous" (*sponte*) in the confession and on the execution of the required *territio* (terrorizing). He pointed to the law: *territio* was to be verbal, the "introduction of the cruel hangman's tools that belong to torture." The *Fiskal* stretched this verbal terror beyond recognition—the torturer actually laid the instruments before her, "bound her hands, and the hangman during the alleged terrorizing always acted as though he were ordered to do the harshest deeds to her."[18] This "verbal" terror was so excessive that to Oldekop it constituted torture in and of itself, a fact that the prosecutors tried to cover up after extracting Grethe's final confession.

Yet Oldekop recognized that whatever errors had occurred and whatever tactics they had used, the prosecution now had produced a final, "freely" given admission of guilt. The advocate knew that he could leave no part of that confession standing.[19] Oldekop even implicated the scribe, Johannes Pilgram, noting that Pilgram began his transcription of Grethe's final confession by describing the torture as "begun but not carried out,"[20] aside from "mildly" (*gelinde*) binding and then quickly releasing her.[21] Oldekop turned to the transcript of the torture session itself, which in his reading was more severe than the final transcript acknowledged. The advocate also argued that, according to legal opinion, the binding or *ligatura* could still be considered a very hard form of torture.[22]

Just as important, for Pilgram to use language such as "mildly" in describing the events would require standing in Schmidt's place. Grethe felt the torture, not Pilgram or anyone else.[23] How, Oldekop asked, could the scribe judge the experience of the fifteen-year-old prisoner? In considering the validity of Oldekop's point here, one must note that Pilgram had in fact witnessed the torture of suspected witches (and would do so again), which could have affected his assessment of the severity of Schmidt's experience.[24] Observing serious torture in other exceptional cases, such as of witchcraft, could affect the perception of pain in the regular criminal process.

Oldekop was not yet done with undermining Grethe's forced confession, however—he circled back to the original problem in the case, the missing corpus delicti. Time and again the inquisitors demanded that Grethe admit the "truth," but they had only the most general idea of what that was (that she was somehow, in some way, a child murderer). Interrogators therefore had used torture not to confirm the truth but to create it through force. Put simply, how could interrogators who did not know what the truth of the crime itself was be sure that Grethe had confessed it?[25]

Yet, astonishingly, Oldekop continued, even the admissions that the prosecution had extracted from Grethe after such laborious and painful efforts proved worthless because the "truth" she "confessed" manifestly contradicted the facts already admitted or established in previous interrogations. On November 8, the judicial personnel asked the tortured prisoner in the final confession why she had hidden her pregnancy and killed her child, to which she answered, "because she wanted to remain a virgin" (in line with the stipulations of *Carolina*, Article 35). The advocate went back to Grethe's first interrogation, in which she not only admitted having sex with Möller but "confirmed in detail" all the circumstances, "by whom, in what place, at what time, in what room, and in what bed."[26] Grethe had openly confessed the sex but adamantly denied the pregnancy. As any "rational person" could conclude, Oldekop argued, the prisoner would never have been so open about her "corruption," especially during the interrogations, if she had child-murder in mind, and even less so if she were trying to "pass for a virgin," as the final confession stated. On this point Oldekop emphasized the puzzling exchanges—solicited by the prosecution—during the early interrogations: after her sexual encounter with Möller, Grethe cut her hair and wore a cap "to acknowledge that she had allowed herself to sleep with someone."[27] The city understood this as a public admission of sexual misconduct. Oldekop noted further that Schmidt had eventually admitted her immoral conduct to her own mother, to Margarethe Hafferland, to Ilse Engelken, and to Philip Becker's wife. And yet now in November, under the pressure of torture, she suddenly professed a desire to appear a maiden?

Another contradiction put the final lie to her "valid" and "free" confession. Oldekop turned to the timing of the alleged deed. Schmidt had confessed that she had borne and killed a baby "in Heinrich Lüdden's house three days before New Year's Day, and not three days after the New

Year's Day, as she had said previously [in fact, she said it twice in the same confession]."[28] Oldekop noted, though, that Grethe's confession flatly contradicted the original testimony of Anna Dedekind, given in August, that she and her husband heard rumors of the pregnancy and confronted Grethe on the Friday *following* the New Year. Oldekop writes with undisguised sarcasm, "Now here thinks a rational man: Because of the supposed pregnancy, Heinrich Lüdden's wife released the prisoner from her service on the Sunday after New Year's. According to this unnatural lie the birth occurred nine days earlier, and in the very same house, in which nine days later the supposed impregnation is said to have been noticed for the first time." To Oldekop, the conclusion was obvious: the news about the presumed pregnancy "had no grounding except in loud women's gossip" (*weiber plauderey*). The same gossip spreading throughout Brunswick explained as well Grethe's mother's "untimely" precaution of reserving a room for a lying-in.[29]

SIGNS OF INNOCENCE

So far, Oldekop's brief concentrated on the prosecution's procedural misconduct. Perhaps the *Fiskal*'s greatest betrayal of their God-given responsibilities, though, lay in never considering the possibility, backed by significant evidence, that Grethe was innocent.[30] This was a serious claim that struck at the heart of the court's own legitimacy. Oldekop, though, did not flinch for a moment—the magistrates "have not even once asked" about signs of innocence but "tossed them behind and entirely out of view."[31]

Oldekop outlined the grounds for Grethe's innocence by turning again to the question of the corpus delicti. There was the testimony of the midwives, who were unanimous in their conviction, following a thorough and specific examination, that Schmidt had never given birth. Following this clear proof of innocence, Grethe should immediately have been set free. Oldekop also used the midwives' decidedly exculpatory testimony in his procedural indictment as well. Rather than accept the findings of their own expert witnesses, the *Fiskal* then turned instead to city physician Laurence Gieseler in an attempt to impeach their testimony. The law, Oldekop asserted, specified the use of "knowledgeable women" in such matters; the most Gieseler, who never himself examined Grethe, could do was cast some general doubt on the midwives' sworn and specific claims. His testimony provided no positive basis for torturing Grethe. The prosecution used Gieseler's statement to turn the midwives' examination (and the law) upside down: Grethe had to be tortured not because she was probably guilty, but because she was only "probably" innocent. Oldekop noted as well that Gieseler was present when the midwives made their report yet said nothing to contradict it. Only when pressed (according to Oldekop) by an overzealous and prejudiced prosecution did Gieseler present the affidavit doubting their examination results.

Indeed, the prosecution's very zeal to convict Grethe at all costs was, to Oldekop, a strong argument for Schmidt's innocence. For all its efforts, the *Fiskal* obviously found no good case in Brunswick—why else would investigators have gone to Gross Schwülper to inquire (of the Hagemans, presumably) whether Grethe might have had a child there around the beginning of February? Finding nothing there, the prosecution brought its "evil" determination back to Brunswick and to the "most false and contradictory assertions" about a birth in the house of Heinrich Lüdden and his wife.[32]

In the testimony concerning what happened in the Lüdden/Dedekind house itself, Oldekop found another sign of Grethe's innocence: "in the bed, and in the entire house, where she supposedly bore and then killed the child, neither the house-father nor the house-mother . . . nor any servant noticed even the smallest sign of a birth." In fact, the room where the prisoner supposedly committed the "falsely imputed deed" was so close to the room where her employers slept that "nothing secret or quiet, much less the alleged birth and evildoing" could take place there without being heard or noticed. But, if Grethe's final confession was to be believed, Heinrich Lüdden and his wife only got wind of the pregnancy through gossip and confronted Grethe in their house *after* the child's alleged birth.

Most compelling in Grethe's favor was the absurdity of the prosecution's contradictory claims: the argument that Grethe's baby was born three days before Anna Dedekind even believed her pregnant, the topsy-turvy use of the midwives' testimony, the prosecution's swinging back and forth from Brunswick to Gross Schwülper in search of a corpus delicti. Among the most puzzling absurdities of all, though, concerned Grethe's open admission of sex with Andreas Möller. If she were really pregnant and plotting a terrible crime to hide her shame, as the *Carolina* expected infanticides to do, she would simultaneously have denied the sex altogether. She must instead have been telling the truth about the sex while honestly denying the pregnancy—resisting prosecutorial pressure until torture did her in.

Oldekop employed the same logic to defuse some of the most damaging and irrefutable testimony against Grethe—her mother's decision to find a room in Neubrücke and her alleged attempt at "shaking down" Margarethe Hafferland. Fitting these pieces together, the advocate acknowledged that Ilse Leuthgen, hearing and apparently believing the rumors and accusations about her daughter, had unwisely sought a place for childbirth.

Oldekop, though, turned this information to his advantage—by their panicked reaction, the Schmidt women had made it impossible to hide the supposed infanticide. No rational person would proceed with a murder after leaving such an incriminating trail to follow and explain. As to Hafferland's statement that the Schmidts had tried to pry one hundred gulden from her stepson, Oldekop suggested that, if true (which he doubted), these poor simple people might have been tempted by the possibility of making more money than they had ever imagined by *faking* both the pregnancy and the lying-in.

Oldekop even argued that Grethe Schmidt's low status—a poor oxherd's daughter now working as a poor serving girl—made it unlikely that she would attach much importance to her dishonor with Möller. It was far more probable that she would view her sexual encounter with a rich man as an opportunity for supporting herself. Möller had the means to make good his mistake. Why would Grethe suddenly reject the opportunity to make her life comfortable in order to fake a virginity that she had obviously not cared about in the first place? Oldekop, it appears, was quite willing to ascribe bad motives to his clients—if doing so would save Grethe's life.

After all this, though, Oldekop was not yet done. In a short addendum to his long brief, he adduced one more very telling sign that the confession was false and that Grethe Schmidt was innocent of any crime save manufacturing lies to placate her torturers. In the final confession, Grethe recounted the childbirth itself, in which the baby presented itself after about a quarter hour, feet first. She "gripped the child with both hands, first by the legs and then the torso, and pulled it out of her." It was, therefore, a breech birth. Oldekop jumped on the description: "All women who have brought children into the world, as well as all those who have heard or read about it, understand . . . that this extorted falsehood is truly an impossibility and runs contrary to nature: because namely the child, when it has its correct position at birth, gradually comes to the world with its head first, and with the torso and legs following. When otherwise, especially when a child comes with the legs first, so that they can be grabbed . . . the mother and child cannot be separated, or this can happen only with great effort and urgency and with the help and advice of another person."[33] In other words, the birth, as Grethe had described it under duress, would have been painful and difficult even with the help of others and was nearly impossible to accomplish alone. Oldekop concluded that it simply could not have happened. Grethe's flawed confession came at the end of a terrifying and coercive interrogation, following a long period in which the defendant had had no contact of any sort with the outside world, with parents or relatives or friends. Even the hardest criminal would not have been able to resist. And yet even under these circumstances, Oldekop argued, the best the city could achieve was a mendacious, contradictory, impossible admission of guilt.[34]

So ended the first stage of the case for the defense. Oldekop now sought redress—no final confession could undo the injury the *Fiskal* had wrought. Thus the city should be required to make good the damages from torture, long and false incarceration, and as prescribed in the *Carolina*, place responsibility squarely on the shoulders of the *Fiskal* for launching such calumnies against Grethe and the Schmidt family.

Connections

What to make of Oldekop's arguments and claims? This is a question that can only be answered in conjunction with the prosecution's response. What is clear is that the defense advocate had no intention of backing down on either legal or factual grounds. Equally clear is the fact that his forceful, strident language and his claim of "prosecutorial misconduct" hit a nerve in the city of Brunswick. Just days after receiving Oldekop's brief, a terse letter circulated in the city offices, complaining of the scurrilous and slanderous language employed by the advocate to describe the criminal process and to accuse officials of malfeasance.[35]

With a confession in hand but a legal brief to answer, the magistrates turned once again to the University of Helmstedt. On December 23, they sent Oldekop's brief and asked for a full opinion from the assembled faculty. Certainly they asked about Oldekop's arguments, but the bulk of the request concerned his "insufferable" language and his accusations that the *Fiskal* was engaged in a "futile," "illegal" process that violated "natural law and God's Word," entirely out of "envy at her innocence," "bloodthirstiness," and "craving her death." The city protested that Oldekop was trying to defame and diminish the prosecutors themselves, and the council requested an opinion about what to do about him and his false claim that Schmidt had gone undefended. On that subject the city council noted that the family had not until the last minute asked for a defense, nor had they pleaded poverty, nor was it clear that they were so poor as was claimed. Even so, the city had appointed a defender now in the form of the *Fiskal*. Clearly, then, the city was confident enough about its case to begin pondering a punishment for the insubordinate lawyer.[36]

The university's answer, when it came, demonstrated to the city council the university's low regard for "Dr. Oldekop's nullifying fantasy."[37] Despite acknowledging the absence of a carcass, the legal faculty still rejected Oldekop's claim that no solid grounds for torture existed. First,

Grethe's status as a *persona vilis* (person of low status), combined with her *fama* (reputation), justified her arrest. Next, the faculty listed succinctly the evidence establishing probable cause for torture: "The suspect confessed the *concubitum* [intercourse], and concerning her pregnancy, not only did Heinrich Lüdden's wife testify to it, but Gertrude Wilmers stated that she was quite round and had full breasts, and Anna Försten on oath testified that [Grethe] appeared womanly on account of her full breasts. The suspect had gone with Garsen's housemaid to Wendschott with the intention of staying there six weeks; her mother and aunt had also gone to Neubrücke to reserve a room and therefore believed her to be pregnant."[38]

Having justified the torture, even without a corpus delicti, Helmstedt had no problem agreeing with its result. Painful questioning, after all, had resulted in a confession, meeting the conditions of the *Carolina* and opening the way for sentencing and punishment. All of Oldekop's other "apparent objections" were thus null and void: in an *inquisitorial process*, it was not necessary for the defendant or her lawyer to view the evidence or the witnesses beforehand, nor was the city required to permit her relatives and family to visit her. Helmstedt also noted that, even without a corpus delicti, the fact of Grethe's confession confirmed the city's original suspicions. Of course, this was just the procedural abomination that Oldekop had most railed against—that a confession extracted through unjustified torture would then provide a basis for validating torment after the fact. The fact of a confession, though, was always a powerful bulwark for any prosecution. As noted above, it was one reason that criminal appeals were so limited, and Oldekop, a champion of such appeals, may already have had his sights set on attempting one. As to Oldekop's claim that the entire prosecution and testimonies had occurred through some enmity against the Schmidts, Helmstedt demanded that he provide proof.

Unquestionably, then, the legal faculty seemed to vindicate the city's behavior while rejecting the defense case. The university faculty was not done yet, however. They referred to the case as "remarkable" and asked the magistrates to question Grethe further. The faculty wanted to know whether the child had indeed "come into the world with the feet first" and just how Grethe had "grabbed the body and pulled it out of her." Midwives and a respected faculty of medicine should then determine whether "such a birth, and indeed in such a small time, in the alleged manner, could have occurred."[39] The legal faculty also wanted to inquire about Schmidt's age, whether indeed her menses had resumed after the New Year, and to question Lüdden and his wife, under oath, about whether they had noticed any signs of birth. Only then would the university recommend a punishment.

Though the syndic of Brunswick city would later publish this opinion as legal vindication against the sophistry of the irascible and pugnacious advocate, the document was in fact more cautious. Despite upholding the legitimacy of the process, the Helmstedt scholars seemed less convinced by the case itself than they had been when recommending torture in the first place. They also expressed some concern about exculpatory evidence. Why ask about Grethe's age, the resumption of her menses, or about what the Lüddens saw if the case were clear, especially since these were problems that Oldekop had himself raised? Why demand that the city involve again not only the midwives but also an outside medical faculty if no doubt remained about the outcome? Finally, it should be noted that the legal faculty postponed any consideration of Oldekop's behavior and language until after completing the Schmidt case.

To some degree then, the legal faculty left room for doubt on the case of Grethe Schmidt, as they had done when advocating a "humane" torture six weeks earlier. They were also hedging their opinion of Oldekop's language—waiting to see how the matter proceeded before judging the defender. One thing was clear from the city council's appeal to Helmstedt, however. The inquisition and criminal process was no longer limited to Grethe Schmidt. Now Justus Oldekop, in defending her, had himself incurred the city's wrath.

12

The Thick Wilderness of Lies

One full year after the alleged murder to which Grethe Schmidt had confessed under torture, and five months after her arrest, the *Obergericht* constituted from the Brunswick City Council published a new decree:

> On the basis of the now completed testimony and confession, as well as the defense put forward, of Margarethe Schmidt, suspected of infanticide, *the report describing the inspection of the corpse of the dead infant found on the fourth of April will be placed in the record* [italics added], and the *Justizherren* and constable are ordered to interrogate the prisoner yet again over the following questions, without any threat, nor with any encouragement of mercy or amelioration of punishment:
>
> 1. Whether she had her period after the New Year, or whether in fact her shirt was not soiled from the birth itself?
>
> 2. Where, and in what place, in the city or in the countryside, was she delivered of a child?
>
> 3. Whether the child came to the world feet first?
>
> 4. Whether she grabbed it by the feet and body, and pulled it out of her?

The decree further stated that a group of reputable midwives would be asked to comment on the possibility of such a childbirth, and the records would be sent to a respected medical faculty for review.[1]

This new document reflects the city's intensified interest in the manner of the confessed birth, its timing, and Grethe's condition in the aftermath. Most remarkably, though, after months in which no actual victim was produced, the city had suddenly managed to find an infant corpse on which to hang Schmidt's guilt. Since Justus Oldekop's outrage and his legal brief depended largely on the absence of a corpus delicti, in one stroke prosecutors had seemingly undermined the entire defense. The prosecution now added two new and gruesome reports to the file, both dated April 4, 1661: according to the report of Otto Theune, "a small, freshly-born, naked child had been found lying in the Oker River behind Hans Grotien's house."[2] Dutifully Theune questioned Hans Grotien's seventeen-year-old servant Hans Jürgen von Peyne, who had first spotted the child. At five in the morning, while fetching water from the Oker, von Peyne saw something suspicious in an almost dry ditch. Upon closer inspection it turned out to be a naked baby lying dead in the mud at the river's edge.

Eventually the *Bürgermeister* himself went to inspect the situation and found that the child was a girl, fully formed and intact except that the umbilical cord had been torn away. Laurence Gieseler was called in the same day to examine the corpse: "He gives it as his report that the same little child was fully formed, looked red and fresh, and he found no damage either on its head, neck, or body; the navel and cord still fresh and bloody, [the body] had not been long in this world."[3]

Here, then, was potentially the source of public outrage that drove the process against Grethe Schmidt. In fact, as the defense would quickly note, this particular corpse might actually cast even more doubt on the prosecution's evidence, procedures, and motives. A baby's corpse found in the Oker River, in Hagen, at five in the morning—these facts correspond roughly to Grethe's statement that she had borne a baby in Hagen, at the Lüdden house, and then had tossed it in the canal toward evening. The similarities end there, though. Grethe confessed that her baby was a boy. Even more telling was the description of the body: a "newly born" infant, "fresh born," "red and fresh," indicating a recent birth, presumably without time for the corpse to bloat significantly or decay. If the baby were found in this condition on April 4, it could have been in the river only a short while and had most probably died the night before.

In short, the baby girl's corpse found on April 4 could not be the newborn boy Grethe Schmidt had confessed to murdering at the beginning of January 1661. A corpse floating in the Oker River for over three months could not possibly be described as "freshly born." Further, during the five months of testimony, from August to December 1661, there was no mention or sign of the corpse found in April of that year. The *Vogt* of Hagen, Otto Theune, had been involved in both Grethe's arrest and in the discovery of April 4. Laurence Gieseler, in particular, made no effort to connect Grethe to the infant corpse in his testimony in the Schmidt trial. Her advocate, Oldekop, knew nothing about it when he launched his long defense brief—surely even the rumor of an actual corpse would have altered his thinking and his presentation. In discussing the case with the legal faculty of Helmstedt, the prosecutors never once mentioned this corpse.

Why, then, did the city decide, in January 1662 to question Grethe about it? The heart of Oldekop's defense was the absence of the corpus delicti. Though generally supportive of the city, Helmstedt's response may well have unsettled the city council, as the *Obergericht* oversaw the lower court's activities but was also responsible for the more difficult legal matters involved in capital cases, such as communications with the legal faculty. The *Obergericht,* guided by the syndic (the chief legal officer in the city, in this case Johannes Baumgarten), may have looked at the faculty's request for further investigation and the postponement of any punishment of Oldekop as an opening for the defense lawyer. Convinced that they were right about Grethe's guilt and armed with her confession, however extracted, the prosecution decided to reconstruct the case along the lines of the *Carolina*, to forestall further "Oldekoppish" mischief. The importance of reopening the case correctly and not seeming to be on a fishing expedition or pursuing a vendetta is evident in the city's own later account, published in 1664. Unlike the criminal records themselves the *Relation of Fact and Law against Margarethe Schmidt, the Immoral Peasant Girl*, written by the syndics, opens with the discovery of an infant's body on April 4, 1661. This provided the supposed grounds for opening a general inquisition that led specifically to the girl from Gross Schwülper.[4] Clearly, in January 1662, Brunswick's higher court was taking over the direction of the case, even though the daily work of investigation and interrogation continued in the hands of Vellhagen, Theune, and the *Justizherren*. By formulating the case in this way, the court also defined it as inquisitorial, which tightened the magistrates' control over the proceedings and the conduct of the defense, marginalizing Oldekop.

In fact, though, this statement from April helps resolve another mystery—the punishment of an infanticide witnessed in the *Altstadt* by Margarethe Hafferland and Anna Sacharitz, an event at which the two women also saw Grethe Schmidt in great distress. Again, no record exists of this other infanticide in the archives of Brunswick. From the circumstantial testimony, though, it seems clear not only that this was the infanticide that aroused suspicion about Grethe Schmidt but also that the culprit had been caught and punished. On one hand, the city had no real grounds to use it as a way of indicting Schmidt four months later. On the other, another case helps to explain the magistracy's concern about crime. Infanticide was an unusual crime, and the possibility of multiple cases in one year may have created alarm among the city authorities.

Providing the corpus delicti was the first of many steps designed to recast the Schmidt investigation after the fact according to more formal judicial guidelines and the Helmstedt recommendations. The second was to interrogate Grethe one more time, according to the decree of January 8, 1662, followed by a request for additional testimony about the birth from the midwives. Finally, prosecutors would again speak with Grethe's former mistress, Anna Dedekind, and her husband. The magistrates intended each step to move them closer to conviction.

In reality, though, each move in the renewed inquiry brought unintended consequences that twisted the case in a different direction. On January 9, 1662, the prosecutors again confronted Grethe, "without any threat, also without any promise of mercy or lessening punishment."[5] She acknowledged that she had not had a period in January 1661, answered "yes" when asked whether the blood people found on her shirt was from the birth, and confirmed that she had given birth to a child, feet first, on the floor of the Lüdden house in Hagen, and that she had no help. As to her age, she said she was seventeen or eighteen.

Altstadt, January 10, 1662

Prosecutors then turned again to the city midwives for expert testimony. The questions they asked the midwives betrayed a new suspicion, inquiring whether a child could actually be born feet first, in such a short period of time, *without outside help?* Similarly, could a mother *alone and without the help of another grasp the child by its feet and body and pull it out of her?* In other words, the city's response to Grethe's description of a breech birth was not to doubt whether she could have had a baby in that manner, as Oldekop had suggested, but whether she in fact bore the child alone, with no help.

All three midwives agreed that such an unattended birth was improbable. The first (unnamed) midwife thought it "nearly impossible" yet noted that many examples existed of children born feet first, through God's omnipotence. In any case, such a birth was not as hard as when an arm emerged first. As to the question of help, the midwife could not answer without knowing the strength of the woman involved. The second midwife, Magdalena Bellers of the Sack district, claimed that such a birth would be hard indeed, especially if it were a first birth. Bellers's experience told her that of the fifty babies she had witnessed born in such a manner, barely ten or fifteen had survived. As to the other question, perhaps the mother could have brought the child out with hard pressing, but only in a situation of "great anxiety and need." Finally, Jillian Wilckens (one of the midwives who had earlier examined Grethe) testified that only with God's help could such a birth occur quickly, that even with a midwife present there would be much work to do. A head-first birth was much easier. Wilckens agreed with the other *Bademütter*—she did not want to deny the possibility of such a birth occurring unassisted, but it would certainly be difficult.[6]

Just as in previous testimony, the midwives proved cautious in giving definitive answers. Unmistakably, though, all of them were quite skeptical: such a birth was difficult and the chances of a successful live delivery were very small. This might seem a victory for the defense. The prosecution, though, was contemplating another possibility: that Grethe Schmidt might have borne a child as she had confessed, but not alone and without help. Though the midwives were dubious about a successful breech birth under any conditions, they acknowledged that having someone present to help might make a difference.

Hagen, the Lüdden Household, January 10, 1662

After the midwives' testimony, the magistrates reexamined the person who testified first—Anna Dedekind, this time with her husband, Heinrich Lüdden—to explain how it was possible for the events Grethe had described to take place without her employers noticing that something was amiss. Was there no commotion? Did Grethe leave no signs of the birth behind—no bloody stains, no soiled linens? Indeed, this was one of the defense claims that had unsettled the faculty of Helmstedt.

One may recall the vagueness of Dedekind's first deposition on the subject of Grethe's alleged pregnancy: after hearing whispers around town for some time, at Christmas she had decided that the rumor about Grethe's situation must be true. Now Dedekind added that around Christmas Grethe was looking "round in body and pregnant." She testified further that Dedekind's husband had warned the girl that, "if things were as they looked, that she [Schmidt] had best talk [to the Lüddens] about them."[7] Dedekind then affirmed that around New Year's, Grethe was indeed "great with child"—or *grob schwanger*, a phrase that meant near to delivery. In August 1661, Dedekind testified that she believed Schmidt was with child but had no idea how far along the pregnancy was. Five months later, Dedekind appeared more sure.

Heinrich Lüdden himself would only say that Grethe was "quite round" and that he relied on his wife's belief that things "were not right with the girl." Lüdden testified that the couple had wanted to notify Grethe's parents before firing her, "so that the young woman would not attempt some mishap."[8] Lüdden added a new wrinkle: Grethe's father had brought a wagon on Saturday (January 5, 1661), to pick up his daughter's things. Andreas Schmidt, though, claimed to know nothing about the matter—he told the Lüddens to take it up with his wife and left. When Grethe's mother came on Sunday, January 6, she too said she knew nothing but wanted to spend the night with her daughter in order to assess her situation. The next morning, Schmidt's mother admitted that, "Yes her daughter was pregnant, and must be taken somewhere else for she could not remain in Schwülper."[9] The mother asked to stay one more night in the Lüddens' house. When the Schmidts left together on the Monday after New Year's, her employers gave Grethe a piece of bread and a blood sausage, admonishing her truly and sternly to "do the right thing."[10]

The interrogation then turned to the circumstances in the Lüddens' house itself: *where Grethe slept, how far from the couple themselves, and how audible were goings on in the maid's room?* The maid slept in a small alcove, four steps above the Lüddens. It was certainly possible to hear what went on there. *Did the witness observe what the maid was doing in her little room during the evening perhaps two or three days before the New Year?* Nothing, was the reply. *Wasn't the girl gone that evening from about 6:00 until 10:00? Did they not speak sternly with her, wondering why she was going out?* Dedekind had no reason to question the maid, since at that time the girl seldom went in or out. *Did they not hear the same evening around 11:00 from the maid that she was not well? Did they not ask her what was wrong or if she was sick?* They heard nothing from the maid to suggest that she was in bed sick. *The next day did they not see some foul blood where the maid had been and notice it on her shirt as well?* No. *Did they not afterward inspect her bed and storage? And what did they find?* After Grethe's departure several days later, Dedekind went to her room, and one or two days later she inspected the bed and bedclothes to prepare for the new maid. However, she had found nothing unclean.[11]

This was a puzzling interview—in the first place the questioners seemed as suspicious of the Lüddens as of the Schmidts. Was it possible the magistrates thought that the couple were hiding something or might have helped Grethe for their own convenience? More important, if Anna Dedekind, just a few feet away, had noticed or heard nothing—no cries, no blood, no mess—either on the night when Grethe was reportedly enduring a difficult and painful delivery or in the days after the maid left, how likely was Grethe's tale? As if to be sure of this conclusion, the interrogators then went outside to look at the spring where Grethe claimed she had placed the corpse, which supposedly then floated away. They discovered in fact that there was no such pool in front of the Lüddens' house, but in front of another house six paces away.

Despite the contradictory details of the Lüdden interrogation, the investigators seemed unshaken—they had a confession in their pockets, after all, and so had only to work out the factual details. To this end, they arranged a set of confrontations between the accused and various witnesses. The *confrontatio* itself dated from the world of "accusatory process." First would come an encounter between Anna Dedekind and Grethe, to force the prisoner to acknowledge her guilt and give more precise details about the manner and timing of the murder. In the second confrontation, the prosecutors intended for the three midwives of Brunswick to question Grethe and assess her account of the birth itself.[12]

Altstadt Fronerey, January 17, 1662

Officials gathered for what promised to be a climactic moment in the case. Two new magistrates—Heinrich Snellen and Melchior Schmidt—joined Vellhagen and Theune to interrogate Grethe and to conduct the *confrontatio* with the Lüddens. They asked her to restate her answer to the question, *Where and in what place in the city or in the country had she borne her child?*

Grethe responded, though, that she "has in her entire life never had a baby, either in Brunswick or elsewhere, that is to say, she has had no child ever."[13] The *Justizherren* must have been astonished and reminded Schmidt: *Was she not just a few days ago, on the ninth of January, asked this question, and did she not answer that she had borne a baby right here in the city in her loft in the house of Heinrich Lüdden? How can she now deny it?* Grethe replied, "What she reports today, that is the truth, and she dearly wished that she had told the truth from the beginning, that all would be so much better."[14]

Here was a stunning development that caught the prosecution off guard—Schmidt was denying the confession that she had affirmed just one week earlier. Of course, Anna Dedekind and Heinrich Lüdden were present, waiting to confront the suspect. The Lüddens, though, could not testify to a birth and death—in fact, the entire point of the Lüddens' presence at this point was to testify that they had seen no signs of a birth. Dedekind and her husband were more certain of Grethe's pregnancy, however, so prosecutors asked Grethe, *whether then she was at no time pregnant?* "She stubbornly says no."[15]

Brought in to confront Schmidt, Dedekind looked her former maid in the eye and said that around New Year's Day 1661, the prisoner was "great with child." The captive "consistently denied" the accusation: "Gottfried Möller's widow and the prisoner's own mother had said that she was pregnant, therefore she also held herself to be pregnant, because she had not had her period." Heinrich Lüdden too looked Grethe in the eye and said that at the time Schmidt left she had a very "full body." He could not himself say that she was pregnant, "since he did not understand these things." His wife, however, had believed her to be pregnant, as did the prisoner's own mother who, after spending a night with the girl in the house, acknowledged her condition.[16] Grethe, though, now adamantly stood by her account, that for the reasons already stated she also believed that she was pregnant, but she had never had a child.[17]

Suddenly the case was back to square one—no pregnancy, no birth. Indeed, Grethe's admission shed new light on her own state of mind throughout the whole ordeal: because everyone, especially her own mother, told her she was with child, of course she believed them, especially since she was also missing her period. Left to her own counsel, Grethe would not have concluded she was pregnant. Grethe's complete reversal washed out any easy path to the proceeding's resolution or her punishment. The magistrates themselves must have realized that Grethe's original confession was false: if the Lüddens were at all credible, the birth could not have happened at the time or place she had claimed. If the midwives were to be believed, Grethe could not have borne the child in the manner she claimed. Her entire detailed description of events, extracted over months, was in the end a web of falsehoods.

It was Grethe herself, then, who derailed the proceedings designed to condemn her. What caused her sudden change of mind, in the space of just days? The answer can be found in a particular moment a few days earlier. Oldekop's pleas had persuaded Grethe's jailers to allow a family visit. The timing of what happened next is crucial, but only comes to light because of a "postscript" to Oldekop's own petition of January 9, entered into the record on January 10, 1662. According to that postscript, when Grethe's family appeared, the Altstadt *Vogt* Johannes Vellhagen was already in the *Fronerey* questioning her. Oldekop wanted to know what had transpired during this questioning and the family's visit and so was requesting a transcript.[18]

Accordingly, the prosecution provided Johannes Vellhagen's description of what occurred. According to the *Vogt*, the court was questioning Grethe on the four new questions proposed on January 8. While this was happening, Schmidt's father and her uncle, Gehrt Bonte, came to visit her in the *Fronerey*, with Vellhagen staying to oversee the visit. They asked how she was and whether she still had clean clothes. Then her father continued, "If she had had a child, she should say so, but indeed she did not have one in Neubrücke, did she?" Grethe responded (as she often did) with silence alone. Her relatives then told her, "If she had confessed something out of anxiety, fear, or pain, she should say so." At this point, Vellhagen interrupted the family, warning them that "they were not permitted to examine the witness, and thereby give her occasion for other ideas." As her father was leaving, though, he said to Grethe, "You should be calm and wait for your rights."[19]

This exchange may well explain the reason for Grethe's reversal a week later. Oldekop's postscript complained that court officers were haranguing Grethe before her father's arrival. According to Vellhagen, though, this questioning was in fact the more formal deposition of January 9, in which Grethe again acknowledged her guilt. The family, according to this accounting, actually visited on January 9. Grethe then retracted her confession in the next interrogation before confronting the Lüddens on January 17, so only one conclusion is possible. Andreas Schmidt's visit—so far as one can tell, the first visit she had received in five and a half months—was enough to change Grethe's mind about her admissions and course of action.

Certainly the judicial officers believed this to be the case. Their own account, published later, juxtaposed the timing of Grethe's retraction and her family's visit. The prosecutor, though, had accompanied the Schmidts throughout the visit and took care to overhear the conversation that occurred. Their report shows no explicit attempt to encourage Grethe to lie, only her father's encouragement that she tell the truth and wait for her rights. The magistrates interrupted any discussion of particular issues that might sway the girl's testimony. The simplest explanation is of course that after such a long incarceration, the consoling fatherly presence of Andreas Schmidt had somehow bolstered his daughter's resolve, had given her the audacity of hope.

This visit and the city's report demonstrate the impact of the advocate's interventions. Oldekop demanded that even informal conversations between the magistrates and Grethe required transcription—and that the defense had a right to see them. Moreover, by insisting that her family had the right to visit her, Oldekop's efforts paved the way for Grethe's conversation with her father, which seems to have turned the tide on her case.

If this was, as it appears, the first meeting with family or loved ones since her arrest in July, then Grethe had been cut off from outside contact for five and a half months. However else she might have been treated, this isolation was central in persuading her to see things the prosecutors' way. Further, the city's account of the family visit suggests the ease with which court officers had access to Grethe, both formally and informally. One can infer from Oldekop's demand for transcripts of these conversations his suspicion that other informal visits did occur, a charge he was to make more explicitly and graphically later. In the regime of isolation, Grethe Schmidt's only human contacts had been the jailer, the magistrates, and the torturer.

Yet the record reveals more than isolation. After the interrogation of January 8, Grethe was sent back to a "heated" room in the *Fronerey*, where she had been held since late July. As usual, she was chained, either by the foot or the leg, and referring to a "heated room" may suggest that Schmidt was receiving better treatment following her first confession.[20] One can only imagine the relief she felt upon seeing her family again. Yet even that consolation itself was tempered by the threatening presence of the court officers, particularly Johannes Vellhagen. Oldekop's next supplication to the magistrates, on January 29, mentioned that Grethe's aunt, after many attempts, finally received permission to visit her niece. According to the aunt, the presence of Vellhagen "before whom [Grethe] has a continuing fear" so unnerved Grethe that she could not go through with the visit, "however much she wanted to." Oldekop, writing on behalf of Andreas Schmidt, then requested that someone other than Vellhagen be present. Also, he pleaded that such visits should not have such strict time limitations but ought to be permissible for a "half hour or a little bit longer."[21] Even the visits Grethe received, it appears, were painfully brief and overshadowed by the jailer's presence.

Why did Vellhagen inspire such particular fear? He was present at Grethe's first interrogation back in August, so she had a long experience with him already. More to the point, Vellhagen was also in the torture chamber on November 5, when Grethe finally confessed after being threatened and bound. These incidents suggest that Vellhagen had been a principal contact between Grethe and prosecution all along. Indeed, Oldekop wrote later that, according to Grethe, the encounter between her and Vellhagen that her father witnessed as he arrived to visit his daughter was not a formal questioning at all. Instead, Vellhagen spent fifteen minutes with the girl warning her to say nothing—which for Oldekop explained her reluctance to answer her father's questions or even to speak.[22]

Shackled, alone, and in fear—this had been Grethe's world for half a year. Small wonder to Oldekop that she should quake in the presence of the judicial officers, or that she would make a false confession. The lawyer was seeking to pierce through the regimen of intimidation that in his view had given the city such control over the prisoner. Reducing Grethe's fear and isolation would allow her to testify truthfully. Complete and free access to the records of what went on during Grethe's ordeal could only help the defense by pointing to the prosecution's legal tactics.

Oldekop's stance reflected his expansive and unusually adversarial approach to criminal law. For the prosecution, though, the prisoner's isolation and fear were a legitimate part of the process itself—the guilty murderess ought to be afraid. Both body and soul *should* fear the wrath of a just God unless by confessing the truth she protect her immortal soul from eternal torment. The advocate and the magistrates were fighting over different visions of the criminal process. As the case moved to yet another, perhaps final stage, the stakes grew higher for both sides—and the tactics became more extreme.

By that time, though, in another strange twist, Oldekop was officially and suddenly gone—at least as far as Brunswick was concerned. The issues were money and access. The city government stood by its decision to allow only an extensive inspection of the acts, to which Oldekop had already objected. The Schmidts had also rejected the city's offer of a defense from within the *Fiskal* itself in favor of their chosen advocate. When the advocate, through Andreas Schmidt, began to suggest that his fees should come from the city's coffers as essential to Grethe's right to a defense, the city's attitude hardened. Because of the poverty of the Schmidt family, the city council had offered a defense ex officio. They had no intention of providing a salary for a freely chosen advocate, especially one whose "insubordination" and intemperate language had already incensed the authorities and whose obstreperousness—they believed—had led to Grethe recanting her confession. Perhaps this explains both the city council's decision not to loosen the "visitation rules," with their time limits and the continued presence of Johannes Vellhagen.

Nevertheless, the authorities were at least noncommittal about compensation. On January 31, they asked that the advocate present them with his costs.[23] On February 5, Oldekop outlined a potential salary. It was interesting indeed—fiftty thalers total, of which twenty were to be paid by Andreas Möller, the "seducer" (*Stuprator*) who had "deflowered" Grethe. This was a novel idea in the case, and it suggests as well that Oldekop may have been contemplating a lawsuit against the Möller family. For now, though, the "extended" Schmidt family had labored to gather a sum of twelve thalers, leaving eighteen. Oldekop noted as well that his *Deductions of Innocence* alone cost him thirty thalers, not to mention his other work on the case. For now, though, he would be satisfied with eighteen thalers, with the proviso that Andreas Schmidt could seek the other twenty later.[24]

On February 7, the city council rejected the advocate's request for payment, arguing that since he was retained by the family and not the city they owed him nothing. Whatever reimbursement he was entitled to would be determined according to the government's standard regulations.[25] Oldekop responded by accusing the city council of retracting the promise to pay stated in the decree of January 31. Then, not so subtly, he wrote in the name of the family: "Also the advocate, who otherwise will not be obligated to further work nor responsible for doing it, should be paid from public funds."[26]

This veiled threat was probably a tactical mistake. Clearly the city council was delighted to rid themselves of this "difficult" man. They chose to interpret it to mean that Oldekop was withdrawing his services. On February 14, they decreed that Oldekop was no longer going to "bother" the city with his "cranky incitations," and because he would introduce nothing further, the prosecution should send the Schmidt files on to the legal faculty for review.[27] The city council had just written him out of the case, meaning that his access to court records was at an end. For Grethe Schmidt, it meant that the next round of escalating interrogations would receive no review from her chosen defense. Of course, again, by law the court itself could provide for her defense. There is no evidence that, in Oldekop's absence, the city council stepped in to help her.

13

The Way to a Confession

And so, the interrogatory process began again. On March 12, 1662, the city council announced its decision to reexamine Grethe Schmidt. They had several questions focusing on why she recanted the November confession, which she had repeated again on January 9. The magistrates' intent was clear: "in case the accused is not ready to confess immediately, she will once again be given over to torture, but in a humane fashion."[1] The rapidly unfolding events of March show that the prosecution had laid out an elaborate plan, reaching beyond Grethe herself, in order to guarantee the outcome.

ALTSTADT FRONEREY, MARCH 13, 1662

Gathering in the *Fronerey* again, Johannes Vellhagen, Otto Theune, and Johannes Pilgram were joined by two of the judicial lords, Heinrich Schnell and Melchoir Schmidt. Confronted with the questions posed four months earlier, Grethe responded that she could not have known she was pregnant because she was *not* pregnant. She had not had a child, but even if she had, "she would not have had the intention to kill it."[2] Asked why she suddenly abjured a confession she had already repeated three times, Grethe answered in a colloquial dialect, rendered by Pilgram as, "I was afraid that something bad would happen to me."[3] *Who led her to deny and renounce what she numerous times earlier had confessed and admitted? How could she even have thought of such a thing [the murder], which she now renounces and says is not true?* "No one led her to it, she had not had a child, she was quite sure." The tone of Schmidt's answers had begun to fray, whether out of exhaustion or dread at what might come next. The magistrates did not hesitate. Because she would not immediately confess, she was brought back to the dungeon, "to the place of torture." Surrounded by the instruments of torture in a place she must have remembered well,

Grethe Schmidt "did not yet want to confess that she had a living child and according to her own report had killed it."[4]

The interrogators, it appeared, would accept only one answer, which Grethe stubbornly refused to give. Finally, "after repeated questionings," the prosecutors delivered her again into the hands of the *Scharfrichter*, who bound her and locked her shin into legscrews (*Beinschrauben*). This still "humane" form of torture represented an intensification from the thumbscrews employed in November but followed the same pattern—fastening the instruments without going too far at the beginning, stretching out the stages between terror and torture, blending the two stages of terror and torture but stretching out the number of steps when fear left off and pain began. The effect was immediate: "She explained that she once again wanted to tell the truth," and so the torturer released her.[5]

The city quickly returned to the list of questions first posed four and one half months previously. *Did she not know she was pregnant by Andreas Müller?* "Yes, she did know it." *Why did she hide the fact?* "She was not able to say." *Did she not have the intention to kill her child if it should come into the world?* "No." *Did she not bring a living child into the world, and where and in what place?* "In Schwülper in her father's house in the bedroom, in the presence of her mother alone, the child was born into the world, and it was already dead." *Did the child not cry or give off some sound?* "It did not cry, for it was not living but a fully formed dead child, and no one helped her but her mother." Grethe was now admitting a pregnancy and a stillbirth, but not a "living" child. But then came question seven: *Did she not kill the child or otherwise do it harm so that it would not live?* "Yes, for as her mother was fetching water and the suspect was alone, she laid the blanket over the child, and the child cried twice and lived for half an hour."

The interrogators still remained unsatisfied. Schmidt's answer meant that she had "not told the truth to questions four, five, and six." The interrogators "deem[ed] it necessary" to ask again whether she had borne a "living child." "Yes," she said. *Where and in what place?* "In Schwülper in her father's house in her room, in the morning as it was already day, though at what stroke of the bell she did not know because there was no clock in the village." *Did the baby cry (question six)?* "Yes, twice, and it lived for perhaps a half hour, because she covered the child with the blanket so that it would die. Before it came into the world, however, she had not had the notion [to kill it]." *And where had she left it after the killing?* "It was in the earth, in her father's garden, her mother knew well where, in the middle of the garden, it was just a little piece of the garden, and there stood no tree there, the child was wrapped up, and her mother took it from her and with a spade buried it, or so her mother reported to her afterward."

Who helped or advised her? "No one, not even her mother."[6]

Now the prosecution had a new confession, but how different from the first! The discrepancies between her admissions make it impossible to say whether Brunswick had finally succeeded in solving the murder or not. The city, though, did not hesitate to act. On March 14 and 15, the *Bürgermeister* sent separate letters to Claus von Marenholz in Schwülper and to judicial offices in the ducal offices at Giffhorn (in the Lüneburg section of the duchy), detailing Grethe's latest admissions and requesting a search of the Schmidt garden, in hopes of finding the corpus delicti. The letters also solicited help in dealing with her parents, since Grethe had now implicated her mother in the infant's birth and death.[7]

Reports from Giffhorn and Gross Schwülper came back swiftly. Marenholtz reported that early on the morning of March 17, the Count of Rötgesbüttel came with the request that he deliver the oxherd Andreas Schmidt together with his wife to Giffhorn. In the presence of the count, Marenholtz and his men conducted the search for the corpus delicti in the Schmidts' garden. A half day's digging, however, brought nothing, though the searchers had "very carefully gone two spades deep," noting that "according to the testimony the death was supposed to have occurred over one year earlier." That afternoon Marenholz handed over the oxherd and his wife to the count.[8]

From Giffhorn came a similar report, saying that the Schmidt parents rejected any claims of a birth in Gross Schwülper. On March 18, Martin Breyer, one of the duke's officers, conducted a more formal interrogation of Grethe's mother. Ilse remained steadfast in denying the entire matter. Grethe had never told her about the encounter with Andreas Möller, much less that she was pregnant. Instead, it was Margarethe Hafferland who first told Ilse the tale. Ilse then confronted Grethe, who acknowledged that Andreas Möller had "with violence forced the girl to have sex with him"[9]—had raped her—but denied that she was pregnant. Just a year ago, perhaps eight days after the New Year, Grethe Schmidt had returned from Brunswick to her family home. A neighbor's widow asked, "Grethe, are you a virgin?" and then "touched and felt Grethe and said, 'So help me God, you are just as thin as ever.'" Grethe's sister "also felt her and said something similar." According to Ilse, "if her daughter had been pregnant, the baby must have come into the world in Brunswick, for nothing had happened with her in Schwülper—there was no child nursed, much less even come into the world, died, and been by her [Ilse] buried."[10]

Officials then read Grethe's recent confession to her, but she "stood firmly by her previous testimony. Maybe her daughter did say something out of pain, but she knew nothing of it." Breyer then turned to Andreas Schmidt: "As far as he knows, in his house in Gross Schwülper nothing happened. It was instead Johannes Vellhagen [the court officer of Brunswick who so frightened Grethe] and others who told him that the baby came into the world in Brunswick in Heinrich Lüdden's house and was thrown into the ditch. Otherwise he knew nothing."[11]

For Brunswick, this expedition to Gross Schwülper and Giffhorn yielded very little—searching the garden for half a day did not uncover a body, and Grethe's parents stood by their story even in the face of her confession. Andreas Schmidt even reminded questioners that Grethe's first—and very different—confession came not from her, but from the notorious Johannes Vellhagen. Now Andreas was being asked about an entirely different story.

ALTSTADT FRONEREY, MARCH 17, 1662

In the meantime, the required three days had passed, and the prosecutors and the prisoner gathered again for Grethe's new, "unforced" statement. The transcript notes that on March 13, Grethe Schmidt, "in the place of torture, during the process of torture, but nevertheless after being released from the instruments of pain, the bindings and legscrews, which were at the beginning of their application, and therefore without agony and pain, freely confessed to bringing a living child into the world and then covering it with a blanket so that it would smother."[12] The careful notation of the moment was a wary reminder of Oldekop's earlier criticisms. By now, the questions must have been numbingly familiar, and Grethe answered according to the expected form. Asked whether she intended and planned the murder, "She says repeatedly that she had the intention, before the child came into the world, that she would kill it when it came."

The fullest response came to questions seven and eight concerning what she had done with the baby after its birth:

> She killed it and placed the blanket over the mouth, and it was not long before it died. . . . Her mother had gone to fetch water, and when she returned . . . and finally came into the room and asked after the baby, what was it doing? When [Grethe] answered, that it was dead, the mother asked how [she] had done it? [Grethe] answered that the blanket came over the child's mouth, for which the mother struck her and said [she] should not have done harm to the child. [Ilse] left the dead child covered up on the bed with [Grethe] until toward evening, when the mother took it from her and said that she wanted to lay it in the churchyard but instead (as her mother afterward reported) buried it with a spade behind their house in the garden, which was only a small plot without any trees and which they shared with the cowherd and otherwise planted cabbages.

After this statement, told in a matter-of-fact way (in contrast to the disorder of the confession three days earlier), Grethe continued, "[she] did not go into the garden, but eight days later . . . she saw the place where the child was concealed, for the earth was still fresh as though not turned up but was now even with the other ground. Out of anguish [she] could not come any nearer, and knew nothing more than what her mother told her."[13]

This melancholy admission is every bit as wrenching as Grethe's first, but the differences are startling. Now she claimed that the birth and murder took place in Gross Schwülper, not in Brunswick. This would mean that the birth took place well after the beginning of the year and not around New Year's—but she did not specify when, and surprisingly the interrogators did not ask. In this account, the birth did not take place at night—no dramatic holding the baby up and looking at it in the moonlight—but shortly after daybreak. She did not discard the body in the Oker River as first stated but let her mother bury it in the garden. Strangely, the city did not explore the vexing question of the delivery itself. In November, Grethe was adamant about having done everything alone, from birth to burial. In March, though, Ilse was present at her bedside in Gross Schwülper (and presumably helped with the delivery), and Ilse managed to hide and bury the corpse. And now, like a repentant criminal, Grethe expressed anguish and remorse over the deed.

If true, this new confession would resolve a glaring contradiction. All the prosecution witnesses agreed that Grethe—if pregnant—was still pregnant when she left Brunswick on her fateful walk after New Year's Day. If so, no birth occurred in the Lüdden-Dedekind household, and this would explain the absence of blood and noise in Grethe's room. On the other hand, Grethe's first confession was quite explicit in detailing the date, the time, the delivery (a breech birth), and her own actions—lifting the infant to see it in the moonlight, suffocating it with her leg, then waiting until the next day to dispose of the body in the Oker River. If her first confession was not true, it was a quite fanciful and specific account that also fit the authorities' reading of the case at the time. Indeed, until Oldekop's excoriating rebuttal, investigators had displayed no hesitation or doubts about it. Now, though, there was a second confession, much simpler, much more aligned with the prosecution's new understanding of the facts, and involving the Schmidt family itself. This confession was also a more convincing response to the objections Oldekop had raised in Schmidt's defense.

The timing and manner of the birth—if there was one—remained unresolved problems. Just when did it occur? Clearly the new confession would place it after the first week of January 1661, but interrogators did nothing to pin down an exact or even approximate date. This was not a trivial detail. If the infant were conceived in early June (around Pentecost, when the sexual encounter took place), she would have been in her thirty-second week (eight months) at the beginning of January. If the baby was born a month later, as the second confession suggests, it would have been almost full-term and more likely to survive. It would also be much less likely to be a breech birth, since the fetus would possibly have turned by then in the womb.[14]

Despite these problems, Grethe's new confession implicated her mother in the alleged crime, confirming the prosecution's deepest suspicions. Strikingly, though Grethe portrayed her mother as covering for her and disposing of the infant's body, she absolved Ilse of participating in the murder itself. Her mother even hit Grethe for "harming" the child. Was Grethe simply trying to protect her mother? Grethe had admitted a homicidal intent. Was it possible that she deliberately waited until Ilse left to implement a murderous plan? While this interpretation would explain the older woman's rebuke when confronted with a dead baby, it contradicts much of the prior testimony about Ilse: maneuvering in Brunswick, suspiciously renting and then canceling a room for the lying-in, bringing Grethe to Gross Schwülper from Wendschott, and finally reappearing in Brunswick, first to assure Hafferland that Grethe was not really pregnant and then to blackmail the stepmother. These were all matters under Ilse's control, and if the city believed this earlier testimony, they might also have concluded that any plot to commit infanticide originated with her.

There is one more problem Grethe's new confession did not solve, and it was the most significant of all. For all the determined digging, Brunswick still could not produce a corpse. Of course, it had now been a year since the body had allegedly been buried in the garden, so much could have happened. Yet it is also true that the new location of the burial was a strange place to hide a body—in the middle of a vegetable garden shared by two families—one of whom had already testified about their suspicions in the Schmidt case.[15] The absence of a body could damage the prosecution's credibility and the willingness of officials in Giffhorn and Gross Schwülper to cooperate further. With Ilse now implicated and in custody in Giffhorn, however, the *Obergericht* decided to turn daughter against mother and mother against daughter. Prosecutors would confront Grethe with her parents' denials in order to extract a more detailed confession.[16] The city council issued precise instructions to repeat the now familiar interrogation but now to warn Grethe to tell the truth, "otherwise [something] very unfortunate for her could easily result."[17]

To accompany this threat, the interrogators were to read back to Grethe her previous statements, pressing her on the very details that involved and incriminated her mother.[18] The final instruction showed the true intent of this maneuver: "The captive must be spoken to and especially led to the disposition that, since her mother has *already confessed in a different way, or in the future might say something else* [emphasis added], it might have consequences for her and her mother both, therefore she should be careful and report the honest truth" (*lautere Wahrheit*).[19] The tactic was clear—to coax more out of Grethe, suggest that Grethe's mother had already confessed something else or was likely to in future, with consequences for both. In fact, as the report from Giffhorn demonstrates, Ilse had admitted to nothing new—neither pregnancy, nor birth, nor burial in Gross Schwülper. Her daughter, though, could not know this.

Altstadt Fronerey, March 21, 1662, 4:00 p.m.

The interrogation took place that very afternoon in a room now familiar to Grethe. The judicial personnel she knew too well repeated the council's threat and charged that she "had demonstrated shame neither before God, who was present everywhere, nor for the government and the judicial personnel." In response, Grethe "declared that she would now speak the truth from the depths of her heart, and whatever she was asked about, she would happily say and willingly confess."[20]

No doubt weary of it all, Grethe repeated her most recent confession. Prosecutors then suggested that as her mother "had perhaps already confessed something different or might in the future," she should think carefully and tell the honest truth, because there was "still time." Yet despite "numerous reminders and questions" (the transcript does not specify how much longer the interrogation continued), Grethe clung to her confession, summarized finally by Johannes Pilgram the scribe:

> Lying in her bed in a room on the ground floor of her father's house in Gross Schwülper, in the presence of her mother, she brought into the world a living child, a boy, in the morning when it had already been day for at most one hour. As now the mother went toward Andreas Sivers house to get water to warm and to bathe the child with it, the suspect had in the meantime covered the child with the blanket, so that it would suffocate, and this occurred about a half hour after it was born into the world. When now the mother returned and asked about the child, but learned that she had laid the blanket over the child so that it would die, the mother cuffed her and told her she should have let it be and now what did she want to do with it? And the suspect answered

that the mother should bury it in the garden. The mother let the child lay there [in the bed] until toward evening of the same day, then took it out of the bed, and in the presence of the suspect wrapped it in a linen shroud and, according to the mother's report, in the garden, that is, in the ditch between the suspect's father's and the cowherd's house, buried it.

Pressed a final time with the possibility that her mother had already contradicted this testimony, Grethe repeated, "She knew nothing other than what she has already confessed concerning the nursing and suffocating of the child, and about her mother hiding the smothered corpse. Which report her mother would not, nor in good conscience could not, deny."[21]

In this statement Grethe produced a useful confession—congruent with the law and, in outline at least, fitting the facts as the city had compiled them over months. Whether her admissions could withstand scrutiny and greater testing, though, was another matter. Unlike her earlier admission, she had not specified a date, not even a month, for these events, nor did she describe the birth in any way. And, as was true throughout, her precise descriptions still had not yielded a corpse, despite the city's urgent efforts to find one. At this late stage, though, vagueness might actually work to the prosecution's advantage. Just as important, this last confession once again implicated the mother. From the first stages of the investigation, Brunswick's judicial personnel had heard repeated testimony of Ilse's active involvement. Now, with the daughter's reluctant help, prosecutors were enacting a clever end game that seemed tantalizingly close to snaring the mother as well. The prosecutors quickly pursued their advantage. The day after Grethe's new confession, the court sent a copy of the transcript with a request to confront her mother with it. This letter also solicited a new request for information from yet another possible witness who might have heard something at the oxherd's house the year previously.[22]

GIFFHORN, MARCH 28, 1662

If the prosecutors hoped that their new information would crack the case, Giffhorn's response (March 28) was less enthusiastic. Officials summoned the wife of the cowherd in Gross Schwülper and asked whether, in light of Grethe's confession, she would not like to add to her testimony given the previous October. Ilse, though, would neither add to nor alter her earlier testimony but repeated it "word for word," so precisely there was no reason even to take down the response. This result was another blow to the prosecution's search for the corpus delicti. The alleged infant's birth and death supposedly took place right next door to the cowherd's house, and the body would have been buried in their garden, now dug up in search of a corpse. After all this, the city still did not have a single bit of testimony or evidence to corroborate Grethe's new tale.

Concerning Grethe's mother, officials in Giffhorn were noncommittal, reluctant to proceed as aggressively as the Brunswick court would like. Having read the daughter's confession, they proposed an alternative solution, bringing mother and daughter together in a confrontation at some "neutral" location.[23] The goal would be to have young Schmidt repeat her confession "under the eyes" of her mother, pitting the daughter's shame against the mother's stubbornness, to decide which was stronger. The letter from Giffhorn cautioned, though, that any further decisions would be made, not in Brunswick, but by ducal officials at the Lüneburg chancellery in Celle, because "without special instructions we cannot commit ourselves to [any action], and in such a case we can undertake no long ordeal, since the old woman is suffering from fever and in jail it might worsen or she might even die of it."[24] As to Grethe's mother's testimony, despite renewed admonishments, Ilse Leuthgen remained stubborn in her claim that Grethe had never borne a child in the house in Gross Schwülper. And the lying-in room in Neubrücke? "She reserved it on account of words she heard in Brunswick from the Möller woman," but when the daughter returned home to Gross Schwülper, Ilse realized her condition was different and let her stay home.[25]

This letter from Giffhorn, measured and restrained, suggests that Grethe's confession did not result in a consensus about her guilt. Indeed, new circumstances brought a new degree of complexity. Schmidt's confession that the murder and burial took place in Gross Schwülper shifted the focus of events away from Brunswick and, most important, outside its jurisdiction and reach. To search for the corpse, investigators had to make a request to ducal officials in Giffhorn. The failure of that search raised questions about the veracity of her statement, but now political and diplomatic issues intruded. Why should authorities in Giffhorn or even Gross Schwülper, both under the jurisdiction of the chancellery of the Lüneburg part of the duchy in Celle, comply with further measures for the sake of Brunswick, especially when those requests might have involved the torture of the duke's subjects? This is evident in the reluctance to press the case against Grethe's mother. Officials in Giffhorn also seemed unwilling to allow Grethe Schmidt herself to remain exclusively in the city's hands—their suggestion that she be taken to an "uncontested" place in order to stage a confrontation with her mother meant taking Grethe out of the hands of investigators who had worked so long to resolve the matter in the city. Added to that, ducal authorities reportedly could not find the new witness mentioned by the city—indeed had never heard of him. The city's grasp of the investigation appeared none too convincing.

This might seem mere speculation but for a letter that arrived at the city council from the "Princely Brunswick-Lüneburg Chancellor and Council" at Celle on March 26. Oldekop, it appears, had not been idle, whatever his status in the city of Brunswick. Referring to a complaint made by Andreas Schmidt in Giffhorn, the ducal letter notes that "according to reports of Grethe Schmidt's last testimony through torture, the delict was committed in Schwülper, in the undisputed dominion of the most highly revered prince." As a result, "we hereby request that you allow the prisoner to be taken to an indisputed border place and delivered to officials of Giffhorn, and to send therefore your own explanation so the assigned officers can be instructed concerning the delivery of the prisoner."[26] The wording of this letter mirrors the language and the request to transfer Grethe that Giffhorn officials used two days later.

The letter, which shows that Oldekop and the Schmidts were still in contact, also demonstrates concern about jurisdiction and procedure given Schmidt's new confession. If Grethe committed a crime in Gross Schwülper rather than in Brunswick, then city authorities were precariously close to overstepping their boundaries and trespassing on the jurisdiction of the ducal government itself. Oldekop's move also had another edge: in the continuing political tension between the city and the Welfen dukes, Brunswick's prosecution might now appear as a usurpation of the duke's authority. Conversely, malfeasance in the criminal process might also undermine the city's own claim to independent administration of its affairs.

The Brunswick magistracy's response would be an important test of their relations with the ducal government and of their political and diplomatic skills. In the meantime, however, magistrates treaded more cautiously in dealing with the immediate matters in Giffhorn, where Grethe's mother was incarcerated and where no one had heard of the city's alleged new witness. On March 28 the city council identified him as "Andreas Glindman," who "is reported to have heard a child" in the Schmidt household.[27] Martin Breyer in Giffhorn replied on April 3, reporting that they had indeed found and questioned Andreas Glindman about "what he heard a year ago in the early morning as he passed by the oxherd's house."[28] Breyer then stated that he confronted Schmidt's mother with the information that Glindman "heard a child crying in the house and that a sound came from it." Yet Ilse stubbornly maintained that "her daughter with her or in her house had not nursed a child, if something happened in the city, of that she had no knowledge."[29] Further, the mother stated emphatically, "do with her whatever one will, she neither could nor knew anything more to say."[30]

So Andreas Glindman did exist to say that he heard something in the Schmidt household in the early morning. The judicial lords that same day sent a fuller, more detailed request to Giffhorn, in hopes of finally trapping Grethe's mother and confirming the confession. The city included a number of details to refute Ilse's contention that she knew nothing of what might have happened in Brunswick. She had appeared in Brunswick to spend a night at the Lüdden house specifically to find out whether her daughter was pregnant, a fact she confirmed to the Lüddens. If Ilse knew nothing, why did she then reserve the lying-in room? And why, just at the appropriate time after the sexual encounter when Grethe should be delivering the child, was Grethe in fact laid up sick in bed in her mother's house, at just the moment when Andreas Glindman allegedly heard a baby's cry?

That same day, April 3, the city council responded to the inquiry from the chancellery in Celle. The letter is a clever riposte to the claim that, because the crime was committed in Gross Schwülper, Brunswick had no standing to pursue the case. On the contrary, "the supplicant in this matter himself specifically will not admit that a delict has been committed in Gross Schwülper. We therefore, as indicated, have until now conducted the inquisitional process by our traditions and customs in similar cases, and further, have in the matter acted according to the law."[31] In other words, if the Schmidts would not admit to any crime in Gross Schwülper, how could they claim the city was overstepping its jurisdictional boundary and pursuing a crime committed in the village? Now it was the prosecution's turn to exploit the absence of a corpus delicti. The subtext of this specious but clever claim, of course, is that for the Schmidts to make their case, someone would have to confirm a crime and therefore Grethe's guilt.

The more significant part of the letter concerned Brunswick's own legal traditions and customs. The wording is crucial: "We want to convey to you, Your High-Noble and Merciful lordship, the certain trust, that you will not expect of us any act contrary to the common and ancient traditions of our city, [and] especially because of this [enclosed] explanation, will most mercifully consider the extradition as excused." This apparently submissive response was in fact a polite but firm rejection of the request. Rather than affirm or dispute the ducal inquiry, the authors instead provided a legal explanation that they believed should satisfy questions about the city's behavior without altering it. Second, by referring to their own ancient traditions, they implicitly upheld the legitimacy and independence of Brunswick's judiciary and criminal processes. Indeed, in a final clause the city council asked forgiveness if it was mistaken and awaited further instructions, pledging all the while that it sought to act as a good subject.[32]

This was a fine line for the city council, but it shows the considerable moxie that had enabled Brunswick to weather the aggressiveness of the duchy in the past. Of equal concern, though, suddenly the consequences of this "burdensome" case threatened to expand and embroil the city in political controversy with its sovereign and implacable foe. The *Bürgermeister* and city council knew exactly who to blame, and this accounts for the intense bitterness of the opening response, directed at one unnamed but obvious person for impugning the city's motives and competence: "against the otherwise well-known author of such coarse defamatory writings, we reserve to ourselves the appropriate revenge."[33] This was a threat that Oldekop could not take lightly. He was drawing the city into confrontation with the duchy, and the rulers of Brunswick now viewed him as actively dangerous.

The council's exchange with the ducal chancellor in Celle may have convinced the city magistrates that they must carefully bring the Schmidt case to a swift (and successful) end in order to prevent further meddling. How better to accomplish this than to turn again to a legal faculty for counsel? This time, however, the city sent all the materials, from the beginning of the case up to the response to the ducal administration, to the University of Rinteln. The decision might seem curious, for Rinteln lay 115 kilometers west of Brunswick in the territories of the Counts of Schaumburg and had been a university only since 1621—less distinguished than Helmstedt ("The Athens of the Welfen Dukes"), which was just 35 kilometers away. The city later explained that, since Oldekop had already demanded a new decision from an "impartial" university, Helmstedt was out of the picture. Rinteln, though, lay outside the territories of Brunswick-Lüneburg and would also mean less scrutiny by the duchy's partisans, particularly given the city's own dealings with the administration. After all, Wolfenbüttel was where Duke Augustus held court.

In Gifhorn, meanwhile, Grethe's mother had now been in jail for over a month. When she was finally questioned again on April 15, once again denying any knowledge of a birth, the authorities there treated the matter more seriously. Upon her denials, "the torturer entered and placed before her the instruments belonging to torture, and made clear to her that if she persisted in her stiff-necked attitude she would be brought to torture and painfully handled."[34] Yet the oxherd's wife reacted as one might expect, given all the testimony about her so far:

> One way or another she remained steadfast—she knew of no child, confess
> what [the daughter] might, she had seen no child that had been born from her

daughter, one could do with her what one would. She would like to wish that it were so, that [the daughter] by Andreas Möller was pregnant and had had a child, he was rich enough, and would have had to do right by her daughter.[35]

This last statement again brought Andreas Möller into the case and echoed Gertrude Wilmers's words to Grethe more than a year earlier. It was also one of the arguments adduced by Justus Oldekop in his long defense brief in November 1661 and points up one of the puzzles of this frustrating affair: if the Schmidts were so venal as to try to blackmail Margarethe Hafferland, why not let Grethe have the baby and extract money from Andreas Möller himself? Indeed, as Gertrude Wilmers had made clear, some women in Brunswick would have expected Möller to provide support for a child and its mother. Surely that would have been easier— and much more profitable—than murder.

The Giffhorn transcript, sent to Brunswick, made no comment about how next to proceed. Officials there clearly did not move from terror to torture itself, and it is hard to know whether they were willing to take the next, fateful step. Earlier letters already expressed some impatience with the process and noted that Schmidt's mother was ill. It is also true that moving from the threat of torture to torture was not automatic—the judicial lords of Brunswick themselves had repeatedly solicited academic advice about Grethe's ordeal. Here in Giffhorn, where less was at stake, justifying torture might not be worth the effort and cost it could involve. Later, Oldekop argued that the *Fiskal* was indeed hoping to trap the older Schmidt woman, a claim that Brunswick's government vehemently denied. Brunswick's officials though, despite their grave suspicions that Ilse Leuthgen had masterminded her daughter's murderous misdeeds, may have realized she was out of reach. With time no longer on their side, they were perhaps only seeking to confirm Grethe's confession rather than pursue the mother.

Giffhorn, May 6, 1662

Besides, the judicial lords still had another witness, the mysterious Andreas Glindman of Gross Schwülper. At the city council's request, Martin Breyer of Giffhorn interviewed him formally, using a set of questions drawn up in Brunswick. He affirmed that one year before, he had passed by the Schmidt house: "It was over a year ago, the exact time he did not keep, but when the cry that the post had been robbed came into the village, he was to be sent to the corporal in Adenbüttel . . . he could not actually say whether it was an hour before or after midnight."[36]

Asked whether he had heard a child's cry, Glindman said that, "Just as he came by the oxherd's house, he heard a noise as a small child, once, and not more, upon which he looked back but heard nothing more, so he continued on. He actually does not know whether it was in or outside the house, it came to him however like the voice of a little child, but not more than once."[37]

Then, more specific even: *Upon his sworn oath and conscience, must he not say that he actually heard the voice, that it must have been that of a child's cry?* "It sounded to him as though it were the voice of a little child. Because, however, he heard it only once, he could not actually say, but it did sound like that to him."

From here, Glindman told what he knew of the Schmidts and of rumors in the village about Grethe and a baby. He had seen Grethe "some weeks after, on the eve of Lent, but could not say that Grethe was nursing a child and was its mother, but neither could he deny it. Many people were talking about it." And this became Glindman's refrain for all the subsequent questions about whether a child had been born and murdered, who had done it, where it had been buried—he either did not know anything or could only report numerous rumors among the villagers.[38] Glindman might have been an official, but he was no more willing than anyone else to accuse Grethe outright.

With Glindman's account, the testimony in the case of Grethe Schmidt came to a close on May 6, 1662. He provided a single detail: he heard a sound like a "small child" crying—once and only once—in the oxherd's house. There is no trace of the postal robbery in the record today,[39] but from the statement it is clear that the date was some weeks before Ash Wednesday (February 14), so Candlemas at the beginning of February seems a reasonable conjecture. That date would be consistent with other testimony about the birth. When pressed, though, Glindman could not even be sure that the cry he heard exactly once was in fact an infant, nor did he stop to investigate. Though he saw Grethe a few weeks later, he could not describe her condition in any way.

Most important, though, Glindman's testimony in fact contradicted Grethe's own final confession, according to which the baby was born when it was already light outside and she killed it shortly afterward. In contrast, Glindman specified that he was roused by the robbery and heard the baby's cry either an hour before or after midnight. Either Grethe had fabricated some parts of the story yet again, or Glindman's testimony was wrong. Brunswick's prosecutors had undoubtedly hoped for more. The disparity between what they expected and what Glindman provided suggests that his testimony was a last, frustrating attempt to end the stalemate—the mother refusing to confess even under threat of torture, the daughter imprisoned in Brunswick for a crime now assumed to have been committed elsewhere, the potential witnesses either reluctant or disappointing.

In the midst of this impasse, the response of the legal faculty of Rinteln arrived. Finding it difficult to believe that no trace would be found, the legal faculty suggested yet another twist—that Grethe was now concealing or lying about the place where the body was buried. The faculty at Rinteln recommended keeping her in jail "until the birth of the child and the cause of its death are no longer in doubt." A crucial phrase then follows: "Should the corpus delicti then come to daylight, then the suspect should be charged before a capital criminal court for the crime, and then if she repeats her previous confession she should as a child murderess [infanticide] be punished according to the Criminal Law of Emperor Charles V." The punishment recommended by the *Carolina* could be drowning—or burial alive.[40]

The scholars of Rinteln offered an alternative to these draconian measures: "If at this point she stands by her previous confession, and likewise the corpus delicti does not come to light, then she is to be struck with the rod and eternally banished according to law."[41] Schmidt's life depended entirely on the discovery of a corpse, but under no circumstances would she get off free. Instead, the legal faculty of Rinteln was recommending a lesser penalty that had in fact become common in the seventeenth century, as legal scholars and practitioners grappled with the difficulties resulting from the demand for a confession as the only certain proof in capital cases. As a "suspected infanticide," the best Grethe could hope for was a severe, shameful sentence that would nevertheless leave her alive.

The letter from Rinteln explains the questions posed to Andreas Glindman. The city had hoped to the end for a final and capital conviction. Failing this, however, prosecutors wanted enough corroborating evidence to justify the lesser sentence of "suspected infanticide." And what of Grethe's mother? Should the city try again to coax Martin Breyer in Giffhorn to take another step against her? There was a torturer at hand in Giffhorn, after all.

The prosecution's decision came on May 13, a week after Glindman's testimony. The city council sent the records to yet another legal faculty, this time in Jena, stating, "the murdered child's corpse . . . has not been found in the specified place, *nor is there hope to do so* [emphasis added]." On this point, the city admitted defeat. The reason was not surprising: "because the prisoner's mother was taken into the Prince of Lunebürg's territory, the proposed confrontation with the suspect, her daughter, will not be possible."[42] The idea of the confrontation, however, originated in Giffhorn itself, so the decision to reject it came from Brunswick. The reason for their reluctance is obscure. It is possible, though, that city investigators feared that transferring Grethe out of their jurisdiction would mean an unresolved finish to their long and weary case. Instead the city sought from Jena "a final judgment of Grethe Schmidt, grounded in the law." Unlike their plea to Rinteln, however, the council sought something more. The faculty should "look into Grethe Schmidt's defense counsel, whose insufferable imputations have attacked our civic honor."[43] The city council wanted now to pursue Justus Oldekop and his damaging allegations. To do this, the *Fiskal* first needed a decision against Grethe Schmidt. The university's opinion would vindicate the process and the "ancient customs" that Brunswick was so determined to preserve.

When it came, the University of Jena's opinion affirmed Rinteln's conclusion: "From the enclosed acts it appears that in the stated matters and circumstances the suspect is to be punished with a public whipping and eternal banishment." As for the defense lawyer, "because of offensive words used against the court in his writing, he is to be punished, not lightly, with 20 *Reichsthalers*, and thereby reminded, in future that he is to represent his clients' needs more humbly or to be more respectful of other orders and views."[44]

Outcomes

On June 18, the city pronounced its final judgment. Both the legal faculties of Jena and Rinteln advised labeling Schmidt a "suspected infanticide" and recommended a lesser punishment as a result. All leads exhausted, the prosecutors apparently saw nothing left to gain. The body, if there ever was a body, would never be found, at least not in Brunswick, and the surrounding territories had no reason to follow along the city's dead ends. The judicial lords, the city council, and the *Bürgermeisters* were all tired of the case, the Schmidts, and above all, Justus Oldekop.

Thus, upon the advice of "learned counsel" and as demonstrated by the evidence, Grethe Schmidt, for "suspected infanticide," was to be flogged and permanently exiled from the city of Brunswick and all its territories.[45] At the very least, then, the absence of the corpus delicti and the machinations of her advocate spared Grethe's life. But flogging was no light sentence—after branding, which left a brutal and public mark of dishonor, it was considered to be the worst possible punishment. Floggings were public events designed to chastise and to warn, and in the case of Brunswick they took place at a particular pillar set in the middle of the Hagen market, using either a rope, a whip, or a bundle of wooden rods. Though the sentence did not specify the number, a typical flogging in Germany involved forty lashes.

Before the sentence was carried out, Grethe Schmidt pledged an "oath of truce" known as the *Urphede*. In it she acknowledged and accepted the sentence, absolving the city of Brunswick, its government, judicial officers, and citizens from any blame and ascribing all responsibility to her own crimes. The *Urphede* was a traditional document used to uphold the sentences handed out in court. The convict accepted the sentence and forgave the court, its personnel, and city itself, swearing never to act against them. Traditionally, vengeance was a constant threat in criminal matters, more so in cases brought by accusation rather than by inquisition. The *Urphede* was not exactly a confession but an acknowledgment of the correctness of the process in order to legitimize the court's decision and hopefully forestall vengeance by family, friends, or associates. The *Urphede* did announce the crime, however, and Grethe's statement acknowledged her sentence as a "suspected infanticide."[46]

The sentence was carried out the next day, but before Grethe could be sent away, one final task remained—the bill. On June 19, the keeper of the *Fronerey* in the Altstadt, Marin Reinhard, issued a receipt: "*Anno* 1661 Margarethe Schmidt from Gross Schwülper was brought to us, now the 19th of June *Anno* 1662 she leaves, making 325 days."[47] Reinhard noted that he had received eighty-four thalers in payment, but the receipt does not indicate from whom. At that moment, Grethe Schmidt disappeared—no doubt she returned, bloody and beaten, to her home in Gross Schwülper in the Duchy of Brunswick-Lüneburg. But she was alive.

It is not clear whether Oldekop witnessed the flogging or was anywhere nearby—there is nothing in his writings to suggest that he was, just as it is impossible to know whether he ever met Grethe before her release or even after. By June 19, though, his attention may already have shifted, because the conviction of Grethe Schmidt was not the only decision publicly decreed on June 18, 1662. The wrath of the city was also about to fall on Justus Oldekop.

14

"Even to the Devil Himself"

"The chance for an appeal ought to be extended even
to the devil himself, if he is in court."
—Justus Oldekop[1]

A lengthy, torturous, and bitter criminal process against Grethe Schmidt did little to slake either Justus Oldekop's or the city of Brunswick's thirst for justice and taste for controversy. Whatever the truth about Grethe, it was lost in the angry appeals and lawsuits that were merely the prologue to a vitriolic public exchange that consumed Oldekop until his death in 1667. Only through this wearying controversy did it become clear that, beneath the murder investigation, other issues far removed from the misdeeds of an oxherd's daughter drove the parties to fight over her reputation: the issues of public honor and the politics of autonomy.

The latest and final phase of the tale began at the very moment the city council published its decree against Grethe Schmidt. On June 18, 1662, the *Rat* issued another decree to penalize Oldekop:

> the suspect's defender, because of the offensive words that he employed in his writings against the local court, is to be punished with twenty *Reichsthalers*. We cite and require the same on the 27th to appear before us in court . . . and to take an oath, from here on out to work for his clients' needs in an appropriate manner, or to prepare for other rebukes. *Published before the general council, 18th June 1662.*[2]

The city council had taken the advice of the University of Jena but added humiliation by requiring a hearing and a new oath from the advocate. Oldekop's offense was not simply extreme language but, the council decreed, insubordinate and immodest behavior toward the *Bürgermeister* and the council. The alleged insults are not hard to find. In December 1661, officials had complained to the Helmstedt law faculty about his "harsh and to us almost insufferable words such as open iniquity, affectation, bloodthirstiness, empty illegal proceedings, resentfulness [*missgunst*] of the suspect's innocence, avidity [*begierig*] for her death, premeditated fabrications . . . false imputations, harsh nullities [*nullitäten*] contrary to the law of Nature and God's Word . . . torture applied against all law and reason . . . calumnious process."[3] The city's defenders were convinced of Oldekop's "thirst to defame" them.[4] Helmstedt advised waiting until the Schmidt process was concluded before responding to Oldekop's behavior. Oldekop himself later claimed astonishment, "having employed his pen in this his profession, almost forty years long, in many upper and lower courts, that no one in his entire life had assessed even a single groschen as a punishment."[5]

As his work in the Schmidt case shows, however, Oldekop was not a man to back down. So it is no surprise that on June 27, 1662, rather than greet a chastened and submissive subject at their door, the city council received a letter expressing surprise and dismay at the subpoena, so much so that Oldekop even asked the officer delivering it whether "there has not been some mistake." Why the shock? Because, claimed Oldekop, for more than the past quarter year he had been officially off the case, following the city's refusal to assist the Schmidts in paying his fee. Despite mounting anxiety about the obvious dangers (*pericul*) confronting him, Oldekop argued, "as I never heard that anyone else came in my place to the rescue and defense of the poor prisoner's innocence . . . I finally had to conclude that the word '*Defensor*' meant me and no one else."[6]

Despite his rhetoric, it is of course clear from the record that Oldekop's absence only applied to the proceedings in Brunswick. He was active (and perhaps most effective) outside the city's jurisdiction—in the Lüneburg chancellery at Celle or at Giffhorn, where the conflict over Grethe's mother and her testimony had been fought. Oldekop, though, was also making a larger point: in his official absence, the *Fiskal* had done nothing more to provide for Grethe Schmidt's defense, so that in the decisive months of March and April, Brunswick's prosecutors had unfettered opportunities to force her confession. Oldekop saw here a gross abuse of judicial procedure—the city had neglected its Christian and legal responsibilities to help the prisoner. Just as important, this fact implicitly put the lie to the *Fiskal*'s refusal to pay Oldekop. He was neither too expensive nor obstreperous. The prosecution simply had no real intention of providing assistance to the poor family. And, finally, if Schmidt had in fact gone undefended, Oldekop had grounds for an appeal.

Oldekop's feigned surprise was a seamless part of his own defense. He realized that by simultaneously pronouncing sentence on the young woman and her advocate, city authorities were linking his fate to the girl's, in order to attach the dishonor of her crime and low status to him (later the city would revile him as "that defender of female oxherders"). Oldekop's self-defense required that he vindicate the innocence of Grethe Schmidt.

Not surprisingly, Oldekop also believed that a good offense was the best defense. He wrote that impartial readers would find no excessively belligerent words, for "I have neither set out nor written anything, indeed not the smallest word, which was not demanded by the unavoidable necessity of defending the innocent and avoiding the shedding of innocent blood." Had he written otherwise "and covered over the evil affair with sugar sweets . . . I would have been acting against my conscience and not as an honest, faithful, and conscientious advocate." In his forty years of experience, he had often uncovered "all sorts and many errors and great failings" without authorities taking his corrections badly, except in these "unprecedented" and "wicked" proceedings against Grethe Schmidt. Behind his rhetoric, though, lay a hard-headed strategy to demand the specifics of the case against him and to consider his options. Thus Oldekop pleaded for another fourteen days, after which he would unhesitatingly answer the magistrates' questions.[7]

HAGEN, JULY 31, 1662

Oldekop's plea appeared reasonable, but he waited until the very day of his hearing to seek its postponement. Although reports came to the magistrates from their agents in Wolfenbüttel that something was going on, the *Rat* did not respond to his appeal until July 31, when two letters arrived at the city council in the name of Augustus, Duke of Brunswick-Lüneburg. Later, the city council would argue that Oldekop's letter of June 27 "in truth sought nothing more than to gain time until the princely high court's citation and appeal could arrive."[8]

The duke's two letters were a serious blow to the city. They informed the council that "the most learned, true and dear to us Justus Oldekop" intended to appeal to the princely court "from an invalid or unlawful judgment and fine pronounced by you and against him on the 18th of June."[9] The high court asked the city to present a deposit of fifty thalers to defray expenses and to provide copies of all materials pertinent to the case for the court's use and for the appellant, Justus Oldekop, who should also not be denied the salary due him in the Schmidt matter.[10] Why would the advocate require copies of the case records now? Because Oldekop's own appeal required revisiting the investigation of Grethe Schmidt, of which he had not officially been a part since late February.

The ducal request, though, went beyond demanding the records of the Schmidt case—to include, as well, the prosecution's and the city council's deliberations concerning their strategy.

Brunswick's rulers, fierce defenders of the city's prerogatives and independence, would not accept the possibility of an appeal beyond the city's jurisdiction itself, at least not to the ducal *Hofgericht* at Wolfenbüttel. Oldekop, though, at this point, technically was not appealing the criminal verdict against Grethe but the fine levied against him. His self-defense involved his actions in the Schmidt case, but in his thinking this was a civil matter.

Like his earlier recourse to the duchy on Grethe's behalf, Oldekop's decision to appeal his case vaulted the issue beyond pure legal maneuvers into the realm of territorial politics. As noted in chapter 1, Brunswick's practical autonomy clashed with its legal subservience to the Dukes of Brunswick-Lüneburg. Throughout the late sixteenth and then the seventeenth century, successive rulers sought to bring the unruly city to heel. In the city itself, numerous citizens actually sided with the duchy, especially as the economy declined and the independence of cities seemed anachronistic in the age of absolutist princes. And now Duke Augustus, with the entire duchy in his hands and at the height of his power, reached for more. This was the same Augustus whose ambition to centralize and rule the duchy politically and legally had been apparent in his "Territorial Order" of 1647, affirming ducal authority over courts and justice. As his appetite for the city's liberties intensified throughout the 1660s, Brunswick's magistrates guarded the city's autonomy. As a result, the battle over Grethe Schmidt's fate grew more significant for both sides. On the very date of the ducal decrees—July 31, 1662—authorities in Hagen sent a *Baumeister* (a city official in charge of civic property and order in one of the twelve *Bauerschaften* of Brunswick) to Oldekop with the following terse message: "On the order of the honorable and most wise *Rat*, I have summoned the so-named Doctor Oldekop to appear at the Neustadt *Rathaus* on 1 August, 1662, upon pain of arrest."[11] Oldekop, on August 1, declined the "very harsh" demand, which left him "shocked" and surprised, because this matter was now "under appeal" to the princely high court "and that therefore I can no longer stand and appear before your honors without loss and renunciation of such a helpful benefit of law."[12] The *Baumeister* sent to call for Oldekop returned empty-handed, except for the lawyer's letter of refusal and belated notification of his intent to appeal.

Within an hour, though, the city council again sent officers to confront Oldekop. Now the *Baumeister* (Arendt Deneken of Hagen) had four companions, and they brought very serious news. What Oldekop was now facing was not simply arrest, but *Verfestung*, a practice deeply rooted in medieval

Saxon law. Originally, *Verfestung* included stripping away the distinctions and privileges of rank, leaving the nobleman, for example, to be treated suddenly and roughly as a "tradesman." If the offense included some serious felony, capital punishment might be the outcome. By the seventeenth century, though, *Verfestung* was a consequence of stubborn disobedience to authority—contumacy—and involved a form of public ostracism that might even include territorial exile. The goal was to compel an individual to appear before his lawful superiors, in which case the sentence could be lifted. In the case of absence or flight, the *Verfestung* meant declaring that the fugitive was now an outlaw. It was a serious punishment that struck at the heart of a lifetime of honors and dignity, demonstrating the level of anger that Justus Oldekop had provoked in Brunswick.[13]

The participants gave conflicting accounts of what happened next. According to *Baumeister* Deneken's deposition later that day, he and four others were dispatched to Oldekop's home to warn him to come immediately to the Neustadt *Rathaus* "or this very day the *Verfestung* will go into effect, so he should spare himself contempt and immediately appear in person."[14] The officers found Oldekop on the Bohlweg (one of the main roads of Hagen, heading south from the market) and suggested he might want to return home to hear their message. Oldekop retorted that "they could say it in his house if they were so ordered, he would not go, though."[15] So they told him right there on the street that the city council required him to go to the *Rathaus* right away or he would incur contempt and *Verfestung* immediately. Oldekop would not comply and said he would notify the council in writing that he was appealing to Wolfenbüttel and that he had to consult with others. At that, the *Baumeister* returned to the *Rathaus* in Hagen, where they proclaimed the *Verfestung* and then sent word of it to Oldekop's home, "so that he might pay attention to it and save himself from further misfortune."[16]

Oldekop recounted a more sinister version of these events. Puzzled about the summons of July 31, the lawyer was worried. The command to appear "seemed more and more suspicious and dangerous." As a result, Oldekop resolved to travel as soon as possible to Wolfenbüttel to seek advice. Oldekop was in fact already on his way to Wolfenbüttel when he met the *Baumeister* on the street, now backed up by four other officers. Oldekop, of course, would have none of their bullying and reported that he explained as firmly and decisively as possible that he had answered the city council that morning and must for business purposes make a journey. Nothing deterred the city authorities, though, and the *Baumeister* ordered him to come along immediately, saying, "The matter is closed."[17] The five officers even rode along with him for a while to force his hand. Oldekop finally repeated what he had written in his letter, that he intended to explain himself to the lords, so they should be at peace with him. With that, he turned toward Wolfenbüttel.

According to Oldekop, he had intended to return to Brunswick the next day, ready to resolve these issues through all appropriate measures. When the bells in Brunswick began to ring and solemnly announce the *Verfestung*, with city officers approaching his home to give public warning and notice to his family, Oldekop had already left the city. He would never live in Brunswick again. When, or if, he might return, even for a brief time, was now gravely uncertain.

With Oldekop's last-minute escape to Wolfenbüttel, the dynamic changed. The Brunswick government lost its immediate physical control over the old lawyer. To enforce its edicts against Oldekop now meant reclaiming jurisdiction, but this would involve the city in a series of dangerous maneuvers with the duke. Brunswick had also to deal somehow with the ducal *Hofgericht* and its decision to consider the lawyer's appeal. Simply put, Oldekop's claims and tactics had thoroughly challenged Brunswick's judicial autonomy at precisely the moment when Duke Augustus was chipping away aggressively at the walls of its independence. While it is likely that Oldekop himself recognized the political ramifications of his appeal, it is hard to imagine that the ducal chancellery overlooked the significance of this opportunity.

The precise timing of these events struck a particular nerve in the city. At the end of July 1662, the very moment Oldekop was protesting Brunswick's actions and appealing to the duchy, the city council was renegotiating its "contract" of homage with Duke Augustus himself. Already in February and March, the city had repeatedly rebuffed Duke Augustus's attempt to reaffirm Brunswick's status as a subject city (*Erbstadt*) and get the city to reenact a solemn ceremony of tribute (*Huldigung*) to his titular sovereignty.[18] In 1663, while Oldekop and the city council battled over his fate in court, the *Hofgericht* itself was reorganized. In short, Oldekop's appeal could not have come at a worse time for the city's rulers, who believed they had no choice but to reject or fend off his charges. Oldekop was feeling the public wrath of an increasingly embattled municipal magistracy.

Neustadt Rathaus, September 19, 1662

With Oldekop slipping from their grasp, the city council pondered its next move. Determined not to permit the *Hofgericht* to claim standing in the appeal, the council decided to send a representative to Wolfenbüttel to present copies of the imperial edicts and ducal concessions guaranteeing its judicial independence. By doing so directly but informally, city officials perhaps hoped to avoid a confrontation in court itself and thus any ducal attempt to undermine Brunswick's long-standing and much-prized autonomy, guaranteed by emperors.

Thus on September 23, 1662, the notary Johannes Strübe set off with a witness to Wolfenbüttel. Once there, though, they waited several hours while the secretary of the *Hofgericht* stalled, finally telling them to return the next day. On September 24, the same evasions and postponements occurred again, until the secretary finally refused the documents on the grounds that the matter of Oldekop's appeal was to be settled in court and the city should find a procurator to represent them rather than try to circumvent the legal proceedings. Strübe stood his ground and protested, but to no avail, and so he finally left.

Rebuffed by the *Hofgericht*, Strübe followed up on another duty—to serve a warrant on Oldekop, whom he learned was staying with a son in a house near the Oker River. When the Brunswick contingent knocked, one of Oldekop's sons answered. Soon, though, "the father himself came out to me, and asked whether I could not instead come back in the afternoon, for he had to go out very soon."[19] When Strübe stated his case, though, Oldekop "stumbled backward and repeatedly said he would accept nothing, he would accept nothing, he was not at home and had nothing to do with the city council of Brunswick, if it were an imperial letter from the *Kammer* [*Reichskammergericht*, that is, the Imperial Chamber Court, the high court of appeals in the Habsburg empire], then he would accept it."[20] Strübe persisted, warning Oldekop not to appeal and thereby reject the city's privilege and insult the empire. Oldekop, though, retreated into his quarters, leaving Strübe and his witness to warn the son that these were imperial documents worthy of the highest respect. Oldekop's son also refused to accept them and followed his father inside. The notary and his witness then deposited their materials in a chest next to the lawyer's chambers and withdrew.[21] As they moved down the road, they heard Oldekop calling to them from his window, but feeling they had fulfilled their charge, the pair left the old lawyer to shout into the air behind them.[22]

Strübe's adventure might have cheered city officials determined to thwart Oldekop's appeal either by law or by intimidation. It certainly unsettled the old lawyer to find Brunswick's officials seeking him out with threats and warrants even in Wolfenbüttel. The city council's attempt to avoid legal confrontation with the *Hofgericht*, however, had failed. And it was clear from the diplomatic minuet between Strübe and the *Hofgericht* that the Oldekop case was politically charged. Whether or not the old lawyer intended it, wherever Oldekop went, trouble for Brunswick seemed to follow.

Any satisfaction the city took from Strübe's mission dissipated two months later, when the *Hofgericht* officially rejected Brunswick's arguments and required that the *Rat* present its case through a procurator and in court. From then on, until 1666, the *Hofgericht* in Wolfenbüttel, along with the Imperial Chamber Court, would be clogged with briefs from Oldekop or from the city of Brunswick, requests for acts, and all of the back-and-forth that a legal process could generate. In the midst of this chaos, Oldekop launched both an appeal and a lawsuit against the city in the name of Andreas Schmidt on behalf of Grethe Schmidt.

As seen in the first injunctions promulgated in August 1662, the duchy in Wolfenbüttel appeared inclined to side with Oldekop, at least in appealing the process against him. In its separate opinions, the *Hofgericht* allowed the case to play out in court, ordering the government of Brunswick to provide documents and to share them with Oldekop. In comparison, the Schmidt appeal itself generated much less attention from Oldekop or from the city council. Oldekop and the city council were fighting for their honor, but in court, at least, the conflict centered on Oldekop, even though the appropriateness of the judgment against Grethe was the issue critical to both sides. The city resisted the very idea that such a matter, which according to imperial and ducal decree belonged exclusively to the city, should even be considered outside Brunswick's boundaries. The city council opted for stalling as long as possible while preparing its own set of appeals to the *Reichskammergericht*. The legal case slowed to a glacial pace, marked by Oldekop's frustrated demands for documents and punctuated by decisions on his behalf from Wolfenbüttel followed by refusals and delays from Brunswick. In November 1664, however, the *Hofgericht* ruled in favor of Andreas Schmidt, in the case of *Schmidt v. Brunswick*.[23] Of course the city itself immediately appealed this decision to the *Reichskammergericht*. At least temporarily, though, Oldekop was vindicated.

If Brunswick could not bring Oldekop to heel, though, neither could Oldekop force the city council to come to terms. Physically safe in Wolfenbüttel, Oldekop still complained to the *Hofgericht* that his reputation lay in tatters due to continued harassment by the city. Not only was his family in Brunswick suffering from endless ridicule, but news of Oldekop's disgrace had spread throughout northern Germany and even as far away as Tallinn at the eastern end of the Baltic (present-day Estonia), where one son heard of the news within weeks, criticizing his father for jeopardizing the family's good name. His eldest son, Heinrich Oldekop, also wrote from Bremen: "I could never have hoped that my honored father at such an age would make so grievous a mistake, which would be to the children's welfare a great blow. . . . Nothing in my entire life has brought me such unhappiness as now."[24] Yet for all Oldekop's pleas, writing, and lawsuits, the city had not budged. And there was more to come.

In 1663, in the midst of all this legal dueling, an anonymous tract appeared in Brunswick, claiming to be the *True Description of an unheard of, contrary to God's word, all Law and Natural Reason, Criminal Process, which the* Burgermeister *and* Rat *of the city of Brunswick conducted against a poor innocent peasant's daughter from Gross Schwulber, born in the Principality of Lüneburg, fourteen years old, named Margareta Schmidt, who, falsely accused of infanticide against the known and revealed truth, was left unheard and undefended.* Though the author's name was not mentioned, it was clear that Justus Oldekop had moved his case to print, now pleading not only for Grethe Schmidt but also for his own cause.

The *Wahrhaffte Beschreibung* (*True Description*) along with the city council's reply, *Relatio Facti et Juris*,[25] appear (in manuscript form) in the appeals case by Justus Oldekop in the name of Andreas Schmidt. The documents thus contain a mixture of harsh polemic and dense legal argument. Even in the title of Oldekop's polemic this is evident—that Grethe Schmidt was not only tortured twice but left "undefended" fell under one of the rules permitting appeals in criminal cases. Oldekop's outrage was also focused on his best legal chance at reversing the decision in court. Brunswick's response—written by chief syndic and head of the *Obergericht*, Johann Strauch—referred to the immorality of Grethe Schmidt, which led automatically to suspicion and to the disobedience of her advocate.

Throughout his pamphlet, Oldekop artfully dodged the question of whether he was the *official* advocate for Grethe Schmidt. Of course, he had clearly been helping the family all along. He had even sought to turn the tables—the Brunswick citations consistently referred to him and no one else as Schmidt's defender. What else could he conclude, then, other than that in his absence the magistrates had done nothing to help Grethe Schmidt, thus proving his point. The question of whether Grethe had received any defense without him, from first to last, was one Oldekop would press home repeatedly and constantly. He could point to the first torture of Schmidt, which came as a surprise to him, since he was awaiting a response from the city to his pleas on her behalf. The city had procured new testimony and solicited a response from Helmstedt but gave the Schmidts no chance to respond in a timely manner. The second grave injustice (in Oldekop's thinking) came after his official release from the case. Following that moment, Schmidt was again tortured and interrogated, her mother arrested, the garden in Gross Schwülper searched (to no avail), a final (and dubious) witness called. At what point did the *Obergericht* solicit or provide for any hearing of Schmidt's defense in these months? For Oldekop, this was clear evidence of malfeasance.[26]

For its part, Strauch's tract presented its case in the new format adopted in January, leading with the discovery of a corpse on April 4. The magistracy launched a general inquisition that would eventually lead to Grethe Schmidt whose confession, elicited through a meticulously conducted legal torture, spoke for itself. Not surprisingly, Strauch concentrated both on the correspondence with the legal faculty at Helmstedt (and elsewhere) and on detailing Schmidt's two confessions. By doing so, the city presented a case following a routine and orderly procedure to its inevitable end. Any apparent irregularities (which Strauch would not in any case concede) were incidental, given the fact that Schmidt had confessed to the crime of infanticide, not once but twice. The structure of the case the court presented made no allowance for a lay "accuser" of Grethe Schmidt—the entire record was a matter of general inquisitorial procedure.[27] As noted earlier, this concentrated authority—including the choice and conduct of a defense, if any—in the magistrates' hands. Schmidt's rights and Oldekop's prerogatives could only be judged under these rules and would be found wanting. It must be said, however, that the manuscript records of the case give no hint that, in the absence of Oldekop, the court made any effort to assess the possibility of Schmidt's innocence. In all honesty, one would not expect them to—the case from beginning to end reads like a prosecutor's brief, a fact pointing up the fatal flaw in concentrating so much authority in the hands of a single court.

Underneath the legal arguments between Oldekop and Strauch, though, lay other issues, undeniably professional and probably personal as well. Oldekop objected to the court's decision to send the files of the Schmidt case to the University of Jena for advice as a "non-partisan" legal faculty. In fact, the syndic Johann Strauch, who wrote the response (*Relatio Facti et Juris*) to Oldekop for the city of Brunswick, was himself a graduate of the university. This was not surprising in the somewhat enclosed world of north German Protestant universities and law schools. Strauch, however, had not only received his master's degree at Jena, but after receiving his doctorate he had been on the faculty there from 1652 until 1660, when he came to Brunswick. He had also married (for the second time, in 1654) the daughter of a professor on the Jena legal faculty itself. His continued and close ties to the university and legal faculty make it much harder to reject Oldekop's complaint about partisanship in the court's dealings.[28]

There was yet another issue that would place Oldekop and the syndic firmly against one another. Following his early studies in Jena, Strauch moved to the University of Leipzig, where he was befriended by both the preacher Johann Benedikt Carpzov and the jurist Benedikt Carpzov himself. It was Benedikt Carpzov who helped publish (1647) Strauch's first

serious—and reasonably successful—work on Roman private law. Oldekop, who came to Brunswick at the same time, had just published (1659)
his treatise against Benedikt Carpzov on criminal appeals, and in that
work he (typically) did not withhold his scorn for the Leipzig jurist.

The legal battle over Grethe Schmidt, then, was for Oldekop (and probably Strauch as well) in some ways a proxy contest over the influence and
ideas of the great Saxon jurist himself. This may explain some of the high
and personal level of vitriol in the case (in an era of generally vitriolic
public debate). This should not be stretched too far, however, nor should
it be automatically assumed that, because of Oldekop's sharp critique of
Carpzov, the two were automatically on opposite sides. Oldekop was more
expansive in his approach than Carpzov, and he had serious concerns
about torture under any circumstances. Oldekop, like Carpzov, was deeply
concerned about the possibility of mistakes and of malice in untrained
judges. Oldekop also agreed with Carpzov that torture should not be considered unless the case was strong and the corpus delicti was present. In
fact, Oldekop's work on the Schmidt case frequently cites Carpzov's *Practica Nova*, and he criticizes the city's courts for not following the Saxon jurist's own recommendations in the Schmidt case. Indeed, a powerful part
of his argument both during the process and in his published assessment
was that the courts of Brunswick were violating the processes already laid
down in Saxon law and upheld by jurists such as Benedikt Carpzov. It was
Carpzov, after all, who upheld firmly the principle of favoring the defense
in criminal matters and who had eloquently argued for a fundamental
right to a defense. Carpzov also argued that, in the case of a defendant's
poverty, the state should be willing to assist or even to conduct the defense
itself (though Oldekop opposed this idea). Ironically, then, some of the
most compelling arguments adduced by this opponent of Carpzov in the
Schmidt case came from Benedikt Carpzov himself and not from the pen
of Justus Oldekop.

Oldekop's legal assistance to Grethe Schmidt was also an attempt to
put his own ideas to work in the courts of Lower Saxony—about criminal
process and the rights of the accused to a full defense and about the right
to an appeal. This may explain the high level of quite personal vitriol in the
matter (though public disputes in this century were not polite affairs in any
case). In the Duchy of Brunswick, Oldekop found a court willing to accept
his case, and perhaps thereby establish its standing over the criminal courts
of its supposed tributary, the city of Brunswick.

Both parts of Oldekop's story—the poor young girl undefended and
the honored old man hounded—relayed a single larger tale with political ramifications: the arrogant magistracy of Brunswick trampling less

powerful people over whom the city had no legal authority. As Oldekop presented the case, only the determined intervention of higher and more righteous powers could protect these defenseless subjects. Oldekop was clearly aware of the fault lines in Lower Saxon politics and law—he had skillfully exploited jurisdictional issues while defending Grethe Schmidt. Just as important, Oldekop's flight from Brunswick led him to Wolfenbüttel, where he lived in the protective shadow of the Dukes of Brunswick-Lüneburg until his death. Oldekop had every reason to support the duchy's claims and every opportunity to be in contact with forces already trying to undermine Brunswick's autonomy. As the magistracy of the city succeeded in suppressing Oldekop's book in city after city, the lawyer was able to get it printed yet again, in Wolfenbüttel. It is safe to say that Justus Oldekop had enlisted in the duke's cause. The very title of the *True Description* identified Grethe Schmidt as a "peasant's daughter from Gross Schwülper, born in the Principality of Lüneburg."[29] While Grethe might have worked in Brunswick, she did not belong to it. Instead, she was a subject of Brunswick-Lüneburg. Each injustice against her was therefore an affront to her true overlord as well.

In Oldekop's telling of the tale, Schmidt's youth, simplicity, and poverty magnified the city's responsibility for dealing carefully with her.[30] Instead, looking at this poor young woman, friendless and "abandoned by the whole world, they [the magistrates] have had their will from beginning to end, and done just whatever came into their heads."[31] Oldekop compared the *Fiskal*'s handling of Grethe—an outsider—with their treatment of imprisoned citizens of the city, who allegedly received a defense and their full rights—very different treatment.[32] Because Grethe Schmidt was not a subject of the city and had no patrons there, the magistrates felt no restraint in their actions.

Oldekop extended his rhetorical outrage to the treatment of the Schmidt family, also subjects of the duke. The city's treachery, by his account, was particularly clear in the case of Grethe's mother, whom the prosecution (according to Oldekop) had tried to lure to the city, ostensibly to help her daughter but in reality to imprison them both. As Oldekop described it, "luckily when she arrived in the city she went first to the advocate and indicated she wanted to visit her daughter."[33] The advocate countered by asking whether she perhaps wanted to join Grethe in the dungeon?[34] The wily lawyer had advised Ilse to flee the city and to avoid the whole region of Brunswick until her daughter's own matter was resolved.

Thwarted in the attempt to lure Grethe's mother to Brunswick, the city council had then duped princely officials in nearby Giffhorn into jailing her for nearly ten weeks, subjecting her to the same pressures confronting her daughter, including the threat of torture. Her release only came, with Oldekop's help, from the magnanimous territorial duke himself.[35]

The contrast Oldekop painted between the actions of the city and the duchy could hardly have been clearer. Oldekop wrote that the duke would suffer no lawlessness or evil action but acted carefully and with measure. Brunswick's *Bürgermeister* and his cronies, on the other hand, shamelessly acting against the laws of God and human reason "were hardened in their insanity" and continued to persecute the poor and innocent.[36] According to this account, the prosecutorial injustice against Grethe Schmidt had caused the city's leaders to pursue the whole family through a clandestine prosecution that included the outright deception of the territorial rulers and their courts. When subterfuge failed (through Oldekop's diligence), the city rulers turned to defiance of their true sovereign.[37]

To Oldekop, the magistrates had ceased to act legally or as the legitimate government of the city: "One can be sure that in the entire Roman empire, no leader, even in the smallest village . . . as long as he had not lost his senses or gone stark raving mad, would conduct such shameful barbarisms and unchristian procedures as have the *Bürgermeister* and council of the great, powerful, and famous city of Brunswick."[38] This barbarity threatened the city and the duchy with God's righteous wrath unless someone intervened to wipe the stain of innocent blood from the land.

Oldekop's polemic over the city's abuse of power did not end with the Schmidt family. He also accused the city of perverting justice by persecuting him as well: "The imperial majesty, the electoral princes, and lords in their high courts hold it to be a special privilege that they are not lords of justice but administrators of justice." In contrast, the city leaders had turned the world upside down "and do not want to judge according to justice, but want justice to follow them and their whims."[39] Oldekop took this claim of tyranny past Brunswick's borders: the city also was stepping beyond its jurisdiction and authority. Grethe Schmidt and Gross Schwülper were not subjects of Brunswick, but this did not spare them from the city's wrath. As for Oldekop, he was himself not a subject of the city but of the duke. To attempt to punish him with a heavy fine for disobedience and to consider other punitive measures not only insulted the duke directly but usurped his legitimate authority.

Having laid out the case so vehemently, Oldekop demanded some forceful response to the city, which he claimed had trampled the laws of the empire and the territory. He wondered that the territorial prince and other governments in general were able to tolerate such "arrogant bravado and insolence."[40] Oldekop wrote that if the city of Brunswick could not act justly to counter the tyranny of its council, then the duke and his allies had not only the right but the duty to "correct" the city's actions. Such language was perfectly suited to an aristocratic ruler—such as Duke Augustus—looking to curtail municipal privileges or to assert his rule over unruly subject cities.

Even if Justus Oldekop was politically shrewd in his attack on Brunswick, it is less clear that he was wise. The polemic he advanced was clever but also very dangerous. Legally and politically, the city council could not afford to ignore printed diatribes attacking the integrity and jurisdiction of its courts and charging tyranny and corruption. There was also the question of imperial guarantees of the autonomy of the city's courts. This was a matter of some significance for the empire, which could not simply stand by and watch the violation of its own prerogatives and proclamations. Whatever the merits of the lawyer's case, legally, politically the city's affronted leaders would have no choice but to refute it. And the city council believed it had no other choice than to confront Oldekop's allegations on all fronts and decisively—it could leave no room for doubt about the merits of the case and the character of their opponents. This is precisely what happened to Oldekop's *Wahrhaffte Beschreibing*. In 1664, Brunswick sued to have it declared a slander and to have the copies confiscated.[41] In the meantime, the city council sent requests to other cities in northern Germany and the Hanseatic League requesting that they prohibit publication and also confiscate copies. This included a letter to Bremen, where one of Oldekop's sons lived.[42] Though this case was also never officially resolved, it appears that several cities on friendly terms with Brunswick complied with the city council's request. So the question remains—for now, at least—whether Justus Oldekop's polemical strategy helped either his cause or that of the family he championed. The time has come to answer this question and to settle accounts.

Conclusion

Many Vigorous Enemies

In 1667, in the ducal city of Wolfenbüttel, the court preacher Daetrius Brandanus presided over the funeral of Justus Oldekop, who on February 19 had died at seventy, still living in exile from the city of Brunswick. Brandanus's funeral sermon was then published—like many other funeral sermons—as part of the official commemoration of Oldekop's life and death.[1] The participation of the court preacher is significant in itself as a sign of the duchy's regard for Justus Oldekop. Brandanus had also known Oldekop for twenty-five years from their service together in Hannover and minced no words about him. Oldekop was a man of "good counsel and action," well regarded in Wolfenbüttel and indeed wherever he had lived, in the service of city and duchy. Brandanus, though, trod carefully around the "world-renowned" events of recent years that had brought the lawyer to Wolfenbüttel.[2] In the sermon itself, Brandanus spoke eloquently of Oldekop as a Christian pilgrim in this world, with no lasting place, forced at the end of a long life into exile, to wander until received in Wolfenbüttel by a gracious lord (Duke Augustus). All these wanderings were themselves over as Oldekop was by now received in paradise by an even more gracious and absolute Lord.[3]

Oldekop as Christian pilgrim in exile was one perception. Oldekop, though, was true to himself in death as in life. His choice of a text for his own funeral sermon came from Psalm 38:

> Many are those who are my vigorous enemies;
> > those who hate me without reason are numerous.
> Those who repay my good with evil
> > slander me when I pursue what is good.

From the grave, then, Oldekop continued not only to vindicate his honor but also to vilify his opponents. This was more in line not only with his character, it seems, but also with the events of recent years: his public feud with the city council of Brunswick, the ongoing appeal of his own and Grethe Schmidt's verdicts, and the countersuits by the city for his "frivolous," even malicious, lawsuits. All of it, though, remained unfinished at his end. The success of the Andreas Schmidt appeal in 1664 was only temporary, as the city appealed to the *Reichskammergericht* in Speyer. At least there, the court promised respect for Brunswick's "ancient privileges." All the cases, though, were unresolved at Oldekop's death and afterward dwindled out, to remain forever unsettled. By then, Oldekop's opponent Johannes Strauch was also leaving Brunswick. Apparently disliked for the elegant courtier's demeanor he had polished in Leipzig, Strauch also had to deal with the wishes of his wife who, preferring her father's household to life in the Hanseatic city, moved back to Jena. Strauch had to follow in order to save his marriage.[4] There is no evidence that the Grethe Schmidt case played any role in either Strauch's relations with his employers in Brunswick or his decision to leave. By the time the city of Brunswick fell to the duchy after the siege of 1671, Strauch had been back in Jena for three years.

There can be no final verdict on Grethe Schmidt's innocence or guilt. By standards of modern or early modern proof, the prosecution fell far short—no witnesses to the event, no material evidence to connect her to a crime, and above all, no body. The infant's corpse discovered on April 4 was clearly not Schmidt's child, nor were the authorities under any misconception that it was. That corpse was introduced into the record solely to explain and justify the general investigation of infanticide, which eventually led to Schmidt. Having exhausted the search for a body in the gardens of Gross Schwülper, the city acknowledged at last that its evidence was inconclusive. The investigators' last efforts strained to gather even enough evidence to reach the lesser verdict of "suspected infanticide." In the specific crime of "suspected infanticide" for which she was finally punished, Grethe Schmidt was herself the corpus delicti—her body, her behavior, her profile as a maidservant.

At the same time, some of the testimony is hard to discount, for example the universally acknowledged fact that Grethe's mother, having been with her daughter at the very height of the girl's alleged pregnancy, solicited a lying-in room in Neubrücke, which was later cancelled. The apparently universal suspicions of the city's women suggest that the "court" of public opinion had judged Grethe to be guilty at least of pregnancy. If Grethe was guilty, though, she made a terrible mistake in returning to Brunswick, where the same women would now harbor different and darker suspicions about her. In contrast, other women—the sworn midwives—examined her long after the fact and found the whole story impossible. Their certainty in the matter remains a striking feature of the case overall.

Some may be inclined to conclude that, because Grethe confessed under a relatively "light" torture, suggesting doubts about the case on the part of the Helmstedt faculty, she must have been guilty. Resistance to torture was not unknown in the early modern world.[5] One could of course argue that Grethe had indeed been pregnant, but either miscarried (e.g., in the Dedekind household, where she discussed the mass that she expelled) or that an infant had been stillborn, an option that becomes more or less likely depending on how late it might have occurred. The court showed no interest in this explanation at any point. Even if it were true, though, the magistrates were unlikely to believe it. After all, this was the prevailing excuse of accused women. The narrative of the law powerfully shaped the prosecution's view of the matter, precluding other possible explanations for the events of 1661.

The choices made by the *Fiskal* about Grethe Schmidt are remarkable for what they excluded from consideration. They ignored testimony about the possibility of witchcraft in the form of the straw doll Grethe allegedly hid in Andreas Möller's bed. Investigators never followed up on the possibility of abortion (or witchcraft again) implicit in the testimony of Margarethe Hafferland and the *Fränkische Frau*. This is especially odd, since the possibility of witchcraft would have diminished the problem of the missing corpus delicti. There is also the singular testimony of Margarethe Hafferland concerning the attempt to blackmail her, which implicated not only Grethe herself but her mother and aunt as well. Rather than pursue this striking, even sensational story, the Brunswick *Fiskal* persistently attempted to craft a case that relied entirely on the most typical, even bland, features of the infanticide narrative. One after another, testimony about the behavior of Grethe Schmidt also fell into line with the standard testimony of women throughout Germany. This may reflect the common circumstances for infanticide, especially when focused on women of a certain age and status. It also means, though, that the narrative laid out in the infanticide law shaped the contours of cases everywhere. Making the case may have been more important than the details.

At Oldekop's death, then, little was resolved, although Grethe Schmidt herself was by then probably living in Gross Schwülper, away from the grasp of Brunswick's prosecutors but no doubt dealing with the effects of her lashing. It is not clear to what extent Oldekop's legal intervention affected her fate. Grethe's family, and in particular her mother, certainly had reason to thank Oldekop, for his greatest success was in skillfully maneuvering between city and duchy to keep Ilse away from the city's investigators, who clearly wanted to use mother and daughter against each other. As to Grethe's sentence, whipping or exile were not unknown in such cases, whatever the horrific stipulations of the *Carolina*.[6] The combination of whipping *and* exile was in fact relatively harsh, though.[7] In part, the question of how much of a difference Oldekop made turns on how the *Untergericht* would have viewed Schmidt's first confession in November had the lawyer not demonstrated its impossibility. Would the court have discovered the problems anyway? Once Schmidt admitted a crime, her confession became the driving force in favor of the court's conduct and the investigation. Despite some possible misgivings Helmstedt, especially, consistently pointed to the confession as demonstrating that justice had in fact been done, that is, the truth had emerged.

One should therefore be careful about judging the city's courts. The difficulties of criminal justice were not limited to the city of Brunswick but were in some ways inherent in the inquisitorial procedure itself, as Ulrich Falk and others have suggested. Practices were in fact evolving in a number of ways—this is evident in the case of torture and terror, in which the use of extreme tortures was diminishing. Oldekop's attack on the city council and its personnel for special malice against the Schmidts seems gratuitous—there is no evidence of a particular animus against Schmidt fostered by Margarethe Hafferland and her neighbors. It seems improbable that the city focused on Grethe Schmidt other than as an outsider who fit a particular profile that convinced the judges of her guilt, though this is not to excuse the fact.

The court's great fault lay in its determination to act in a thoroughly prosecutorial fashion rather than as investigators and judges seeking the truth. It is also clear that, in the absence of Oldekop and his demands, the syndics did not concern themselves with providing a defense for Schmidt. From the time Oldekop left the case until Schmidt's punishment, no trace of advocacy for her is in the evidence. And despite all the prosecutors' efforts, they never found a corpse. Their unyielding determination to push forward anyway—and the complicity of the Helmstedt faculty in permitting the matter to continue without the corpus delicti—remains a puzzle. Strikingly, one can very easily read the correspondence and opinions handed down by the faculties of both Rinteln and Jena—particularly the former—as critical of the Helmstedt decision. Rinteln (as noted in chapter 13) explicitly referred to the absence of a corpus delicti as grounds for its recommendation. In asking for an opinion from Jena, the city council admitted failure in the search for a corpse. Punishing Grethe Schmidt for "suspected infanticide" under these particular circumstances was a not uncommon compromise in the seventeenth century. By pointing to the missing corpus delicti, though, Rinteln was undermining the very grounds for torturing Grethe in the first place. As Oldekop claimed, the criminal courts of Brunswick (and the faculty at Helmstedt) had ignored or violated the principles set out by the most famous Saxon jurist of the seventeenth century. Oldekop's statement that he had at first glance been unconcerned about the case, given the absence of a corpse and the midwives' own report about the state of Grethe's body, has about it the ring of truth. The pugnacious old advocate's subsequent outrage had a solid grounding in the law.

As for Oldekop himself, the jurist was prone to exaggeration and astonishing embellishment, as in his description of the bloodthirsty torturer anxious to lay hands on Grethe Schmidt or the other, anonymous, infanticide punished in Brunswick in 1661 ("the hot pincers ripping her flesh"). Oldekop's desire for justice is undeniable, but it is also hard not to see the Schmidt affair as a test case for his legal agenda. Whether one admires Olde-kop or not, clearly he was a feisty, difficult, even choleric (in the medical parlance of the age) man given to hyperbole and vitriol, fully capable of raising the hackles of his opponents.[8] There may, of course, have been more to the story of Oldekop's relationship with the city council or the syndics. Oldekop was unsparing and vehement in criticizing the partisan nature of the Helmstedt legal faculty. Personal and professional conflict would be understandable over the course of long careers conducted in a relatively compact territory, and the prosecutors of Brunswick hinted that Oldekop had a long history of antagonizing magistrates. Evidence for this has not surfaced, however, and the claim must remain speculative.

Aside from its impact on the lives of an impoverished family in a nearly forgotten village long ago or the honor of one old man, the case of Grethe Schmidt illuminates many larger issues for historians of women, law, and early modern Europe. A chief lesson is that no criminal case was immune to the byzantine political culture of seventeenth-century Germany, divided as it was into so many overlapping territories and jurisdictions, which multiplied the potential conflicts. Grethe Schmidt's plight might have seemed irrelevant to the political struggles of the city of Brunswick, but in fact the moment Oldekop took up her cause the potential difficulties became apparent to all the parties involved. All that was required was an ambitious lawyer and an opportunistic duchy seeking to establish its standing and thereby expand its legal reach.

The political context, then, is fundamental to understanding the workings of criminal law in early modern Europe. The Schmidt affair demonstrates that even apparently insignificant cases involving obscure individuals could depend for their outcome on political questions seemingly far removed from the legal issues themselves. Conversely, conflicts between territories could have important ramifications for subjects at whatever place on the social scale. The law itself was flexible enough to enable skilled legal practitioners to employ it on behalf of their clients. The inquisitorial criminal process could seem to be closed to influence from outside, a self-contained investigatory and prosecutorial institution. But the presence of outside counsel could in fact deflect the course of an investigation. However limited, the role of the defense was real and potentially made the process far more dynamic and volatile than a one-sided procedure involving only the *Fiskal*. It remained for lawyers and theorists to make overt the possibilities latent in the laws, something that happened on a wider scale in the eighteenth century. Oldekop, then, was a kind of pioneer in this process.

The same criminal process that served rulers and lawyers also left a tiny opening for lesser folk. Against many odds the Schmidt family, particularly Ilse Leuthgen, managed to turn the law to their advantage and help Grethe. It was the territorial and jurisdictional confusion of northern Germany—and the conflict between the city and the duchy—that enabled the Schmidts to avoid the full pressure of Brunswick's courts. The Schmidts could not have done this without Justus Oldekop, of course, but the case demonstrates that poor families determined to fight for their kin could in fact find a means to do so. Possibly, then, the hero—or the true villain—of the case was the tough, defiant, and resourceful Ilse Leuthgen, who refused to relinquish her daughter's fate to the magistrates of Brunswick.

This close study of a young woman's ordeal reveals another dynamic element in the criminal process—the construction of a criminal identity—with important ramifications for understanding crime and gender in early modern Europe. The Schmidt process occurred at the height of an era of close attention to prosecuting illegitimate sexual relations. Patriarchal in nature, this tendency "was linked to efforts to naturalize maternal love and praise chastity and marriage as women's sole avenues towards respectability."[9] The burden of this trend fell on women, particularly poor single women. As noted in chapter 2, the law itself affirmed a particular narrative that focused on women alone, and in a particular way. In simple fact, then, infanticide was in practice a woman's crime.

Yet the value of the Schmidt case lies less in showing that a crime such as infanticide applied to women almost exclusively (a fact generally accepted today) than in showing how magistrates and authorities adapted the criminal to the crime. It was not enough for Grethe Schmidt to have killed her child—the murder had to be the premeditated outcome of a particular motive that at one stroke damned the culprit as malicious and unnatural while simultaneously focusing on sexual impurity and fornication as the gateway to more egregious behaviors. Grethe Schmidt may or may not have been a murderess, but publicly she provided an object lesson about the dangers of fornication. Indeed, even if the outcome was not exactly what the court sought, and even if Schmidt did not commit the crime of infanticide, her punishment showed quite clearly that a woman who participated in sex outside marriage could suffer, simply from the suspicion to which her immorality gave rise.

As the records demonstrate, the criminal was a work in progress, created by layer upon layer of interrogation, suggestion, and threat. In the testimony, each admission, each step forward added a new layer and became the basis for the next. Slowly, defiance gave way to uncertainty, and then to a further test of Schmidt's resolve, all set against the background of the established infanticide narrative itself. The Schmidt case makes plain that this slow process of unmaking the individual and making the criminal was not limited to the interrogations or torture sessions alone. In Grethe's case, the city's officers had constant and prolonged opportunity to coax, cajole, and threaten the girl for the entire ten months she was in the *Fronerey*, while possibly also coaching her testimony—as in the events surrounding her father's visit in January. Even torture, then, occurred within the framework of constant pressure rather than separately from it.

Recognizing this fact means realizing as well that the recorded words in this or any criminal affair were only the visible, official element of a much more involved process. Schmidt's interrogators had regular access to her, with perhaps more opportunity to "influence" her testimony than the transcripts themselves suggest. Nowhere was this more evident than in Grethe's first "unforced" confession, following her torture in early November. In the required days between coercion and confession, Grethe seemed to have absorbed the court's expectations for her testimony and motives quite well. At a very vulnerable moment in the proceedings, after pain and threat had worked their effect, Grethe was willing to accept her fate from prosecutors who had the means and access to offer it to her unhindered by any other alternative.

When Grethe Schmidt signed the "consent" to her punishment and acknowledged the charge of "suspected infanticide," she went into exile from Brunswick, but she also disappeared from history. Whether she carried her new "identity" as a criminal with her in any way except as a public stigma—in other words, whether the year of confinement and torture marked a permanent "conversion" of her personality and character—is unknowable. The long-term presence of family and familiars may have proved, with time, more powerful than the machinery of the torture chamber. The mark of shame she carried with her might not have burned so deeply into her flesh. On the other hand, the lashes she received would mark her indelibly in public and perhaps cause permanent physical damage as well.

The question of constructing a criminal identity through interrogation and pressure brings us to the question of torture and its significance for the early modern criminal process. The Schmidt experience makes plain that contact, intimidation, and threat were not limited to the interrogations or torture sessions but applied to the entire process from arrest through conviction. One has to contemplate the moment of torture within this much larger context of terror rather than as a separate act.

Looking at the case from a great distance reveals serious gaps in the historical understanding of the "performance practices" of interrogation and torture. In the more bloodless official descriptions of the processes, the torturer "presented" the instruments of pain and warned of their potential use should the suspect not confess. Yet in Schmidt's case, the torturer clearly played a more active role than mere functionary at the wishes of the *Fiskal*. The torturer not only "showed" the instruments to the girl but demonstrated his apparent eagerness to use them by pretending to seize and bind her. Further, we cannot divide the process so easily into discrete events such as "terror" followed by a separate "torture," and while the increasing gradations in practice may have reduced the actual application of physical pain, they also made it more difficult to know where terror left off and torture began. Instead, one phase blended rather seamlessly into the next. This was an important element in Oldekop's defense brief, but it suggests that the dividing lines of the torture process were not so distinct, especially if we incorporate the grim intimidation and isolation that comprised long-term incarceration. If so, then, historians cannot so easily assume that confessions extracted through "mere" threat were any different or more plausible than those that came with "actual" torture.[10] Pain was a real presence throughout the process.

Another conclusion—with modern ramifications—to draw from the Schmidt case concerns the relation between torture and plausibility. The authorities, for their part, relied on torture to tear through the suspect's defenses and pull out "the truth." They assessed the plausibility of the confession in part by the ease with which they coerced it. Grethe had succumbed to "humane" torture, or even the bare threat of "humane" torture. Yet Oldekop noted that both "terror" and "torture" were subjective—it was impossible to assess the degree of pain as experienced by the one tortured. How then could the authorities know just how deeply they had probed or what damage was necessary to produce a confession? Oldekop's point here closely resembles the modern debate over the nature and effects of torture.

More simply, though, the repeated threats and tortures in the Schmidt case make it difficult, if not impossible, to decide what was in fact true or false. If each new session could produce a fresh tale from a suspect who was gradually learning what was and what was not acceptable to authorities, then how could any one version be singled out as the truth? Repeatedly, Grethe recounted strangely intimate details about the birth and infanticide that only she could have known and which made her story plausible, and yet for all their seeming artlessness and authenticity, those details proved to be fabrications. In other words, though terror and torture may have produced at some point along the line a "true" confession, it is impossible to know what that might have been. Reviewing the evidence, it seems impossible to escape Oldekop's own conclusion that, as in witchcraft cases, torture in the Schmidt case helped to create the corpus delicti where none was at hand. Readers here must remember that the personnel in the Schmidt case had dealt with torture before and would do so again. The city and the Duchy of Brunswick had been particularly harsh in dealing with suspected witches—just two years later in Brunswick, the same cast of players prosecuted Tempel Anneke for witchcraft, which resulted in her execution. We might want to ask just how the perceptions of evidence and the experience of torture affected prosecutors' interpretations as they moved from case to case in practice. In the case of Tempel Anneke, alas, a man like Justus Oldekop was no longer around to trouble the system.

Grethe's tale contains yet one more unresolvable but fascinating puzzle. Grethe's first confession was demonstrably false in almost every way, yet it contained so much detail that it reads, not like the frenzied outpouring of a distressed woman but almost as a fully imagined fantasy. Raising the child to gaze at it in the moonlight and determine its sex was a startling moment and, since she later confessed to killing the infant in daylight instead, could not have come from the "actual" birth. At some point during the isolation, fear, and pain, it is possible that Grethe Schmidt—innocent or not—began to imagine herself as an infanticide. The law's narrative may have indeed become her own, but this very fact again makes the ultimate truth impossible to know. Or was there another, still untold, story to bind up all the loose ends and tell what really happened in January or February 1661? If so, it must remain as elusive as the alleged corpse in the garden or the river. Despite the voluminous arguments of male lawyers and judges alike, what went on in the mind and body of a fifteen-year-old girl remains at the heart of the story.

Notes

INTRODUCTION

1. Otto Ulbricht, "Kindsmord in der Frühen Neuzeit," in *Frauen in der Geschichte des Rechts: Von der Frühen Neuzeit bis zur Gegenwart*, ed. Ute Gerhard (Munich: C. H. Beck, 1999), 242. Ulbricht's invaluable work on infanticide is outlined in English in "Infanticide in Eighteenth-Century Germany," in *The German Underworld: Deviants and Outcasts in German History*, ed. Richard Evans (London: Routledge, 1988), 108–40.

2. Johann Strauch, *Acten gemässe Relatio Facti et Juris Uber den zu Braunschweig Wider Margareten Schmieds/ Eine Stuprirte Bauer-Magd/ in puncto verdächtigen Kindermords geführten Inquisitions* (Halberstadt, 1665), title page.

3. Richard van Dülmen, *Theatre of Horror: Crime and Punishment in Early Modern Germany* (Cambridge: Polity Press, 1990), 9–10; Bernd Roeck, "Criminal Procedure in the Holy Roman Empire," *International Association for the History of Crime and Criminal Justice Bulletin* 18 (1993): 24–25.

4. Roeck, "Criminal Procedure," 35–36. See Wolfgang Behringer, "Mörder, Diebe, Ehebrecher: Verbrechen und Strafen in Kurbayern vom 16. bis 18. Jahrhundert," in *Verbrechen, Strafen, und soziale Kontrolle: Studien zur historischen Kulturforschung*, ed. Richard van Dülmen (Frankfurt: Fischer Taschenbuch Verlag, 1990), 85–132.

5. Richard van Dülmen, *Frauen vor Gericht: Kindsmord in der Frühen Neuzeit* (Frankfurt: Fischer Taschenbuch Verlag, 1991), 8.

6. For a recent survey of infanticide globally, see Brigitte H. Bechtold and Donna Cooper Graves, eds., *Killing Infants: Studies in the Worldwide Practice of Infanticide* (Lewiston, NY: Edwin Mellen Press, 2006).

7. Populations suffering from hunger and poverty seek to suppress births either by contraception or by controlling marriage. When these methods fail, parents may correct the problem through infanticide. For a brief survey of the debate over infanticide and population control, see Pier Paolo Viazzo, "Mortality, Fertility, and Family," in *The History of the European Family*, ed. David Kertzer and Marzio Barbagli (New Haven: Yale University Press, 2001), 1:157–90, esp. 178–79. Advocates of the population limitation theory include Lawrence Stone, *The Family, Sex, and Marriage in England 1500–1800* (London: Weidenfeld & Nicolson, 1977); William L. Langer, "Checks on Population Growth: 1750–1850," *Scientific American* 226, no. 2 (1972): 92–99.

8. This latter practice, focusing on the choice to kill *female* children, has received the most extensive recent attention from scholars ranging across the globe from Asia to the United States, and covering most periods of history, from Graeco-Roman antiquity until today. For claims about "femicide" in European antiquity, see Sarah Pomeroy, *Families in Classical and Hellenistic Greece: Representations and Realities* (Oxford: Oxford University Press, 1998); and Sarah Pomeroy et al., *Ancient Greece: A Political, Social, and Cultural History*, 2nd ed. (New York: Oxford University Press, 2007).

9. Keith Wrightson, "Infanticide in European History," *Criminal Justice History* 3 (1982): esp. 14–15. See also Viazzo, "Mortality, Fertility, and Family," 178–79.

10. Peter C. Hoffer and N. E. H. Hull, *Murdering Mothers: Infanticide in England and New England, 1558–1803* (New York: New York University Press, 1981).

11. Ulbricht, "Kindsmord in der Frühen Neuzeit," 246.

12. Viazzo, "Mortality, Fertility, and Family," 178–79. Even in ancient Greece and Rome, though, there is little direct evidence for a higher rate of female infanticide and numerous claims against it. Wayne Ingalls, "Demography and Dowries: Perspectives on Female Infanticide in Classical Greece," *Phoenix* 56, nos. 3–4 (2002): 246–54.

13. G. Hanlon, "L'infanticidio di coppie sposate in Toscana nella prima eta moderna," *Quaderni Storici* 113 (2003): 453–98. I am grateful to Wolfgang Mueller for discussion on the use of sources for early modern family planning.

14. Ulbricht, *Kindsmord und Aufklärung in Deutschland* (Munich: Oldenbourg, 1990),177.

15. Viazzo, "Mortality, Fertility, and Family," 177.

16. Ibid.

17. Ibid., 179. David Kertzer has found some evidence hinting at gendered rates of abandonment: "Clearly, fifteenth-century Florentine parents were more eager to abandon girls than boys. Almost wherever we can find information, the pattern is the same: in the early days of the foundling homes girls were much more likely to be abandoned than boys." By the nineteenth century, however, "Where abandonment was limited almost entirely to illegitimate children, and where virtually all illegitimate children were abandoned, girls were no more likely to be abandoned than boys." Kertzer, *Sacrificed for Honor: Italian Infant Abandonment and the Politics of Reproductive Control* (Boston: Beacon Press, 1993), 111.

18. For the comparison between France and the German lands, see Ulbricht, *Kindsmord und Aufklärung*, 185–87.

19. For an analysis of the role of killing children as part of a "blood libel" against Jews and other outsiders, but extended to Protestants and Catholics during the sixteenth century, see Luc Racaut, "Accusations of Infanticide on the Eve of the French Wars of Religion," in *Infanticide: Historical Perspectives on Child Murder and Concealment*, ed. Mark Jackson (Aldershot: Ashgate, 2002), 18–34.

20. For an illuminating account of sexual and reproductive crimes—including infanticide—in early modern Venice, see Joanne M. Ferraro, *Nefarious Crimes, Contested Justice: Illicit Sex and Infanticide in the Republic of Venice, 1557–1789* (Baltimore: Johns Hopkins University Press, 2008). For England and New England, see Hoffer and Hull, *Murdering Mothers*; on sixteenth- and seventeenth-century Germany, see Richard van Dülmen, *Frauen vor Gericht*; and Ulinka Rublack, *The Crimes of Women in Early Modern Germany* (Oxford: Clarendon Press, 1999), 163–96. The most comprehensive discussion of late seventeenth- and eighteenth-century German infanticide is Otto Ulbricht, *Kindsmord und Aufklärung*.

21. Mark Jackson, *New-Born Child Murder: Women, Illegitimacy, and the Courts in Eighteenth-Century England* (Manchester: Manchester University Press, 1996).

22. Alfred Soman, trans., "Anatomy of an Infanticide Trial: The Case of Marie-Jeanne Bartonnet (1742)," in *Changing Identities in Early Modern France*, ed. Michael Wolfe (Durham, NC: Duke University Press, 1996), 250.

23. Jackson, *New-Born Child Murder*, 32.

24. Soman, "Anatomy of an Infanticide Trial," 248–49.

25. Heinrich Gwinner and Gustav Radbruch, *Geschichte des Verbrechens: Versuch einer historischen Kriminologie* (Stuttgart: Koehler, 1951), 242, cited in Isabel

Hull, *Sexuality, State, and Civil Society in Germany, 1700–1815* (Ithaca: Cornell University Press, 1996), 111.

26. Rebekka Habermas and Tanja Hommen have edited the court proceedings in the case of Susanna Margarethe Brandt. See Habermas and Hommen, *Das Frankfurter Gretchen: Der Prozeß gegen die Kindsmörderin Susanna Margaretha Brandt* (Munich: Beck, 1999).

27. As Richard van Dülmen notes, from the historical attention received, one might be tempted to think that, at the height of the witch hunts, no other crime existed: *Frauen vor Gericht*, 113n3.

28. Ibid., 59–60.

29. Ibid., 71–72.

30. Rublack, *Crimes of Women*, 192.

31. *Acta inquisitionis wider die unverehelichte Anna Mack aus Braunschweig wegen angeschuldigten Kindermordes 1677*, Stadtarchiv Braunschweig CV 102; *Acta inquisitiones wider Katharene Mundt aus Braunschweig wegen angeschuldigten Kindermordes 1693*, Stadtarchiv Braunschweig CV 108.

32. Authorities mandated punishment for individuals who did not report pregnant single women or who harbored, hired, or helped women who might fall under suspicion. Dülmen, *Frauen vor Gericht*, 73.

33. One recent and convincing example is Govind P. Sreenivasan, *The Peasants of Ottobeuren, 1487–1726: A Rural Society in Early Modern Europe* (Cambridge: Cambridge University Press, 2004).

34. Ulbricht, "Kindsmörderinnen vor Gericht: Verteidigungsstragien von Frauen in Norddeutschland, 1680–1810," in *Mit den Waffen der Justiz: Zur Kriminalitätsgeschichte des Spätmittelalters und der Frühen Neuzeit*, ed. Andreas Blauert and Gerd Schwerhoff (Frankfurt: Fischer Taschenbuch Verlag, 1993), 61.

35. The issue of the defense has gained some traction in the last decade, in particular through the groundbreaking work of Ulrich Falk, "Zur Geschichte der Strafverteidigung: Aktuelle Beobachtungen und rechtshistorische Grundlagen," *Zeitschrift der Savigny-Stiftung für Rechtsgeschichte, Germanistische Abteilung* 117 (2000): 395–449, and "Vom Unzeitigen Rennen, Sich Sperren und Disputieren: Eine Fallstudie zur Verteidigung im Hexenprozeß," in *Vom Unfug des Hexen-Processes: Gegner der Hexenverfolgungen von Johann Weyer bis Friedrich Spee*, ed. Hartmut Lehmann and Otto Ulbricht, Wolfenbütteler Forschungen 55 (Wiesbaden: Harrassowitz, 1992), 284–305. By contrast, in important earlier studies, neither John Langbein, *Prosecuting Crime in the Renaissance: England, Germany, France* (Cambridge: Harvard University Press, 1974), nor Eberhard Schmidt, *Einführung in die Geschichte der deutschen Strafrechtspflege*, 3rd ed. (Göttingen: Vandenhoeck & Ruprecht, 1995) treats the question of a defense.

36. Alexander Ignor, *Geschichte des Strafprozesses in Deutschland, 1532–1846: Von der Carolina Karls V. bis zu den Reformen des Vormärz* (Paderborn: F. Schöningh, 2002), 78–83. See also Hinrich Rüping, *Der Grundsatz des rechtlichen Gehörs und seine Bedeutung im Strafverfahren*, Strafrechtliche Abhandlungen—Neue Folge 26 (Berlin: Dunker & Humblot, 1976), 59.

37. Rüping, *Grundsatz des rechtlichen Gehörs*, 49–50; Heinz Lieberich and Heinrich Mitteis, *Deutsche Rechtsgeschichte: Ein Studienbuch*, 19th ed. (Munich: Beck, 1992), 404. Ulrich Falk, though, details carefully the ways in which mid-seventeenth century commentators—particularly the oft-maligned Benedikt Carpzov—argued in

favor of a wider right to defense. See "Zur Geschichte der Strafverteidigung," 409–19.

38. On the disadvantages faced by lawyers in the early modern period, see Albrecht Cordes, "Anwalt," in *Handwörterbuch zur deutschen Rechtsgeschichte* (hereafter *HRG*), ed. Albrecht Cordes and Wolfgang Stammler, 2nd ed. (Berlin: Schmidt, 2008): 1:259–61.

39. Despite numerous criminal records in German archives, the documentation of a full-blown defense in such depth is an infrequent occurrence before the eighteenth century. Ulbricht has detailed the workings of the infanticide defense both in "Kindsmörderinnen vor Gericht," and in "Landesverweisung für Kindsmord—milde Strafen in harter Zeit? Ein Stegeberger Fall aus dem Jahre 1684," in *Mare Balticum: Beiträge zur Geschichte des Ostseeraumes in Mittelalter und Neuzeit; Festschrift zum 65. Geburtstag von Erich Hoffmann*, ed. Werner Paravicini et al., Kieler historische Studien 36 (Sigmaringen: Jan Thorbecke, 1992), 261–78.

40. Even in so detailed an account as Thomas Robisheaux's recent *The Last Witch of Langenburg: Murder in a German Village*, there is little mention of an active defense because inquisitorial authorities considered themselves to be investigators of the truth rather than partisans of one side or another. Thomas Robisheaux, *The Last Witch of Langenburg: Murder in a German Village* (New York: W. W. Norton & Company, 2009). The entire transcript of the Tempel Anneke case is available in Peter Morton, ed., *The Trial of Tempel Anneke: Records of a Witchcraft Trial in Brunswick, Germany, 1663* (Peterborough, ON: Broadview Press, 2006.).

41. The history of torture is, of course, voluminous. To mention two salient examples in English, Edward Peters has constructed a very clear and useful survey of the history of torture in *Torture* (Philadelphia: University of Pennsylvania Press, 1996). For an exceptionally insightful account of the logic of early modern torture, see Lisa Silverman, *Tortured Subjects: Pain, Truth, and the Body in Early Modern France* (Chicago: Chicago University Press, 2001). A recent and careful account concerning early modern Germany is Robert Zagolla, *Folter und Hexenprozess: Die strafrechtliche Spruchpraxis der Juristenfakultät Rostock im 17. Jahrhundert*, Hexenforschung 11 (Bielefeld: Verlag für Regionalgeschichte, 2007).

1—In Brunswick, near Hannover City

1. Jürgen Schlumbohm, *Lebensläufe, Familien, Höfe: Die Bauern und Heuerleute des Osnabrückischen Kirchspiels Belm in proto-industrieller Zeit, 1650–1860* (Göttingen: Vandenhoeck & Ruprecht, 1994), 152–55; John Knodel, *Demographic Behavior in the Past: A Study of Fourteen German Village Populations in the Eighteenth and Nineteenth Centuries* (Cambridge: Cambridge University Press, 1988), 42–45.

2. Schlumbohm, *Lebensläufe*, 159.

3. Ibid., 187.

4. Ibid., 185.

5. Christian Pfister, *Bevölkerungsgeschichte und historische Demographie 1500–1800*, Enzyklopädie deutscher Geschichte 28 (Munich: Oldenbourg, 1994), 36; Schlumbohm, *Lebensläufe*, 160–64.

6. Theo Bosse, ed., *Die Register und Kataster der Ämter Gifhorn, Fallersleben, und Isenhagen ab 1563/64* (Gifhorn: Landkreis Gifhorn, 1988), 14.

7. In numerous tax and census rolls from Lower Saxony, the herders often make no appearance, and when they do, frequently their names are not mentioned, only

their positions, along with the "contribution" expected of them (for example, for provisioning troops in time of war). Bosse, *Die Register und Kataster*, 308–12.

8. Ulrike Gleixner, *"Das Mensch" und "der Kerl": Die Konstruktion von Geschlecht in Unzuchtsverfahren der Frühen Neuzeit, 1700–1760* (Frankfurt: Campus, 1994), 41.

9. Herders performed other duties in villages or perhaps had to help others, such as pastors, with chores, either because they owed the duty to their "lords" or, if hired by a free village, they were contracted to do so, or perhaps just because the pay was so low that extra jobs were necessary to buy bread. See Louis Carlen, *Das Recht der Hirten: Zur Rechtsgeschichte d. Hirten in Deutschland, Österreich u. d. Schweiz* (Innsbruck: Österr. Kommissionsbuch, 1970), 71.

10. Rudolf Wissell, *Des Alten Handwerks Recht und Gewohnheit 1* (Berlin: Colloquium Verlag, 1971), 148–49. On the question of honor, see especially Kathy Stuart, *Defiled Trades and Social Outcasts: Honor and Ritual Pollution in Early Modern Germany* (Cambridge: Cambridge University Press, 1999); Richard van Dülmen, *Der ehrlose Mensch: Unehrlichkeit und soziale Ausgrenzung in der Frühen Neuzeit* (Cologne: Böhlau, 1999); Werner Danckert, *Unehrliche Leute: Die Verfemten Berufe* (Bern: Francke, 1963).

11. Wissell, *Des Alten Handwerks*, 174.

12. Dülmen, *Der ehrlose Mensch*, 35; Wissell, *Des Alten Handwerks*, 173.

13. Carlen, *Das Recht der Hirten*, 73.

14. Stadtarchiv Braunschweig *BIII.17.9* (hereafter and throughout as *BIII.17.9*), fol. 37R.

15. Richard van Dülmen, *Kultur und Alltag in der Frühen Neuzeit* (Munich: C. H. Beck, 1990), 1:122.

16. In Protestant territories, moralists and preachers included worldly rulers and employers among those to be revered under the fourth commandment's "Honor thy Father and thy Mother." Renate Dürr, *Mägde in der Stadt: Das Beispiel Schwäbisch Hall in der Frühen Neuzeit* (Frankfurt: Campus Verlag, 1995), 80.

17. Justus Oldekop, *Warhaffte Beschreibung/ Eines nie erhörten/ unchristlichen/ wider Gottes Wort/ alle Rechte/ und natürliche Vernunfft lauffenden peinlichen Processus, welchen Bürgermeister und Raht der Stadt Braunschweig/ wider eine arme unschüldige Bawren Tochter/ von Grossen Schwülber . . . von vierzehen Jahren/ Margareta Schmidts genant/ eines . . . fälschlich zugemessenen Kindermohrts halber . . . Anno 1661. und 1662. geführt und exequirt.* (Wolfenbüttel: Bismarck, 1664). The original was published quickly and without a publisher or place of publication in 1663. This chapter quotes the corrected version of 1664, hereafter *WB*.

18. *BIII.17.9*, 30R.

19. Merry E. Wiesner, "Having Her Own Smoke: Employment and Independence for Singlewomen in Germany, 1400–1750," in *Singlewomen in the European Past, 1250–1800*, ed. Judith M. Bennett and Amy M. Froide (Philadelphia: University of Pennsylvania Press, 1999), 192–216.

20. As Merry Wiesner notes, "Given the economic security, legal advantages, and higher social status that marriage promised, it is not surprising that marriage was the goal of most women and men." Ibid., 199

21. Olwen Hufton, *The Prospect before Her: A History of Women in Western Europe* (New York: Alfred Knopf, 1996–), 1:61.

22. Wiesner, "Having Her Own Smoke," 202.

23. Maryanne Kowaleski, "Singlewomen in Medieval and Early Modern Europe:

The Demographic Perspective," in *Singlewomen in the European Past*, 53. Sheilagh Ogilvie's research on Württemberg shows that between 1635 and 1834, 14 percent of women never married, with the averages growing higher over the course of the seventeenth and eighteenth centuries. See Sheilagh Ogilvie, *A Bitter Living: Women, Markets, and Social Capital in Early Modern Germany* (Oxford: Oxford University Press, 2003), 40–41; Antoinette Fauve-Chamoux, "Marriage, Widowhood, and Divorce," in *The History of the European Family*, ed. David Kertzer and Marzio Barbagli (New Haven: Yale University Press, 2001), 1:225–27.

24. Ogilvie, *A Bitter Living*, 41; Fauve-Chamoux, "Marriage, Widowhood, and Divorce," 224.

25. Lyndal Roper, *Witch Craze: Terror and Fantasy in Baroque Germany* (New Haven: Yale University Press, 2002), 129–33.

26. Christian Pfister, "The Population of Late Medieval and Early Modern Germany," in *Germany: A New Social and Economic History*, ed. Bob Scribner and Sheilagh Ogilvie (London: Arnold, 1996), 1:44; Ogilvie, *A Bitter Living*, 51–53.

27. Ogilvie, *A Bitter Living*, 268–71; for general attitudes toward single people in early modern Germany, see Wiesner, "Having Her Own Smoke," 196–99.

28. Wolfgang Behringer, *Witchcraft Persecutions in Bavaria: Popular Magic, Religious Zealotry, and Reason of State in Early Modern Europe* (Cambridge: Cambridge University Press, 1997), 331.

29. Judith A. Bennett and Amy M. Froide, "A Singular Past," in *Singlewomen in the European Past*, 14; Roper, *Witch Craze*, 161. Roper notes that most of the older women accused of witchcraft had at some point borne children. See also Alison Rowlands, "Witchcraft and Old Women in Early Modern Germany," *Past & Present* 173 (November 2001): 50–89.

30. Schlumbohm, *Lebensläufe*, 338; Hufton, *Prospect before Her*, 1:70–71. For a detailed analysis of ages at which children were considered economically "useful" in the Württemberg region, see Sheilagh Ogilvie, *A Bitter Living*, 99–101.

31. Normally speaking, children leaving before the age of fourteen indicated either parental death or extreme poverty. Dürr, *Mägde in der Stadt*, 157–60.

32. Hufton, *Prospect before Her*, 1:71.

33. Maryanne Kowaleski writes eloquently of this fleeting time of independence. See her "Singlewomen in Medieval and Early Modern Europe," 40. See also Schlumbohm, *Lebensläufe*, 361.

34. Wiesner, "Having Her Own Smoke," 200.

35. Ibid., 197.

36. Alternatively, by the fifteenth century, some cities had employment agents, usually women, to mediate the job search. See Merry Wiesner, *Working Women in Renaissance Germany* (New Brunswick, NJ: Rutgers University Press, 1986), 83–85.

37. Kowaleski, "Singlewomen in Medieval and Early Modern Europe," 40.

38. Paul Münch, *Lebensformen in der Frühen Neuzeit* (Frankfurt: Propyläen, 1992), 50; Dülmen, *Kultur und Alltag*, 2:62–63.

39. Werner Spiess, *Geschichte der Stadt Braunschweig im Nachmittelalter: Vom Ausgang des Mittelalters bis zum Ende der Stadtfreiheit, 1491–1671* (Brunswick: Waisenhaus-Buchdruckerei und Verlag, 1966), 2:396.

40. Werner Spiess, ed., *Braunschweigisches Bürger- und Gewerbe-Verzeichnis für das Jahr 11* (Brunswick: J. H. Meyer, 1942), 75.

41. Ibid., 7.

42. Spiess, *Geschichte der Stadt Braunschweig*, 1:203–8; Edeltraut Hundertmark, *Stadtgeographie von Braunschweig* (Oldenburg: G. Stalling, 1941), 9:31.

43. Karl Bader and Gerhard Dilcher refer to a city like Brunswick as an "autonomous city," rather than a "free city." See Karl Bader and Gerhard Dilcher, *Deutsche Rechtsgeschichte: Land und Stadt—Bürger und Bauer im alten Europa* (Berlin: Springer, 1999), 754.

44. Ibid.

45. Spiess, *Geschichte der Stadt Braunschweig*, 1:152–76; Bader and Dilcher argue that a number of Brunswick's prominent citizens were coming to find that the city's autonomy had outlived its usefulness. Bader and Dilcher, *Deutsche Rechtsgeschichte*, 754.

46. Wolfgang Meibeyer, ed., *Die Bevölkerungsverteilung in der Stadt Braunschweig 1758* (Braunschweig: Bauverwaltung, 1967), 142, 148.

47. Hufton, *Prospect before Her*, 1:77–78.

48. Ibid., 1:76.

49. Werner Spiess, ed., *Braunschweigisches Bürger- und Gewerbe-Verzeichnis für das Jahr 1671* (Braunschweig: J .H. Meyer, 1942).

50. Stadtarchiv Braunschweig E152, Pfarrkirche St. Martin, Teil 1: *Trauungen und Taufen, 1613–1626*: F026R, F177R; Stadtarchiv Braunschweig E153, Pfarrkirche St. Martin, *Kopulierte und Verstorbene, 1627–1647*: F564R. It seems likely that Gottfried Möller himself was a relatively recent arrival in Brunswick, because on April 30, 1620, a Gottfried Muller from Hamburg was registered in the Altstadt as a new citizen. That this was the same as Möller cannot be confirmed, but the sequence of swearing the oath of citizenship, followed by a marriage in June and the birth of a child less than two years later, is perhaps too coincidental to discount.

51. Hufton, *Prospect before Her*, 1:80.

52. Johann Zedler, *Großes Vollständiges Universal-Lexikon* (Leipzig, 1754), 10:1287.

53. See, for example, the *Mägdeschelte*, which first appeared in 1684. Durr, *Mägde in der Stadt*, 96–97.

54. Wiesner, "Having Her Own Smoke," 200–201.

55. On disciplining recalcitrant domestics, see Zedler, *Großes Vollständiges Universal-Lexikon*, 10:1287. As Sheilagh Ogilvie writes, "Communities tolerated young women as servants and daughters living with parents, but ejected them if they set up independently as *Eigenbötlerinnen*, threatened to burden the poor rate, caused conflict in households, violated norms such as Sabbath observance, created sexual temptations for local men, were reported as promiscuous, or brought poor reputations from other communities. Similar examples exist from other parts of pre-industrial Germany." Ogilvie, *A Bitter Living*, 136.

2—Anatomy of a Crime

1. On the original meaning of the term *Scharfrichter*, see Jacob and Wilhelm Grimm et al., *Deutsches Worterbuch*, 16 vols. (Leipzig: Hirzel, 1854–1960), 14:2196–97. For the idea of "sharp justice" see, for example, the funeral sermon preached by Johann Benedikt Carpzov at the funeral of Christoph Heintze, executioner of Leipzig, in 1696: "they are also called sharp judges, for they judge with fire and sword, with gallows and the wheel." Johann Benedikt Carpzov, *Ertheilter Unterricht von den*

Scharffrichtern (Leipzig: Lanckisch, 1701), 25. This Carpzov's uncle, the Saxon jurist Benedikt, also defended the "honor" of the *Scharfrichter* as God's representative and he therefore should not ask the condemned for forgiveness. Benedikt Carpzov, *Peinlicher Sächsischer Inquisition- und Achts Proces darauß zuvernehmen, wann, wie und welcher Gestalt von der Obrigkeit ex officio wider die delinquenten und Verbrechere zu inquiriren, so wol auch wieder die Flüchtigen mit der Acht zuverfahren* (Frankfurt: Presse, 1653), title 12, article 2.

2. On the history of the executioner generally, see H. Schuhmann, "Henker," in *HRG*, 2:75–77; Jutta Nowosadtko, *Scharfrichter und Abdecker: Der Alltag zweier "unehrlicher Berufe" in der Frühen Neuzeit* (Paderborn: Ferdinand Schöningh, 1994), 49–64.

3. See, for example, Johann Benedikt Carpzov's sermon over Heintze: "And in this fashion God is the Higher Judge, the Government is the Lower Judge, and the *Scharffrichter*, who executes the judgment, he is the executing judge." Carpzov, *Ertheilter Unterricht*, 25.

4. On prison conditions and treatment, see Dülmen, *Theatre of Horror*, 10–12.

5. On the role and responsibilities of the advocate, see chapter 10.

6. For a general discussion of the definition of infanticide, see the introduction above.

7. The Virginia Statute runs as follows: "(A.) Any person who knowingly performs partial birth infanticide and thereby kills a human infant is guilty of a Class 4 felony. (B.) For the purposes of this section, "partial birth infanticide" means any deliberate act that (i) is intended to kill a human infant who has been born alive, but who has not been completely extracted or expelled from its mother, and that (ii) does kill such infant, regardless of whether death occurs before or after extraction or expulsion from its mother has been completed." <http://leg1.state.va.us/000/cod/18.2-71.1.HTM>. In 2003, the U.S. Congress passed the *Partial Birth Abortion Ban Act of 2003*, claiming in part that partial birth abortion "blurs the line between abortion and infanticide in the killing of a partially-born child just inches from birth." <http://news.findlaw.com/hdocs/docs/abortion/2003s3.html> The congressional statute does not, however, define infanticide in any way.

8. "Infanticide Act 1938 (c. 36)," *UK Statute Law Database*. <http://www.statutelaw.gov.uk/content.aspx?LegType=All+Legislation&title=infanticide+act+&Year=1938&searchEnacted=0&extentMatchOnly=0&confersPower=0&blanketAmendment=0&sortAlpha=0&TYPE=QS&PageNumber=1&NavFrom=0&parentActiveTextDocId=1085464&ActiveTextDocId=1085465&filesize=414>; Brenda Barton, "When Murdering Hands Rock the Cradle: An Overview of America's Treatment of Infanticidal Mothers," *Southern Methodist University Law Review* 51 (1998): 596; Ania Wilczynski, "Infanticide," *Encyclopedia of Women in Crime*, ed. Nicole Hahn Rafter (Phoenix: Oryx Press, 2000): 114–16; Elizabeth Rapaport, "Mad Women and Desperate Girls: Infanticide and Child Murder in Law and Myth," *Fordham Urban Law Journal* 33, no. 2 (2006): 527–69. Barton notes the diverse ways in which current psychiatry has defined this "imbalance," which on the whole, American juries have proved reluctant to accept.

9. Otto Ulbricht, "Kindsmord in der Frühen Neuzeit," 235–36.

10. "In den Jahrhunderten zwischen Reformation und Aufklärung galt der Kinsmord al eine, wenn nicht gar als die Greueltat par excellence." Ibid., 235.

11. Gustav Radbruch, ed., *Die Peinliche Gerichtsordnung Kaiser Karls V. von*

1532 (Stuttgart: Reclam, 1975), article 131, 87–88. Hereafter referred to as *Carolina*. Except where noted, all translations from the *Carolina* are by the author.

12. Stadtarchiv Braunschweig CV 108, f. 1–70.

13. By the seventeenth century, Ulinka Rublack notes, "Infanticide had become a totally unforgivable crime, and women were almost certain to be beheaded for having killed a living child." *Crimes of Women*, 165.

14. For a brief history of the *Constitutio Criminalis Carolina*, see Rolf Lieberwirth, "Constitutio Criminalis Carolina," in *HRG*, 1:885–90; Rüping, *Grundriß der Strafrechtsgeschichte*, 3rd ed. (Munich: Beck, 1998), 124ff. For a recent survey of the *Carolina*'s pre-history and development, see Ignor, *Geschichte des Strafprozesses*, 41–82. A classic exposition of the *Inquisitionsprozess* is Eberhard Schmidt, *Einführung in die Geschichte*.

15. *Carolina*, article 35, translated by John Langbein in *Prosecuting Crime*, 277; Wilhelm Wächtershauser, *Das Verbrechen des Kindesmordes im Zeitalter der Aufklärung: Eine rechtsgeschichtliche Untersuchung der dogmatischen, prozessualen und rechtssoziologischen Aspekte* (Berlin: E. Schmidt, 1973), 59–71.

16. *Carolina*, article 131; Wächtershäuser, *Kindesmordes*, 153.

17. Otto Ulbricht, "Kindsmord in der Frühen Neuzeit," 236.

18. Wächtershäuser, *Kindesmordes*, 63.

19. Ibid.

20. Ibid.

21. Benedikt Carpzov, quoted in Ulbricht, "Kindsmord in der Frühen Neuzeit," 244.

22. Wächtershäuser, *Kindesmordes*, 65–66.

23. Isabel Hull, *Sexuality, State, and Civil Society*, 114.

24. Otto Ulbricht notes that authorities seldom displayed any interest in the sexual partners of accused women unless suspecting them of participation in the murder itself. *Kindsmord und Aufklärung*, 77.

25. Ulbricht, "Kindsmord in der Frühen Neuzeit," 240–41; Ulbricht, *Kindsmord und Aufklärung*, 31. Ulbricht summarizes his findings in English in "Infanticide in Eighteenth-Century Germany," 111–12. Rublack, *Crimes of Women*, 164; Clemens Zimmerman, "Behörigs Orthen angezeigt: Kindsmörderinnen in der ländlichen Gesellschaft Württembergs, 1581–1972," *Medizin, Gesellschaft, und Geschichte* 10 (1998): 81.

26. Ulbricht, "Kindsmord in der Frühen Neuzeit," 244–45.

27. This was also true of the other fantastic crime that exercised the legal imagination of the seventeenth century—witchcraft. Lyndal Roper's *Witch Craze* lays out the overall process and the methods employed. For a particular and striking example involving multiple layers of German society, see Thomas Robisheaux, *Last Witch of Langenburg*.

28. Ulinka Rublack discusses the relationship between an idealized motherhood and the increasing severity of infanticide punishments in the seventeenth century. See Rublack, *Crimes of Women*, 165–67, 170–72.

29. In the precise words of James A. Brundage, Alexander's decretal *Veniens ad nos* "ruled that a valid marriage might be contracted either by the free and voluntary exchange of present consent between persons of legal age who were free to marry each other, or by the free and voluntary exchange of future consent between two parties legally able to marry one another, if that consent was ratified by subsequent sexual intercourse." James A. Brundage, *Law, Sex, and Christian Society in Medieval Europe*

(Chicago: University of Chicago Press, 1987), 334.

30. Ibid., 552–53.

31. Isabell Hull, "Sexualstrafrecht und geschlechtsspezifische Normen in den deutschen Staaten des 17. und 18. Jahrhunderts," in *Frauen in der Geschichte des Rechts: Von der Frühen Neuzeit bis zur Gegenwart*, ed. Ute Gerhard (Munich: C. H. Beck, 1999), 220.

32. Gleixner, *"Das Mensch" und "der Kerl,"* 10–11.

33. Stefan Breit, *"Leichtfertigkeit" und ländliche Gesellschaft: Voreheliche Sexualität in der Frühen Neuzeit* (Munich: Oldenbourg, 1991), 134–35.

34. Hull, "Sexualstrafrecht," 226–27.

35. Gleixner, *"Das Mensch" und "der Kerl,"* 447–60.

36. "Should someone through force, food, or drink, abort a woman's living child, or make a man or woman unfruitful and should such evil intentionally and with malice aforethought occur, then should the man with sword, as a murderer, and the woman be drowned or otherwise put to death. Should, however, a child, that was not living, be aborted by a woman, then the judge should take counsel about the punishment with learned legal scholars or others how to fulfill this ordinance." *Carolina*, article 133, 89.

37. See Wolfgang P. Müller, *Die Abtreibung: Anfänge der Kriminalisierung, 1140–1650* (Cologne: Böhlau, 2000), esp. 121–33; Günter Jerouschek, *Lebensschutz und Lebensbeginn: Kulturgeschichte der Abtreibungsverbots* (Tübingen: Edition Diskord, 2002).

38. "When intentionally through drink or otherwise the unborn child that was living in the mother's body is aborted, the woman and whoever helped her with drink or in some other way should be put to death with the sword. Should however the child not be living, and such took place under halfway following conception, or should that which was taken for the abortion have no effect, or if the aborted was not a child, they should be vigorously struck with the whip, or punished with banishment or prison, according to the form of the crime." *Kursächsischen Constitutionen von 1572* (Dresden edition, 1578), quoted in Jerouschek, *Lebensschutz und Lebensbeginn*, 255.

39. Ibid.

40. Ulbricht, "Kindsmord in der Frühen Neuzeit," 242.

41. Richard van Dülmen and Otto Ulbricht bring very different perspectives—and statistics—to bear here. Dülmen notes a marked spike in prosecutions and death sentences in cities as diverse as Danzig and Nürnberg, while Ulbricht, focusing on Schleswig-Holstein and Brandenburg-Prussia, sees both little change and an increase of milder punishments, such as exile. See Dülmen, *Frauen vor Gericht*, 58–72, and Ulbricht, "Kindsmord in der Frühen Neuzeit," 242; also Ulbricht, *Kindsmord und Aufklärung*, 176–88.

42. Ulinka Rublack is particularly astute in pointing up the "gendered" character of homicide prosecutions and punishments in relation to the pervasiveness of male violence. See *Crimes of Women*, 167–68; Ulbricht, "Kindsmord in der Frühen Neuzeit," 238–39.

43. Ulbricht, "Kindsmord in der Frühen Neuzeit," 241.

44. Ogilvie, *A Bitter Living*, 268–71.

45. See Renate Dürr's account of the *Hausväterliteratur* and its discussion of the morals and dangers of maids in the city, in *Mägde in der Stadt*, 54–108, 220–65.

3—A GIRL, PURPORTEDLY A MAIDEN

1. Otto Ulbricht notes the incongruity of having men question and sit in judgment upon women in matters that were normally held to be women's terrain, and about which men seemed quite uncertain, even squeamish. Ulbricht, "Kindsmörderinnen vor Gericht," 57.

2. Ulrike Ludwig, *Das Herz der Justitia: Gestaltungspotentiale territorialer Herrschaft in der Strafrechts- und Gnadenpraxis am Beispiel Kursachsens, 1548–1648* (Constance: UVK Verlagsgesellschaft, 2008), 65, traces the process through a graphic. The most telling difference concerned the relative possibility of conducting a defense, with ramifications that will be discussed below (chapter 10).

3. For the structure of the Brunswick court system, see Werner Spiess, "Die Gerichtsverfassung der Stadt Braunschweig zur Hansezeit," *Beitraege zur Geschichte des Gerichtswesens im Lande Braunschweig* 14 (1954): 39–77, esp. 64–77. For an introduction to the processes of courts and "justice" in early modern Europe, see Julius R. Ruff, *Violence in Early Modern Europe* (Cambridge: Cambridge University Press, 2001), 73–116; and Dülmen, *Theatre of Horror*, 5–23. A fuller treatment of the legal history itself appears in Langbein, *Prosecuting Crime*, 129–209.

4. Two examples of the trend are Johannes Brunnemann, whose *Tractatus* was translated into German in the late seventeenth century, and the renowned Benedikt Carpzov, whose *Peinlicher Sächsischer Inquisition und Achts-Process* appeared in 1638. Carpzov's introduction eloquently explains his purpose—to help new and inexperienced judges to avoid mistakes that could lead to convicting the innocent, freeing the guilty, and not least causing unnecessary expenses to the court. The edition used in the present book is the reprint from 1653.

5. Bayerische Akademie der Wissenschaften, *Allgemeine deutsche Biographie* (Leipzig: Duncker und Humblot, 1893), 36:529.

6. Ludwig, *Das Herz der Justitia*, 64–66.

7. Langbein, *Prosecuting Crime*, 179–80.

8. Holzhauer, "Geständnis," in *HRG*, 1:1636–37.

9. Ibid., 1:1637; Ignor, *Geschichte des Strafprozesses*, 66–71.

10. Schmidt, *Einführung in die Geschichte*, 204. Carpzov's influence here was decisive, though it did not go unchallenged by jurists, notably Justus Oldekop, whose significance for the Schmidt case will be discussed below (chapter 10).

11. *Der Rat der Stadt BS gegen Dr. Justus Oldekop (Verteidiger in dem Kriminalprozeß gegen Margarethe Schmidt wegen Kindestötung) wegen Verleumdung des städtischen Justizwesens 1661–1666, BIII.17.9*, 5R–5V.

12. As a way of making the somewhat convoluted German language practice of "indirect speech" more accessible to an English reading audience, and as a way of keeping the questions clearly separated from responses, I have paraphrased the questions and placed them in italics throughout the book.

13. *BIII.17.9*, 5V.

14. "[A]nfänglich hatte sie so nicht gemercket, dann sie hette gemeinet, Captiva wehre darzu noch zu Jung, weiln aber die Leuthe hatten beginnen daran zu /: münckeln /: zusagen, hatte sie genauer achtung auff sie, Captivam gegeben, und umb Weihnachten hinauß eigentlich gemercket, daß Captiva schwanger were, zumahln seithero sie dieselben für eine Magdt gehabt, nicht an ihr versturet worden, daß sie ihr Menses und Zeit nicht gehabt." Ibid., 6R.

15. "Saget ja, sie und ihr Mann Heinrich Lüdden hatten Captivam vorgehabt, und sie wegen der vermerckten schwängerung ernstlich zureden gesetzet, und daß were ihres behalts am Freytage Abends umb Zehen Uhr, nach diesen Neuen Jahres Tag geschehen, aldiweilen Captiva aber durchauß nichts bekennen noch gestehen wollen, und weder Ja noch nein sagen wollen." Ibid., 6R–6V.

16. "[D]ie Mütter aber geantwortet, daß sie nicht darzu künte, und ihre Tochter fragen wolte, darauff auch mit der Tochter desselben Sontages wie sie herein kommen, nach der Mittages malzeit außgangen, und nicht wider zu Hause kommen were, biß gegen Abend." Ibid., 6V.

17. "[D]a dann die Mütter gestanden daß es mit ihrer Tochter, itziger Captiva, anders were." Ibid.

18. "[The mother] were auch des folgenden tages alßdan Montag, wiederumb naher Schwülber gangen, und die Tochter /: weil Zeugin dieselbe ohne daß bey so beschaffene Sache nicht behalten wollen :/ mit sich dahin genommen, und ein mehres nicht berichtet alß daß es ein Reuter gethan haben solte. Inmassen Zeugin auch nicht wieder dernach fragen mügen." Ibid.

19. "Saget, sie könne nicht anders sagen, alß daß sie Margarethe Schmidts, itzige Captivam für Schwanger und geschwängert gehalten, inmassen sie auch durch derselben Mütter reden, das es nemblich ein Reuter gethan haben solte, in ihrer meinung hernacher gesterket worden were, ob Captiva aber grobschwanger, und wie hoch die Zeit /: a tempore conceptionis :/ mit ihr gewesen, zu demmahle wie sie mit der Mütter von hir naher Schwülber gangen, das könte Zeugin nicht sagen." *BIII.17.9*, 7R.

20. The interrogation of Grethe Schmidt can be compared to those detailed in Ulbricht, "Kindsmörderinnen vor Gericht."

21. *BIII.17.9*, 13V. She referred to her father as a "Hüter."

22. Ibid., 14R.

23. "Saget, in Gottfried Möllers Wittiben Hauße auff der breiten Strassen, und zwar auff Andreas Möllers des Sohns seiner Kammer, nahe vor deßen Stüben, auff seinen Bette, wo er sie hingelegt, denn sie hette ihre Luft gebrauchet." Ibid.

24. "Andreas Möllers, der Sohn im Hauß." Ibid.

25. "Saget, ein Tag oder zwey vor Pfingsten, das vorigen 1660sten Jahres, und were nur ein eintziges mahl, und sonsten kein congresses mehr geschehen. Wie wohl sie nicht in abreden seyn könte, daß er sie vorhero, zu weilen geküßet, und ihr in den Büsen gegriffen." Ibid.

26. "Saget hette kein geldt dafür bekommen, und hette ihr Andreas Möller damalß auff dem bette gesaget, das sie es niemandt sagen solte, es würde ihr nicht schaden." Ibid.

27. Literally, "a head with bad fruit."

28. "Wenn es gleich des Kopfs halber nicht geschehen were, hetten sie es dennoch thun wollen." *BIII.17.9*, 14V.

29. "Darumb daß die Lüddische dafür gehalten, daß es mit der Captiva nicht recht were, maßen ihre Nachbaren, die gemelte Lüddische nicht nennen wollen, solches gesaget hetten." Ibid.

30. "Saget, in der alten Garßen Hauße, beym Katherinen Kirchhoffe, da selbst were Gottfried Möllers Wittibe gewesen, und sie, itzige Captivam gefraget, ob sie mit ihrem Stieffsohn zu schaffen gehabt, und ob sie baldt ins Kindelbette Kommen wolte?

Sie Captive aber hette ihr der Mollerschen, in beyseyn ihrer herein gefoderten und gekommenen Mütter von Schwulber, geantwortet, daß sie zwar mit ihrem Stiff Sohne Andreas Möllers zu schaffen gehabt habe, aber von keinem Kindt oder Kindelbette wüßte." *BIII.17.9*, 14V–15R.

31. "Saget, hier in der Stadt nicht, sondern zur Newen brücken, dann ihre Mütter und der Schwester, die Krügersche zu Schwülber, were ihr Captive ohnewissend, dahin gangen, und beym Ambstmanne angehalten, daß sie daselbst bey iemanden seyn mügte, welches ihren auch, wie Captiva hernach vernommene, versprochen worden." Ibid., 15R.

32. Ibid.

33. "Sie habe kein kind jemals gehabt, auch kein von Andreas Möllers." Ibid.

34. "Vorhero, hette sie dieselbe alle vier Wochen gehabt, post coitionem aber hette es sich damit geändert, daß es um die funfte oder sechste Woche, ja wohl umb die siebende Woche komme." *BIII.17.9*, 15V.

35. "Saget, einen Tag, nach negste erlebten Neuen Jahres Tag, abends wie sie in Lüddens Hauß zum Bette gehen wollen, und albereits zu liegen kommen, war etwas so roth, etwas doch nicht gar dicke, und kaum als ein finger lang gewesen, von ihr gangen . . . dieses Werck, was ietzerzehlten maßen, von ihr kommen, hatte sie in ein Tüchlein gebunden, und es die nacht darin behalten, das folgenden Tages aber ümb 4 uhr nachmittages, hatte sie es, vor Lüddens Thur, sambt dem Tüchlein in den graben, ins Waßer geworffen, ob es nun geschwommen, oder zu grunde gangen, darauff hatte sie keine Ansicht gegeben." Ibid.

36. *BIII.17.9*, 16R.

37. Ibid.

38. "Captiva nicht schwanger . . . maßen es sonsten etwas, maßen es obbeschriebe, von ihr kommen." *BIII.17.9*, 17R.

39. Ibid., 12R–V.

40. Ibid., 37R.

41. Ibid., 38R.

42. "Wenn sich ein Jungfraw oder Magdt lest beschlaffen und Schwanger wird/ Sol sie baldt/ wenn sie ire schuldt vormerckt ein Schleiger auffsetzen und tragen." *Der Stadt Braunschweig Ordnunge/ ire Christliche Religion/ auch allerhandt Criminal/ Straff und Policey sachen betreffendt* (Magdeburg: Kirchner, 1579), 25. On the custom of the *Strohkranz*, at least for Franconia (rather than northern Germany) see Hans Moser, "Jungfernkranz und Strohkranz," in *Das Recht der kleinen Leute: Beitr. zur rechtliche Volkskunde*, ed. Konrad Köstlin and Kai Detlev Sievers (Berlin: E. Schmidt, 1976),140–61; Merry E. Wiesner-Hanks, *Christianity and Sexuality in the Early Modern World: Regulating Desire, Reforming Practice* (London: Routledge, 1999), 83–85.

43. Justus Oldekop, *Ex Facto & Iure Außführliche und gründliche Wiederlegung . . . und gantz unwarhafften falschen Relation* (Halberstadt: Kolwald Erben, 1665), 16. Whether this custom was in fact true or not remains unclear.

44. "Wenn es gleich des Kopffs halber nicht geschehen, hette sie es dennoch thun wollen." *BIII.17.9*, 14V.

45. In medieval Cologne and elsewhere, prostitutes were required to wear a red veil or headcovering. See Franz Irsigler and Arnold Lassotta, *Bettler und Gaukler, Dirnen und Henkler: Aussenseiter in einer mittelalterlichen Stadt; Köln, 1300–1600* (Munich: Deutscher Taschenbuch Verlag, 1989), 196.

4—FAMILY VALUES

1. *Der Stadt Braunschweig Ordnunge jre christliche Religion auch allerhandt Criminal Straff vnd Policey-Sachen betreffendt : beradtschlagt vnd eindrechtiglich bewilligt vnd angenomen von einem erbarn Rathe, Rathsgeschworenen, Zehenmannen, Geschockten, Gildemeistern vnd Haubtleuten der Stadt Braunschweig vor sich vnd von wegen der gantzen gemeinen Bürgerschaft darselbst* (Magdeburg: Wolfgang Kirchner, 1579), 46, title 34.

2. Isabel Hull makes a forceful distinction between the statistics and the literary narrative, with its consequences for women and gender relations, in *Sexuality, State, and Civil Society*, 111–16, 280–85. As noted above in chapters 1 and 2, Renate Dürr explains the view of moralists that maidservants were a danger to the godly household precisely because they inspired and hoped for sexual misconduct. On the contrary, Ulbricht notes for the north in the eighteenth century that of eighty-eight male partners he traced, only thirteen were employers of servants and only three were the sons of employers. Ulbricht, *Kindsmord und Aufklärung*, 76–78, following Wächtershäuser, *Verbrechen des Kindesmordes*, 122f.

3. *BIII.17.9*, 27R.

4. As noted in chapter 2, however, officials were relatively uninterested in the fathers, unless they were suspected of participating in the murder.

5. *BIII.17.9*, 20R.

6. Ibid.

7. "[D]erentwegen Sie, aus Haß gegen das gottlose wesen, bewegen worden, daß Sie Zeugin, ihrer alten Magdt zugeredet, dieselbe, das gottlose Weibstücke, itzige Captivam, auff der Dehle hette rechtschaffen auffschlagen sollen." *BIII.17.9*, 20V.

8. "Sie Zeugin darauff geantwortet, daß sie, wo sie wollte nur hingehen solte, Zeugin wolte mit ihr und ihren gehen, durchaus nichts zuthun haben." *BIII.17.9*, 21R.

9. Ibid.

10. *BIII.17.9*, 21V.

11. "[D]ann es ihren hette wohl belohnet werden sollen." Ibid.

12. *BIII.17.9*, 22R.

13. Ibid., 22V.

14. "Es were aber herr Möller (Andreas Möller mit welchem die Captiva ihfrem gestandnüß nach fleischlich zuschaffen gehabt) in die Stuben kommen, und Zeugin, in praesentia derselben, alß seiner Stieffmütter, angeredet und gefraget, Ob Sie Grethen, itzige Captivam, mit nach Wendtschodt zu ihren Vatter nehmen wollte, dass es sechs Wochen aldar bliebe, die Leuthe die sageten, dass es beschaffen were." Ibid.

15. Ibid.

16. *BIII.17.9*, 23R.

17. "Allein es were Captiva ihr Vatter, das folgenden Freytages zu Abend naher Wendtschodt kommen, und sie des Sonnabends fruhe, wie es zu tagen beginnet, mit sich hin weg, dem Vorgeben nach, nacher Schwülber mit genommen, mit vermelden er geben einem Hünde wohl etwas, so wollte er seinem Kinde wohl selbst zu essen geben." Ibid., 23V.

18. Ibid., 24R.

19. Saget, wiße es in warheit nicht mehr, ob sie auß eigner Vorsorge in möller Hauß gangen were, oder ob es ihr Von iemand geheisen worden." Ibid.

20. "[D]och erinnerte sich Zeugin endlich daß es ihr von der alten garsin ge-

heisen, daß sie nach Gottfried Möllers wittiben gehen sollte, dann sonsten Captivam Mütter . . . dahin gehen wollen." *BIII.17.9*, 24V.

21. Ibid.

22. "In Summa, es hettet Captiva nicht zu gelaßen, und were nicht anzusehen gewesen, daß sie eine Jungfer were." *BIII.17.9*, 25R.

23. "Captiva ihr etwas streitmehrig /: widerspenstig :/ fürkommen." Ibid., 26R.

24. "Weil nun Captiva alles Verleugnet, hatte ihr Zeugin ernstlich zugeredet, und ihr ins gesichts gesaget, ob sie auch etwa, was anders [und nichts guts] im sinne damit hette, sie solte darzu Verdacht seyn und die Warheit sagen, wie es mit ihr beschaffen were." Ibid., 26V.

25. "Hirauff hette Captiva geantwortet, sie hette mit demselben [Andreas Möller] nichts mehr zu thun, alß einen guten Tag, und guten weg, Zeugin aber ihr dahingegen geredet, wann denn so wehre, und sie mit ihne nichts zu thun hette, noch gegen ihr bekandt, seyn wolte, könte sie Zeugin nicht mehr thun, und solte Captiva nur hinlauffen." Ibid.

26. "[W]ere ihre Mutter herein in der alten garsin Hauß kommen, und hette sich sehr übel angestellet." Ibid.

27. "[H]ette der Captiva Mutter, ihr Zeugin wieder berichtet, daß sie, ihre Tochter vorgehabt, und dieselbe bekant hette, daß 'sie von niemanden, alß von der Mollersen ihrem Sohn /:Andreas Möller :/ wüßte." *BIII.17.9*, 27R.

28. "[E]r dennoch nicht hoffen wolte, daß es so mit ihr were, uff allen fall aber Schimpff zu verhüten, mügte Zeugin bedacht seyn, wie daß Mensch, itzige Captiva etwa an einen ort hinauß gebracht, und versorget würde, dann er alles bezahlen wolte, hette auch selbst alßfort den Vorschlag gethan, ob itzige Captiva, nicht an den ort wo Ilsgn / [:nemblich naher Wendtschodt] Ilse Engelcken, der alten garsin Magdt :/ her wehre, gebracht werden könte, und der Zeit daselbst erwarten." *BIII.17.9*, 27V.

29. Ibid.

30. "[S]elbst ein Maul gesperren macheten, eher dann sie sehen, wie es mit Captiva werden mügte." *BIII.17.9*, 28V.

31. Ibid. See the letter from Neubrücke in chapter 3 for apparent corroboration of this fact.

32. "Wie nun Zeugin geantwortet, daß Sie ihnen nichts gestunde, für ihre Person auch nichts geloben könte." Ibid.

33. "Mutter und dero Schwester vernohmen laßen, Sie als fort nach der breiten Straße, und sonderlich die krügerische voran gehen, und alda einen solchen allarm machen, machen daß die gantze Straße wachen werden solte." *BIII.17.9*, 29R.

34. "Als nun Zeugin naher Hause gangen, und solche der beeden Weiber reden, ihrem Sohne berichtet, hette sich derselbe also ercläret und erböthen, Wann erst die Zeit herbey kehme, und seiner rechnung nach, eintreffen würde, so solten sie es haben." Ibid.

35. "[H]offete Zeugin nicht, daß sie hiermit gesündiget hette, dann alles was geschehen, umb Verhütung Schimpffe geschehen were, und umb ihres Stieffsohnes seel. Vatters, der trefflich viel auff ihm gehalten, und große Hoffnung für demselben getragenen, hette geschehen were." *BIII.17.9*, 29V.

36. Ibid.

37. "Sie sich einsmahls auff eine Pferdt gesetzet, und am Sonnabendt darauff übers Marckt geritten, daß es viel auffsehens gegeben, und ihr Zeugin nicht wenig verdroßen." *BIII.17.9*, 30R.

38. Ibid.

39. "[W]ie Captiva naher Wendtschott gangen, denn Captive ziemlich rund anzusehen gewesen were." *BIII.17.9*, 30V.

40. "[E]rinnerte sich Zeugin, daß Sie Captivam zu dammahle, wie sie dieselbe zum ersten mahle, umb die newe Jahres Zeit, in der garsin Haus fodern laßen, Captiva aber nichts gestehen wollen, angreiffen und (sonderlich vorm Leibe) begreiffen wollen, allein Captiva hette sie nicht ansehen wollen, hette auch nicht leiden wollen, das Zeugin sie angegriffen, sondern hette mit beeden handen, der Zeugen Handt von sich gestoßen und abgewendet." *BIII.17.9*, 31R.

41. "[E]rinnerte sich Zeugin noch wohl, wie Captiva in ihren Hause noch gedienet, daß sie hingangen an den Wenden graben in das Hauß, alwo ihre Schwester zu demmahle dedienet, und sich wegen auß fahrenden bösen Feuchtigkeiten auff dem Haupte, ihre Haare abschneiden laßen." *BIII.17.9*, 31V.

42. "Befraget, ob sie nicht von der Captiva, wie Sie dieselbe auff dem Steine Wege in der Breite Straßen stehend, und sich nach ihrem Hause umbschawen gesehen, geredet, daß Captiva vor lengst ihre Straffe, oder der gleiche Straffe verdienet hatte, oder was dieselbe sonst würdig were?" Ibid.

43. "Zeugen aber (der bey ihr gestandenen Frawen) nicht mehr darauff geantwortet, alß daß Sie gesaget, daß möchten Sie nemblich grethe und die ihrigen verantworten, wann die gedachte wehtage und Zäne schmertzen was böses oder Verdechtiges gewesen weren." *BIII.17.9*, 32R.

44. "[S]ie würde derselben ohne Zweiffel, di hand auff dem Leib geleget, und solches erkundet haben." Ibid., 32V.

45. "Captiva Mutter, zur Antwort geben, daß es wohl nicht anders seyn würde, alß das grethe schwanger were, dann ihr, itziger Captiva die beine gar dicke geschwollen gewesen, daß Sie kaum ihre Strümpffe, salva venia, zu setzen, außziehen connen . . . , daß Sie aber ihrer Tochter Leib befühlt, und daß ein lebendiges Kind, bey ihr sich gereget, empfunden haben solte, deßwere nicht geschehen." Ibid.

46. "Als Zeugin aber weiter gefraget, ob Captiva es dann umb Martini zum ersten mahle gemercket, hirauff hette Captiva weder Ja noch Nein gesaget, daß mann es horen könne." Ibid., 33R.

5—COMMON REPUTE

1. Rumor was frequently the beginning of a set of suspicions that might prompt the authorities to act. See Ulbricht, "Landesverweisung für Kindsmord," 263f, for a case that began in just this way. With Schmidt, though, the rumors that prompted official action came some seven months after the alleged murder.

2. Ulinka Rublack notes that upper-class women were more restrained in crossing class barriers to gossip: *Crimes of Women*, 18–19. Below that level, though, the Schmidt case shows prosperous widows trading information with women well below their class. For an overview on the importance of reputation in medieval and Renaissance Europe, see Thelma S. Fenster and Daniel Lord Smail, eds., *Fama: The Politics of Talk and Reputation in Medieval Europe* (Ithaca: Cornell University Press, 2003).

3. In her excellent account of gossip, reputation, and crime, Ulinka Rublack notes the serious attention women and men alike gave to separating mere malice from knowledge: *Crimes of Women*, 22. In the Schmidt case, though, the ease with which one rumor ran into another suggests that the trail and control of rumors was much more diffuse.

4. Merry Wiesner, "Having Her Own Smoke," 206–8, describes the various occupations of women and widows forced to find their own incomes on the margins of a guild-dominated urban economy, as well as the disrepute they experienced.

5. "[S]ehet, da stehet eure alte Magdt, gretha, was mag die itzo wohl gedencken [und zu diesen reden were Zeugin bewegen worden], weil die Leuthe sageten, daß es derselben so Frawenhafftig zuließe." *BIII.17.9*, 34R.

6. "Ja was mag es freÿlich dencken. Sonsten aber hatten die zusehen in gemein, einer zu dem anders geredet, daß wohl manche darunter sein mügte, die es eben als verdienet hette." Ibid., 34R–V.

7. "[B]erichtet daß eine Magdt, nemblich itzige Captiva Margarethe Schmidt, bey dem Spielmanne in Sacke /:bey Hauß Bordtfeldten :/ in den Dienst kommen were, der lieste es gar Frawenhafftig zu." Ibid., 35V.

8. "Zeugin ferner erzehlet, daß sie, auff einen dorffe, welches Zeugin nicht zu nennen wüste, gewesen, in einem Hause, welches Zeugin ihres behalts, von der Captiva ihres Vatters Hause, nicht weit gewesen seyn mügte, woselbst der Captive ihre kleine Schwester hinkommen, und der Lohmännschen, welche vielleicht mit ihme bekandt, zu verstehen gegeben, daß ihre Schwester die itzige Captiva krank were, und es derselben im Leibe wehe thete. Ob nun gedachte Lohmanns Wittibe, etwas auß den gemeinen reden, so draüßen zur newebrügken und sonsten von Captiva, in schwange gangen seyn mügten, vernommen, und mit fleiße nach grethen, der itzigen Captiva, bey dem kleinen Mägdtgen gefraget, daß könte Zeugin nicht wißen, dann die Lohmännsche hette Captivam, zu der zeit albereits, wie dieselbe in Gottfried Möllers Wittibes Haüße gedienet, und in Zeugin Mannes Haüß zu weilen, schue zu flicken gebracht." Ibid., 34V–35R.

9. "[D]aß sie einen vollen Büsen gehabt, und ihr Zeugin dahere etwas frawenhafftig fürkommen sey." Ibid., 35R.

10. Ibid.

11. "[D]aß sie wohl dabey thet." *BIII.17.9*, 39V.

12. "[W]as etwa der heilige Christ bescheret hette, sehen solte." Ibid.

13. In her callback testimony the next day, Wilmers corrected this statement somewhat, saying that she could not remember exactly whether Margarethe had come on the day summoned or sometime thereafter. *BIII.17.9*, 44R.

14 Ibid 40R

15. "Ihr auch fürgehalten, daß sie darzu verdacht seyn, und wohl dabey thun solte." Ibid.

16. "[H]atte Zeugen von ihr haben wollen, das sie Captiva, ihr der Zeugin ins gesichte sehen sollen, welches Captiva aber auch nicht thun wollen, sonder ihr gesichte und augen, ein mahl wie das ander nieder geschlagen." Ibid.

17. *BIII.17.9*, 44R.

18. "[D]amit es die Mägdte nicht hören sollen, geredet." Ibid., 43R.

19. "[W]ie sie hette mit Andreas Möller, weiln der gleichwohl ein fürnehmer Kerl were, zusammen kommen könne, fragte." Ibid., 43R–V.

20. "*Phui!* daß der Dicke Kerl hinder dem Kacheloffen sase, und sie nun also weitern /:wandern:/ müste." Ibid., 43V.

21. "[S]ie und Möllers damahlige andere Mägdt, ein stroh kind gemachtet, und es Andreas Möller in sein Bette geleget, er Möller aber daselbe des folgenden morgens wieder umb von einander gemachet, und die itzige Captivam darzu gerissen, und wie sie roth worden, ihr Zugeredet, daß sie sich nicht verjagen /:erschreken:/ solte." Ibid., 44R.

22. It is tempting to consider the episode of the straw doll as an instance of attempted magic, especially in a world and territory so attuned to witchcraft and witchcraft trials. The magistrates, however, never mentioned this moment again, so they most likely saw it as a prank. Curiously, the other maid in the Hafferland house was never called to witness, either to this event or to other potential goings-on with Andreas Möller.

23. "[D]aß ihrer Tochter Grethe, itziger Captiva Waßer, bey einer Frauen, Zeugin meinung nach, bey der Fränkschen ein Hagen, besehen laßen, und die selbe frawe gesaget hette, daß ihre Tochter nicht schwanger, sondern derselben auffgeschlagen were." *BIII.17.9*, 47R.

24. Ibid., 45R.

25. "[D]ie Weiber lange warten solten, biß sie eine solche Schein oder Schreiben bekohmen." Ibid., 45V.

26. *BIII.17.9*, 47R.

27. "[E]ttwa einen tranck verfertighet, was sie für krauterey, und sonsten mehr dazu gebrauchet, wofur der tranck gutt, od genützet, was, oder wie viel sie dafür an gelde bekommen?" *BIII.17.9*, 47R.

28. "[B]erichtet, daß zwar woll leutte kähmen, die Ihr das Waßer zu besehen brächtten, könnte sich aber nichts erinnern, noch besinnen, daß dero Zeitt Ihr ein Waßer zubesehen, von einer frawen von Schwülber sollte gebracht sein, zumahl sie darauff keine Achttung gebe, wohin oder woher die leutte kähmen, und gehoreten . . . auch manniches mahl selber nicht bekandt, sie fragtte sie auch seltten darumb." Ibid., 47V.

29. "Nein, das were nicht geschehen, sie machtte mannichen Menschen woll einen Trunck, der ein Leber und Lungen Schaden, oder ander gebrechen und Mangel im Leibe hette, da sie den mannichen Menschen geringe Mittel gebrauchtt, die dann demselben, durch Gottes Gnade geholffen, daß sie aber solcher gestaltt, wie sie gefraget würde, träncke machtt haben sollte, das köntte und sollte niemand mitt wahrheitt Ihr nachsagen, sie wäre nunmehr eine alte kummerliche frawe, sie wüste umb solche händel nicht, hette auch mitt solchen sachen nichts zuschaffen, dafür sollte sie Gott im hohen Himmel bewahren, wüste also, hochbetewrlich außagend, hervon nichts zuberichten." Ibid., 47V–48R.

30. Morton, *The Trial of Tempel Anneke*.

6—Corpus Delicti

1. Ulinka Rublack powerfully describes the diverse attitudes and beliefs concerning pregnancy and its social and gendered meanings, in "Pregnancy, Childbirth, and the Female Body in Early Modern Germany," *Past & Present* 150, no. 1 (1996): 84–110.

2. Rublack, *Crimes of Women*, 176.

3. Ulbricht, "Kindsmörderinnen vor Gericht," 65–66. Ulbricht notes that the claim of a sudden, unexpected birth was a standard feature of suspects' attempt to defend themselves.

4. Barbara Duden, *Disembodying Women: Perspectives on Pregnancy and the Unborn* (Cambridge: Harvard University Press, 1993), 11.

5. Ibid., 53.

6. Ibid., 54.

7. Angus McLaren, *Reproductive Rituals: The Perception of Fertility in England from the Sixteenth to the Nineteenth Century* (London: Methuen, 1984), 23; Duden, *Disembodying Women*, 15, citing Marjorie Nicolson, *Science and Imagination* (1956): 165ff.

8. Lois N. Magner, *A History of the Life Sciences* (New York: M. Dekker, 1994), 172.

9. McLaren, *Reproductive Rituals*, 16; Magner, *History*, 172.

10. McLaren, *Reproductive Rituals*, 17.

11. Aristotle, *Generation of Animals*, II. IV (739b, 21–25), quoted in Duden, *Disembodying Women*, 56.

12. As Barbara Duden notes, "From the historical beginnings of Western medicine, the womb has been seen as a two-handled vessel used by nature for cheese making." Duden, *Disembodying Women*, 56.

13. Robert Willis, trans., *The Works of William Harvey* (1847), 294, quoted in McLaren, *Reproductive Rituals*, 18.

14. Magner, *History*, 177–79.

15. Ibid., 183.

16. Konstantinos Kapparis, *Abortion in the Ancient World* (London: Duckworth Academic, 2002), 39.

17. McLaren, *Reproductive Rituals*, 108.

18. Jacques Gélis, *History of Childbirth: Fertility, Pregnancy, and Birth in Early Modern Europe*, trans. Rosemary Morris (Cambridge: Polity Press, 1996), 58–59. Gélis, though, does not distinguish between the learned and unlearned tradition, nor does he argue over time periods.

19. Eva Labouvie, *Andere Umstände: Eine Kulturgeschichte der Geburt* (Cologne: Böhlau,1999), 21–23.

20. Barbara Duden, *The Woman beneath the Skin: A Doctor's Patients in Eighteenth-Century Germany* (Cambridge: Harvard University Press, 1991), 35, citing Sandra Ott, "Aristotle among the Basques: The 'Cheese-Analogy' of Conception," *Man* 14 (1979): 699–711; Emmanuel LeRoy Ladurie, *Montaillou: The Promised Land of Error* (New York: G. Braziller, 1978), 172–73.

21. Ott, "Aristotle among the Basques," 708.

22. Duden, *Woman beneath the Skin*, 162.

23. Gélis, *History of Childbirth*, 58, citing J. Duval, *Des Hermaphrodits, Accouchemens des Femmes et Traitement qui est Requis pour les Relever en Santé, et bien Élever leurs Enfants* (Rouen: De l'imprimerie de David Geuffroy, 1612), 6.

24. Justine Siegemundin, *The Court Midwife*, ed. and trans. Lynne Tatlock (Chicago: University of Chicago Press, 2005). For a very effective discussion of diagnosis and the "ambiguities of female bodily processes," see Ulinka Rublack, *Crimes of Women*, 174–79.

25. This according to the seventeenth-century French midwife Louise Bourgeoise. For the general uncertainty of diagnosis in French history, see Cathy McClive, "'The Hidden Truths of the Belly: The Uncertainties of Pregnancy in Early Modern Europe," *Social History of Medicine* 15, no. 2 (2002): 212.

26. The French surgeon Cosme Viardel claimed that four early signs demonstrated a pregnancy: "the little shiver" felt during a fertile intercourse; the closing of the "neck of the womb"; the end of menstruation; and the swelling of breasts. Gélis, *History of Childbirth*, 46.

27. Rublack, "The Public Body: Policing Abortion in Early Modern Germany," in *Gender Relations in German History: Power, Agency, and Experience from the Sixteenth to the Twentieth Century*, ed. Lynn Abrams and Elizabeth Harvey (Durham, NC: Duke University Press, 1997), 59; Gélis, *History of Childbirth*, 46.

28. Labouvie, *Andere Umstände*, 14–16.

29. Rublack, *Crimes of Women*, 174, 177.

30. Duden, *Woman beneath the Skin*, 160.

31. "[I]st unter andern auch gar eine betrügliche und ungegründete Meinung/ daß mann schliessen will/ wenn in denen ersten Monaten die Monatliche Reinigung fortginge/ so sey ein Weib nicht schwanger/ oder wenn in diesen Monaten gedachte Reinigung aussen bliebe/ so sey ein Weib schwanger/ zumal solches dieser beyden Gegentheil selbst in der That widerspricht/ in dem bey gewissen schwangern Weibes-Personen diese Reinigung im ersten und andern Monat nicht allein nicht aussen bleibet/ sondern auch ohne Schaden der Frucht in gewöhnlicher Ordnung wolh fortgehet/ biß zur Helffte ihres schwanger seyns/ deren Exempel bey Weibern/ die lebendige/ meistens Männliches Gechlechts und gesunde Kinder bracht haben/ nicht unbekant sind: Hingegen ist das Gegentheil auch mehr als zu viel bekant." Johann Georg Sommer, *Nothwendiger Hebammen-unterricht* (Jena: Birckner, 1676), 15–16.

32. Paulo Zacchia, *Pauli Zacchiae, medici Romani, Quaestiones medico-legales: in quibus eae materiae medicae, quae ad legales facultates videntur pertinere, proponuntur, pertractantur, resolvuntur* (Amsterdam: Blaeu, 1651), 65.

33. Rublack, *Crimes of Women*, 177.

34. Duden, *Woman beneath the Skin*, 159–60.

35. Ibid., 160; Rublack, *Crimes of Women*, 175, describes the civic doctor of Constance prescribing a "purgative" for dropsy, only to have the unmarried woman in great surprise give birth two weeks later. Of course, one can also look at cases like this with suspicion about what the woman actually knew and the doctor really assumed.

36. Duden, 161.

37. Rublack, "The Public Body," 60. Modern observation also demonstrates that during times of malnourishment and famine, a woman might cease to menstruate.

38. Rublack, *Crimes of Women*, 176.

39. According to modern reckoning, women experiencing their first pregnancy frequently feel the first movements somewhere between eighteen and twenty weeks. Women who have had a child occasionally experience movement as early as thirteen to fifteen weeks. David Bainbridge, *Making Babies: The Science of Pregnancy* (Cambridge: Harvard University Press, 2001), 134.

40. Gélis, *History of Childbirth*, 48.

41. Rublack, "The Public Body," 59–60.

42. Rublack, *Crimes of Women*, 176.

43. McClive, "Hidden Truths," 218.

44. Siegemundin, *The Court Midwife*, 47–48.

45. Judith M. Richards, *Mary Tudor* (London: Routledge, 2008), 173–79.

46. Rublack, "The Public Body," 60; McClive, "Hidden Truths," 219–20.

47. Ibid. Today these might be identified as hydatidiform moles, nonviable embryos growing in the womb. See Vinay Kumar, Nelso Fausto, and Abul Abbas, et al., *Robbins and Cotran Pathologic Basis of Disease*, 7th ed. (Philadelphia: Elsevier Saunders, 2005), 1110.

48. Bainbridge, *Making Babies*, 117–18.

49. Rublack, "The Public Body," 60.

50. Siegemundin, *The Court Midwife*, 49–51.

51. McClive, "Hidden Truths," 219, quoting Louise Bourgeois, *Observations diverses sur la Sterilité, Perte de Fruict, Foecondité, Accouchements, et Maladies des Femmes, et Enfants Nouveaux Naiz* (Paris: Saugrain, 1617), 54, 91.

52. Gélis, *History of Childbirth*, 48.

53. Labouvie, *Andere Umstände*, 25–26.

7—KNOWLEDGEABLE WOMEN

1. *Carolina*, article 35.

2. Ibid.

3. Erwin H. Ackerknecht, "Midwives as Experts in Court," *Bulletin of the New York Academy of Medicine* 52, no. 10 (1976): 1225.

4. Ibid., 1226.

5. Wendy Arons, translator's introduction to *When Midwifery Became the Male Physician's Province: The Sixteenth Century Handbook; The Rose Garden for Pregnant Women and Midwives* by Eucharius Rösslin (Jefferson, NC: McFarland & Company, 1994), 5.

6. Ibid., 6.

7. Mary Lindemann, *Medicine and Society in Early Modern Europe* (Cambridge: Cambridge University Press, 1999), 220. On the relation between midwives and male doctors, see the recent work of Monica Green, *Making Women's Medicine Masculine: The Rise of Male Authority in Pre-modern Gynaecology* (New York: Oxford University Press, 2008).

8. Ibid., 223.

9. Arons, *Midwifery*, 6.

10. Eva Labouvie, *Beistand ins Kindsnoten: Hebammen und weibliche Kultur auf dem Land, 1550–1910* (Frankfurt: Campus, 1999), 101.

11. Gélis, *History of Childbirth*, 103–4; Lindemann, *Medicine and Society*, 221.

12. Lindemann, *Medicine and Society*, 116.

13. Labouvie, *Beistand ins Kindsnoten*, 74–75; Gélis, *History of Childbirth*, 105–7.

14. Labouvie, *Beistand ins Kindsnoten*, 75.

15. Merry Wiesner, "The Midwives of South Germany and the Public/Private Dichotomy," in *The Art of Midwifery: Early Modern Midwives in Europe*, ed. Hilary Marland (London: Routledge, 1993), 82.

16. Ibid., 83.

17. Ibid., 83–84.

18. Lynne Tatlock, "*Speculum Feminarum*: Gendered Perspectives on Obstetrics and Gynecology in Early Modern Germany," *Signs* 17, no. 4 (1992): 732–34. See also Duden, *Woman beneath the Skin*, 83–85, 99–103. On barber surgeons, see F. C. Wille, *Über Stand und Ausbildung der Hebammen im 17. und 18. Jahrhundert in Chur-Brandenburg* (Berlin, 1934), 7, cited in Tatlock, "*Speculuam Feminarum*," 733.

19. Tatlock, "*Speculum Feminarum*," 733–34.

20. Gélis, *History of Childbirth*, 107.

21. Ibid.

22. Erwin H. Ackerknecht, "Zur Geschichte der Hebammen," *Gesnerus* 31 (1974): 182.

23. "Es bestehet aber solches vornemblich darinn/ daß sie Gottes Wort fleissig hören/ das hochwürdige Abendmahl zu rechter Zeit brauchen/ die Christliche Information Stunden fleissig besuchen/ und was sie gefallet und gelernet/ zum Glauben und Christlichem Leben anwenden. Hingegen sol aller Aberglauben und Mißbrauch Gottes Namens und Worts/ (so wider das erste und andere Gebot Gottes läufft)/ als da ist Segensprechen/ characteren oder Buchstaben/ Zeichen/ sonderliche Gebährden und Creutz machen/ Ablosung des Näbeleins mit gewissen Fragen und Antworten/ anhängen etlicher sonderbahren Dinge/ wider das Abergläubische Beruffen der Kinder/ bespitzen vor oder nach dem Bade/ und dergleichen/ nicht alleine an ihnen selbsten gänzlich verboten seyn/ sondern auch/ wenn sie dergleichen unChristliches und tadel hafftes Beginnen an andern Leuten vermercken/ solen sie dieselben ernstlich davon abmahnen/ auch allen falls dem Pfarrer oder Obrigkeit anzeigen." *Nothwendig- und nützlicher Unterricht, so wol vor Jedermänniglichen, als sonderlich vor die bestellten Wehemütter oder Heb-ammen im Fürstenthumb Gotha . . . Auff sonderbahre fürstliche Anordnung und gnädigen Befelch zusammen getragen und gestellet von denen verordneten Medicis zu Gotha* (Gotha: Johann Michael Schalln, 1658), para. 1.

24. "Sollen die Bade-Mütter keine abergläubigische Worte/ Geberde/ oder Segnerey gebrauchen/ sondern das Werck von GOtt/ und andächtigem Gebet anfangen/ auch damit mitteln und schliessen." *Unterricht vor die Heb-Ammen, oder Bade-Mütter, in der Stadt Braunschweig* (Braunschweig: Zilliger, 1686).

25. Labouvie, *Beistand in Kindsnoten*, 88–89.

26. Ackerknecht, "Zur Geschichte der Hebammen," 184–85.

27. Labouvie, *Beistand in Kindsnoten*, 89.

28. Ackerknecht, "Zur Geschichte der Hebammen," 184.

29. Ibid., 182–83.

30. So, for example, in Gotha, "Should there be too little flow of blood, and the proper cleansing not follow, then she should, through gentle means, such as bayleaves, muscat flowers, ginger, saffron, or rosemary, given in warm beer or wine, coax the blood. Purgative and other strong expulsive means, however, without the advice and permission of a doctor, are not to be used." *Nothwendig- und nützlicher Unterricht*, para. 39.

31. Wiesner, "Midwives," 85–86.

32. "[S]o sollen die Bade Mütter sich keiner Tauffe unterstehen/ oder anmassen/ sondern zu GOTT andächtig beten/ auch die andern gegenwärtige Frauen vermahnen/ nebst ihr/ das Kindlein durchs Gebet dem lieben Gotte fürzutragen/ und aufzuopffern." Braunschweig, *Bademütter Ordnung 1686*, para. 8.

33. "Wann aber es mit der Gebuhrt so unglücklich gienge/ dass das Kindlein sein Leben einbüssen müste/ sollen die Bade-Mütter GOTT dem HErrn/ wann die Entbindung geschehen/ gleichwol dancken/ auch die Kindbetterin aufs beste trösten/ dass Kindlein/ welches sie GOTT im Gebet fleissig befohlen/ sey von demselben zu Gnaden angenommen/ und also ihre Arbeit nicht vergebens: Da auch GOtt der HERR es so schickte/ dass die gebährende Frau selbst ihre Augen darüber zuthun müste/ sollen die Bade-Mütter/ wann sie solches mercken/ denen Männern/ und anwesenden Frauen mit guter Weise es an die Hand geben/ damit sie sich desto besser in GOttes Willen ergeben/ und zum seligen Ende/ mit andächtigem Gebet/ auch Herzuforderung des Predigers/ und Bestellung ihres Hauses/ anschicken können." *Bademütter Ordnung 1686*, para. 13.

34. "Item/ sie soll wissen/ wenn sie in die Angst und Noht kommt/ dass ihr Gott gnädiglich solches habe aufgelegt/ da er zu Eva sprach/ Gen. 3. Ich wil dir Kummers zuschaffen/ wenn du schwanger wirst. Du solt deine Kinder mit Kummer zur Welt bringen. Ist das nicht gnädige Straffe? Ich höre wol/ dass er viel sagt von Kummer/ er sagt aber darbey/ dass er sie woll schwanger machen/ und ihr Kinder geben. Wo ist ein Weib/ das solchs nicht begehrt/ wenn auch noch so viel Noht verhanden wäre? Was nichts kost/ das gilt auch nichts. Darum wenn das Weib nach Gottes Wort glaubt/ dass ihr solchs hab GOtt gnädiglich aufgelegt/ die Angst und Noht/ oder ihr Creuz so zu tragen/ so hat Gott an dem Weibe in ihren grossen Nöhten ein grosses Wolgefallen/ als er auch ein unmässig Wolgefallen hatte in seinem eingebohrnen Sohne/ unserm Herrn Jesu Christo/ da er sein Creuz trug/ und must leiden. Denn Gott der Vater hat ihm dasselbe aufgelegt/ dem war er gehorsam." *Bademütter Ordnung 1686*, appendix.

35. Ulrike Gleixner, "Die 'Gute' und die 'Böse': Hebammen als Amtsfrauen auf dem Land (Altmark/Brandenburg, 18. Jahrhundert)," in *Weiber, Menscher, Frauenzimmer: Frauen in der ländlichen Gesellschaft, 1500–1800*, ed. Heide Wunder (Göttingen: Vandenhoeck & Ruprecht, 1996), 103–4.

36. Traditional medical knowledge could, however, cut both ways. Seventeenth-century forensic medicine treatises considered with great respect the Hippocratic belief that pregnancy was a seven-month affair, potentially providing a two-month cushion for nervous potential fathers. See, for example, Paul Amman, *Medicina critica, sive decisoria, centuria casuum medicinalium in concilio Facult. Med. Lips.* (Leipzig: Hertz, 1670), 30–33.

37. Wiesner, "Midwives," 86–87.

38. Gleixner, "Die 'Gute' und die 'Böse'," 108.

39. The parallels to torture were not coincidental.

40. *Braunschweig Ordnung 1686*, para. 14 and oath.

41. On this subject, see Ulrike Gleixner, "Die 'Gute' und die 'Böse'," 96–122.

42. Fischer-Homberger, *Medizin vor Gericht: Gerichtmedizin von d. Renaissance bis zur Aufklärung* (Bern: Huber, 1983), 59–60.

43. Ibid., 56.

44. Gleixner, "Die 'Gute' und die 'Böse'," 103–4.

45. This is true not only in forensic medicine commentaries. Handbooks for midwives also state that milk can appear in women of all physical states and ages. Johannes Muralt's instruction book, though published later than the Schmidt case, is a good example: "Observation demonstrates the opposite, that [women] of sixty and seventy years carry milk and yet no menstruation. There are men who are seen to carry milk and newborn children whose breasts are full of milk. Should a woman claim not to be pregnant, and yet carry milk in her breast, one should not make an unconsidered judgment, but wait out the time and then decide. If someone has harmed her child, and claims to be innocent, then her breasts can be visited, and also the stomach observed, to see whether it is newly creased . . . one will soon discover the truth." Johannes Muralt, *Kinder- Und Hebam[m]en-Büchlein: Oder Wolgegründeter Underricht/ wie sich die Wehemüttern und Vorgängerin[n]en gegen Schwangern Weiberen in der Geburt . . . zu verhalten haben* (Basel: König, 1697), 48.

46. Gleixner, "Die 'Gute' und die 'Böse'," 104.

47. "Grete Voges/ Franz Stacken Sehl. nachgelassene Wittwe/ vor jetzo bestellete Bademutter in der Neustadt/ ist ihre Bademutter Eydes/ und sonsten in Praesentia Herrn D. Laurentii Gieselers des Phisici, erinnert worden/ und hat berichtet/ daß sie

auff empfangenen Befehl die jetzige Captivam Margaretha Schmidts in Augenschein genommen/ und collum & ostium Matricis, mittels einen Handgriff/ und wie es diese Sache erforderte/ nach Müglichket exploriret/ da sie dann befunden/ daß die Geburts Glieder bey der Captiva also arctiret und verschlossen gewesen/ daß dieselbe ihr/ der Bademutter Meinung nach/ niemals ein Kind gehabt/ weniger ein Kind durch den Ort niemals zur Welt kommen sey.

"Befragt: Woher sie solches wissen könne? Saget: Wann sie bey eine Person käme/ so allbereits eins oder mehr Kinder zur Welt gebracht hätte/ daß es sich dann viel anders hätte/ dann diese Captiva an dem Ort ganz und gar verschlossen wäre.

"Illian Wilcken/ Henning Cordes Haußfrau/ geschworne Bademutter in der Neustadt/ admonita, berichtet/ daß sie auff empfangenen Befehl/ die Captivam, Margarethen Schmidts/ an ihren Beinen/ allwo die Weibespersonen nach der Geburts Zeit blaue Adern zu haben pflegten/ imgleichen an ihren Brüsten und umb ihren Nabel besehen/ aber nichts/ insonder aber an der Geburts-Stelle die Captivam befunden/ daß sie an Wirbeln und Geburts-Knochen ganz unverletzt gewesen/ und sich alles an der Gefangenin also eräuget/ daß sie/ die Bademutter/ für ihre Person nicht sagen könte/ daß von Captiva jemals ein Kind zur Welt gebohren/ und das die Mutter bey der Captiva von itzo noch wol verschlossen gewesen sey." *BIII.17.9*, 49R–V.

48. "[S]ie zwar, die itzige Captivam, wegen des vollen Büsens fuer frawenhafftig angesehen, und solches zu obgemeltes Hillebrandes frawen gesaget hette. Ibid., 50R.

49. Ibid., 50V.

8—Legal Maneuvering and the Question of Torture

1. *BIII.17.9*, 53R–54R.

2. *WB*, 5.

3. *BIII.17.9*, 55R.

4. Ibid., 56R–V.

5. On blood, pregnancy, and menstruation, see chapter 6, above.

6. This is one of the few places where the records remark upon an age disparity between the two parties, confirming that the Andreas Möller, born in 1621 (and therefore thirty-eight years old when the sex occurred in 1660), was indeed the correct person.

7. Justus Oldekop, *Ex Facto & Iure Außführliche und gründliche Wiederlegung/ der wider Ihn/ und seine vorige SchutzSchrifft/ von Burgermeistern und Raht der Stadt Braunschweig/ Abgeflossenen 1664. Jahrs . . . in offenem Druck außgesprengeter Ehrenverleumbderscher Schmäheschrifft/ und gantz unwahrhafften falschen Relation* (Halberstadt: Erben, 1665), 36. This is Oldekop's response to the city's own published attack. Oldekop later gathered his original pamphlet, the city's response, and his final vindication, publishing all together as *Ungehewres Inivstitiae Monstrum Burgermeistere und Raths der Stadt Braunschweig* (Celle: Zeitz, 1665).

8. *BIII.17.9*, 58R.

9. Ibid., 63R–V.

10. Ibid., 71R: The last phrase reads, "sie schlechte einfältige Hirtenleuthe wehren, die niemahls keinen Eidte geleistet, es auch nicht verstünden, massen sie täglich bey den Viehe in Holtze und Feldt zubrächten entschüldigen wollen."

11. Ibid., 71V.

12. Ibid.

13. *BIII.17.9*, 72R.

14. Ibid., 72R–V.

15. Ibid., 73V–74R.

9—Terror, Torture, and Grethe Schmidt

1. The exact text reads: "Meister Hans ihr werdet wol was an ihr zutrecken kriegen/ sie ist zimlich dicke; Da hat demselben der Hencker hinwieder geantwortet; Ich wil mich daran versuchen/ waß ich daran kan. Worauff derselbe untershciedlich zu der Gefangenen gesagt: Komestu under meine Hand ich werde dich nicht lose angreiffen/ wiltu nicht bekennen/ ich wil dich so lange ziehen uss der Leiter, daß man mit einem Licht durch dich sol hersehen." *WB*, 9.

2. *BIII.17.9*, 75R–76R.

3. Robert Zagolla, *Folter und Hexenprozess: Die strafrechtliche Spruchpraxis der Juristenfakultät Rostock im 17. Jahrhundert* (Bielefeld: Verlag für Regionalgeschichte, 2007), 78–81, notes that in Rostock the number of cases sent to the university for advice was never much higher than 50 percent and generally much lower.

4. Ibid., 26–27.

5. For Carpzov's instructions, see Benedikt Carpzov, *Peinlicher Sächsischer Inquisition- und Achts Proces Darauß zuvernehmen, Wann, wie und welcher Gestalt von der Obrigkeit ex officio wider die delinquenten und Verbrechere zu inquiriren, so wol auch wieder die Flüchtigen mit der Acht zuverfahren* (Frankfurt: Presse, 1653), title 10. Carpzov assumed that the records should be sent to a legal faculty, and he prescribed the form in which the opinion was to be framed. For a discussion of Carpzov's torture rules, see Ulrich Falk, *Zur Folter im deutschen Strafprozeß: Das Regelungsmodell von Benedict Carpzov (1595–1666)*, Forum historiae iuris, <http://www.rewi.hu-berlin. de>. For a balanced and judicious discussion of Carpzov himself and his work, see Thomas Robisheaux, "Zur Rezeption Benedict Carpzovs im 17. Jahrhundert," in *Hexenprozesse und Gerichtspraxis*, ed. Herbert Eiden and Rita Voltmer (Trier: Paulinus Verlag, 2002), 527–43. The stages leading to torture are traced briefly in Rublack, *Crimes of Women*, 54–56, and Ruff, *Violence in Early Modern Europe*, 94–96. Richard van Dülmen gives a fuller account in *Theater of Horror*, 17–19. The most complete account for this period in German is Zagolla, *Folter und Hexenprozess*, esp. 147–317.

6. *BIII.17.9*, 78R–V.

7. On the significance of recommending a "bearable" punishment, see Falk, "Vom unzeitigen Rennen," 299; also in Falk, "Zur Geschichte der Strafverteidigung," 424.

8. In Van Dülmen's outline of the torture process, this preliminary, more "humane" phase was itself part of the process, which moved to more extreme measures should the suspect persist in his or her hard-headedness. An individual who survived those pains was judged to be innocent and set free. Many people appear to have given in during the first round of "lighter" pain. Dülmen, *Theater of Horror*, 19–20.

9. *BIII.17.9*, 77R.

10. Benedikt Carpzov, *Peinlicher Sächsicher Inquisition*, 138, title X.

11. "Saget, hette kein Kind gehabt/ darumb sie auch keines umbgebracht/ was in Heinrich Lüdden Hause am Wenden Graben/ massen sie vor diesem allbereit bekand haette/ von ihr abgangen/ sey kein Kind . . . sondern mit Ehren zu melden/

ein rohtfärbiger Zeher Unflat/ etwas zween finger lang gewesen/ welchen sie mit dem Hembde/ vor Lüdden Thür auf der Füllen im Graben/ des Nachmittages umb vier Uhr/ salva venia, zusetzen außgewaschen." *BIII.17.9*, 79V.

12. Ibid., 83R: "[I]st sie mit Vorstellung des Scharfrichters und deren zur Peinligkeit gehörigen Instrumenten terriret, und, gleich sie würklich damit angegriffen werden solte, ernstliche Bedrew- und Anstellung gethan, und Sie unter dessen, nochmals über obgedachte in Decreto sub Num. Actor. 30 enthaltene Articulos, mit sonderlicher Ermahnung fleissig befraget . . . werden."

13. Ibid., 83R–V.

14. Ibid., 85R.

15. Ibid., 85R–V.

16. Ibid., 85V.

17. "[D]er Scharfrichter auch, als ob er würcklich angreifen wolte, sich zu ihr genähret." *BIII.17.9*, 85V.

18. "[W]ann sie darumb sterben solte, das das Kind tod von ihr zur Welt kommen were." Ibid., 85V.

19. Ibid.

20. According to Otto Ulbricht's evidence, in some 50–60 percent of cases, women at first claimed that the infant was stillborn. "Kindsmörderinnen vor Gericht," 64–65.

21. Ruff, *Violence in Early Modern Europe*, 95. Ruff also notes the numerous people exempt from torture to demonstrate that the practice was not as widespread as imagined. Schmidt's own defender would later base his defense on the fact that Grethe was too young to be tortured—fourteen, though her age cannot be decisively determined and the city's magistrates believed her to be around fifteen at the time. Ulrike Ludwig notes a relatively small percentage of individuals either tortured or terrorized in electoral Saxony during the century between 1548–1648: out of 750 cases studied, only 5 percent went to a "full" torture, while another 4 percent were "terrorized" or underwent "first" torture. On the other hand, Ludwig is careful to contrast these figures to much higher torture rates in Bavaria and Rostock (on the Baltic Sea). Ludwig, *Das Herz der Justitia*, 69. In contrast, Robert Zagolla notes the differences in incidence from territory to territory, noting that torture by law applied only to serious crimes. Citing the higher frequency of torture in Rostock and its apparent increase following 1685, Zagolla states that no one can make an authoritative claim about the trend or incidence of torture in the seventeenth century: *Folter und Hexenprozess*, 64–65.

22. Johann Strauch, *Acten gemässe Relatio Facti et Juris Uber den zu Braunschweig Wider Margareten Schmieds/ Eine Stuprirte Bauer-Magd/ in puncto verdächtigen Kindermords geführten Inquisitions: Wie auch wider dero Advocatum D. Justum Oldekoppen . . . Ungehorsams halber vollstreckten Verfestungs-Proceß . . . benanten Advocato, und dessen in Druck gegebener Famos-Schrifft entgegen gesetzet/ Von denen zum peinlichen Sachen verordneten Gerichten daselbsten* (Halberstadt: Kolwald Erben, 1665), 24.

23. *BIII.17.9*, 87R.

24. "[D]as Kind sey nicht lebendig zur Welt kommen, hette kein lebendig Kind zur Welt gebohren, sondern es were todt von ihr auff die Welt kommen, wiewohl sichs acht Tage vorher, und des Tages zuvor ehe es zur Welt kommen, bey ihr gereget hette und zwar an der rechten Seite/ in ihrem Leibe, umb Elff Uhr aber dieselbe Nacht, etwa drey viertel Stunden vorhero ehe es zur Welt kommen, und sie etliche mal albereits

das wehe gehabt, hette es sich mitten in ihrem Leibe gereget, hette sich auch hernacher wie es zur Welt kommen in der Geburth ein klein wenig gereget, und hette es bey einer halber viertel Stunde gewehret, ehe es aus der Geburt an die Welt kommen, und hätte sie solches Kind vore erst bey seinen Beinen, und dann beym Leibe mit ihren beeden Händen gefasset, und von sich gezogen, es in die Luken in den Mondenschein getragen, und es besehen, aber nicht befunden/ daß es gelebet wie es nun zu tode kommen/ das wuste sie nicht. Dann wie sie gefühlet daß das Kind von ihr, aber kein Leben darinn were, were sie nach deme es klein wenig bey ihr im Bette, and der rechten Seiten in die Länge gelegen, bald auff gestanden, und es in der Luken beym Mondenschein besehen/ aber kein Leben darin befunden." Ibid., 87V.

25. Ulbricht, "Kindsmörderinnen vor Gericht," 82–83.

26. *BIII.17.9*, 87V–88R.

27. "[H]at sie gütlich bekandt, daß sich das Kind, wie es auff die Weldt gekommen gewesen ein wenig nur noch gereget, und ein klein wenig /: zwischen ihren beinen ligende:/ geginset, zwey oder drey mahl, sie aber were gantz mat gewesen, daß sie sich nicht mehr wegen konnen, wie sie nun kurtz darauff sich umb wenden, und nach dem Kinde sehen wollen, were sie gewahr worden daß ihr rechtes Bein dem Kindt auff dem gesichte gelegen, derentwegen sie das Bein stracks zu rucke gezogen, aber gewahr worden, daß das Kind Todt were. Hette wohl eine viertel Stunde gelebet, und hette sie nicht gewußt, daß sie dem Kinde ihr bein auff das Angesichte geleget gehabt." Ibid, 88V.

28. "Endlich . . . hat sie bekandt, daß sie das Kind, mit dem Beine auff vorberichtete maße umbgebracht, und ihr die gedanken gekommen weren, wie das Kind lebendig zur weldt gebohren gewesen, hette es aber darumb an die Luhke in den Mondern schein gebracht, daß sie sehen wollen, ob noch Leben darin were. Wann es noch lebendig gewesen were, hette sie es nicht umbringen wollen, allein sie hette kein leben mehr darin befunden und were es ein Knäblein gewesen, welches sie des ander Morgens für Heinrich Lüdden Thür, in den Wenden graben in Waßer gewerffe, daß es, weiln das Waßer etwas groß gewesen, mit wegfließen müß." Ibid., 88V–89R.

29. Ibid., 89R–V.

30. "BEY DER AM 5. Novembris negsthin angestelleten, aber nicht an ihr effectuirten Tortur, aüssgenommen, die Schnürung womit sie anfänglich (jedennoch gelinde) angegriffen, aber bald wiederiimb davon lossgelassen," Ibid., 91R.

31. In many cases, women gave in under the pressure of the terror alone. Ulbricht, "Kindsmörderinnen vor Gericht," 83–84. Schmidt may therefore have actually withstood a more *severe* torment than many others.

32. "[I]n güte bestanden und bekand hat, dass Sie in Heinrich Lüdden Hause, am Wenden graben drey tage, nach dem Neuen Jahres Tage dieses 1661sten Jahres, des Nachtes ümb Elff üh, ein lebendiges Kind, welches, alss es schon zur Weldt gebracht, noch etliche mahl geginset, oder wie ein Kätzgen gemauet, in ihrem Bette, vor ihres Hausherren Schlaff Kammer, gebohren und demselben ihr rechtes Bein übers gesicht aüff den Mund geleget habe, dass es erstecken müssen." *BIII.17.9*, 91R.

33. "[I]st Sie bestendig dabey verblieben, dass Sie das Kind mit ihrer rechten beine also vorsetzlich gedempffet und ümbgebracht habe." Ibid., 91V.

34. Ibid.

35. "[U]nd wie Sie jetzo recht Besinnete, nicht drey Tage nacht, besondern drey Tage vor dem Newen Jahres Tage." Ibid.

36. *BIII.17.9*, 92R.

37. Ibid.

38. "[D]arümb hette sie es gethan, dass Sie gern Jüngfer bleiben wolle, und es nich auss kommen sollen." Ibid.

39. *BIII.17.9*, 93R.

40. Ibid., 92V.

41. Ibid., 93R.

42. Ulbricht, "Kindsmörderinnen vor Gericht," 75.

10—CASE FOR A DEFENSE

1. *BIII.17.9*, 93R–95V.

2. Ulrich Falk gives a coherent review of the law and its commentators from the sixteenth through the nineteenth centuries. See "Zur Geschichte der Strafverteidigung."

3. Rüping, *Der Grundsatz des rechtlichen*, 49f.

4. Albrecht Cordes & Gerhard Buchda, "Anwalt," *HRG*, 1:259. On the history of lawyers in Germany in general, see Adolf Weissler, *Geschichte der Rechtsanwaltschaft* (1905; repr., Frankfurt: Sauer & Auvermann, 1967).

5. "Außführung der Unschuld vor der peinliche frage zu ermahnen, und weitherer Handlung daruff," *Carolina*, article 47, 53–54. See also Rüping, *Grundsatz des rechtlichen*, 52. The *Carolina*'s emphasis on the right to a defense is a result of its grounding in Roman law. See Rüping, "Die Carolina in der strafrechtlichen Kommentarliteratur," in *Strafrecht, Strafprozess, und Rezeption: Grundlagen, Entwickling, und Wirkung der Constitutio Criminalis Carolina*, ed. Friedrich-Christian Schroeder and Peter Landau (Frankfurt: Klostermann, 1984), 168.

6. "Von Offnung der Kundtschafft," *Carolina*, article 73, 63–64. On this point, see Ignor, *Geschichte des Strafprozesses*, 80–81.

7. Ludwig, *Das Herz der Justitita*, 66–67.

8. "In such a case that the accused denies the alleged crime, it should be demanded of him, whether he can produce evidence that he is innocent of the charged misdeed." *Carolina*, article 47, 53.

9. Johann Friedrich Henschel, "Die Strafverteidigung im Inquisitionsprozeß des 18. und im Anklageprozeß des 19. Jahrhunderts" (PhD diss., Freiburg University, 1972), 13.

10. Benedikt Carpzov, *Peinlicher Sächsischer Inquisition*, title 8, article 1, 116.

11. Ibid.

12. Ibid., title 8, article 1, 117.

13. Carpzov and Brunnemann follow article 47 of the *Carolina*. See Brunnemann, *Tractatus juridicus de processu fori legitime instituendo et abbreviando, litiorumqve anfractibus praescindendis: ex jure communi, ordinationibus judiciorum & nuperrimo recessu imperii*, 2nd ed. (Celle, 1659), 137. It should be noted here that the Brunswick-Lüneburg *Hofgericht* in Wolfenbüttel ringingly endorsed the state's obligation to assume the costs for poverty-stricken parties: *Hoffgerichts Ordnung: Des Durchleuchtigen Hochgebornen Fürsten/ vnd Herrn/ Herrn Juliussen/ Hertzogs zu Braunschweig vnd Lüneburg* (Wolfenbüttel: Horn, 1571), article 12. On the other hand, Ulrich Falk's examination of the defense in a number of witchcraft cases is more pessimistic. The possibility of a defense lay largely in the hands of those who could afford it. Falk, "Vom unzeitigen Rennen," 283–84.

14. Carpzov, *Peinlicher Sächsischer Inquisition*, title 8, article 2, 118; see also title 6, articles 3 and 4, 99–100.

15. Ibid., title 8, article 4, 120.

16. Falk notes that Carpzov's own writings help explain why Leipzig was in fact a relatively lenient and mild territory. Falk, "Zur Geschichte der Strafverteidigung," 412.

17. Rüping, *Der Grundsatz des rechtlichen*, 49.

18. Ulrich Falk notes the discrepancy between the language of the *Carolina* and realities of the early modern period: "Vom unzeitigen Rennen," 282–83.

19. Once a process began, a suspect became an "object of justice" rather than an active participant. Mitteis and Lieberich, *Deutsche Rechtsgeschichte*, 404.

20. Rüping, *Der Grundsatz des rechtlichen*, 49–50. As noted in the introduction, it is striking that two serious and important histories of inquisitorial process virtually ignore the question of a defense: Langbein, *Prosecuting Crime*, and Schmidt, *Einführung in die Geschichte*. Ulrich Falk notes the "fatal logic and historical tendency" of a process that concentrated all the duties of judge, prosecutor, and defense lawyer in a single person or institution. Falk, "Vom unzeitigen Rennen," 283.

21. According to Rüping, for Carpzov "the inquisitorial process permitted a defense in order better to investigate the material truth." Rüping, *Der Grundsatz des rechtlichen*, 56.

22. Ignor, *Geschichte des Strafprozesses*, 124. See Carpzov, *Peinlicher Sächsischer Inquisition*, title 8, article 2, 118.

23. Ulrich Falk, "Von unzeitigen Rennen," 281–305.

24. As one proponent of strong defense practices put it, "Then if a prisoner does not know what kind of testimony each witness has given, how can he bring a sufficient defense against it?" Christoph Andreas Blumblacher, *Commentarius In Kayser Carl deß Fünfften/ und deß Heil. Röm. Reichs Peinliche Halß-Gerichts-Ordnung* (Saltzburg: Mayr, 1670), 138.

25. "The most significant right of defense is the right to inspect the records. A glimpse into the records is a glimpse through the curtain." Ignor, *Geschichte des Strafprozess*, 81.

26. Brunnemann, *Tractatus juridicus*, 136–39.

27. Ludwig, *Das Herz der Justitia*, 66.

28. Carpzov, *Peinlicher Sächsischer Inquisition*, title 8, article 3, 122.

29. Ibid., 123.

30. Brunnemann, *Tractatus juridicus*, 138–40.

31. The *Policey Ordnung* dealt with frivolous criminal complaints against otherwise honorable citizens, and it is not immediately clear whether the customary practice of reviewing the documents in the presence of the court was not an attempt to allow honorable citizens to clear up matters and influence decisions of judges in a rather informal fashion.

32. Brunnemann, *Tractatus juridicus*, chapter 8, 139.

33. See Gerald Strauss, *Law, Resistance, and the State: The Opposition to Roman Law in Reformation Germany* (Princeton: Princeton University Press, 1986), 3–30. For a contemporary example, see the Brunswick-Lüneburg *Hoffgerichts Ordnung*, title 10, 18.

34. Zagolla, *Folter und Hexenprozess*, 474.

35. Mitteis and Lieberich, *Deutsche Rechtsgeschichte*, 379.

36. Rüping, "Die Carolina in der Strafrechtlichen Kommentarliteratur," in

Strafrecht, Strafprozess, und Rezeption: Grundlagen, Entwickling, und Wirkung der Constitutio Criminalis Carolina, ed. Friedrich-Christian Schroeder and Peter Landau (Frankfurt: Klostermann, 1984), 268.

37. Falk, "Von unzeitigen Rennen," 283.

38. Blumblacher, *Commentarius*, chapter 47, 142–43.

39. Peter Oestmann notes that Justus Oldekop was one of the theorists who, early on, proposed permitting appeals on substantive grounds to the *Reischkammergericht* (the Imperial Chamber Court). Peter Oestmann, *Hexenprozesse am Reichskammergericht* (Cologne: Böhlau, 1997), 349–50. In this, Oldekop was nearly contemporary with Friedrich Spee, the great critic of witchcraft proceedings.

40. Carpzov himself conceded the significant right of an appeal in Roman law but argued that it was not applicable to German practice. Zagolla, *Folter und Hexenprozess*, 474. Oldekop was less attuned to the so-called *usus modernus*, in which jurists tried to adapt Roman law to more traditional Germanic law.

41. There is surprisingly little about Oldekop and his work in the historical literature. See Karl Henning Oldekop, "Justus Oldekop, ein streitbarer Jurist im 17. Jahrhundert," *Braunschweigische Heimat* (1973): 8–14. Joachim Lehrmann, in his popular survey, *Hexenverfolgung in Hannover-Calenberg (und Calenberg-Göttingen): vom Wahn bis zur Aufklärung* (Lehrte/Hannover: Lehrmann, 2005), 227–50, briefly surveys Oldekop's work on the Schmidt case while focusing on and championing Oldekop's work against Carpzov on the witch question, calling the Hildesheim lawyer a hero and precursor to the Enlightenment.

42. *BIII.17.9*, 97R.

43. Ibid., 98R.

11—NOT EVEN A SOW

1. *WB*, 68.
2. Oldekop, *Ex Facto & Iure*, 68.
3. Ibid.
4. *WB*, 5.
5. "Die Warheit ist bitter." *WB*, 6.
6. *BIII.17.9*, 98R–143V. Oldekop later published the brief in his *Wahrhafte Beschreibung* (1663), and the following discussion refers to the printed version.
7. *WB*, 63.
8. Ibid., 69–70.
9. *Carolina*, article 188, translated by John Langbein in *Prosecuting Crime*, 301.
10. *WB*, 66.
11. See chapter 3.
12. "Und als die rigidi Examinatores gradatim die Antwort darauff bekommen/ welche sie gerne hören wollen/ haben sie ferner Captivam befrag: Ob sie dann das Jenige/ so izt berichter massen von ihr kommen/ für kein Kind hielte/ und wovon das dasselbe bey ihr zu tode kommen? Item: Wann sie keine Handen an das Kind gelegt und es ertödtet hätte? Ob sie dann vorher Träncke eingenommen?" *WB*, 70.
13. "Bey der letzten Tortur, wie die Examinatores alles haben erzwungen/ und durch die Tortur herauß bracht/ was sie gerne haben wolten/ haben dieselbe pro abundanti annoch dies Captiosam quaestionem, duas enunciationes conteninetem, welche mit einer responsion nicht beantwortet werden können/ an die Gepeinigte

gethan: Nemlich: Ob es ihr auch leidt wäre/ daß sie ihr eigen Kind auß Vorsatz umbgebracht habe? Worin so viel astute begriffen/ daß man die Gefangene zu einer vorsetzlichen Kinder-Mörderinnen machen wollen/ worauff der Torquirten auch Angst und Bange worden (massen ab der eilfertigen abgezwungener Antwort leicht abzunehmen) ehe sie Ja dazu gesagt/ und wider sich selbst (bona cum venia) gelogen hat." Ibid.

14. "Dagegen halte man nun gegenwertigen Casum der verübten Tortur, worin nicht einmahl ein einziges rechtmässiges Indicium verhanden/ weniger legitime probirt. So findet sich offenbahrlich/wie jämmerlich/ erbärmlich/ nichtiglich and widerrechtlich/ wider das armes gefanges junges Mensch verfahren/ und dasuff ihre abgezwunge vermeinte Confession, wann sie auch vielmehr gesagt hätte/ nicht einer kalten Bonen wehrt zu achten." *WB,* 71.

15. "[E]s fast nicht anders scheinet/ als wann derselbe der Gefangenen die befundene Unschuld mißgönnete/ nach ihrem Tode ganz begierig sey/ und alles Dichten und Trachten dahin anstelle/ daß die selbe ihrer Unschuld nicht geniessen/ sondern einen Weg wie den andern des Henckers Hand nicht entgehen solte." Ibid., 74.

16. "Als er aber die Sachen daselbst unklar und falsch befunden/ hat ers auff eine andere Manier versucht/ sich gewendet/ und die unerhörte/ nichtige und widerrechtliche territion und Tortur." Ibid., 74–75.

17. "Aber mit solchem regeriren würde derselbe sich ferner prostituiren/ die nullitates damit accumuliren." Ibid., 72.

18. "[B]ey den vermeinten und genandten verbalibus territionibus, nemblich die Vorstellung der grawsamen Hencker-Instrument zur Tortur gehörig/ der Gefangenen vorgelegt/ ihr die Hände geschnüret/ und der Hencker allemahl bey den vermeinten territionibus sich also gebähret/ als wen er auffs schärffste sie zu peinigen befehliger were." Ibid.

19. *WB,* 79.

20. *BIII.17.9,* 91R.

21. "[A]usgenommen die Schnurung, womit sie anfänglich angegriffen, aber bald wiederumb davon loßgelaßen." Ibid.; *WB,* 79–80.

22. "Zu dem kan die Schnürung, in specie, oder ligatura auch wol eine gar harte tortura seyn." *WB,* 80.

23. "Das aber dem protocollisten . . . zu schreiben beliebet/ Captiva wäre mit der Schnürung gelinde angegriffen/ muß man zwar an seinen Orth gestellet seyn lassen. Er kan aber ja davon nichts gewisses Zeugen/ wie gelinde oder wehe der Gefangenen die Schnürung habe gethan: Diese hats gefühlet und kein ander." Ibid.

24. The very same personnel who tortured Grethe Schmidt for infanticide, for example, were involved in a witchcraft case just two years later. See Morton, *Trial of Tempel Anneke.*

25. *WB,* 84–85.

26. "Welches ja und Gestandnuß sie dazu mit allen umbständen/ von wem/ an wass ohrt/ und zu waß Zeit/ auch in welcher Cammer/ in welchem Bette/ außfürlich bekräfftiget." Ibid., 86.

27. "[S]o hätte es doch thun/ nemlich eine Müze tragen wollen: Zu verstehen deswegen/ weil sie sich hätte lassen beschlaffen." Ibid.

28. "[I]n Heinrich Lüdden Hauße/ drey Tage vor dem Newen Jahrs Tage/ noch lauffenden 1661. Jahrs/ und nicht drey Tage nach dem Newen Jahrs Tage/ wie sie vorhin gesagt." Ibid. This refers to Margarethe's statement in *BIII.17.9,* 91V, "correct-

ing" Grethe's admission under threat of torture, *BIII.17.9*, 84R. Both statements would prove highly problematic.

29. "Die Geburt ist nach diesem unnatürlichen mendacio neun Tage vorher gangen/ und zwar in demselben Hause/ da man neun Tage hernach die vermeinte impregnation allererst vorgeben und vermercket haben wil/ Das die unter die Leute kommene nach-Rede/ von vorgegebener Schwängerung/ keinen Grund habe/ sondern von lauter Weiber-Plaudereyen/ und der Gefangenen Mutter unbesonnenet unzeitiger Vorsorge/ des Kind-Bettes halber/ herrürhe / ist allenthalben gnugsam abzunehmen/ auch zum Theil ab der Antwort Heinrich Lüdden Ehe-Frawen/ *ad interrog. 27 in actis sub n. 2.*" *WB*, 88.

30. See chapter 8, above.

31. "[J]a nicht einmahl darnach gefragt/ sonder denselben hinter sich geworffen/ und ganz aus den Augen gesetzet." *WB*, 88.

32. Ibid., 90–91.

33. "Allen Weibern aber/ welche Kinder zur Welt getragen und gebohren/ auch allen so davon gehört oder gelesen haben/ verstehen diß Werck weit besser und anders/ daß dieses extorquirtes mendacium eine wahre Unmüglichkeit sey/ und wider die Natur lauffe: Weil nemlich die Kinder /wann es mit der Geburt seine rechte natürliche Beschaffenheit hat/ allemahl mit dem Kopff vorher/ und dann mit folgendem Leib und Beinen zur Welt kommen: Wans aber anderst ist/ zuvor auß wann ein Kind mit den Beinen vorher kompt/ daß dasselbe daran kan gefasset werden wie unschuldig torquirte aus Marter / reverenter/ gelogen/ so kommen Mutten und Kind nicht von einander/ oder da mit grosser Not ander Hülffe und Raht geschaffet wird/ muß doch eins/ wo nicht beyde bleiben. Welches ohne grosse Quaal und Schmerzen nicht kan zugehen." Ibid., 94–95.

34. *WB*, 95.

35. *BIII.17.9*, 147R–148V.

36. Strauch, *Acten gemässe Relatio Facti*, 29–31; *BIII.17.9*, 147R–V.

37. Strauch, *Acten gemässe Relatio Facti*, 31.

38. *BIII.17.9*, 149R–V.

39. "[O]b solche Geburt/ und zwar in so geringer Zeit/ angegebener massen/ habe geschehen können/ zu vernehmen." Ibid., 150V.

12—The Thick Wilderness of Lies

1. *BIII.17.9*, 150R.

2. Ibid., 157R.

3. Ibid., 160R.

4. Strauch, *Acten gemässe Relatio Facti*, 1–2.

5. *BIII.17.9*, 161R.

6. Ibid., 162R.

7. "[W]ann es also beschaffen/ wie es das Ansehen hette/ daß sie es von sich sagen solte." Ibid., 168R–V.

8. "[D]amit das junge Weibstücke nicht ein Unglück anrichtete." Ibid., 171R.

9. "Ja es würde wol nicht anders seyn/ als daß ihre Tochter Schwanger were/ müste sich derowegen nach einer Herberge umbthun/dann zu Schwülber könte sie nicht bleiben." Ibid., 171V.

10. "[S]ie . . . wol darbey thun solte." Ibid., 172R.

11. Ibid., 169R–V.

12. Ibid., 177R.

13. Ibid., 179R.

14. Ibid.

15. *BIII.17.9*, 179V.

16. "Es were nicht anders/ ihre Tochter/ ietzo Inhafftirte/ were schwanger." Ibid., 180R.

17. "Captiva wiederholet ihren ietzo gethanen Bericht/ daß sie selber aus vorangezeigter Ursache es dafür gehalten/ daß sie schwanger gewesen/ wiewol sie niemals ein Kind gehabt." Ibid.

18. *BIII.17.9*, 176R (postscript acta 45).

19. Ibid., 178R–V.

20. Ibid., 161V.

21. Ibid., 184R.

22. *WB*, 22.

23. *BIII.17.9*, 185R.

24. Ibid.,186R–187R.

25. Ibid.,188R.

26. Ibid.,189R.

27. Ibid.,181R.

13—The Way to a Confession

1. *BIII.17.9*, 196R.

2. "Wann es so mit ihr were gewesen/ daß sie hette ein kind haben sollen/ hätte sie dasselbe umbzubringen keinen Vorsatz gehabt." Ibid., 203R.

3. "Saget formalibus verbis? Mek was bange/ dat mek wat do lehen sheien/ das ist/ mir war bange/ das mir etwas were zu leide geschehen." Ibid., 203V.

4. Ibid., 204R.

5. Ibid., 204V.

6. Ibid., 204V–205R.

7. Ibid., 206R–207R.

8. Ibid., 214R–V.

9. "[D]as Andreas Müller in abwesen der Mutter sie mit Gewalt zum Beyschlaff gezwungen." Ibid., 216R.

10. Ibid.

11. "Sagt/ daß seines wissens zu Grossen Schwülper in seiner Behausung nichts vorgangen:/ sondern es hetten Johann Vellhagen und andere ihm gesagt/ das Kind were in Braunschweig in Heinrich Lüdde Hause am Graben zu Welt kommen/ ob deme also/ wisse er nicht/ zu Schwülper in seinem Hauß were nichts vorgangen noch geschehen." Ibid., 216V.

12. Ibid., 210R.

13. Saget Ja, Sie habe es ümbgebracht, und demselben, das Decke Bette über dem Mond gezogen, und habe es nicht lange gewesen, da sey es Todt gewesen . . . Ihre Mutter habe waßer geholet, und wie sie einkommen, sey dieselbe noch ein wenig auff der Tehle geblieben und endlich in die Stuben kommen, und habe nach dem Kinde gefraget, was es mache? Wie nun Inquisitin geantwortet, daß es Todt sey, hette die Mutter gefraget, wie es Inquisitin gemachet hette, hette Inquisitin geantwortet, daß

decke bette were dem Kind auff die Mundt gekommen, derentwegen ihre Mutte mit ihr gekiffen und gesaget, Inquisitin hette dem Kinde nichts solle zu leide thun, hette das ertödete Kind auch bey Inquisitin auffen Bette verdecket ligen laßen, biß gegen dem Abendt, da es die Mutter von ihr genommen, und gesaget, daß sie es auff den Kirchhoff wolte begraben laßen, das Kindt aber /:wie die Mutter ihr nach berichtet hette:/ hinter ihrem Häuse in den garten, welches nur ein kleiner Platz ohne Bäume were, und an ihren und des Kührten Häuse so herginge, auff welchen sie sonst Kohl Pflantzen gehabt hetten, mit einen Spaden eingegraben. Und were Inquisitin sie der den Zeit nicht in dem garten sondern 8 Tage hernacher wie es geschehen gewesen nur davor gewesen und sie den ort gesehen, wo das Kind hin verscharret, dann die Erde were noch frisch, wiewohl sie nicht auffgeschlagen, sondern dem anderem Lande gleich eben gewesen, und Inquisitin für Wehmuht nicht können näher hin zugehen. Und wüßte Inquisitin nichts mehr herumb, alß was ihre die Mutter gesaget daß hette ihr niemand geholffen noch Rath gegeben. Ibid., 210V–211R.

14. Modern statistics indicate a high incidence of breech deliveries in premature situations, decreasing markedly as the term nears. Lone Krebs, "Breech at Term: Early and Late Consequences of Mode of Delivery," *Danish Medical Bulleten* 52, no. 4 (2005): 234–52.

15. These would be the Hagemans, interviewed in chapter 8, above.

16. Strauch, *Acten gemässe Relatio Facti*, 66.

17. *BIII.17.9*, 220R.

18. "[W]ann es zu dem Punct (des Kindes Genesung/ item, daß das Kind in Abwesen ihrer Mutter umbgebracht/ dann daß ihr Mutter das Kind begraben/ und zwar an dem bezeichnetem Orte) kompt." Ibid.

19. "Muß Captivae wol zugeredet/ und insonderheit zu Gemüthe geführet werden/ daß/ dafern ihre Mutter schon auff eine andere Art bekennet hette/ oder ins künfftig noch anders sagen würde/ Es über sie ind ihre Mutter beyde außkommen dürffte/ darum sie sich vorsehen/ und die lautere Warheit berichten solte." Ibid.

20. "Als nun Captiva auff vorgethanes ernstes zureden/ und beschehenen Vorweiß, daß sie in viel stücken die Warheit gesparet/ und erdichtete Dinge und theils offenbahre Lügen/ wieder ihr besser wisen und Gewissen fürzubringen/ weder für Gott/ der allenthalben zugegen were/ noch für der lieben Obrigkeit und denen Gerichts-Personen scheu getragen hette/ sich erkläret/ daß sie nunmehro von Grund ihres Herzens die Warheit reden/ und worüber sie befraget würde/ gerne sagen und willig bekennen wolte." *BIII.17.9*, 220V.

21. "Als daß sie gesaget, Sie hette zu Großen Schwülber in ihrer Vattern Häuse in der Stüben, auff der Erden auffen Bette liegen, in bey seyn ihrer Mutter, und sonsten niemand mehr, ein lebedigen Kind, ein Knäblein zur Weldt geborhen, des Morgens, Wie es meistens eine Stunde lang albereits Tag gewesen were. Wie nun ihre Mutter nach Andreas Sivers Hoffe gangen, und Waßer holen wollen, umb daßelbige warm zu Machen und das Kind damit zu baden, hette Inquisitin dem Kind inmitteß des Decke bette übergezogen, daß es gedempffet, und were dieses etwa eine halbe Stunde hernach, als es zur Welt geborhen gewesen, geschehen, Als nun die Mutter kommen, und nach dem Kinde gefraget, aber von Inquisitin vernommen, daß Sie dem Kinde das Bette übergeleget, daß es dempffen müssen, hette die Mutter gekiffen, und zu Inquisitin gesaget, das hette sie sollen bleiben laßen, was Inquisitin damit anfangen wolle, und wie Inquisitin geantwortet, daß die Mutter es begraben solte in den garten, hette die Mutter das Kind biß gegen den Abend deßelben Tages ligen laßen dernach

es von Bette weg genommen, es in praentia der Inquisitin in einen Leinen Lacken gewickelt, und, ihrer Berichte nach, in dem garten, nemblich auff das Grabland zwuischen Inquisitin Vatters und des Kühhirten häuse an den Vorbezeichneten ort begraben." Ibid., 222V–223R.

    22. Ibid., 224R.

    23. "Die Herren werden woll wißen, wie in solche Sache weiter zu verfahren sie, von unsere Person hieltens dafür, wan Tochter und Mütter an einen gewißen und ohnstreitigen ort, künten zusammen gebracht, gegen einander *confrontiert,* und gehöret werden. . . ." Ibid., 225V.

    24. Ibid.

    25. "[I]hre Tochter alda zu Gruß Schwulper in ihrer Behausung keines kindes genesung weniger von ihr begraben worden, daß sie zu Neubrücke vor die Tochter Herberge bestellet, hatte sie uf die Worte so sie zu Braunschweig von der Müllerschen und sonsten gehört, gethan. Wie aber ihre Tochter zu Hause kommen, und sie solche anders befunden, hatte die bei sich behalten." *BIII.17.9,* 226R.

    26. Ibid., 232R–V.

    27. Ibid., 227R.

    28. "[H]aben wir Andreas Glindmann vor unß bescheiden undt ermahnet die warheit zusagen, waß er vorm Jahr alß er deß morgens früh, vor deß ochsenhirten Hauße voruber gangen gehöret." Ibid., 228R.

    29. "[S]ie bleibt aber dabei daß ihre tochter bei ihr oder in ihrer Wohnung keines Kindeß genesen." Ibid.

    30. "[W]ere in der Stadt etwaß geschehen, davon hette sie keine wissenschafft man müchte mit ihr machen waß man wolte, so könte oder wüste sie nicht anderß zusagen." Ibid.

    31. *BIII.17.9,* 229R.

    32. Ibid., 229R–V.

    33. Ibid., 229V.

    34. "[D]er Scharfrichter herein kommen, die zur Tortur gehörige Instrumenta ihr vergelegt, und ihr dabei angedeutet, daß woferne sie bei ihrer Halßtarrigkeit bleiben würde sie uff die Folter gebracht und peinlich angriffen worden solte." Ibid., 234R.

    35. "Sie ist aber einen weg wie den andern bestendig dabei gebliben. Sie wuste vom keinem Kinde, sie müchte bekandt haben waß sie wolle, sie hette kein Kind gesehen, welches von ihrer tochter gebehren, man müchte mit ihr machen waß man wolle. Sie müchte wünschen, daß [Grethe] von Andreas Möllern schwanger gewesen, undt ein Kindt gehabt, der wehre reich genug, hetter ihrer tochter woll gerecht werden müssen." Ibid., 236V. This statement is from the transcript of the interrogation itself, rather than the report forwarded to Brunswick.

    36. Ibid., 247R.

    37. Ibid., 247V.

    38. Ibid., 247V–248R.

    39. Records of Glindmann's testimony and of the postal robbery would presumably be handled in the chancellery in Celle and now would rest in the main state archive in Hannover rather than in the territorial archives of Lower Saxony located in Wolfenbüttel. According to the archivists in Hannover, no records remain in the archive of such a robbery, nor any of the testimony in the Schmidt case.

    40. *BIII.17.9,* 235R–V.

41. Ibid., 235V.
42. *BIII.17.9*, 249R.
43. Ibid.
44. *BIII.17.9*, 251R.
45. Ibid., 253R.
46. Ibid., 252R.
47. Ibid., 256R.

14—"Even to the Devil Himself"

1. "[E]tiam diabolo, si esset in judicio, appellatio concedi deberet." Justus Olde-kop, *Contra Benedictum Carpzovium: Tractatus Duo; Primus de appellatione in causis criminalibus, alter Decades tres quaestiunum ad processum criminalem necessarium* (Bremen: Köhler, 1659), 8.

2. "[D]er Inquisitin Defensor, wegen der anzüglichen Worte/ so er in seinen Schrifften wider hiesiges Gericht geführet/ mit zwanzig Reichs-Thalern zu bestraffen: [Wir] zu dem denselben citiren und erfordern/ auf den 27. hujus vor uns gerichtlich zu erscheinen/ und . . . und Anlobung zu thun/ hinführo seiner clienten Notthurfft bescheidentlich einzubringen/ oder andern einsehens und Verordnung gewerthig zu seyn." *BIII.17.9*, 255R.

3. "[Z]iemlichen harten und uns fast unleidentlichen Worten begangener of-fenbahrer Iniquitet, affecten, Blutdürstigkeit/ nichtigen und wiederrechtlichen Proce-direns, Mißgunst Inquisitae Unschuld/ Begierigkeit ihres Todes/ vorsetzliches dichten und trachten/ sie ihrer Unschuld nicht geniessen zulassen/ fälschlicher Imputationen, wider das Recht der Natur und Gottes Wort hart anlauffender nulliteten, Bemühung/ sie in Unglück zu stürzen/ und zu einem erschrecklichen unverdientem supplicio zubringen/ wider alle Rechte und Vernunfft angethaner torturae, falscher unverant-wortlicher Anklage/ calumniosi processus, und was des Unfugs mehr/ uns/ unter der Person des Fiscalis, als Obrigkeit pungiret und bezüchtiget." *BIII.17.9*, 147R–V..

4. Strauch, *Acten gemässe Relatio Facti*, 76.

5. *WB*, 41.

6. *BIII.17.9*, 257R.

7. Ibid., 257R–260V.

8. Strauch, *Acten gemässe Relatio Facti*, 82.

9. *BIII.17.9*, 263R.

10. Ibid., 263R–V.

11. Ibid., 275R; Strauch, *Acten gemässe Relatio Facti*, 82.

12. Ibid., 273R.

13. For a brief discussion of the history of the *Verfestung* in English, see Carl Ludwig von Bar et al., *A History of Continental Criminal Law* (Boston: Little, Brown, 1916), 112–14. See also Malcolm Letts, "The *Sachsenspiegel* and Its Illustrators," *Law Quarterly Review* 33 (1933): 570–71.

14. *BIII.17.9*, 276R; Strauch, *Acten gemässe Relatio Facti*, 82.

15. "[D]arauff D. Oldekopff geantwortet/ Sie könten es wol in sein Hauß sa-gen/ Ille Nein/ weren befehliget Ihm es anzudeuten." *BIII.17.9*, 276V; Strauch, *Acten gemässe Relatio Facti*, 82.

16. "[A]uch wann dieselbe vollenstrecket/ in D. Oldekopffs Wohnunge andeuten daß die Verfestung nunmehr geschehen/ er möchte sich darnach achten/ und vor fern-

erer Ungelegenheit hüten." *BIII.17.9*, 276V; Strauch, *Acten gemässe Relatio Facti*, 83.

17. "[D]er Bawermeister . . . trit wieder alles Vermuthen zu ihm/ mit Anzeige: Die Herrn liessen ihn zu Rathause citiren, in der Persohn zuerscheinen/ so bald mit ihnen hinauff zugehen und sich vor grossem Schmpff zu hüten/ es wäre sonsten derselbe schon geschlossen." *WB*, 43.

18. Spiess, *Geschichte der Stadt Braunschweig*, 1:205.

19. "[I]st anfangs deßen Sohn, baldt aber daruff der Vater selbst zu mir heraußkommen, und zu mir gesagt, Ob Ich nicht uffen Nachmittag wider kommen müchte, müßte bald außgehen." *BIII.17.9*, 317R.

20. Ibid., 317R–V.

21. Ibid., 317V.

22. Ibid., 318R.

23. These materials are in the Landesarchiv Niedersachsen Wolfenbüttel, under the call number 6 Alt. 852–54.

24. *BIII.17.9*, 346R.

25. *WB*; Strauch, *Acten gemässe Relatio Facti*. See note 2 above.

26. *WB*, 14.

27. *Acten gemässe Relatio Facti*, 1–4.

28. On Strauch, see the *Allgemeine deutsche Biographie* 36 (1893): 528–31. Oldekop would refer directly to Strauch's long association with the legal faculty of Jena in his final published answer, seeking to impeach the sentence against Grethe Schmidt and the fine levied against him. See Oldekop, *Ex Facto et Jure*, part II, 3.

29. *WB*.

30. Ibid., 20.

31. Ibid., 28–29.

32. Ibid., 18.

33. Ibid., 10.

34. Ibid.

35. *WB*, 16.

36. Ibid.

37. *WB*, 26.

38. Ibid., 27.

39. Ibid., 53–54.

40. Ibid., 59.

41. The records for this appeal are found in Stadtarchiv Braunschweig, *BIV.15b.27* and Niedersächsisches Landesarchiv Wolfenbüttel.

42. Stadtarchiv Braunschweig, *BIV.15b.27*: 7R–13R.

CONCLUSION

1. Daetrius Brandanus, *Sonderbare Klagrede . . . Leichenpredigt auff Justi Olde Koppen* (Bremen, 1668).

2. "[Z]uletzt aber/ wie bekant und fast Weltkündig worden/ in grosse difficultäten und Widerwertigkeiten gerahten/ daß Er sich endlich anhero in diese Fürstliche Residentz- und Verstung Wolfenbüttel unter S. Hoch-Füstl. D. gnädigsten Schutz zu begen/ genötiget worden. Von welchem beschwerlichen Handel und weitleuftigen Process/ den Er dieser wegen bisher geführet/ etwas in specie anzuführen/ gehöret nicht an diesen Ort." Ibid., 37.

3. "Weil er nach Gottes willen und Schickung an unterschiedenen Orten seinen Lebens-lauf biß in das zimlich hohe Alter fortsetzen und als ein Pilgrim herumb wandern müssen/ da es Ihm dann auff solcher seiner Wallfaht an mancherley Ungewitter/ Ungemach/ Widerwertigkeit/ Noht und Gefahr nicht gemangelt/ . . . massn er noch zuletzt als bey einem sonderbahren Ungewitter in diese Fürstliche Residentz-Stade seine Zuflucht genommen." Ibid., 5.

4. *Allgemeine deutsche Biographie*, 36, 530.

5. Ulrich Falk, citing Böhm's study of criminal records in Leipzig, notes that in Carpzov's time, one-third of the sentences to torture end with the suspect refusing to confess. "Geschichte der Strafverteigidung," 422.

6. Ulbricht, "Landesverweisung für Kindsmord," 261. Ulbricht makes a strong case for exile as perhaps the more likely punishment for infanticides in northern Germany. See ibid., 276–77.

7. In Ulrike Ludwig's profile of electoral Saxony from 1548 to 1648, fourteen women were punished for infanticide—two were executed and eight were exiled either temporarily or permanently. Four of the convicted were both whipped and permanently exiled. Ludwig, *Herz der Justitia*, 90.

8. Joachim Lehrmann may overstate both Oldekop's heroism and his Enlightened attitudes, but he acknowledges Oldekop's affinity for controversy. *Hexenverfolgung*, 229.

9. Rublack, *Crimes of Women*, 255–56.

10. On this question of threat and its relation to torture itself in a modern context, see John T. Parry, "Escalation and Necessity: Defining Torture at Home and Abroad," in *Torture: A Collection*, ed. Sanford Levinson (Oxford: Oxford University Press, 2004), 145–64: "The purposeful infliction of severe pain, whether or not accompanied by the threat of escalation, is torture. But so too is a practice that lasts relatively briefly and causes less than severe pain, if it does so against a background of total control and potential escalation that asserts the state's dominance over the victim. The difference between wall-standing and the rack is a matter of degree, not of kind. . . . Thus, torture is not merely the infliction of severe pain to gather information or punish. Rather, torture is also the infliction of potentially escalating pain for purposes that include dominating the victim and ascribing responsibility to the victim for the pain incurred. This definition broadens the Convention's carefully negotiated definition of torture and deliberately blurs the uneasy distinction between torture and cruel, inhuman, or degrading treatment or punishment."

Bibliography

PRIMARY SOURCES

Unpublished Sources

Stadtarchiv Braunschweig (City Archive, Brunswick)

ALTES RATSARCHIV, HOF UND REICHSKAMMERGERICHT

BIII.17.9–10: *Der Rat der Stadt BS gegen Dr. Justus Oldekop (Verteidiger in dem Kriminalprozeß gegen Margarethe Schmidt wegen Kindestötung) wegen Verleumdung des städtischen Justizwesens.* Volume 9: 1661–1666 (572 folio leaves) and Volume 10: 1666 (161 folio leaves).

BIV.2f.9: *Andreas Schmidt Ochsenhirte zu Groß-Schwülper (sowie dessen Patron Dr. Justus Oldekopf) gegen die Stadt Braunschweig wegen Verurteilung und Bestrafung seiner des Kindesmordes beschuldigten Tochter Margaretha 1662–1665* (163 folio leaves).

BIV.15b.27: *Proceß wider den Advocaten Dr. iur. Justus Oldekopp aus Braunschweig wegen seiner Schmähschrift gegen Rat, Consulenten und Gerichtspersonen der Stadt 1663–1666* (259 folio leaves).

ÄLTERES MAGISTRATSARCHIV, PROZESSAKTEN

CV 102: *Acta inquisitionis wider die unverehelichte Anna Mack aus Braunschweig wegen angeschuldigten Kindermordes 1677.*

CV 108: *Acta inquisitiones wider Katharene Mundt aus Braunschweig wegen angeschuldigten Kindermordes 1693.*

Das Niedersächsische Landesarchiv, Wolfenbüttel (Lower Saxony Territorial Archives, Wolfenbüttel)

REICHSKAMMERGERICHT

6 Alt. Nr. 852: *Bürgermeister und Rat der Stadt Braunschweig gegen Dr. Justus Oldekopp in Wolfenbüttel und alle Buchdrucker in Jena, Halberstadt, Wittenberg, Leipzig, Frankfurt und Nürnberg wegen Beleidigung in Schriften. Rotulus 1666–1667. Prozeß ohne Abschluß.*

6 Alt. Nr. 853: *Bürgermeister und Rat der Stadt Braunschweig gegen Dr. Justus Oldekopp in Wolfenbüttel wegen Anrufung des Hofgerichts in Wolfenbüttel. Rotulus 1666. Prozeß ohne Abschluß.*

6 Alt. Nr. 854: *Bürgermeister und Rat der Stadt Braunschweig (Bekl.) gegen Andreas Schmidt in Groß-Schwülper (Kl.) wegen Strafprozeß gegen Klägers Tochter Margarete wegen angeblicher Kindestötung. Band 1: Klage Andreas Schmidt vor dem Hofgericht in Wolfenbüttel gegen die Stadt Braunschweig wegen des gegen seine Tochter eingeleiteten Strafprozesses.*

6 Alt. Nr. 855: *Bürgermeister und Rat der Stadt Braunschweig (Bekl.) gegen Andreas*

Schmidt in Groß-Schwülper (Kl.) wegen Strafprozeß gegen Klägers Tochter Margarete wegen angeblicher Kindestötung. Band 2: Berufung der Stadt Braunschweig vor dem RKG gegen den Bescheid in Band 1.

Published Sources

Amman, Paul. *Medicina critica, sive decisoria, centuria casuum medicinalium in concilio Facult. Med. Lips.* Leipzig: Hertz, 1670.

August, Duke of Braunschweig-Lüneburg. *Unsers Augusti Von Gottes Gnaden Herzogs zu Bruns-wyg und Lunä-Burg, . . . erneuerte und vermeerte Hof-Gerichts-Ordnung . . . Samt beigefügten Kayserlichen Privilegiis de non appellando.* Wolfenbüttel: Stern, 1663.

Blumblacher, Christoph Andreas. *Commentarius in Kayser Carl deß Fünfften / und deß Heil. Röm. Reichs Peinliche Halß-Gerichts-Ordnung.* Saltzburg: Mayr, 1670.

Bosse, Theo. *Die Register und Kataster der Ämter Gifhorn, Fallersleben und Isenhagen ab 1563/64.* Gifhorn: Landkreis Gifhorn, 1988.

Brandanus, Daetrius. *Sonderbare Klagrede . . . Leichenpredigt auff Justus Olde Koppen.* Bremen, 1668.

Brunnemann, Johannes. *Johann Brunnemanns Weyl. Chur-Fürstl. Brandenb. Raths und Ordinarii der Juristen Facultät zu Franckfurt an der Oder Anleitung zu vorsichtigen Anstellung des Inquisitions Processes: Itzo erstlich allen Gerichts-Obrigkeiten und Verwaltern, welche der Peinlichen Rechte nicht genugsahm kundig, zur nöthigen Information heraus gegeben von J. S. S. D.* Halle: Renger, 1697.

———. *Tractatus juridicus de processu fori legitime instituendo et abbreviando, litiorumqve anfractibus praescindendis: ex jure communi, ordinationibus judiciorum & nuperrimo recessu imperii.* 2nd ed. Celle, 1659.

Carpzov, Benedikt. *Peinlicher Sächsischer Inquisition- und Achts Proces darauß zuvernehmen, wann, wie und welcher Gestalt von der Obrigkeit ex officio wider die delinquenten und Verbrechere zu inquiriren, so wol auch wieder die Flüchtigen mit der Acht zuverfahren.* Frankfurt, 1653.

———. *Practica nova imperialis saxonica rerum criminalium . . . decisiones exhibens.* 3 vols. Wittenberg, 1635.

Carpzov, Johann Benedikt. *Ertheilter Unterricht von den Scharffrichtern . . . [Leichenpredigt auf Christoph Heintze, Nachrichter in Leipzig, +1. Feb. 1696].* Leipzig: Lanckisch, 1701.

Habermas, Rebekka, and Tanja Hommen, eds. *Das Frankfurter Gretchen: Der Prozeß gegen die Kindsmörderin Susanna Margaretha Brandt.* Munich: Beck, 1999.

Kursächsischen Constitutionen von 1572. Dresden, 1578.

Morton, Peter, ed. *The Trial of Tempel Anneke: Records of a Witchcraft Trial in Brunswick, Germany, 1663.* Peterborough, ON: Broadview Press, 2006.

Muralt, Johannes von. *Kinder- Und Hebam[m]en-Büchlein: Oder Wolgegründeter Underricht/ wie sich die Wehemüttern und Vorgängerin[n]en gegen Schwangern Weiberen in der Geburt . . . zu verhalten haben.* Basel: König, 1697.

Nothwendig- und neutzlicher Vnterricht/ So wol vor jedermaenniglichen/ als sonderlich vor die bestellten Wehemuetter oder Heb-ammen im Füstenthumb Gotha: Wornach sich dieselbige . . . alles Fleisses richen und achten sollen; Auff sonderbahre Fürstliche Anordnung . . . zusammen getragen und gestellet Von denen verordneten Medcis zu Gotha. Gotha: Johann Michael Schalln, 1658.

Oldekop, Justus. *Cautelarum Criminalium sylloge practica, in quâ Consiliariis & Maleficiorum Iudicibus aeque, atq[ue] Advocatis scitu utiles & pernecessariae admonitiones in materia criminali praescribuntur.* Brunswick: Gruberianus, 1633.

———. *Contra Benedictum Carpzovium: tractatus duo; Primus de appellatione in causis criminalibus, alter Decades tres quaestiunum ad processum criminalem necessarium.* Bremen: Köhler, 1659.

———. *Ex Facto & Iure Außführliche und gründliche Wiederlegung/ der wider Ihn/ und seine vorige SchutzSchrifft/ von Burgermeistern und Raht der Stadt Braunschweig/ Abgeflossenen 1664. Jahrs . . . in offenem Druck außgesprengeter Ehrenverleumbderscher Schmäheschrifft/ und gantz unwahrhafften falschen Relation.* Halberstadt: Kolwald Erben, 1665.

———. *Observationes criminales practicae: congestae, & in quinque titulos, quos versa indicat pagina, speciatim tributae.* Bremen: Köhler, 1654.

———. *Politischer Unterricht für die Rahtsherren in Städten und Communen: Wie dieselbe zu der Ehre Gottes, gemeiner Stadt Wolfahrt, und Erhaltung ihres selbst eigenen respects, ihr Ampt führen sollen.* Gosslar: Duncker, 1634.

———. *Tractatus de appellatione in Causis criminalibus . . . cum annexis quaestionibus nonnullis ad processum necessarii, post praefationem indicatis.* Halberstadt: Colwald, 1655.

———. *Ungehewres Inivstitiae Monstrum Burgermeistere und Raths der Stadt Braunschweig: Bestehent in dreyen unterschiedlichen Schrifften/ Welche seynd: Erstlich/ Die Warhaffte Beschreibung der begangenen Braunschweigschen Barbarischen Ubelthaten an ihnen selbst: Zum Andern/ Des Raths zu Braunschweig Schmähaffte Beantwortung und Calumnien Gedichte/ Wodurch sie sothane grewliche Mißhandelungen zu entschuldigen . . . vormeinen: Vors Dritte/ Solcher vormeinten Beantwortung/ ex facto & jure gründliche Wiederlegung . . . Allen . . . Menschen . . . in offenen Truck herauß gegeben.* Celle: Zeitz, 1665.

———. *Warhaffte Beschreibung eines nie erhörten, Unchristlichen, wieder Gottes Wort, alle Rechte und natürliche Vernunfft laufenden Peinlichen Processus, welcher Bürgermeister und Raht der Stadt Braunschweig wieder eine arme unschüldige Bawren Tochter, von Grossen Schwülber . . . von vierzehen Jahren, Margareta Schmidts genant, eines . . . fälschlich zugemessenen Kindermohrts halber Anno 1661 und 1662 geführt und exequirt.* Wolfenbüttel: Bißmarck, 1663.

———. *Warhaffte Beschreibung/ Eines nie erhörten/ unchristlichen/ wider Gottes Wort/ alle Rechte/ und natürliche Vernunfft lauffenden peinlichen Processus, welchen Bürgermeister und Raht der Stadt Braunschweig/ wider eine arme unschüldige Bawren Tochter/ von Grossen Schwülber . . . von vierzehen Jahren/ Margareta Schmidts genant/ eines . . . fälschlich zugemessenen Kindermohrts halber . . . Anno 1661. und 1662. geführt und exequirt. Dann auch/ Welcher gestalt gedachte Bürgermeister und Raht benanter . . . Margareten Schmidts . . . dienenden Advocatum Barbarisch tractirt . . . haben . . . Mit . . . Appendice, Von dem verbottenem heimlichem Westphälischem Blut-Gerichte . . . von jetztgedachtem Advocato zum andern mahl in offenem Truck herauß geben . . . corrigirt.* 2nd, corrected edition. Wolfenbüttel: Bißmarck, 1664.

Radbruch, Gustav, ed. *Die Peinliche Gerichtsordnung Kaiser Karls V. von 1532.* Stuttgart: Reclam, 1975.

Rösslin, Eucharius. *When Midwifery Became the Male Physician's Province: The Sixteenth Century Handbook; The Rose Garden for Pregnant Women and Midwives.*

Translated by Wendy Arons. Jefferson, NC: McFarland, 1994.

Siegemundin, Justina. *Die Chur-Brandenburgische Hoff-Wehe-Mutter, Das ist: Ein höchst nöthiger Unterricht, von schweren und unrecht-stehenden Geburten, in einem Gespräch vorgestellet wie nehmlich, durch Göttlichen Beystand eine wohl-unterrichtete und geübte Wehe-Mutter mit Verstand und geschickter Hand, dergleichen verhüten, oder wanns Noth ist, das Kind wenden könne; Durch vieler Jahre Ubung, selbst erfahren und wahr befunden.* Cölln am Spree: Liebpert, 1690.

———. *The Court Midwife.* Edited and translated by Lynne Tatlock. Chicago: University of Chicago Press, 2005.

Spiess, Werner, ed. *Braunschweigisches Bürger- und Gewerbe-Verzeichnis für das Jahr 1671.* Braunschweig: J. H. Meyer, 1942.

Der Stadt Braunschweig Ordnunge jre christliche Religion auch allerhandt Criminal Straff vnd Policey-Sachen betreffendt: beradtschlagt vnd eindrechtiglich bewilligt vnd angenomen von einem erbarn Rathe, Rathsgeschworenen, Zehenmannen, Geschockten, Gildemeistern vnd Haubtleuten der Stadt Braunschweig vor sich vnd von wegen der gantzen gemeinen Bürgerschaft darselbst. Magdeburg: Wolfgang Kirchner, 1579.

Strauch, Johann. Acten gemässe Relatio Facti et Juris Uber den zu Braunschweig Wider Margareten Schmieds/ Eine Stuprirte Bauer-Magd/ in puncto verdächtigen Kindermords geführten Inquisitions: Wie auch wider dero Advocatum D. Justum Olde-koppen . . . Ungehorsams halber vollstreckten Verfestungs-Proceß . . . benanten Advocato, und dessen in Druck gegebener Famos-Schrifft entgegen gesetzet/ Von denen zum peinlichen Sachen verordneten Gerichten daselbsten. Halberstadt: Kolwald Erben, 1665.

Unterricht vor die Heb-Ammen, oder Bade-Mütter, in der Stadt Braunschweig. Brunswick, Zilliger, 1686.

Zacchia, Paulo. *Pauli Zacchiae, medici Romani, Quaestiones medico-legales: In quibus eae materiae medicae, quae ad legales facultates videntur pertinere, proponuntur, pertractantur, resolvuntur.* Amsterdam: Blaeu, 1651.

Zedler, Johann. *Großes Vollständiges Universal-Lexikon.* Vol. 10. Leipzig, 1754.

Secondary Sources

Ackerknecht, Erwin H. "Midwives as Experts in Court." *Bulletin of the New York Academy of Medicine* 52, no. 10 (1976): 1224–28.

———. "Zur Geschichte der Hebammen." *Gesnerus* 31 (1974): 181–92.

Albrecht, Peter. "Das Zeitalter der Aufgeklärten Absolutismus (1735–1806)." In *Die braunschweigische Landesgeschichte: Jahrtausendrückblick einer Region,* ed. Horst-Rüdiger Jarck and Gerhard Schildt, 575–610. Brunswick: Appelhans Verlag, 2000.

Bader, Karl S., and Gerhard Dilcher. *Deutsche Rechtsgeschichte: Land und Stadt—Bürger und Bauer im alten Europa.* Berlin: Springer, 1999.

Bainbridge, David A. *Making Babies: The Science of Pregnancy.* Cambridge: Harvard University Press, 2001.

Barton, Brenda. "When Murdering Hands Rock the Cradle: An Overview of America's Treatment of Infanticidal Mothers." *Southern Methodist University Law Review* 51 (1998): 591–619.

Baumann, Anette. *Advokaten und Prokuratoren: Anwälte am Reichskammergericht (1690–1806).* Cologne: Böhlau, 2006.

Bechtold, Brigitte, and Donna Cooper Graves, eds. *Killing Infants: Studies in the Worldwide Practice of Infanticide.* Lewiston, NY: Edwin Mellen Press, 2006.

Behringer, Wolfgang. "Mörder, Diebe, Ehebrecher: Verbrechen und Strafen in Kurbayern vom 16. bis 18. Jahrhundert." In *Verbrechen, Strafen und soziale Kontrolle: Studien zur historischen Kulturforschung*, ed. Richard van Dülmen, 85–132. Frankfurt: Fischer Taschenbuch Verlag, 1990.

———. *Witchcraft Persecutions in Bavaria: Popular Magic, Religious Zealotry, and Reason of State in Early Modern Europe.* Cambridge: Cambridge University Press, 1997.

Bennett, Judith M., and Amy M. Froide, eds. *Singlewomen in the European Past, 1250–1800.* Philadelphia: University of Pennsylvania Press, 1999.

Bepler, Jill. "Literatur und Buchkultur." In *Die braunschweigische Landesgeschichte Jahrtausendrückblick einer Region*, ed. Horst-Rüdiger Jarck and Gerhard Schildt, 611–28. Brunswick: Appelhans Verlag, 2000.

Breit, Stefan. *"Leichtfertigkeit" und Ländliche Gesellschaft: Voreheliche Sexualität in der Frühen Neuzeit.* Munich: Oldenbourg, 1991.

Brundage, James A. *Sex, Law, and Marriage in the Middle Ages.* Aldershot: Variorum, 1993.

Carlen, Louis. *Das Recht der Hirten: Zur Rechtsgeschichte d. Hirten in Deutschland, Österreich u. d. Schweiz.* Studien Zur Rechts-, Wirtschafts- und Kulturgeschichte 7. Veröffentlichungen der Universität Innsbruck 64. Innsbruck: Österr. Kommissionsbuch, 1970.

Cordes, Albrecht. "Anwalt." In *Handwörterbuch zur deutschen Rechtsgeschichte*, ed. Albrecht Cordes and Wolfgang Stammler, 1:259–61. 2nd ed. Berlin: Schmidt, 2008.

Danckert, Werner. *Unehrliche Leute: Die verfemten Berufe.* Bern: Francke, 1963.

Duden, Barbara. *Disembodying Women: Perspectives on Pregnancy and the Unborn.* Cambridge: Harvard University Press, 1993.

———. *The Woman beneath the Skin: A Doctor's Patients in Eighteenth-Century Germany.* Cambridge: Harvard University Press, 1991.

Duden, Barbara, Jürgen Schlumbohm, and Patrice Veit, eds. *Geschichte des Ungeborenen: Zur Erfahrungs- und Wisssenschaftsgeschichte der Schwangerschaft, 17.–20. Jahrhundert.* Göttingen: Vandenhoeck & Ruprecht, 2002.

Dülmen, Richard van. *Der ehrlose Mensch: Unehrlichkeit und soziale Ausgrenzung in der Frühen Neuzeit.* Cologne: Böhlau, 1999.

———. *Frauen vor Gericht: Kindsmord in der Frühen Neuzeit.* Frankfurt: Fischer Taschenbuch Verlag, 1991.

———. *Kultur und Alltag in der Frühen Neuzeit.* 3 vols. Munich: C. H. Beck, 1990–1999.

———. *Theatre of Horror: Crime and Punishment in Early Modern Germany.* Cambridge: Polity Press, 1990.

Dürr, Renate. *Mägde in der Stadt: Das Beispiel Schwäbisch Hall in der Frühen Neuzeit.* Frankfurt: Campus Verlag, 1995.

Erler, Adalbert, Ekkehard Kaufmann, and Wolfgang Stammler, eds. *Handwörterbuch zur deutschen Rechtsgeschichte (HRG).* 4 vols. Berlin: E. Schmidt, 1971–.

Evans, Richard I. *Rituals of Retribution: Capital Punishment in Germany, 1600–1987.* Oxford: Oxford University Press, 1996.

———, ed. *The German Underworld: Deviants and Outcasts in German History.* London: Routledge, 1988.

Falk, Ulrich. "Vom Unzeitigen Rennen, Sich Sperren und Disputieren: Eine Fallstudie zur Verteidigung im Hexenprozeß." In *Vom Unfug des Hexen-Processes: Gegner der Hexenverfolgungen von Johann Weyer bis Friedrich Spee*, ed. Hartmut Lehmann and Otto Ulbricht, 281–305. Wolfenbütteler Forschungen 55. Wiesbaden: Harrassowitz, 1992.

———. *Zur Folter im deutschen Strafprozeß: Das Regelungsmodell von Benedict Carpzov (1595–1666)*. Forum historiae iuris. <http://fhi.rg.mpg.de/articles/0106falk-folter.htm>

———. "Zur Geschichte der Strafverteidigung: Aktuelle Beobachtungen und rechtshistorische Grundlagen." *Zeitschrift der Savigny-Stiftung für Rechtsgeschichte, Germanistische Abteilung* 117 (2000): 395–449.

Fauve-Chamoux, Antoinette. "Marriage, Widowhood, and Divorce." In *The History of the European Family*, ed. David Kertzer and Marzio Barbagli, 1:221–56. New Haven: Yale University Press, 2001.

Fenster, Thelma S., and Daniel Lord Smail, eds. *Fama: The Politics of Talk and Reputation in Medieval Europe*. Ithaca: Cornell University Press, 2003.

Ferraro, Joanne Marie. *Nefarious Crimes, Contested Justice: Illicit Sex and Infanticide in the Republic of Venice, 1557–1789*. Baltimore: Johns Hopkins University Press, 2008.

Fischer-Homberger, Esther. *Medizin vor Gericht: Gerichtsmedizin von d. Renaissance bis zur Aufklärung*. Bern: Huber, 1983.

Gélis, Jacques. *History of Childbirth: Fertility, Pregnancy, and Birth in Early Modern Europe*. Translated by Rosemary Morris. Cambridge: Polity Press, 1996.

Gerhard, Ute, ed. *Frauen in der Geschichte des Rechts: Von der Frühen Neuzeit bis zur Gegenwart*. Munich: C. H. Beck, 1999.

Gleixner, Ulrike. "*Die 'Gute' und die 'Böse': Hebammen als Amtsfrauen auf dem Land (Altmark/Brandenburg, 18. Jahrhundert)*." In *Weiber, Menscher, Frauenzimmer: Frauen in der ländlichen Gesellschaft, 1500–1800*, ed. Heide Wunder, 96–123. Göttingen: Vandenhoeck & Ruprecht, 1996.

———. "*Das Mensch" und "der Kerl": Die Konstruktion von Geschlecht in Unzuchtsverfahren der Frühen Neuzeit (1700–1760)*. Frankfurt: Campus, 1994.

Gleixner, Ulrike, and Marion W. Gray. *Gender in Transition: Discourse and Practice in German-Speaking Europe, 1750–1830*. Ann Arbor: University of Michigan Press, 2006.

Green, Monica. *Making Women's Medicine Masculine: The Rise of Male Authority in Pre-modern Gynaecology*. New York: Oxford University Press, 2008.

Gwinner, Heinrich, and Gustav Radbruch. *Geschichte des Verbrechens: Versuch einer historischen Kriminologie*. Stuttgart: Koehler, 1951.

Hanlon, Gregory. "L'infanticidio di coppie sposate in Toscana nella prima eta moderna." *Quaderni storici* 113 (2003): 453–98.

Henschel, Johann Friedrich. "Die Strafverteidigung im Inquisitionsprozeß des 18. und im Anklageprozeß des 19. Jahrhunderts." PhD diss., Freiburg University, 1972.

Heydenreuter, Reinhard. *Kriminalgeschichte Bayerns: Von den Anfängen bis ins 20. Jahrhundert*. Regensburg: Pustet, 2008.

Hippel, Wolfgang von. *Armut, Unterschichten, Randgruppen in der Frühen Neuzeit*. Munich: Oldenbourg, 1995.

Hoffer, Peter Charles, and N. E. H. Hull. *Murdering Mothers: Infanticide in England and New England, 1558–1803*. New York: New York University Press, 1981.

Holzhauser, H. "Gestaendnis." In *Handwörterbuch zur deutschen Rechtsgeschichte*, ed. Albrecht Cordes, 1:326–35. 2nd ed. Berlin: Erich Schmidt Verlag, 2008.

Hufton, Olwen H. *The Prospect before Her: A History of Women in Western Europe.* Vol. 1. New York: Alfred Knopf, 1996–.

Hull, Isabel. *Sexuality, State, and Civil Society in Germany, 1700–1815.* Ithaca: Cornell University Press, 1996.

———. "Sexualstrafrecht und geschlechtsspezifische normen in den deutschen Staaten des 17. und 18. Jahrhunderts." In *Frauen in der Geschichte des Rechts: Von der Frühen Neuzeit bis zur Gegenwart*, ed. Ute Gerhard, 221–34. Munich: C. H. Beck, 1999.

Hundertmark, Edeltraut. *Stadtgeographie von Braunschweig.* Oldenburg: G. Stalling, 1941.

Ignor, Alexander. *Geschichte des Strafprozesses in Deutschland, 1532–1846: Von der Carolina Karls V. bis zu den Reformen des Vormärz.* Paderborn: F. Schöningh, 2002.

Ingalls, Wayne. "Demography and Dowries: Perspectives on Female Infanticide in Classical Greece." *Phoenix* 56, nos. 3–4 (2002): 246–54.

Irsigler, Franz, and Arnold Lassotta, eds. *Bettler und Gaukler, Dirnen und Henker: Aussenseiter in einer mittelalterlichen Stadt; Köln, 1300–1600.* Munich: Deutscher Taschenbuch Verlag, 1989.

Jackson, Mark. *Infanticide: Historical Perspectives on Child Murder and Concealment, 1550–2000.* Aldershot: Ashgate, 2002.

———. *New-Born Child Murder: Women, Illegitimacy, and the Courts in Eighteenth-Century England.* Manchester: Manchester University Press, 1996.

Jarck, Horst-Rüdiger. "Die Dreißigjährige Krieg." In *Die braunschweigische Landesgeschichte Jahrtausendrückblick einer Region*, ed. Horst-Rüdiger Jarck and Gerhard Schildt, 513–35. Brunswick: Appelhans Verlag, 2000.

Jarck, Horst-Rüdiger, and Gerhard Schildt, eds. *Die braunschweigische Landesgeschichte Jahrtausendrückblick einer Region.* Brunswick: Appelhans Verlag, 2000.

Jerouschek, Günter. *Lebensschutz und Lebensbeginn: Kulturgeschichte des Abtreibungsverbots.* Tübingen: Edition Diskord, 2002.

Kapparis, Konstantinos. *Abortion in the Ancient World.* London: Duckworth Academic, 2002.

Kertzer, David. *Sacrificed for Honor: Italian Infant Abandonment and the Politics of Reproductive Control.* Boston: Beacon Press, 1993.

Kertzer, David I., and Marzio Barbagli. *The History of the European Family.* 3 vols. New Haven: Yale University Press, 2001–2003.

Knodel, John E. *Demographic Behavior in the Past: A Study of Fourteen German Village Populations in the Eighteenth and Nineteenth Centuries.* Cambridge: Cambridge University Press, 1988.

Kowaleski, Maryanne. "Singlewomen in Medieval and Early Modern Europe: The Demographic Perspective." In *Singlewomen in the European Past, 1250–1800*, ed. Judith M. Bennett and Amy M. Froide, 38–81. Philadelphia: University of Pennsylvania Press, 1999.

Kumar, Vinay, Nelso Fausto, Abul Abbas, et al. *Robbins and Cotran Pathologic Basis of Disease.* 7th ed. Philadelphia: Elsevier Saunders, 2005.

Labouvie, Eva. *Andere Umstände: Eine Kulturgeschichte der Geburt.* 2nd, rev. ed. Cologne: Böhlau, 2000.

———. *Beistand in Kindsnöten: Hebammen und weibliche Kultur auf dem Land, 1550–1910*. Frankfurt: Campus, 1999.

Langbein, John H. *Prosecuting Crime in the Renaissance: England, Germany, France*. Cambridge: Harvard University Press, 1974.

———. *Torture and the Law of Proof*. Chicago: University of Chicago Press, 1977.

Langer, William L. "Checks on Population Growth, 1750–1850." *Scientific American* 226, no. 2 (1972): 92–99.

Lehmann, Hartmut, and Otto Ulbricht, eds. *Vom Unfug des Hexen-Processes: Gegner der Hexenverfolgungen von Johann Weyer bis Friedrich Spee*. Wolfenbütteler Forschungen 55. Wiesbaden: Harrassowitz, 1992.

Le Roy Ladurie, Emmanuel. *Montaillou: The Promised Land of Error*. New York: G. Braziller, 1978.

Lieberich, Heinz, and Heinrich Mitteis. *Deutsche Rechtsgeschichte: Ein Studienbuch*. 19th ed. Munich: Beck, 1992.

Lieberwirth, Rolf. "Constitutio Criminalis Carolina." In *Handwörterbuch zur deutschen Rechtsgeschichte*, ed. Albrecht Cordes and Wolfgang Stammler, 1:885–90. 2nd ed. Berlin: Schmidt, 2008.

Lindemann, Mary. *Medicine and Society in Early Modern Europe*. Cambridge: Cambridge University Press, 1999.

Ludwig, Ulrike. *Das Herz der Justitia: Gestaltungspotentiale territorialer Herrschaft in der Strafrechts- und Gnadenpraxis am Beispiel Kursachsens, 1548–1648*. Konflikte und Kultur—Historische Perspektiven 16. Constance: UVK Verlagsgesellschaft, 2008.

Magner, Lois N. *A History of the Life Sciences*. New York: M. Dekker, 1994.

Marland, Hilary. *The Art of Midwifery: Early Modern Midwives in Europe*. London: Routledge, 1993.

McClive, Kathy. "The Hidden Truths of the Belly: The Uncertainties of Pregnancy in Early Modern Europe." *Social History of Medicine* 15, no. 2 (2002): 209–27.

McLaren, Angus. *A History of Contraception: From Antiquity to the Present Day*. Oxford: Blackwell, 1990.

———. *Reproductive Rituals: The Perception of Fertility in England from the Sixteenth to the Nineteenth Century*. London: Methuen, 1984.

McManners, John. *Death and the Enlightenment: Changing Attitudes to Death among Christians and Unbelievers in Eighteenth-Century France*. Oxford: Clarendon Press, 1981.

Meibeyer, Wolfgang, ed. *Die Bevölkerungsverteilung in der Stadt Braunschweig 1758*. Braunschweig: Bauverwaltung, 1967.

Meumann, Markus. *Findelkinder, Waisenhäuser, Kindsmord: Unversorgte Kinder in der frühneuzeitlichen Gesellschaft*. Munich: Oldenbourg, 1995.

Moser, Hans. "Jungfernkranz und Strohkranz." In *Das Recht der kleinen Leute: Beitr. zur rechtliche Volkskunde*, ed. Konrad Köstlin and Kai Detlev Sievers, 140–61. Berlin: E. Schmidt, 1976.

Müller, Wolfgang Peter. *Die Abtreibung: Anfänge der Kriminalisierung, 1140–1650*. Cologne: Böhlau, 2000.

Münch, Paul. *Lebensformen in der Frühen Neuzeit*. Frankfurt: Propyläen, 1992.

Nowosadtko, Jutta. *Scharfrichter und Abdecker: Der Alltag zweier "unehrlicher Berufe" in der Frühen Neuzeit*. Paderborn: Ferdinand Schöningh, 1994.

Oestmann, Peter. *Hexenprozesse am Reichskammergericht*. Quellen und Forschungen zur höchsten Gerichtsbarkeit im alten Reich 31. Cologne: Böhlau, 1997.

Ogilvie, Sheilagh C. *A Bitter Living: Women, Markets, and Social Capital in Early Modern Germany*. Oxford: Oxford University Press, 2003.

Ohnsorge, Werner. "Zur Geschichte der Kanzlei und des Hofgerichts zu Wolfenbüttel im 16. und 17. Jahrhundert." *Beiträge zur Geschichte des Gerichtswesens im Lande Braunschweig* 14 (1954): 9–37.

Oldekop, Karl Henning. "Justus Oldekop, ein streitbarer Jurist im 17. Jahrhundert." *Braunschweigische Heimat* (1973): 8–14.

Ott, Sandra. "Aristotle among the Basques: The 'Cheese Analogy' of Conception." *Man* 14 (1979): 699–711.

Parry, John T. "Escalation and Necessity: Defining Torture at Home and Abroad." In *Torture: A Collection*, ed. Sanford Levinson, 145–64. Oxford: Oxford University Press, 2004.

Peters, Edward. *Torture*. Philadelphia: University of Pennsylvania Press, 1996.

Pfister, Christian. *Bevölkerungsgeschichte und historische Demographie, 1500–1800*. Enzyklopädie deutscher Geschichte 28. Munich: Oldenbourg, 1994.

———. "The Population of Late Medieval and Early Modern Germany." In *Germany: A New Social and Economic History*, ed. Robert W. Scribner and Sheilagh C. Ogilvie. Vol. 1. London: Arnold, 1996.

Pomeroy, Sarah B. *Families in Classical and Hellenistic Greece: Representations and Realities*. Oxford: Oxford University Press, 1998.

Pomeroy, Sarah B., et al. *Ancient Greece: A Political, Social, and Cultural History*. 2nd ed. New York: Oxford University Press, 2007.

Racaut, Luc. "Accusations of Infanticide on the Eve of the French Wars of Religion." In *Infanticide: Historical Perspectives on Child Murder and Concealment*, ed. Mark Jackson, 18–34. Aldershot: Ashgate, 2002.

Rapaport, Elizabeth. "Mad Women and Desperate Girls: Infanticide and Child Murder in Law and Myth." *Fordham Urban Law Journal* 33, no. 2 (2006): 527–69.

Reidemeister, Sophie, and Werner Spiess. *Genealogien Braunschweiger Patrizier- und Ratsgeschlechter aus der Zeit der Selbständigkeit der Stadt (vor 1671)*. Werkstücke aus Museum, Archiv und Bibliothek der Stadt Braunschweig 12. Brunswick: J. H. Meyer, 1948.

Richards, Judith M. *Mary Tudor*. London: Routledge, 2008.

Robisheaux, Thomas. *The Last Witch of Langenburg: Murder in a German Village*. New York: W. W. Norton, 2009.

———. "Zur Rezeption Benedikt Carpzovs im 17. Jahrhundert." In *Hexenprozesse und Gerichtspraxis*, ed. Herbert Eiden and Rita Voltmer, 527–43. Trierer Hexenprozesse: Quellen und Darstellungen 6. Trier: Paulinus Verlag, 2002.

Roeck, Bernd. "Criminal Procedure in the Holy Roman Empire." *International Association for the History of Crime and Criminal Justice Bulletin* 18 (1993): 21–40.

Röemer, Christof. "Das Zeitalter des Hochabsolutismus (1635–1735)." In *Die braunschweigische Landesgeschichte Jahrtausendrückblick einer Region*, ed. Horst-Rüdiger Jarck and Gerhard Schildt, 535–75. Brunswick: Appelhans Verlag, 2000.

Roper, Lyndal. *Witch Craze: Terror and Fantasy in Baroque Germany*. New Haven: Yale University Press, 2004.

Rowlands, Alison. "Witchcraft and Old Women in Early Modern Germany." *Past & Present* 173 (November 2001): 50–89.

Rublack, Ulinka. *The Crimes of Women in Early Modern Germany*. Oxford: Clarendon Press, 1999.

———. *Gender in Early Modern German History*. Cambridge: Cambridge University Press, 2002.

———. "Pregnancy, Childbirth, and the Female Body in Early Modern Germany." *Past & Present* 150, no. 1 (1996): 84–110.

———. "The Public Body: Policing Abortion in Early Modern Germany." In *Gender Relations in German History: Power, Agency, and Experience from the Sixteenth to the Twentieth Century*, ed. Lynn Abrams and Elizabeth Harvey, 57–79. Durham, NC: Duke University Press, 1997.

Ruff, Julius R. *Violence in Early Modern Europe*. Cambridge: Cambridge University Press, 2001.

Rüping, Hinrich. "Die *Carolina* in der Strafrechtlichen Kommentarliteratur." In *Strafrecht, Strafprozess, und Rezeption: Grundlagen, Entwickling, und Wirkung der Constitutio Criminalis Carolina*, ed. Friedrich-Christian Schroeder and Peter Landau, 161–76. Frankfurt: Klostermann, 1984.

———. *Grundriss der Strafrechtsgeschichte*. 3rd ed. Munich: Beck, 1998.

———. *Der Grundsatz des rechtlichen Gehörs und seine Bedeutung im Strafverfahren*. Strafrechtliche Abhandlungen—Neue Folge. Vol. 26. Berlin: Dunker & Humblot, 1976.

Schlumbohm, Jürgen. *Lebensläufe, Familien, Höfe: Die Bauern und Heuerleute des Osnabrückischen Kirschspiels Belm in proto-industrieller Zeit, 1650–1860*. Göttingen: Vandenhoeck & Ruprecht, 1994.

Schmidt, Eberhard. *Einführung in die Geschichte der deutschen Strafrechtspflege*. 3rd ed. Göttingen: Vandenhoeck & Ruprecht, 1995.

Schuhmann, H. "Henker." In *Handwörterbuch zur deutschen Rechtsgeschichte*, ed. Adalbert Erler, Ekkehard Kaufmann, and Wolfgang Stammler, 2:75–77. Berlin: Schmidt, 1978.

Scribner, Robert L., and Sheilagh C. Ogilvie. *Germany: A New Social and Economic History*. 3 vols. London: Arnold, 1996–2003.

Silverman, Lisa. *Tortured Subjects: Pain, Truth, and the Body in Early Modern France*. Chicago: Chicago University Press, 2001.

Soman, Alfred, trans. "Anatomy of an Infanticide Trial: The Case of Marie-Jeanne Bartonnet (1742)." In *Changing Identities in Early Modern France*, ed. Michael Wolfe, 248–72. Durham, NC: Duke University Press.

Spiess, Werner. *Braunschweig: Die Verfassung und Verwaltung der mittelalterlichen Stadt*. Hildesheim: A. Lax, 1949.

———. "Die Gerichtsverfassung der Stadt Braunschweig zur Hansezeit (bis 1671)." *Beitraege zur Geschichte des Gerichtswesens im Lande Braunschweig* 14 (1954): 39–77.

———. *Geschichte der Stadt Braunschweig im Nachmittelalter: Vom Ausgang des Mittelalters bis zum Ende der Stadtfreiheit, 1491–1671*. 2 vols. Brunswick: Waisenhaus-Buchdruckerei und Verlag, 1966.

———. *Von Vechelde: Die Geschichte einer Braunschweiger Patrizierfamilie, 1332–1864*. Werkstücke Aus Museum, Archiv und Bibliothek der Stadt Braunschweig 13. Brunswick: Waisenhaus-Buchdruckerei, 1951.

Sreenivasan, Govind P. *The Peasants of Ottobeuren, 1487–1726: A Rural Society in Early Modern Europe*. Cambridge: Cambridge University Press, 2004.

Stone, Lawrence. *The Family, Sex, and Marriage in England, 1500–1800*. London: Weidenfeld & Nicolson, 1977.

Strauss, Gerald. *Law, Resistance, and the State: The Opposition to Roman Law in Reformation Germany*. Princeton: Princeton University Press, 1986.

Stuart, Kathy. *Defiled Trades and Social Outcasts: Honor and Ritual Pollution in Early Modern Germany*. Cambridge: Cambridge University Press, 1999.

Tatlock, Lynne. "*Speculum Feminarum*: Gendered Perspectives on Obstetrics and Gynecology in Early Modern Germany." *Signs* 17, no. 4 (1992): 725–60.

Ulbricht, Otto. "Infanticide in Eighteenth-Century Germany." In *The German Underworld: Deviants and Outcasts in German History*, ed. Richard Evans, 108–40. London: Routledge, 1988.

———. "Kindsmörderinnen vor Gericht: Verteidigungsstragien von Frauen in Norddeutschland, 1680–1810." In *Mit den Waffen der Justiz: Zur Kriminalitätsgeschichte des Spätmittelalters und der Frühen Neuzeit*, ed. Andreas Blauert and Gerd Schwerhoff, 54–85. Frankfurt: Fischer Taschenbuch Verlag, 1993.

———."Kindsmord in der Frühen Neuzeit." In *Frauen in der Geschichte des Rechts: Von der Frühen Neuzeit bis zur Gegenwart*, ed. Ute Gerhard, 235–47. Munich: C. H. Beck, 1999.

———. *Kindsmord und Aufklärung in Deutschland*. Munich: Oldenbourg, 1990.

———."Landesverweisung für Kindsmord—milde Strafen in harter Zeit? Ein Stegeberger Fall aus dem Jahre 1684." In *Mare Balticum: Beiträge zur Geschichte des Ostseeraumes in Mittelalter und Neuzeit; Festschrift zum 65. Geburtstag von Erich Hoffmann*, ed. Werner Paravicini et al., 261–78. Kieler historische Studien 36. Sigmaringen: Jan Thorbecke, 1992.

Viazzo, Pier Paolo. "Mortality, Fertility, and Family." In *The History of the European Family*, ed. David Kertzer and Marzio Barbagli, 1:157–90. New Haven: Yale University Press, 2001.

Wächtershäuser, Wilhelm. *Das Verbrechen des Kindesmordes im Zeitalter der Aufklärung: Eine rechtsgeschichtliche Untersuchung der dogmatischen, prozessualen und rechtssoziologischen Aspekte*. Quellen und Forschungen zur Strafrechtsgeschichte 3. Berlin: E. Schmidt, 1973.

Weissler, Adolf. *Geschichte der Rechtsanwaltschaft*. Leipzig, 1905. Reprint, Frankfurt: Sauer & Auvermann, 1967.

Wiesner, Merry E. "Having Her Own Smoke: Employment and Independence for Singlewomen in Germany, 1400–1750." In *Singlewomen in the European Past, 1250–1800*, ed. Judith M. Bennett and Amy M. Froide, 192–216. Philadelphia: University of Pennsylvania Press, 1999.

———. "The Midwives of South Germany and the Public/Private Dichotomy." In *The Art of Midwifery: Early Modern Midwives in Europe*, ed. Hilary Marland, 77–94. London: Routledge, 1993.

———. *Working Women in Renaissance Germany*. New Brunswick, NJ: Rutgers University Press, 1986.

Wiesner-Hanks, Merry E. *Christianity and Sexuality in the Early Modern World: Regulating Desire, Reforming Practice*. London: Routledge, 1999.

Wilczynski, Ania. "Infanticide." In *Encyclopedia of Women in Crime*, ed. Nicole Hahn Rafter, 114–16. Phoenix: Oryx Press, 2000.

Wissell, Rudolf. *Des alten Handwerks Recht und Gewohnheit 1*. Berlin: Colloquium Verlag, 1971.

Wrightson, Keith. "Infanticide in European History." *Criminal Justice History* 3 (1982): 1–20.

Wunder, Heide, ed. *Weiber, Menscher, Frauenzimmer: Frauen in der ländlichen Gesell-schaft, 1500–1800.* Göttingen: Vandenhoeck & Ruprecht, 1996.

Zagolla, Robert. *Folter und Hexenprozess: Die strafrechtliche Spruchpraxis der Juristen-fakultät Rostock im 17. Jahrhundert.* Hexenforschung 11. Bielefeld: Verlag für Regionalgeschichte, 2007.

Zimmerman, Clemens. "Kindsmörderinnen in der ländlichen Gesellschaft Würt-tembergs, 1581–1972." *Medizin, Gesellschaft, und Geschichte* 10 (1998): 67–101.

Index

abandonment: gendered rates of, 214n17; infant, as "indirect" infanticide, 8–9

abortion: penalties for, 222nn36, 38; possibility of, 206; purgative for, 83; statutes on, 40–41

Absolutist princes, powers of, 193

accusatorial process: role of court in, 141; transition from, 140; wider defense rights in, 143

advocate: compensation of, 171; complaimts about language of, 158; legitimizing role of, 145; written legal arguments by, 140

Akteneinsicht (inspection of the records), restrictions on, 143–44

Amann, Paul, 117

animation, moment of, 90

Anneke, Tempel, prosecution of for witchcraft, 13, 212

appeal: Andreas Schmidt's, 197, 205; *Hofgericht,* role in, 95–97; limitations on right to, 144; *Reichskammergericht,* role in, 47, 145; territorial politics of, 193. *See also* Carpzov, Benedikt; Oldekop, Justus; Schmidt, Grethe, case of

Aristotle: gestation theory of, 88–89, 91; position of on animation, 90

Augustus, Duke of Brunswick-Lüneburg, 3, 29; ambitions of, 203; letters of to city council, 192, 193; "Territorial Order" of 1647 by, 193

baptism, emergency, 101, 104

Baumgarten, Johannes, 163

Becker, Philip, 75

blood: role of, 102–3, "stagnant," 92, 93. *See also* conception; menstruation

body, problematic disposal of, 8

Bonte, Gehrt, 168

Bourgeois, Louise, 95

Brandanus, Daetrius, 204

Brandt, Susanna Margarethe, 134

Braunschweig. *See* Brunswick

breast feeding, 19

breech birth, 157, 178; incidence of, 246n14; midwives' testimony on, 164–65; reinvestigation of, 159

Breyer, Martin, 175–76

Brunneman, Johannes, 144, 223n4

Brunswick, 25–30; brewing in, 28; citizenship in, 25; in conflict with duchy, 184, 193; defense of, 29; description of, 25; divisive internal conflicts in, 29; as "free" city, 29; in international trade, 28; practical autonomy but legal subservice of, 193; professions in, 28; rule of law in, 34–39; size of, 25–28; suit of against Oldekop, 203; traditions and customs of, 183. *See also* city council

Brunswick-Lüneburg Chancellor and Council: letter from requesting Grethe's transfer, 181–82; city council response to, 183–84

Brunswick-Lüneburg, duchy of, 29, 202–3

Carolina, the, 9; Article 6 on limited use of torture, 151; Article 35 on examination of single women, 107; Article 47, basic right to criminal defense in, 140; Article 73, right in to inspect and question evidence, 140, 143; Article 188 on source of complaint, 151; on consultation with legal experts, 124; infanticide in, 35–36, 38; promulgation of as watershed, 11; strict controls on torture in, 129

Carpzov, Benedikt, 37, 124, 199–200; as champion of clarifying legal pocess, 141; on futility of defense, 142; influence of, 200; Oldekop's scorn for, 200; as opponent of right to appeal, 47, 144; on option to exclude advocate, 144, 146; on quickening of fetus, 41; reputation of as witch hunter, 141;

on right to defense, 141, 142; time
pressure on advocate recommended
by, 143; works of, 223n4
Carpzov, Johann Benedikt, 199; on
"sharp justice," 219n1
case study, advantages of, 4–5
Cautelarum criminalium (Oldekop), 146
Cautio criminalis (Spees), 146
Charles V (Holy Roman Emperor), 35
childbirth: contradiuction in hour of
alleged, 178; religious aspects of,
104–5
"childhood," restricted meaning of, 21
child labor, necessity of among poor, 21
churches, Christian: attempt of to
regulate midwives, 101, 103; control
over marriage by, 39
cities and states, political relations
between, 3, 4. *See also* territories
city council: attempt of to lure Ilse
to Brunswick, 201–2; decree of to
penalize Oldekop, 12, 190; judicial
independence of, 195–96. *See also*
magistrates; *Obergericht*
conception, 88–91; as fertilization of
eggs, 89; popular traditions about,
90–91; role of blood in theories of,
92–93; William Harvey on, 89
confession: Grethe's new, jurisdictional
concerns in, 182, 183; as requirement
for conviction, 46, 142; as validating
torture after the fact, 159
confrontatio: between accused and
witnesses, 167–68; proposed between
mother and daughter, 187–88
congressus, midwives and, 100
*Constitutio Criminalis Carolina. See
Carolina,* the
Constitutions for Electoral Saxony,
abortion in, 41
corpse, discovery of infant female, 162,
163
corpus delicti: absence of, 150, 178, 183,
207; creation of by court, 151–52;
futile search for, 156, 175
Corpus Juris Iustiniani, duties of
midwives in, 100
costs, payment of, 189

courts: growth of secular, 42; as prosecutors, 207. *See also* individual courts;
judiciary
crime, history of, 5
criminal complaints, frivolous, 241n31
criminal law: of Holy Roman Empire, 3,
9; as mirror of magistrates' anxieties,
43; Oldekop's adversarial approach to,
171; political control of, in sixteenth
and seventeenth century Germany,
13, 14, 139–40, 208
criminal process: different visions of,
171; infanticide in, 34, 35; inquisitorial, 44; torture as focus of, 46–47

De Appellatione in Causus Criminalibus
(Oldekop),145
*Decades tres Quaestionum ad processum
Criminalem necessarim* (Oldekop), 145
Dedekind, Anna, 32; confrontation of
with Grethe, 167–68; on Grethe's
physical signs of pregnancy, 96; initial
testimony of, 47–50, 58; reexamina-
tion of, 165–67
defense: advocates for the, 145–47; brief
by, 150–55; court's reluctance to
appoint, 149; deep-seated suspicion
of, 144; fluid role of, 12; infrequency
of, 216n39; initial response of to first
interrogations, 113–16; potential for
criminal, 6, 111; of poverty-stricken,
141, 144; procedural restraints on,
142–43; right to a, 139–45; shackling
of by inquisitorial judges, 142; types
of representation, 140; uncertainty
about, 140
Denekind (*Baumeister*), 194
dishonor, consequences of, 20
domestic service: as acceptable employment, 24; age of entering, 23; critical
attitude toward, 96; persons in as
potential seducers, 31, 226n2; risks
of, 24; scope of, 30
Duden, Barbara, 87
Dülmen, Richard van, 10

Engelken, Margarethe, 24, 31; testimony
of, 61–64